JOHN F. D'AMICO teaches history at George Mason University in Fairfax, Virginia.

D0894037

RENAISSANCE HUMANISM
IN PAPAL ROME

THE JOHNS HOPKINS UNIVERSITY
STUDIES IN HISTORICAL AND POLITICAL SCIENCE
101st Series (1983)

1. Renaissance Humanism in Papal Rome: Humanists and Churchmen on the Eve of the Reformation. *By John F. D'Amico*

RENAISSANCE HUMANISM IN PAPAL ROME

Humanists and Churchmen on the Eve of the Reformation

JOHN F. D'AMICO

The Johns Hopkins University Press
Baltimore and London

This book has been brought to publication with the generous
assistance of the National Endowment for the Humanities.

The Johns Hopkins University Press, Baltimore, Maryland 21218
The Johns Hopkins Press Ltd., London

Library of Congress Cataloging in Publication Data

D'Amico, John F.
    Renaissance humanism in papal Rome.

    · (Johns Hopkins University studies in historical and
political science; 101st ser., 1)
    Includes bibliographical references and index.
    1. Humanism. 2. Renaissance—Italy—Rome. 3. Rome—
(Italy)—Intellectual life. 4. Catholic Church. Curia
Romana. I. Title. II. Series.
B778.D35 1983   945'.63206   82–49059
ISBN 0-8018-2860-0

B
778
.D35
1983

DILECTIS PARENTIBUS MEIS
DICATUS

Contents

Acknowledgments   xi
Introduction   xiii

PART I
ROMAN HUMANISTS

1 *Humanist Prelates and Curialists*   3
2 *Curial Households and the Humanists*   38
3 *Humanist Families in Rome*   61
4 *The Roman Academies*   89

PART II
HUMANIST THEOLOGIANS IN ROME

5 *The Idiom of Roman Humanism*   115
6 *Classicism in Humanist Theology*   144
7 *Scriptural Skepticism*   169
8 *A Moderate Classicism*   189
9 *Roman Humanism and Curial Reform*   212

Conclusion   238
Notes   241
Index   323

Acknowledgments

Over the years many personal and intellectual debts have been incurred. I began this study approximately a decade ago when Prof. Marvin B. Becker suggested that I work on a Rome-related topic, and it first appeared as a thesis presented at the University of Rochester in 1977. Prof. Becker encouraged me to turn the original manuscript into something broader, and both he and Betty Becker have offered me hospitality at important periods. Profs. Donald R. Kelley, A. William Salamone, and Perez Zagorin of the Department of History; Profs. Philip Berk and Frederick Locke of the Department of Foreign and Comparative Languages and Linguistics of the University of Rochester; and my then fellow graduate students Drs. James Folts and Bernard McLane read and commented on the early version of this study. I have benefited from discussions on humanism and Renaissance Rome with Profs. Charles Trinkaus, Marcella Grendler, Nelson Minnich, Kathleen Weil-Garris, John O'Malley, and Werner Gundersheimer; the last two read parts of the manuscript. Prof. Paul F. Grendler patiently read and reread the manuscript at various stages in an effort to infuse the whole with intellectual rigor. Mr. Alfred J. Marion, Jr., brought a keen editorial eye to the text and purged it of many infelicities and inconsistencies. Profs. Paul O. Kristeller and Richard Goldthwaite read the entire manuscript and offered valuable suggestions. Prof. Kristeller's incomparable knowledge of Renaissance humanism saved me from many errors. I am grateful to all these scholars for their friendship and assistance.

In the past decade many financial obligations have accumulated. A NDEA Fellowship from the University of Rochester and a Rome Prize Fellowship from the American Academy in Rome allowed me to begin and complete work on my thesis. Summer grants from the Center for Reformation Research and the Newberry Library enabled me to pursue related projects. A NEH Fellowship administered through the Villa I Tatti provided the opportunity, *inter alia,* to begin the task of reshaping the manuscript, and a Mellon Post-Doctoral Fellowship in the Humanities at the University of Pennsylvania permitted me to make some final additions even while I was beginning a new project. The financial assistance of all these institutions made it possible for me to continue my work and to remain in academic life.

Many libraries and interlibrary loan offices have aided my research. I have benefited from the collections in the major libraries of Rome, Florence, and Volterra; indeed, most of my time in Italy was spent in the Vatican Library, where I made many new friends. The interlibrary loan staffs of the University of Rochester, especially Ms. Ann Schertz, of the University of Illinois, of the University of Pennsylvania, and of George Mason University obtained many unusual books and articles for me. George Mason University also provided valuable secretarial support.

I have been especially happy in my relations with the Johns Hopkins University Press and wish to express my gratitude to Henry Y. K. Tom, Social Sciences Editor, for showing an early and continued interest in this book.

The dedication expresses my first and final debt.

Introduction

"There is the language of Florence, which we use when we are the creatures of history; but there is also the vocabulary of Rome which we must learn to use when we are the bearers or creatures of history; and in Rome there is especially the vocabulary of the Ara Coeli and the Campidoglio. I do not know that they are inexhaustible, but their voices have been pleading for a long human time."[1] Part of that "long human time" was the High Renaissance, when the Ara Coeli (transformed into Santa Maria in Aracoeli) and the Campidoglio symbolized the two poles of Rome. The Church of Santa Maria in Aracoeli, a symbol of Christianity, and the Campidoglio, the ancient seat of imperial Rome, helped to create the speech of the self-appointed custodians and interpreters of history. However, that history and its idiom have been less perfectly mastered by Renaissance historians than the language of Florence, with its more secular, republican, and bourgeois vocabulary and syntax. While it would be facile and inaccurate to overemphasize the divergences between these two languages, there were substantial differences in their intellectual, political, and social qualities. This study seeks to propose an interpretation of Roman humanism which will make that Roman speech in its special Renaissance dialect a little more comprehensible.

The history of Rome in the quattro- and early cinquecento has only recently attracted the attention of American Renaissance historians. They are far behind the art historians and European scholars in projecting High Renaissance Rome as a unique entity worthy of intense research. This neglect includes Roman humanism and, *a fortiori,* its relationship to the city's religious character. Most studies of Renaissance humanism concentrate on Florence and, apart from making passing reference to Nicholas V and the Roman Academy, ignore Rome. Yet Rome offers a very successful example of humanism's ability to accommodate to a particular political, social, and religious ambience. Moreover, Rome became the center for Italian humanism in the last decade of the quattrocento and the first decades of the cinquecento, when Florence and other Italian states were subjected to severe political and military pressures after the French invasion of 1494. Roman humanism, nurtured in a unique Roman environment, had a special position in Renaissance intellectual history. In order to understand its special character, this study will concentrate on the points where humanism and the pervasive religious character of Rome coincided. Since humanism and humanists are the topics of this study, a clear definition of terms is necessary. Humanism was an intellectual movement devoted to the *studia humanitatis,* i.e., those literary, historical, and moral studies which developed from a renewed interest in ancient Greek and (especially) Latin writings and civilization.[2] This was predicated on the belief that these studies laid the basis for a new, more immediate reinterpretation of contemporary culture. Humanists, in pursuit of these ideals, produced literary pieces (especially poetry and orations) and theories, histories, commentaries on ancient writers, translations, and moral treatises, all based on classical ideas and language. This did not require a rejection, in their entirety, of medieval ideals and precepts, but it did subject all aspects of life and thought to classical standards. Ancient writers provided the language, style, examples, and context through which these men expressed their thoughts on contemporary problems and desires. Humanism, therefore, provided a cultural context in which men could judge and adjust their world to new circumstances.

As a comprehensive cultural movement, humanism naturally had to contend with the religious precepts of its day.[3] In this there was always the possibility of tension, since humanism was essentially a secular movement concerned with human acts separate from any metaphysical or theological implications. Indeed, early quattrocento humanists, such as Salutati, Poggio, and Bruni, generally displayed a strong antipathy toward technical theological speculation since its theories seemed to them unresponsive to their human interests. These humanists tended to judge religious questions by the moral principles they discovered in their classical authorities. However, in the course of the quattrocento the humanists, or at least many of them, found themselves more and more willing to expand the area of their moral concerns and discuss a variety of theological and religious questions. This resulted from changes in the type of material (such as Greek patristic and Neo-Platonic writings) available to them and as a natural consequence of their broader involvement in contemporary problems. Theological expertise never became the center of Italian humanist activity, nor did it ever constitute an essential element in defining humanism. Nevertheless, religious and certain broad theological questions did enter into the repertoire of some humanists, and this was especially true of Rome in the latter half of the quattrocento.

Despite this increased interest in and willingness to discuss religion in quattrocento Rome, there has been little serious consideration of the consequent ideas and writings in modern scholarship, with a handful of important exceptions.[4] Generally, however, the religious thought of the intellectual elite (which either did not belong to or was independent of the religious orders) in the very institutional center of the Western Church on the eve of the Reformation has been ignored. There are a variety of reasons for this situation.

Rome's political-ecclesiastical establishments have deflected the attention of interested scholars toward the study of the papacy and its policies. Those who have focused on Rome's theological and ecclesiological developments have centered their attention on the established theological traditions of the religious orders and the canon lawyers, rather than on those intellectuals who were primarily litterateurs and historians and only secondarily theologians. Further, historians have emphasized the derivative quality of early quattrocento Roman humanism, a time when displaced Florentines and Tuscans, having no particular identity with Rome, dominated. Such a generalization, however, does not hold for the period after the 1450s. Moreover, the intellectual interests of Roman humanists, especially their devotion to an imitative, classically formed Latin style, do not appeal to modern sensibilities concerned with orginality. Further, the society that Roman humanists made their own is equally foreign to modern preferences. In order to secure a place for themselves in Roman society, the Roman humanists had to become increasingly clerical in their number and more orthodox in their thought. This society contrasted sharply with the Florentine model, with its secular and republican-civic qualities. All these "defects" of Roman humanism, from the point of view of modern scholars, become more acute when the historian chooses to concentrate on the religious writings of the humanists.

A further impediment to the study of Roman humanism and its religious thought stems from the tradition that portrayed Roman humanism as the center of Renaissance neopaganism. While modern scholarship has generally put to rest the theme of neopaganism in the Renaissance, it has nevertheless left a heritage that continues to plague Roman Renaissance history by rendering several elements in its religious life somehow unworthy of serious consideration. This attitude has received circumstantial reinforcement from the moral laxity of many of Rome's clergy. Indeed, religious and moral irregularity seemed to mark clerical Rome. Yet, it would be incorrect to extrapolate from this condition a rejection of Christianity and a longing for the pagan gods. Despite the apparent inability of papal Rome to live up to Christian principles, some Roman humanists seriously expounded the essentials of Christian morality and thought. These ideals as reformulated by the humanists, and not the immorality that Rome harbored, concern us.

An important source for this negative assessment of Rome's intellectuals comes from a major Renaissance figure. In his polemics with the Roman Ciceronians and most particularly in his masterful satire the *Ciceronianus* (1528), Desiderius Erasmus stigmatized Rome as a center of paganism in both word and deed. Whatever the motivations for Erasmus's negative judgment (and they will be discussed in detail in Chapter 5), his strictures have helped to deflect many from investigating Roman humanism, particularly its religious thought. In his attacks Erasmus did provide later scholars with a key to understanding Roman humanism by highlighting the close cultural identification between linguistic and religious orthodoxy—an identification that in its Roman formulation was unique. Suffice it to say here that Roman humanists did not advocate the repaganization of life, and that many of them exhibited a spirituality that reflected, and was limited by, their environment and intellectual interests. However, the cultural and religious values to which Rome's humanists responded did differ from those of Erasmus and his followers.

In a similar manner the identification of Roman humanism with papal policies against the Reformation has led scholars to judge it as an unsuccessful intellectual movement. While Roman humanists certainly supported papal policy for the most part, they did not formulate it and had certain reservations toward it. In general, Roman humanists were curialists, dependent on the papal establishment, and they participated in the papal offensive against the reformers. As papal defenders, the humanists offered literary works that mirrored their own estimation of papal claims and their self-appointed role as defenders of Western culture. Their ultimate weakness in the face of the Reformation and its new ideals should not overshadow the sincerity of their desire to explain and defend their relations with the ecclesiastical establishment.

Whatever the traditions surrounding the investigation of Roman humanism and its religious thought, there can be little doubt that it successfully adapted itself to Roman society. This adaptability produced what other scholars and I have called "curial humanism"; this term describes the connection between humanism and the governmental and financial structures of Renaissance Rome, which centered on the Curia Romana and the papal and other semiofficial courts. Roman humanism stands out as a spectacularly successful example of the accommodation of Renaissance intellectuals to their political and social surroundings, and of their transformation from outsiders to major defenders of the status quo.

Insofar as adaptability is the key element in understanding and evaluating Roman humanism, it is all the more important to place Roman humanism securely in its political and social context. This has required extensive discussions of the governmental and social institutions of Renaissance Rome and the Church. However, these analyses are selective. I have concentrated on those aspects of the Curia and Roman society which related directly to humanists and how they responded to them.

Since this study proposes an interpretation of Roman humanism, it must choose those elements which support its major propositions most clearly. The unique qualities of Roman humanism rather than the common elements of Renaissance humanism have been emphasized. In order to expose both the social-political ambience of Roman humanism and its special relations to Rome's religious character, this study is divided into two parts. Part I, consisting of Chapters 1–4, sketches the institutional, social, and general intellectual settings of Renaissance Rome. It begins with a consideration of humanist advancement in the Church hierarchy in Rome and the Curia Romana. In this treatment of the Curia special attention is given to the secretarial and similar offices that employed the most prominent humanists. Chapter 2 is devoted to the various households (*familiae*) or courts of the popes, cardinals, and rich laymen which offered humanists many employment opportunities and the means for social integration. Chapter 3 takes up the social position and career opportunities of the humanists' natural families. Here the goal is to show how humanists modified their familial ambitions to fit into the clerical-curial world of Rome and to provide some examples of this process. Chapter 4 sketches the types of social-institutional assemblies the Roman humanists invented as means of engaging in intellectual and scholarly discourse and for arriving at intellectual consensus.

Part II, Chapters 5–9, concentrates on the humanists as exponents of the religious character of Rome. Chapter 5 proposes a framework within which one may understand the humanists as defenders of Rome's religious and ecclesiological prominence. It attempts to demonstrate how the humanists coalesced their literary-scholarly and religious-clerical opinions into an ideology. Chapters 6, 7, and 8 provide detailed discussions of the moral and theological writings of three representative humanists. These men—Paolo Cortesi, Adriano Castellesi, and Raffaele Maffei—are examined because they represent the salient characteristics that one can identify as central to Roman humanism. They were successful curialists, active in Rome from the 1480s to the second decade of the cinquecento. They knew Rome's traditions well. Their intellectual development was characteristic of other humanists; they had been educated, at least in part, in Rome and were not members of religious orders. They had been intellectually formed by Rome's literary principles and standards. Finally, they all enjoyed international reputations for their humanist activity. They each contributed works of literary, historical, or philological value, and their religious writings were an important element in their humanism. Chapter 9 details the reform thought of the humanists at the point where their curial background and their religious-moral ideals coincided and often clashed. An attempt has been made to show both the extent to which the Roman humanists were conscious of the abuses of the Church and the Curia and the need to rectify them, and the reasons why they as participants in the institutions criticized did not propose any realistic solutions.

A natural yardstick with which to judge any interpretation of Roman humanism is the Florentine experience. This study tries to show where the two differed and where Rome modified humanistic elements to correspond to its special situation. A thorough comparison has not been attempted since my desire has been to establish the integrity of Roman humanism and not merely to discuss it as a deviation from an ideal type. Roman humanism grew on the foundations of Florentine humanism; however, it did not fashion itself in opposition to it, but blended in with Roman social and political-religious surroundings in order to create a unique intellectual movement.

PART I
ROMAN HUMANISTS

1

Humanist Prelates and Curialists

Roman humanism required little more than a century to develop its unique physiognomy and to suffer a premature end.[1] It grew dialectically by responding, on the one hand, to the limits imposed by a theocratically organized society and, on the other, to the traditions of Florentine humanism and its tendencies toward civic humanism and Neo-Platonism. The entry of Martin V into Rome in 1420 and the sack of the city in 1527 mark the limits of this extended century. When Martin arrived, Rome was an intellectual backwater, a victim of neglect resulting from the papacy's long absence at Avignon and the chaos of the subsequent Great Schism.[2] Naturally humanism did not come suddenly to Rome in the entourage of Martin V. Several prominent humanists had been active in the Curia Romana and in Rome before Martin's arrival, and some humanist traditions were established tentatively during the years of the Great Schism. These traditions did not reflect the unique elements of Roman life, nor did the disorganization that afflicted the Curia and Rome equally allow the humanists to establish easily permanent homes there before 1420.[3] However, humanism prospered so markedly after the reestablishment of the papacy that by the pontificate of Leo X (1513–1521) Rome had become the center of a group of confident intellectuals who interpreted cultural values for the mixed audiences of Rome. During this period Roman humanism developed from a fragile Florentine transplant into the dominant Italian form.

Within the limits of this century, a major subdivision dating from approximately 1475 until about 1520 stands out. In that period humanism triumphed in a Rome that had become a focal point of Italian intellectual activity. Drawn first to Rome by its classical associations and ruins, humanists developed certain definite characteristics which had been only embryonic in the previous decades. These characteristics differed from those of Florentine humanism, though Roman humanists often had Florentine or Tuscan origins. As with Florentine humanism, the Roman variety expressed cultural values derived from the reinterpretation of classical antiquity and its application to contemporary society. Unlike Florentine humanism, which grew within a republican and secular ambience, Roman humanism responded to the needs of a uniquely constituted clerical-courtly society. The resulting entity was distinct from the values of civic humanism since the individual could not affect Roman government or society. It differed further from the intellectual world of the Italian courts that were organized around secular patronage; these were in great part destroyed or greatly diminished in the military, political, and social upheavals resulting from the French invasion of Italy in 1494.[4]

❧ I ❧

Roman humanism can best be defined as curial, i.e., dependent upon the patronage of a court or courts. In Rome this term broadly signified the Roman Court, which included the papal *familia,* or household, the Curia Romana with its various branches or offices, and the several satellite courts of cardinals and other rich prelates and laymen.[5] Although aristocratic government had been increasing throughout Italy since the trecento, a process which accelerated in the quattro- and cinquecento, Rome had always had her courts and aristocrats. The various constituent elements of the Roman court centered in one form or another on the authority and person of the reigning pontiff. The Curia and the cardinals and the curial bureaucracy did not depend solely on the will of the pope but continued along well-established lines from pontificate to pontificate. Within limits, court life could express itself in a variety of forms since by the second half of the quattrocento Rome enjoyed sufficient income from papal revenues and from monies originating in the papal states to fund diverse activities; after the pontificate of Nicholas V (1447–1455), a political stability greater than that of most other Italian governments also developed.

Roman curial humanism cannot be equated simply with other court-dominated centers of humanism like Naples, Urbino, or Ferrara. Roman society was constituted and ruled unlike any other, its most distinctive quality being its control by the clerics. The clergy held the real power and determined the political, cultural, and intellectual life of the city. They provided most of the major employment opportunities in Rome and brought into the city the revenues on which all depended directly or indirectly. Even Rome's civil government was appointed and controlled by the pope and his advisers. This clerical monopoly assured that whatever might prevail in Rome had to come to terms with the clergy and its interests whether in the realms of hieratic worship, scholarship, and oratory or in the supervision of a European-wide administration. A clerical dictatorship limited the avenues of expression and

required a conformity that could prove stultifying if applied in a tyran-
nical manner. This dominance did not destroy intellectual and artistic
life in Rome since there was a laxity in clerical life and a lack of a clear
line of demarcation between clerical and secular elements. Men in orders
at whatever level (with the exception of those who belonged to the
mendicant and other religious orders) often did not differ appreciably
from their secular brothers in their intellectual and social habits. The
passing from one state to the other was not a difficult one to maneuver.
In an age before uniform seminary education, clerics and laymen were
often indistinguishable.

The humanists' ability to function in Rome's clerical society reflected
a significant change in humanism itself during the last decades of the
fifteenth century.[6] In response to the ambiguities of a scholarly existence and the need for economic security, many humanists were greatly
attracted to clerical life in some form. This was so especially if it offered
a benefice with no residency requirement. A close connection between
humanism and the clerical state developed; indeed, we may speak of a
relative "clericalization" of humanism. Humanists saw no threat to
their intellectual interests if they found it advisable to take orders. Any
concept of "vocation" was obviously weak in such a circumstance, and
the vagueness of the religious content of the minor orders made their
acceptance easy since there was little need to alter established lay behavior. In Rome this tendency was intensified by a movement within
the Curia to staff exclusively with clerics those offices which earlier in
the century had been open to laymen. Lay status thereby became
increasingly an impediment to advancement to an individual seeking his
fortune in Rome. This clericalization was not unique to Rome, only
more pervasive there. Angelo Poliziano was in minor orders, Marsilio
Ficino a priest, Pico della Mirandola an apostolic protonotary and in
minor orders, and Baldassare Castiglione, also in orders, served as a
papal nuncio. Some prelates were at times more renowned as men of
letters than as clerics.

Naturally, Roman clerical society was exclusively male and celibate
at the official level; women had no openly acknowledged place in it.
The official Roman *familia,* or household, for example, was a hybrid
entity, usually created to satisfy the pope's or a prelate's official and
domestic needs but untouched by the feminine; it lacked any natural
binding force save careerism. Also, marriage had an ambiguous position
in Roman society since it could effectively block advancement in the
bureaucracy as the Curia became increasingly clericalized. To compen-
sate for this sexual-social imbalance, Roman society accepted the role
of the courtesan and open concubinage. Rome was famous for her large

number of prostitutes, of varying social status, and some learned men naturally sought out women who could fill their intellectual and emotional as well as their physical needs. A few beautiful, learned courtesans such as the famous Imperia ran the equivalent of salons, which attracted humanists and learned prelates.[7] Consequently, concubinage and illegitimacy actually assumed a quasi-official status, reflecting a widespread tendency in the fourteenth and fifteenth centuries to ignore the prohibition against a married clergy.[8] The close-knit family of Cardinal Rodrigo Borgia, later Alexander VI, is the most famous case of the weakness of clerical celibacy; it exemplifies how Roman society accepted improper alliances among the rich and powerful as well as among the lower ranks. Innocent VIII, to the scandal of many, originated the practice of official recognition of illegitimate papal offspring. The need to marry papal children well and to find for them suitable positions consumed increasingly large amounts of papal time and finances. As in feudal society, illegitimacy held no final disabling character since the popes could, and did, easily legitimize. Alexander VI legitimized his son, Cesare Borgia, in order to create him a cardinal. When Leo X became pope, he appointed his illegitimate cousin, Giulio, to the cardinalate and later made him vice-chancellor of the Church; when Giulio became pope, his *datarius* and chief adviser was the illegitimate Gian Matteo Giberti.

This sexual imbalance affected humanism in several ways. First, on a purely formal level, it limited the material a humanist could discuss when approaching a clerical patron or the official court. Humanists could not propose to Roman society the ideal of Alberti's family, whose generations of young and old, male and female, lived in natural union.[9] This sexual peculiarity also had the effect of encouraging laymen employed in the Curia Romana or by prelates to delay marriage until late in life or to accept minor orders for career purposes (although certain of the minor orders were compatible with marriage), and this naturally stimulated concubinage. Often those who did marry kept their families away from Rome and its scandals, an expedient that conveniently allowed them a putative celibate status. The ambiguities of official celibacy are seen in the case of certain curial officials, e.g., judges, who, although married and the fathers of children, had to dress and comport themselves as clerics for the purposes of their offices. In such a situation a lenient attitude toward canonical rules is not surprising.

Within this male-oriented society, Roman intellectuals adapted their interests to reflect the concerns of the Curia and the clergy. Both in acknowledgment of this need and as a reflection of their own literary prejudices, Roman humanists concentrated their talents on Latin. Latin remained the official language of all curial business till the end of the quattrocento, and all papal letters and official documents of the Curia were in Latin. This emphasis on Latin both helped to attract humanists to Rome and was instrumental in integrating them into Roman society. Humanists communicated with each other and their supporters and addressed the world almost exclusively in Latin prose and poetry. The nature and development of the Latin language was an important topic for Roman humanists.[10] Vernacular prose had only a minor position among them, with the exception of Marc'Antonio Altieri (1450-1532), although there was greater interest in Italian poetry.[11] This concentration on Latin within the curial bureaucracy assured an audience for the poetry, orations, histories, and classical editions and commentaries humanists produced.

A further characteristic of Roman society, and one related to the dominance of Latin, was its cosmopolitanism. This was a medieval inheritance. In great part the trend continued into the Renaissance, even though in the quattrocento the Curia as a whole was becoming more and more Italian.[12] Indeed, Roman society was remarkably non-Roman. Italians from other sections of Italy—most notably Naples and Tuscany—and non-Italians—Frenchmen, Germans, and Spaniards in particular—gave Rome a special flavor.[13] They came to Rome to do business in the Curia or to see the religious and classical sites, or to find permanent employment. Some spent only a short time there, while others lived the greater part of their adult lives in Rome. In some ways the bureaucracy actively encouraged cosmopolitanism. When Sixtus IV in 1472 reorganized the auditors of the *Sacra Romana Rota*—a judicial office—and fixed their number at twelve, he also divided their membership among the important Western and Italian states.[14] It is ironic that the most famous humanist of Roman birth and from a well-established curial family, Lorenzo Valla (1407-1457), spent most of his productive life outside Rome and received an important curial post in Rome only toward the end of his life.[15] His feuding with other humanist members of the Curia, while based on literary disagreements, was not without its civic element.

A conspicuous example of a foreigner's success in Rome is the career of the German humanist Jacob Questenberg (*ca.* 1470-*ca.* 1524).[16] During forty years in the Curia, from the pontificate of Innocent VIII to that of Clement VII, Questenberg rose from papal scriptor to apostolic protonotary and a cleric of the College of Cardinals—a financial post—while at the same time holding several German benefices. His nationality did not inhibit his enjoying close support from the popes he served. He also held a degree in law, which facilitated his entrance and advancement in the bureaucracy. Learned in Greek and Latin, he devoted his free time to classical scholarship and poetry and actively participated in the intellectual life of the city. While there were no doubt many examples of tension between Italians and non-Italians, Questenberg's experiences show that Roman society was probably more open to national differences than any other in Western Europe.

❧ II ❧

With its clerical predominance, Roman society could not help but be strictly hierarchical. Everyone had a superior to whom he had to answer and upon whom he often depended for his livelihood. At the summit of this hierarchy stood the pope, the theoretically absolute monarch of the city and the Church (at least so curial propagandists maintained). Since all authority related directly or indirectly to the pontiff, the popes played important roles in the history of Roman humanism, even if only indirectly. In general, the popes vacillated in their attitudes toward humanism.[17] Even though few harsh doubts were registered about the humanists and their values (the major exception being Paul II), there was no continuous program of papal support until the end of the quattrocento. It would be wrong to picture the Renaissance papacy as a wholehearted supporter of humanist learning. Rather, the popes' attitudes were pragmatic. They willingly accepted the literary talents of the humanists and usually allowed them to engage in their intellectual interests on their own time without interference. The career of Aeneas Silvius Piccolomini (1405-1464),[18] an internationally respected humanist, papal official, bishop, cardinal, and finally pope, Pius II (1458), proves that humanistic fame in itself posed no noticeable impediment to ecclesiastical and curial advancement. In like manner, humanistic ability per se never sufficed to move a pope to advance a man far up in the bureaucracy. The popes of the quattrocento were either political creatures or men of scholastic backgrounds rather than literary ones, with the exception of Nicholas V and Pius II. Yet Sixtus IV (1471-1484),[19] a Franciscan and Scholastic theologian with no predilection for humanistic studies before his election, was more important as a patron of humanism in Rome than Pius II.

The popes realized early on that humanism could have administrative and political advantages.[20] The humanists could broadcast papal political positions. They did so during the Great Schism and during the extended struggles with the reform councils through their writings and through their secretarial skills. They were especially valuable as ambassadors to hostile or wavering courts.[21] In their desire to reestablish their position as equals to secular governments, some popes felt that support of humanistic learning, like a grand building program, was one means of self-advertisement. Several popes realized the political value of humanism in presenting the papal court as a cultural force equal to, if not greater than, any secular court. In so doing the papacy sought to achieve an intellectual and cultural leadership of Western Europe partly through the agency of humanism.

Both Martin V (1417-1431) and Eugenius IV (1431-1447) were too involved in reestablishing the papacy in Rome and rebuilding its political and financial structures in often hostile civic and international surroundings to concern themselves with the intellectual ambience of the city. Nevertheless, they were generally open to humanism and employed many humanists in the papal bureaucracy.[22] The pontificate of Nicholas V (1447-1455)[23] marked humanism's first major advance in Rome and in the Curia Romana. Nicholas established a policy of open support of humanism which was to continue in later pontificates. In his prepapal years Nicholas had carefully studied classical and Christian authors, patristic and Scholastic theologians, and had intimate connections with Florentine humanism. He was, however, more a lover of books and learning than an independent scholar. His experience in church politics, especially in the Unionist Council of Florence (1439), where humanist knowledge of Greek proved valuable, helped him to realize the value of humanist learning to the papacy and the Church.[24] His devotion to Latin and Greek scholarship, especially his desire to have translations made of the Greek classical and patristic masterpieces, made him employ noted humanists as translators; in payment he often offered the humanists posts in the Curia as well as monetary gifts.[25] Nicholas's humanistic patronage formed part of his general plan to remake Rome into the cultural center of Europe. This program included the foundation of the new papal library, which Sixtus IV would perfect, and the rebuilding of the Vatican and the refurbishing of the old St. Peter's, a prototype for Julius II's great building schemes. In Nicholas's eyes humanism, like architecture, was another form of patronage which spread the glory of its patron—a view shared by Nicholas's close friend Cosimo de' Medici.[26]

Of the succeeding popes, Calixtus III (1455-1458), a Spaniard by birth and canon lawyer by training, and Pius II (1458-1464)[27] devoted their time and energies to the preparation of a crusade against the Turks which never materialized and to the advancement of their own families. The Venetian Paul II (1464-1471)[28] had a much deeper interest in artistic matters than in literature and viewed Roman humanism as

politically and religiously suspect. However, humanism suffered no lasting reverses during these pontificates. The humanists remained important members of the Curia. Even the notorious suppression of the
Roman Academy by Paul II did not cause humanists to flee Rome.[29]
The Curia had become too dependent on humanist expertise to reject
it, and the humanists were too attracted to its professional opportunities to forsake Rome.

The full significance of Nicholas's use of humanist learning became
clear only under Sixtus IV. Sixtus's pontificate advanced humanism's
place in Rome and at the papal court. This did not mean that Sixtus
himself had either a great love or understanding of humanistic scholarship but rather that it formed an element in his grandiose conception
of the papacy.[30] Under Sixtus humanism prospered because it contributed to the pope's intention of establishing the papacy as a great secular
power. Whatever the reasons for Sixtus's patronage of humanists, it was
real and important. Building on the program laid out by Nicholas, Sixtus advanced the model of a papacy involved in humanistic, artistic,
and architectural patronage which would be perfected by his nephew
Julius II.

Sixtus's two immediate successors, Innocent VIII (1484-1492) and
Alexander VI (1492-1503), were generally uninterested in humanistic
studies.[31] Innocent, a weak individual, devoted most of his energies to
marrying off his son. Alexander, with similar familial concerns, employed a few humanists in important positions, but usually his requirements for support were political, not intellectual. These two popes in
no way hindered humanism, which continued to advance in the Curia
despite the low moral tone of these pontificates. Pius III (1503)[32]
ruled for only a month. As a cardinal, Pius (the nephew of Pius II) had
been an important supporter of humanists and humanistically inclined
prelates, and it is possible that, had he lived longer, his reign as pope
might have witnessed a flowering of humanism.

Julius II (1503-1513),[33] probably the strongest personality to sit on
the papal throne during the Renaissance, followed his uncle Sixtus's
program of exploiting humanism and the arts for essentially political
purposes. Although his patronage of the arts is better known and played
a more obvious part in his pontificate, humanism also had an important
role in defining the cultural ambitions of Julian Rome. Again, the
pope's personal interests or expertise in humanistic learning were less
important than his willingness to allow it to develop freely. If the humanist Raffaele Maffei was correct in maintaining that Julius was indifferent to learning and did not even bother to read the titles of the
books dedicated to him, then Julius was obviously capable of ignoring

humanists whenever it suited his purposes.[34] However, the same Maffei also observed that Julius could appreciate well-written Latin poetry.[35] Julius was too shrewd a politician to have been either ignorant of or indifferent to the cultural vitality of Renaissance Rome. He knew well that humanism, like the architecture of Bramante, the painting of Raphael, and the sculpture of Michelangelo, represented the cultural and intellectual avant-garde, and he did not miss the opportunity to capitalize on it. Julius had been a careful student during his years of apprenticeship under Sixtus, and he seems to have known the political value of cultural patronage.

Leo X (1513-1521)[36] has generally enjoyed the reputation of a great humanist pope. While there is a certain truth in this, the limits of Leo's pontificate, in all areas, have become clearer as a result of more recent research.[37] Certainly none of his predecessors, with the exception of Pius II, could claim to have had as thorough a humanist training. Leo could boast as a tutor no less a scholar than Poliziano.[38] His humanistic patronage, even in his own day, was legendary. In many ways his pontificate marked both the zenith of official recognition of humanism and the first signs of its decay. Leo could be generous with his patronage, but not always wise. He gave official recognition to humanism, especially in selecting two Ciceronian stylists, Pietro Bembo and Jacopo Sadoleto, as his private secretaries. He had a seemingly unlimited appetite for neo-Latin verse and could himself spin a good Latin lyric extemporaneously.[39] However, by the end of Leo's reign some humanists felt constricted and a few left Rome sensing the limits of Leo's overextended treasury and fruitless foreign policy as well as the increasing pressure brought to bear on Rome and its humanism by religious confrontations.[40]

Adrian VI's brief pontificate (1522-1523) cut papal patronage and frustrated humanist hopes for continued papal largesse.[41] The bitterness on the part of the humanists and Roman curialists generally toward Adrian was extreme and completely out of proportion with any act on the pontiff's part, however.[42] Adrian's conservative and careful financial procedures and his desire to reform the Curia and the Church contrasted sharply with his predecessor's financial profligacy (especially in military matters) and laissez-faire administration and as a result damned him in the eyes of the Romans. Despite the warmest of receptions by the Roman humanists upon his election, Clement VII (1523-1534),[43] Leo's cousin and major adviser, merely watched as the intellectual dominance of Rome passed away, too weak and indecisive to do anything to halt the situation. His disastrous foreign policy, which wavered between pro-French and pro-Spanish support, culminated in the sack of

Rome and marked the end of High Renaissance Roman culture. The sack interrupted Roman life and ended the confidence of Renaissance humanism.

Papal favor toward humanism was neither continuous nor uniform, but it was always informed by the various popes' policy needs. Political exigencies, financial problems, and family pressures could impede the ability or will of a pope to advance cultural interests, while his personality and education could prove inimical to the essentially secular concerns of humanist study of ancient culture and literature. Still, given all these qualifications, papal support manifested itself at certain decisive moments. Nicholas's patronage, which came just as the papacy finally regained stability, identified humanist culture with elements of papal policy. Sixtus repaired whatever damage was done to humanism and humanists by Paul II's attack on the Roman Academy and reaffirmed Nicholas's identification. Julius's and Leo's support coincided with reverses suffered by humanism as a result of the political and social upheavals Italian states experienced at the end of the quattrocento, especially Florence. Under the aegis of these popes, Italian humanism received a world-center stage for its intellectual and cultural manifestations and secured a prominent place for certain of its representatives. Papal Rome thereby became the last stronghold for the Latin humanism of the quattrocento.

❧ III ❧

The papacy could set the cultural and intellectual pace of Renaissance Rome, but it was erratic in its support of humanism. However, when a pontiff who was unfriendly or indifferent to humanism reigned, humanists could elicit support from the resident cardinals and prelates and even secure membership in their number. Indeed, a fair index of humanism's success in Rome is the extent to which humanists advanced to the episcopate, as well as the extent to which high prelates accepted humanist patronage as a requirement of their position. When discussing the prelates of Rome, it must be remembered that they differed from their equals throughout Europe. They were part of the central administrative apparatus of the Church rather than diocesan leaders. They did not reside in their dioceses. Further, while they had to resign their curial offices when they were appointed bishops, a dispensation from this requirement was also obtainable. They preferred the cosmopolitan society of Rome to life in a provincial Italian or northern European city. These men were conscious of their position in the center of Western Christendom and tended to overestimate their importance and influence. They formed an elite within an elite and generally were better educated than other clerics and prelates.[44]

A number of humanists became bishops in Renaissance Rome. With a few exceptions, those who did rise to the episcopacy either had important prelate-friends or had demonstrated loyal curial service. Usually humanist training and talents provided them with the first step in their careers. It guaranteed them the necessary qualifications to act as secretaries to prelates or to fill curial posts. If they were successful as poets or orators or produced important examples of scholarship, these could provide them with additional claims to preference. Generally they depended on their proven administrative or diplomatic abilities or upon their political connections for the final step to a bishopric. Whatever other factors contributed to their success, those humanists who did enter the hierarchical elite demonstrated a definite cultural hegemony.

The career of Niccolò Perotti (1429-1480)[45] exemplifies the intermingling of scholarly and political-curial characteristics necessary for a successful humanist bishop. Perotti received a good humanist education, studying with the famous humanist teachers Vittorino da Feltre and Guarino da Verona. He came to Rome in 1447 and entered the service of Cardinal Bessarion, with whom he remained until the cardinal's death. His knowledge of Greek allowed him to undertake a series of translations of ancient and patristic Greek texts for Nicholas V. His relationship with Bessarion and his translations won him the post of apostolic secretary in 1455. The next year he began a diplomatic career when he was sent to Naples on an embassy. Like other curialists, Perotti realized the value of clerical status for purposes of advancement and he took holy orders in 1456. His ecclesiastical career was as successful as his curial one, culminating in 1458 with the archbishopric of Siponto. Diplomacy remained an important element in his career, including missions to Mantua, Germany, and Venice. A major advance came with his appointment to the governorships of Viterbo (1464-1469), Spoleto (1471-1472), and Perugia (1474-1477). Unfortunately he could not overcome the civic factionalism common to the papal states, and his administration proved unsuccessful. After his tenure in Perugia, Perotti retired from active civic life and devoted his time to study. Perotti's humanistic production was substantial. He translated extensively from Greek, especially moral and historical works, wrote a grammatical treatise, a life of Cardinal Bessarion, and commentaries on classical writers. Essentially a philologist who loved words, his greatest contribution to scholarship was the *Cornucopia, sive commentaria linguae latinae.* In form the *Cornucopia* was a grand commentary on

Martial, but in content it was an enormously erudite study of the Latin language.

Perotti experienced the often heavy administrative duties that could be imposed on a curial humanist. Others were able to exploit their ecclesiastical status more completely to further their intellectual and scholarly interests. One such man was Giovanni Andrea Bussi (1417–1475).[46] Bussi came from a well-established family in Vigevano in Lombardy. As a youth he studied in Paris and in Mantua with Vittorino da Feltre; he subsequently taught school in Genoa before going to Rome. In 1451 he became an acolyte for Nicholas V, which indicates that he was at least in minor orders by that date. Other offices and honors followed: a canonate in Milan worth 24 florins (1455), a post in the papal *familia* of Calixtus III, and a deanship in Santa Maria in Via Lata in Rome. A major advance in his career came when Cardinal Nicholas of Cusa chose him as his secretary. The German cardinal must have trusted Bussi's scholarly abilities, for he permitted him to correct his writings. Pius II created Bussi bishop of Acci in Corsica (1461) while allowing him to keep a commendary abbacy in Milan since Acci was a poor diocese. In 1464 Pius appointed Bussi vicar of the archdiocese of Genoa and in 1466 translated him to the bishopric of Aleria, also in Corsica. Bussi even had some diplomatic responsibilities, accompanying Juan de Carvajal on an embassy to Venice. Later Sixtus IV appointed him one of his secretaries and director of the papal library (1472).

For all his curial and ecclesiastical activities, Bussi devoted most of his energies to scholarship. His most valuable contribution was as editor for the German printers Sweynheym and Pannartz, an association which began in 1468.[47] Bussi was one of the first humanists to take an active part in the recently introduced press. Inspired by his employer Nicholas of Cusa, Bussi collaborated in the editing of a variety of texts. Especially prominent among his productions were editions of Platonistic writings and Greek translations. His association with Bessarion partly accounts for these interests. Noteworthy is the large number of *editiones principes* he produced, including works by Cicero, Caesar, Vergil, Ovid, Strabo, Lucan, Cyprian, Silius Italicus, Aulus Gellius, Jerome, Leo the Great, Aquinas, and Nicholas of Lyra. Cardinal Pietro Riario, the favorite nephew of Sixtus IV, employed Bussi in a project to establish a library in his palace at SS. Apostoli, a forerunner to Sixtus's library. However, Bussi seems not to have been very active in the project and the library never materialized.

A final example will further indicate the political dangers of curial service. Giannantonio Campano (1429–1477)[48] came from a modest family from Caserta, near Naples. He studied in Naples, Siena, and

Perugia and taught rhetoric at Perugia's university. He came to Rome as Perugia's ambassador to congratulate Calixtus III and Pius II upon their elections. His literary abilities brought him into contact with important curial cardinals and associates of Pius II, including cardinals Filippo Calandrini, Jacopo Ammannati-Piccolomini, Alessandro Oliva, and Francesco Todeschini-Piccolomini. Like his brother Angelo, who belonged to the household of Cardinal Angelo Capranica, Campano served as secretary to Cardinal Liva and in the *familia* of Todeschini-Piccolomini. His poetic talents attracted the attention of Pius II, who named him bishop of Crotone in Calabria in 1462 and in the following year transferred him to the see of Teramo in the Abruzzi. Although a member of the Roman Academy, Campano did not suffer from Paul II's suppression of that humanist group. Indeed, Paul was unsuccessful in soliciting Campano's services as his biographer, but sent him on a legation to Germany in 1471. Upon the ascension of Sixtus IV, Campano obtained the support of the favorite papal nephew, Cardinal Pietro Riario. Sixtus appointed Campano to the governorship of Todi in 1472, of Foligno and Assisi in 1473, and of Città di Castello in 1474. While serving in the last-named post, he unwisely defended Niccolò Vitelli, the *signore* of Città di Castello, against Sixtus's attacks. His insubordination earned him dismissal from office and the loss of papal favor. Campano spent the last years of his life in his diocese in Teramo.

Campano was a prominent figure in Rome's intellectual circles. Like Bussi he was an early contributor to the Roman press. He worked for the German publisher Ulrich Hahn as a corrector of texts. He was especially prized by his contemporaries for his oratorical and poetic skills. As noted above, Pius II especially valued his poetic production. The pope had such confidence in Campano's literary skills that he gave him the duty of correcting his memoirs, the *Commentarii rerum memorabilium.* His poetry covered a wide range of topics: praise of his friends and patrons; devotional religious themes; and erotic, even homosexual, verse. His literary accomplishments also included biographies of Braccio da Montone and Pius II. Like Bussi and Perotti, Campano owed his initial success to his humanistic talents and contacts, and like Perotti, he floundered on the internal politics of the papal states.

The list of humanist bishops in Rome could easily be extended, but that is unnecessary here. The pattern is clear. A humanist could aspire to a bishopric, but only occasionally was it a reward for his learning, and his duties could be exacting. Access to a cardinalate, however, was much more restricted. (Although a cardinal, unlike a bishop, did not have to be a priest, he did have to be in minor orders.) The red hat was not a gift handed out lightly by a pope to a good poet, editor, or scholar. Humanistic talents trailed formidable political or personal qualifications in the selection of a cardinal. Men were created cardinals because of their long, faithful service in the Curia; their close, usually familial, relationship to the reigning pope or an important secular ruler; their outstanding service in a religious order; or, finally, to meet the needs of particular political situations.[49] When we find a humanist in the College of Cardinals, we must look to determinative considerations other than his humanist scholarship.

Whatever their other qualifications, a few—very few—cardinals owed their early success to their humanistic abilities. This rarity requires that we look closely at the career of such an individual in order to determine the place of humanistic scholarship in the intellectual and political life of a high Roman cleric. One man stands out as a prime candidate for such consideration, Adriano Castellesi of Corneto (Tarquinia), near Rome (1458-1522?).[50] Castellesi enjoyed a European-wide reputation as a Latin stylist and a minor one as a Hebrew scholar, but his literary productions followed his promotion to the cardinalate. He published all his major writings after his selection as a cardinal in 1503, while functioning at the highest level of papal politics and diplomacy.

Almost no information exists on Castellesi's early life in Corneto. We know that he came to Rome through the aid of a cleric-uncle who introduced him to the powerful Cardinal Rodrigo Borgia, and that he subsequently entered the Curia. Learned in Latin, Greek, and Hebrew, he belonged to a group of young curial humanists, mostly Tuscan by birth, who were working their way up in the curial bureaucracy in the 1480s and 1490s. Included in this group were Tommaso Fedra Inghirami, Raffaele Maffei (1451-1522), both from Volterra, and Paolo Cortesi (1465-1510). All these men successfully united their humanist scholarship with their offices and established Italian and European reputations while making their fortune through curial revenues.

Beginning in the 1480s, Castellesi held several curial offices in his steady rise through the bureaucracy. He served first as solicitor of apostolic letters, then as a notary in the *Camera Apostolica* (a post that cost him 1,000 ducats), a cleric of the *Camera,* a papal scriptor, the collector of Peter's pence in England, an apostolic secretary, the treasurer-general of the Church, and an apostolic protonotary.[51] Most of these posts represent a good cross section of the types of curial posts humanists found most congenial to their talents. Castellesi also had diplomatic experiences and served on special missions to Scotland (1489) and France (1498). A crisis in his early career came when he contracted to marry a relative of his colleague Fedra Inghirami. He subsequently reconsidered, opted for clerical status, and received a papal annulment (1487).[52]

Like other curialists, Castellesi realized the need to take holy orders in order to advance in the Curia and the Church.

Perhaps as a compensation for his decision not to marry, as well as an acknowledgment of his literary and oratorical talents and of his connections to the powerful Borgias, the pope dispatched Castellesi to Scotland on a diplomatic mission to settle a civil war in 1489. Changed political circumstances, however, stranded him in England and brought him the unexpected opportunity to secure the patronage of the king of England, Henry VII.[53] Castellesi spent two years in England and obtained royal support for the posts of collector of Peter's pence in England and orator, or representative, of the English nation in the Curia.[54] His service to England earned him the bishoprics of Hereford (1502) and Bath and Wells (1503).[55] The esteem of the English king, close relations with the German imperial faction in Rome, and friendship with the Borgia pope resulted in Castellesi's appointment as private secretary to Pope Alexander in succession to Bartolomeo Florido (1497).[56] As Alexander's private secretary Castellesi was privy to the pope's secrets, or so some of his contemporaries believed. Despite this seemingly compromising position, Castellesi's friend the humanist Raffaele Maffei praised him for avoiding the moral ambiguities of Alexandrine Rome.[57] Alexander elevated Castellesi to the cardinalate shortly before his death in 1503.[58] As a cardinal Castellesi was considered one of the richer members of the college.[59] He was obviously successful in taking advantage of his various posts since his wealth was based exclusively on his curial and ecclesiastical offices.

As a humanist Castellesi represented the favored curial Latin style, Ciceronianism. He produced a Latin phrase book, *De modo loquendi* (1507),[60] which offered abundant examples of proper Latin form based in great part on Cicero. It was popular in the sixteenth century as a textbook, especially when combined with Castellesi's *De sermone latino* (1516),[61] a short history of the development of the Latin language. As a man of letters Castellesi befriended foreign intellectuals, including the German Hebraist Johannes Reuchlin and the English humanist and churchman John Fisher.[62] As a Hebrew scholar, Castellesi attempted to translate part of the Scriptures directly from Hebrew into Latin.[63] He was an accomplished poet and was widely respected for his Latin verse.[64] He collected a series of theological statements from the writings of the four Latin doctors of the Church and used them in the *De Vera Philosophia* (1507), a treatise attacking theologians' dependence on human reason.[65] This last work is an important source for fideistic tendencies among Roman humanists. Despite his busy political career, Castellesi found the time to produce some literary and scholarly pieces, even if they were relatively short (apart from the poetry, they were in great part collections of material rather than original compositions).

Castellesi made several disastrous errors in his political life. He fled Rome in September 1507 when Julius II learned of a derogatory remark he had made about him to the English king.[66] Castellesi feared Julius's wrath and sought refuge in Austria, where he cultivated closer relations with Emperor Maximilian. Castellesi even seconded Maximilian's plan to have himself elected pope while still emperor.[67] Julius's death in 1513 allowed Castellesi to return to Rome and take part in the conclave that elected Leo X. In the first years of the new pontificate, Castellesi enjoyed papal favor and was able to regain some of his lost influence at the papal court. As a sign of papal favor, he might have received special economic privileges in Ancona.[68] His political and economic positions collapsed, however, when he was implicated in the conspiracy of the cardinals to poison Leo in 1517.[69] Although he seems to have been innocent of any wrongdoing, Castellesi was forced to pay 25,000 ducats as punishment. Not trusting Leo's willingness to forgive even for a large cash sum, Castellesi took flight once again, this time seeking asylum in Venice, whose government Castellesi had consistently cultivated. Castellesi's rejection of papal calls to return to Rome allowed his enemies, led by Cardinal Thomas Wolsey, who coveted Castellesi's English benefices, to convince the pope to deprive the cardinal of his red hat. This was accomplished in June 1518. Castellesi devoted his last years in Venice to continued study of Hebrew and theology. He died, probably early in 1522, the victim of a robbery attempt by a servant while returning to Rome to participate in the conclave following Leo's death.[70]

Castellesi's life was exceptionally dramatic and was unique in combining politics and humanistic scholarship at such a high level. While only his poetry was original, as a whole his writings do reveal a sensitivity to current intellectual trends. He even joined scholarship with politics. Franceso Todeschini-Piccolomini, for example, humanist patron and cardinal-protector of the English nation, to whom Castellesi dedicated a derivative piece on canon law, the *De Romanae Ecclesiae potestate* (*ca.* 1492), was in a position to assist Castellesi in his relations with the English.[71] Castellesi also dedicated his *De Vera Philosophia* to Henry VII and the *De sermone latino* to Charles of Spain, the grandson of Emperor Maximilian. His amassed wealth allowed him to build a grand palace in Rome[72] and to act as a patron to other humanists. Among these humanists was Polydore Vergil, the later historian of the English nation whom Castellesi introduced into England as subcollector of Peter's pence.[73] Few men in early sixteenth-century

Rome blended their intellectual and political careers as successfully as Castellesi.

When one looks more deeply into the history of the Renaissance cardinalate, few other humanists stand out.[74] Cardinals Francesco Todeschini and Jacopo Ammannati[75] were relatives of Pope Pius II and used his family name, Piccolomini; their humanist credentials were incidental to their promotion. The famous Cardinal Bessarion received his red hat for his willingness to abandon Orthodoxy for Latin Christianity.[76] Cardinal Bernardo Dovizi of Bibbiena (1470–1520), a famous Italian playwright, was Leo X's primary political adviser in the early years of his pontificate.[77] These and other humanist prelates did not depend on scholarly or literary criteria for their success.

Few humanists commanded such nonhumanistic requirements to rise to a bishopric and fewer still to a cardinalate. Rather, most were relegated to lesser positions either in the *familia,* or household, of the rich Roman prelates (a topic that will be discussed more fully below) or in teaching at the University of Rome (called the *Sapienza*), as private tutors or in the city's elementary schools. However, by far the most important employment prospects for the humanists were the various offices of the Curia Romana. Naturally only a minority of the employees of the Curia, even at the most literate levels, were humanists. Nevertheless, it is valid to connect the Curia with humanism because of the important role the Curia played in humanist life and humanism's effects on the cultural tendencies of the members of the Curia.

❦ IV ❦

Bureaucratic organization characterized Renaissance Rome more than any other Western European society. The need to staff the myriad offices of the Curia Romana attracted to Rome from all parts of Europe men whose lives were affected by its demands and its opportunities. The Renaissance Curia reflected centuries of centralization within the late medieval Church and experienced major reorganization as a result of the dislocations brought about by the Great Schism and the increased demands made on the Church's administrative center throughout the quattrocento. Since the Curia played such a central role in Renaissance Roman life and humanism, it is necessary to explain its workings in some detail. Of course, any sketch of such a complex organism as the Curia must ignore many complicated elements and treat its offices as static when in fact they were dynamic.

The Renaissance Curia remained very much a medieval institution that had grown pragmatically in response to the increasing demands made upon it. Nevertheless, it did display certain salient characteristics of modern bureaucracies.[78] First, its various offices assumed ever more specific jurisdictions, dividing power along judicial, administrative, and financial lines. The process was a slow one, however, and any one office could include all three elements. This functional division increased at the end of the sixteenth century when Sixtus V (1585-1590) reformed the offices of the Curia and reorganized them into congregations and tribunals. Second, the Curia operated along hierarchically organized lines of authority. Subordinates answered to specifically designated superiors in performing their duties. Even among those who were in the same office and executed the same or similar tasks, a hierarchical arrangement prevailed. In this the Curia mirrored accurately its ecclesiastical origins. Third, the Curia lived by producing formal documents. Lower officials generated a variety of written documents that expressed the decisions of the pope and the bureaucracy, and these officials were paid in cash for their work. Fourth, expert training, whether legal, theological, or secretarial, defined the qualifications for career advancement, although this was blunted by the venality of offices. Fifth, the offices were governed by well-established rules which directed the actions of the bureaucrats and against which their work could be judged. Each new pope issued compilations of rules and regulations such as the *Regulae Cancellariae Apostolicae,* which informed both the curialists and their clients of the organization's requirements.

These modern, rationalized bureaucratic features were counterbalanced by a number of factors. The pope had the theoretical power to act independently of the bureaucracy's regular procedures whenever he wished. He could create or abolish offices as well as abrogate their laws and rules. Many curialists developed lucrative careers by holding more than one curial post. To an extent this frustrated the smooth functioning of the bureaucracy. The holding of extracurial ecclesiastical benefices (even if in great part the responsibilities entailed were delegated) further divided curialists' attention. Similarly, the prevalence of the venality of offices undermined the efficiency of the organization. Still, with all these limiting factors, the size and organization of the Curia made it probably the most complex and certainly the most international government in Western Europe.

A complex structure such as the Curia required a large number of learned men to do its paper work and to settle legal disputes.[79] This educational requirement naturally attracted humanists to Rome, and at one time or another many were bureaucrats. A talented young man with a good knowledge of Latin or with a degree in law, especially if he had good connections or, in the latter half of the quattrocento, enough money to buy an office, could find a socially and financially rewarding niche in Rome. While the Curia was hardly a model of a meritocracy, it did realize the desirability of advancing its learned employees. Membership in the bureaucracy required that the humanists accept and follow the rules that governed their offices. As a natural consequence of this a certain conservative attitude toward the Curia's rules and traditions informed its employees' attitudes, including the humanists'.

As the central judicial, financial, and administrative body of the Church, the Curia Romana experienced the natural increases and alterations of any bureaucracy, and these changes opened opportunities for new men to enter the offices.[80] The Curia's functions increased throughout the Middle Ages. The Avignon papacy had continued the process of consolidating and expanding curial power, and even the setbacks of the Great Schism and the conciliar attempts to limit the Curia's power and size could not halt the process. The Curia grew as a result of the papacy's position as the court of final appeal in spiritual and temporal matters, through its ability to dispense or forgive from ecclesiastical or civil censures or impediments, and by means of its claim to control the distribution of a wide variety of ecclesiastical offices throughout Europe.[81] Historically these powers and prerogatives evolved in response to Christians' seeking forgiveness for their sins or legitimization of their ecclesiastical authority from the pope. In order to meet these requests the papacy and the canon lawyers created a variety of rules and exceptions that could be applied only by the Holy See through the machinery of the Curia. The normal procedure consisted of the petitioner's submitting a request or supplication to the pope, who then issued his decision in the form of a rescript, called in general *litterae apostolicae,* which was then communicated to the interested party.[82] For the requested justice or favor (called *gratia*) bestowed, a tax, or payment, was charged; in theory, the charge was made for the document containing the dispensation of favor and not for the act itself. These charges, which originated as free-will donations, subsequently became standardized and obligatory.[83] This arrangement obviously appealed to many Christians since the initiative for most papal documents came from outside the Curia, and thus the volume of business increased throughout the Renaissance.

At the head of the Curia stood the pope and his assistants, the cardinals. Together they supervised directly or indirectly the bureaucracy's departments. Distinct from the Curia was the papal *familia,* or household, although there was some overlap between the two. The papal household was essentially a separate entity, but depended on

DIAGRAM OF THE RENAISSANCE CURIA ROMANA

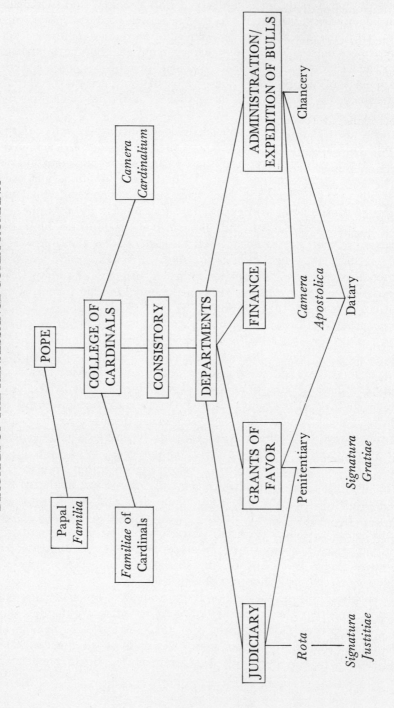

the reigning pontiff and lacked, to an extent, the independent existence of the curial offices. Naturally not all the cardinals resided in Rome and assisted in the administration of the Curia. Those cardinals who lived in the city helped govern the Church and supervise the Curia by participating in the consistory, which made policy and decided certain legal questions. Some cardinals supervised specific curial offices; e.g., the cardinal vice-chancellor directed the chancery. Finally, the cardinals, either collectively or individually, exercised judicial duties bestowed on them by the pope. As an independent body the College of Cardinals had its own separate department for the collection and distribution of common monies, the *Camera Collegii Cardinalium.*[84]

The Renaissance Curia can be viewed most profitably as a series of offices or bureaus with overlapping functions. The first was judicial. A variety of courts or tribunals existed to settle both spiritual and temporal questions that had been appealed to the Holy See. As judicial entities they could hear testimony and issue final decisions. In the highest court, the consistory, the pope and the cardinals were assisted by consistorial advocates, who presented the cases.[85] The cardinals individually also had their own courts, but these were limited in personnel and jurisdiction.[86] Other judicial cases came under the jurisdiction of the *Sacra Romana Rota* and the *Signatura justitiae.* The *Rota* (or *Audientia causarum apostolici palatii*) consisted of judges, or *auditores,* who were formed into a college in 1472 by Sixtus IV, who fixed their number at twelve and divided them among various nations.[87] The *auditores* dealt with questions of minor importance, questions that did not require the direct intercession of the pope. Assistant notaries helped the *auditores* draw up the necessary documents. The *Signatura justitiae* (which formed a unit with the *Signatura gratiae* for most of the quattrocento) developed from the need to sign each supplication once the pope had made his decision. The *Signatura justitiae* possessed ordinary jurisdiction over legal problems raised by a supplication that did not demand papal intervention. The cardinal prefect, who headed the *Signatura,* supervised the work of the *referendarii,* or legal experts, who also helped to determine the fees charged.[88]

Besides these specifically judicial tribunals, there were also offices in the other bureaus of the Curia which acted as courts coincident with their other duties. The *Camera Apostolica* regulated disputes arising from its financial tasks. Also in the *Camera* were the *auditor generalis* and the procurators.[89] The *Audientia litterarum apostolicarum* in the apostolic chancery judged the meaning of chancery bulls when one of the parties questioned the interpretation.[90]

The offices within the second division of the Curia were an extension of the judicial division. Unlike the offices just described, however, these bureaus dealt with the *forum internum,* i.e., questions of conscience, and with the distribution of papal favors, or graces (*gratiae*). The *gratiae* were given to individuals upon petition to the pope. They were free-will gifts on the part of the pope since the petitioner had no claim to them. They included dispensations, indulgences, and honors. The most important offices within this division of the Curia were the *Sacra Penitentiaria Apostolica,* or apostolic penitentiary, the *Signatura gratiae,* and to a lesser extent the datary. The penitentiary dealt originally with the forgiveness of sins.[91] It grew from the ancient custom of penitents' coming to Rome to obtain forgiveness for their sins from the pope. As the number of petitioners increased, the pope appointed lesser penitentiaries to hear confessions and grant absolution. Throughout the Middle Ages more and more requests for forgiveness were directed to Rome, and the pope reserved a variety of cases for his adjudication. In the quattrocento the grand penitentiaries, usually cardinals, expanded their authority to include the granting of privileges and other dispensations. They supervised a large staff made up of auditors, correctors, scriptors, procurators, and lesser penitentiaries. The *Signatura gratiae* regulated requests for grace of an extraordinary nature and was empowered to bypass the established law that could nullify the requested favor.[92]

The third function of the Curia was financial. The major financial bureau was the *Camera Apostolica,* or the apostolic chamber.[93] The *Camera* had the responsibility of collecting from spiritual and temporal sources monies due to the Holy See, such as annates and Peter's pence; directing the pope's personal finances; and governing the papal states.[94] At the head of the *Camera Apostolica* was the cardinal camerarius, or chamberlain, who with the treasurer-general of the Roman Church (*Thesaurarius generalis Ecclesiae Romanae*) and the clerics of the *Camera,* seven active members (*de numero*) with assistants and other (*supernumerii*) members, formed the *Collegium Camerae.* Among the other functionaries who reflected the diverse financial, judicial, and administrative aspects of this bureau were the *Depositarius generalis* (banker), the *Auditor generalis,* the collectors of Peter's pence, notaries, the governor of the city of Rome (who was also the vice-chancellor), as well as the advocates and procurators of the fisc. The *Camera* controlled the revenues accruing from the papal states; these funds became the major source of monies for the papacy during the Renaissance, outdistancing monies collected for the pope's spiritual gifts. Other offices in the Curia also had financial aspects. The datary and the penitentiary (two offices that developed greatly in authority and power in the Renaissance) collected certain monies, as did the papal household, or *familia.*

The fourth division of the Curia, the general administrative section, concerned the expedition or issuance of the papal letters, especially the solemn bulls, by the *Cancellaria Apostolica,* or apostolic chancery.[95] Until the quattrocento the chancery had a monopoly on issuing papal bulls. However, as the various other bureaus began to issue their own bulls and as some of the papal correspondence became the duty of the papal secretaries, the chancery retained control of only those bulls reflecting public decisions made in the consistory, certain decisions from other offices, and the graces granted by the pope. These included the consistory's judicial statements, the nominations of cardinals and bishops, the papers relating to beatification and canonization, and certain magisterial documents. Since the validity of papal decisions depended on their proper form, the chancery was naturally concerned with correct form and language, and was conservative in its attitude. It functioned according to a set of rules issued by each new pope, the *Regulae Cancellariae Apostolicae.*[96]

Ironically, as the chancery lost many of its duties and the popes reformed it under pressure from the councils, the number of its employees actually increased. At the head of the chancery stood the cardinal vice-chancellor (the office of chancellor had disappeared); below him were the twelve apostolic protonotaries, functionary and honorary.[97] The other members of the chancery had specific duties relating to producing or policing the bulls. For example, a body of *correctores litterarum apostolicarum* corrected legal documents issued by the chancery,[98] and the *collectores taxae plumbi,* numbering 104 under Alexander VI, guarded the bulls until they were retrieved by the interested party and the taxes were paid.[99] Humanists could be found among these officials and in the other chancery offices.

The chancery had several ways of issuing its bulls, or *litterae apostolicae.*[100] The normal manner, called *per viam ordinariam* or *per viam Cancellariae,* followed the established chancery rules for the production of bulls. All others were sent *per viam extraordinariam.* The bulls *per viam secretam* or *per viam camerae* or *de camera* (referring to the papal *camera,* not the *Camera Apostolica*) concerned a cardinal or some other high official. They were drawn up by the papal secretaries and were exempt from the normal chancery charges. The *litterae per viam Curiae* or *de Curia* regulated the functioning of the bureaucracy; they were directed to some bureau or curial official and thus did not leave the Curia. Finally, in a separate category distinct from the bulls were the papal briefs produced by the papal secretaries (which will be discussed separately).

It might prove useful to follow a bull *per viam ordinariam* through the various stages of its production.[101] Since the bulls issued by the chancery were usually responses to petitions directed to the pope, the process commenced with the presentation to the pope of a supplication by a *referendarius.* Once the pope had given his decision, the petition was countersigned by the vice-chancellor and dated by the *datarius.* The signed petition was then entered into a register of supplications by a cleric of the registry, where a copy was made. The original was sent to the vice-chancellor in the chancery (a separate palace) and the process of shortening the supplication and producing the final bull began. The abbreviators produced the "concept," or shortened form, stating the facts and the pope's decision. The abbreviators then sent the concept, now called a "minute," to the *rescribendarius,* who was chosen from the *scriptores litterarum apostolicarum* to write a good copy of the bull. Other specially designated scriptors, the *computator* and *auscultator,* also checked the new form. The abbreviators had the responsibility of checking the work of the scriptors, and if they found it wanting, could return the new copy for rewriting. The rewritten product was read to the officials of the chancery, called the *audientia publica,* and if any controversy arose concerning its meaning, a legal decision was rendered by the *auditores litterarum contradictarum.* Once all the supervisors had approved of the newly composed and executed bull, it passed to the *fratres barbati,* or *bullatores,* usually two illiterate Cistercians (illiterate so they could not tamper with the text) from the monastery of Fossanova (actually under the jurisdiction of the *Camera Apostolica*), who affixed the seal. Julius II included laymen among the *bullatores,* most notably Bramante and Sebastiano del Piombo. Next, the appropriate charges were calculated. Finally, the finished bull was registered by an official under the *magister registri* and given into the care of the *collectores taxae plumbi.* For each step in this process a fee was assessed.

Such a complex system of producing papal bulls enabled the bureaucracy to maintain strict control over authenticity and prevent falsifications. Counterfeiting papal documents was no doubt a profitable sideline, but the Curia acted harshly to maintain its integrity. The extent of such illicit activity is uncertain. Perhaps the most famous instance of the counterfeiting of papal bulls concerned Bartolomeo Florido, the archbishop of Cosenza and private secretary to Alexander VI.[102] He was accused and convicted of counterfeiting, deprived of his office and ecclesiastical rank, and imprisoned in Castel Sant'Angelo (1497). He died a few months after his confinement, but his contemporaries judged him fortunate, for counterfeiting was a capital offense.

The Curia was a dynamic institution. Throughout the Renaissance the papacy moved to organize those bureaucrats performing the same function into colleges with their own rights and duties, a process that was especially prominent in the chancery.[103] This rationalizing process helped to define the individual subgroups in the Curia and to clarify lines of authority, and as a consequence, the hierarchical structure of the Curia became even stronger. The collegial system also expedited another major Renaissance administrative innovation, the venality of offices.[104]

The beginnings of venality of offices in the Curia are uncertain, but the practice may have originated in the pontificate of Boniface IX (1389–1404). At first venality was a private matter between individuals and lacked official license. The procedure was simple: a curialist resigned his office in favor of another qualified individual and received a payment. In time the practice became official and the *Camera Apostolica* charged a fee for permission to resign and to succeed. Eventually this procedure became fixed and even included offices vacated by death. By the time of the pontificate of Sixtus IV most nonspiritual offices in the chancery, apostolic chamber, and penitentiary were venal. Venality arose from the Curia's need to increase its revenues and remained a part of that institution until 1901. To the purchaser or purchasers, venality functioned as an investment yielding interest or as a type of annuity, while to the Curia it was essentially a variety of funded debt.

The chief institution controlling the selling of offices was the datary.[105] The *datarius*'s proximity to the pope when dating rescripts earned him the pope's confidence. The popes began to assign special duties to the *datarius,* including financial ones. Nicholas V, for example, empowered him to pay the papal librarian. The *datarius* assisted in fixing the fees for certain bulls. Sixtus IV gave to him the task of calculating the prices for venal offices. By 1480 the *datarius* controlled the books, or registers, that listed the fixed prices, collected the money, and held it for the personal use of the pontiff.

The number of venal offices and their prices grew throughout the quattrocento. In the cinquecento Julius II extended venality to noncurial offices, a procedure that was continued more systematically by his successor. Leo increased the number of existing venal offices and created new ones, including honorary ones that existed only for the purpose of raising money. Under Sixtus IV the number had grown from 300 to 625; under Julius II it grew to 936, and finally under Leo it reached 2,232.[106] According to a 1514 price list for curial offices, an auditorship in the *Camera Apostolica* cost 1,000 ducats; a notaryship in the *Camera,* 2,500; a scriptorship of apostolic letters in the chancery, 2,700; an abbreviatorship, 1,000; and an archivist of the Curia, 1,800.[107] Such high prices naturally limited the availability of most posts since an individual had to have a substantial income to make the original investment. The income curialists received from their offices also increased over the years. The secretaries received approximately 250–300 ducats in 1415, 350 in 1487, and 500 in 1513. Correctors in the chancery received 200 ducats during the Great Schism and 1,200 in the 1520s.[108] By the year 1520 the Curia had accumulated some two and a half million ducats from venal offices and paid out 300,000 scudi (or approximately 275,000 ducats).[109] Obviously the Curia could not easily dispense with such a sizable income, even though venality ultimately harmed the institution.

Venality not only brought much money into the Curia; it also guaranteed a conservative attitude on the part of the bureaucrats who paid for their offices and it decreased the bureaucracy's efficiency. The resulting increase in costs was passed on to the petitioners. These developments help to explain the view of the Curia as an inefficient and money-hungry organization living off the faithful, an opinion that had important political and religious consequences in the sixteenth century. Indeed, the bureaucracy itself realized the evil effects of the multiple officeholding that accompanied venality. Officials holding more than one office were accused of not doing their duty or of doing it poorly. The chancery especially suffered since an official could slow the expedition of bulls by not doing his duty promptly.[110] For all of this, the humanists kept apace with others in purchasing curial offices.

The process of creating new offices was not always an easy one for a pontiff. A pope could reverse his predecessor's moves, and the bureaucracy could bring pressure to guard its own interests if it felt the pope threatened them. Pius II, for example, created the *Collegium abbreviatorum apostolicorum,* which included some humanists. Paul II, Pius's successor, dissolved the office, while Sixtus IV refounded it.[111] In 1483 Sixtus IV established the 72-member *Collegium notariorum Curiae Romanae,* granting it a monopoly on all notarial duties in the Curia. Although notaries had always held an important place in curial business, in giving them a monopoly the pope infringed on other offices. The bureaucracy effected the revocation of Sixtus's decree in 1484. However, Sixtus's nephew, Julius II, a stronger personality with a greater familiarity with the workings of the Curia, reestablished the essentials of Sixtus's plan by creating the *Collegium scriptorum archivi Curiae Romanae,* an office with 101 members.[112]

Within the Curia the chancery offered the humanists the best employment prospects. Chancery posts called for the type of education humanists commanded, but they did not require university training. Within the Curia certain positions were popular among the humanists. The *scriptores litterarum apostolicarum* especially attracted many humanists. One source of this appeal was the size of the office; there were 101 scriptorships. The humanists easily satisfied the position's Latin and calligraphical requirements. A scriptorship, a relatively low-ranking office, was often the first post a humanist held in his progress through the Curia.[113]

Higher in the hierarchy was the office of abbreviator.[114] The *abbreviatores litterarum apostolicarum* prepared the "minute," or short version of a bull, and helped to supervise the writing of its final form. They were divided into two groups, the *abbreviatores de prima visione* (i.e., those who first checked the form of the bulls drawn up by the scriptors) and the *abbreviatores assistentes Vice-Cancellerio in expeditione litterarum apostolicarum in Cancelleria* (i.e., those who joined with the vice-chancellor in a second review [*secunda visio*] of the bull). The latter were also divided into the *abbreviatores de parco majori,* who drew up the "minutes," and the *abbreviatores de parco minori,* who helped with the "minutes" and calculated the fees. Their titles refer to the placement of their desks in the chancery. In 1463 Pius II organized the abbreviators without reference to type into a college with its own chapel and statutes, set their number at seventy, and made the office venal. As noted above, Paul II dissolved the college, but in 1479 Sixtus IV reestablished it with seventy-two members, twelve *de parco majori,* twenty-two *de parco minori,* and thirty-eight *de prima visione.* At the beginning of the sixteenth century the office cost 500 ducats. In keeping with the general curial tendency, Calixtus III excluded married men from holding the abbreviatorship *de parco minori;* Pius II in his reorganization required that all abbreviators be clerics. Despite this clerical prejudice, humanists were found in their ranks.

The most prominent chancery post open to the humanists was the apostolic secretariat.[115] The secretaryship ranked above the scriptorship, and humanist membership in it testifies to the strength of humanism in the Renaissance Curia. The secretaries served directly under the pope and prepared his "briefs" on diplomatic, political, and private matters. The papal brief was one of the major innovations of the late medieval chancery.[116] It received its name from the shortened form that distinguished it from the formal, longer bulls issued by the chancery.

Production of the briefs appealed to the humanists because it was carried out without the stricture of following the facts laid out in a supplication, which in the case of bulls determined the final form. Humanists could therefore demonstrate their talents in original Latin composition. Significantly, the secretaries were the first curialists to adopt the new humanist calligraphy.[117] This innovation both reflected humanist influence in the secretariat and rendered the humanists best qualified for the position. Like many other curial offices, the secretariat experienced great changes in its constitution and membership during the Renaissance.

Secretaries first appeared during the Avignon papacy.[118] Originally they were merely scriptors detached from the chancery to aid the pontiff in dispatching letters that for reasons of secrecy or speed could not follow the normal chancery procedures. In time, these scriptors developed a special relationship to the pope and became increasingly independent of the chancery. For most of the quattrocento the secretaries numbered six (although this varied) and had the simple title *secretarii apostolici.* Each pope selected one secretary as his chief adviser and as leader of the other secretaries. This private (*domesticus,* or *intimus*) secretary wrote the pope's most important briefs. No major alteration in the secretariat occurred until the pontificate of Innocent VIII. In his bull *Non debet reprehensibile* (1487), Innocent enlarged the *Collegium secretariorum apostolicorum* from the customary six positions to thirty.[119] He divided this large body into two sections, the *secretarii apostolici* and the *secretarii domestici,* the latter usually being two in number. The domestic, or private, secretaries had the closest relationship to the pope and even lived in the papal palace. As a consequence of their personal dependence on the reigning pontiff, they enjoyed tenure only for the reign of that pope or until dismissed by him. The other secretaries could continue from one pontificate to another. A further refinement of the secretariat's organization occurred in 1513 when Leo X chose one of the private secretaries as the *secretarius major* to deal with special political correspondence.

The secretariat could be a financially rewarding post since its members might hold other offices and preferments concurrently and could receive monies from the issuance of certain chancery documents. The close contact with the pope made the office a prominent one and its holder, if a cleric, an obvious candidate for ecclesiastical advancement. It was this prominence and opportunity for financial reward which also attracted humanists to the secretariat and made it so important in the history of humanism in the Curia. A number of well-known humanists held the office in the early quattrocento. Perhaps the most famous humanist secretary was Poggio Bracciolini (1380–1459).[120] Other significant humanists in the secretariat from the first years of the quattrocento through the pontificate of Eugenius IV were Leonardo Bruni, Flavio Biondo, Antonio Loschi, and George of Trebizond.[121]

In time the humanists came to consider the secretariat uniquely their own. Proof of this attitude comes from a series of encounters between the secretaries and the consistorial advocates over precedence in religious processions. In a hierarchical institution such as the Curia, position in official ceremonies provided an important index of relative importance and naturally became a cause of contention. The consistorial advocates were lawyers who argued cases before the consistory. Although they were professional jurists, some advocates did favor humanist learning.[122] The dispute between the humanist secretaries and the advocates first arose during the reign of Martin V when Poggio Bracciolini and Leonardo Bruni defended the secretary's claims to precedence. The controversy resurfaced under Pius II, who issued precedence directives favoring the senior advocate.[123] The most important discussion of the controversy occurred under Sixtus IV when Jacopo Gherardi of Volterra (1434–1516)[124] and Sigismondo dei Conti (d. 1512)[125] defended the secretariat in 1471. They argued their cases before a special commission of four cardinals empowered to hear the opposing views. In their written defenses Gherardi and dei Conti emphasized the literary qualities of the secretariat and denied the advocates' claims to precedence based on their legal training. Both men discussed the secretariat from a specifically humanistic point of view.

Gherardi addressed his memorial to the cardinalate commission.[126] He argued that the secretaries were superior to the advocates by virtue of the importance of their duties and the fame of their membership. In serving the pope, the secretaries dealt with the general welfare of Christendom, the *salus publica,* whereas the advocates concerned themselves with cases relating to individuals, the *salus privata.* Unlike the advocates, the secretaries did not receive their position automatically by virtue of a doctoral degree but rather as a result of their proving their abilities. A secretary required greater skill because he helped to determine war and peace and the relations among the rulers of Europe. Above all, concluded Gherardi, the secretaries must be orators. Obviously basing his argument on the Ciceronian ideal of the orator, Gherardi maintained that the secretaries required a knowledge of all fields, including law, while the lawyers were ignorant of other specialties.[127] Gherardi's arguments led to the conclusion that the apostolic secretaries must be humanists. In his memorandum Gherardi proclaimed that the broad literary and historical culture of the humanists, as against the narrow professionalism of the degreed lawyers, was proper to the curial bureaucracy.

Addressing the pope directly, dei Conti[128] used essentially the same attacks on the advocates' professionalism and the same defenses of the secretaries' abilities as Gherardi. Dei Conti, however, emphasized even more strongly the humanistic attributes of the secretaries. The secretaries' proximity to the pope and their need for broad learning made them comparable to the ancient royal advisers, in dei Conti's opinion.[129] Like the ancients, the secretaries were educated in eloquence and represented the virtues of the orator. As masters of the *ars dicendi,* the secretaries conveyed the pope's words to the world.[130] Dei Conti provided a list of famous recent humanist secretaries to support this argument.[131] His memorandum concluded with a plea to Sixtus to maintain his patronage of learned humanists. They would guarantee the pope's search for immortality through their writings better than monuments made of stone. Sixtus need only look to the model of his great predecessor Nicholas V, who supported so many learned men.[132] Despite Gherardi's and dei Conti's pleas, Sixtus followed Pius's decree and gave the senior advocate precedence over the senior secretary, but he ordered the remaining secretaries and advocates to march together in cermonies according to the respective seniority of their offices.[133]

Both Gherardi and dei Conti set forth ideal pictures. Despite their claims, not all the secretaries were humanists. Popes with little humanistic interest might well favor their countrymen or clients with little literary reputation, although men with literary and scholarly talents were never completely ignored. Certainly Nicholas V's fame rests as much on his architectural programs as on his support for learned men. Still, there was a certain truth to Gherardi's and dei Conti's arguments. The very literary talents necessary for the office guaranteed that humanists would be prominent among the secretaries and provide the office with a special quality.

The strong humanist character of the secretariat can be demonstrated in a short accounting of the secretaries of two quattrocento popes, Pius II and Sixtus IV. Since the secretaries for both these popes have recently been studied in detail, we have a fairly accurate picture of them and their activities.[134] Moreover, these popes deserve special attention because they succeeded in staffing the secretariat with a good cross section of Roman humanists in the second half of the quattrocento.

Pius II appointed twelve secretaries during his reign.[135] Of these, eleven can definitely be identified as humanists or as men with strong humanist connections.[136] One, Jacopo Ammannati-Piccolomini (1422–1479), was created a cardinal by Pius (although this was as much for personal reasons as for his curial service);[137] two, Leonardo Dati (1408–1472) and Niccolò Perotti (1429–1489), eventually became bishops.[138] Sixtus appointed thirteen humanists to the post of secretary.[139] Although not all of these men were major figures, a few did distinguish themselves as scholars of worth, including Jacopo Gherardi and Sigismondo dei Conti, both of whom wrote histories of contemporary Rome. Also noteworthy were Domizio Calderini (1446–1478), an important humanist commentator on classical writers who served Cardinal Bessarion as a secretary and taught at the University of Rome;[140] and Giovanni Andrea Bussi, whose service to the printers in Rome has already been noted.[141] Some secretaries, including Gaspare Biondo (d. 1493),[142] Andreas of Trebizond (d. 1490),[143] Marcello dei Rustici (d. 1481),[144] Leonardo Dati,[145] and Lianoro dei Lianori (d. 1478),[146] served as secretaries under both Sixtus and Paul II, while Dati and dei Rustici also served under Paul II. All but Dati and Lianori were members of curial families with previous connections to the Curia. More significant, the fathers of Biondo, dei Rustici, Trebizond, and Francesco Loschi had served as secretaries under previous pontiffs and had enjoyed the reputation of scholars. This indicates a definite *lay* humanist presence in the secretariat in the quattrocento, compared to the cinquecento, when clerical status became a requirement for all secretaries.

Not all those who held a secretaryship took an active part in its duties. Honorary posts were not unknown, usually being bestowed on men who had distinguished themselves in some service to the pope.[147] Some humanists were just too busy with other duties, such as teaching, to function effectively as secretaries. A few were dispatched on embassies that limited their time in Rome.[148] Financially, the office could be very rewarding. Leonardo Grifo (d. 1486),[149] Sixtus's domestic secretary, accrued a large number of benefices in addition to his curial posts, and he was a wealthy man at the time of his death. Although fuller lists for later periods would make the humanist character of the secretariat in the other pontificates equally evident, it should be clear from this accounting that a definite tendency to appoint humanists to the secretariat existed in the Renaissance.[150]

Certainly the duties of an active secretary placed a definite limit on the amount of time a man could devote to scholarship, and in fact they hampered the scholarly careers of several secretaries.[151] Still, the financial rewards of the office could provide the leisure for study and writing after retirement. Gherardi's career demonstrates this. He was secretary to both Cardinal Ammannati-Piccolomini (Pius II's secretary) and Sixtus IV, as well as a papal diplomat under Innocent VIII. Later he served as a tutor in Rome to Cardinal Giovanni de' Medici, who made him

bishop of Segni (1512) and then bishop of Aquino (1513). After his
retirement from papal service, Gherardi wrote an important account of
his years in Rome.[152]

The high point of humanist success in the Curia, at least symbolically,
was Leo's appointment of Jacopo Sadoleto (1477-1547)[153] and Pietro
Bembo (1470-1547)[154] to the domestic secretariat. Their selection was
an acknowledgment of the triumph of Ciceronian Latinity within the
Curia. Papal bulls were probably never formulated as classically as
they were under these two secretaries.[155] Sadoleto was the son of
a professor of law and grew up in Modena and Ferrara; he came to
Rome in about 1500. In Rome he entered the *familia* of Cardinal
Oliviero Caraffa of Naples, a cleric noted for his strict morals. Sadoleto
established himself as one of the best Latin stylists among the younger
humanists in Rome, and his contemporaries praised him for his poem
on the recently discovered Laocoön (1506). Bembo came from a noble
Venetian family, and his father had once served as Venetian ambassador
to Rome. Bembo enjoyed a formidable literary reputation even before
his appointment to the secretariat. Both men represented the cultivated
life of Roman humanism in its academic and curial settings. From the
secretariat, both advanced in the clerical hierarchy. Sadoleto was made
bishop of Carpentras (1517), and the humanistically educated Paul III
created both men cardinals (Sadoleto in 1536 and Bembo in 1539).
Bembo exemplified those who entered upon an ecclesiastical career
without any personal religious sensitivity.

The choice of humanists to staff the papal secretariat highlighted a
major development in humanism and Renaissance government. Political
leaders had come to recognize the administrative and diplomatic services the humanists could render. The humanists, in turn, considered
their learning, in properly classical and especially Ciceronian fashion,
appropriate to any governmental activity. The preference in Renaissance states for humanists in chancery positions cut across political
philosophies. In addition to the papal theocracy, the Florentine republic and the Neapolitan monarchy selected humanists to fill their important secretarial and chancery posts. In all three cases the humanists
exploited the desire to have fluent Latinists in the chancery to express
the governments' views in eloquent periods and to use the new humanistic forms as part of a program of administrative rationalization. In
Florence, a tradition of humanist chancellors originated with Coluccio
Salutati (who had once sought employment in the Curia) and continued
with Leonardo Bruni, Poggio Bracciolini (each of whom had held a
papal secretariat), and Bartolomeo Scala.[156] In Naples, the choice of

humanist secretaries reflected the desire of the kings to exploit humanist learning as part of a program to help legitimize their rule and to have an alternative to the feudal aristocracy from which to select administrative personnel. Without doubt the most significant example of a Neapolitan humanist secretary was Giovanni Pontano (1429-1503), who also served as a royal tutor and ambassador.[157] Similarly, these governments appreciated humanists as ambassadors to foreign courts, where they could explain their governments' positions in good Latin. The choice of humanists for official posts by these three diverse governments proves both the acceptance of humanist talents on the part of the political bureaucracies and leaders and the adaptability of the humanists to the political realities of quattrocento Italy.

❧ VI ❧

Any consideration of the place of humanists in the curial bureaucracy should not ignore what was the most prominent scholarly post open to a humanist, the papal librarianship. Only a few humanists could hold either a librarianship or one of the auxiliary posts connected to the library. Nevertheless, in fulfilling their duties, these librarians and their assistants had extensive contact with their fellow humanists. In a sense they represented a purer form of humanism within the curial ambience. These early humanist librarians did much to give the Vatican Library its early organization and to initiate its career as one of the great scholarly libraries of Europe and one of the most important depositories for humanistic writings.[158]

While the Vatican library, as we know it today, had its official beginnings with Sixtus IV, it is generally acknowledged that Nicholas V's library, which contained a large collection of Greek and Latin manuscripts, was the prototype for the Sixtine Library.[159] Since Nicholas was a great lover of books and had helped his friend Cosimo de' Medici organize his library, it was natural that Nicholas would choose for his librarian a man with substantial scholarly credentials. His choice was Giovanni Tortelli (*ca.* 1400-1466).[160] Tortelli, a Florentine who had studied Greek in the East and devoted his life to scholarship, translated several classical and patristic Greek writings and commented on classical authors. He was a capable scholar and is best remembered for his encyclopedic study of classical vocabulary, the *Orthographia.*[161]

When Sixtus established his library in 1475, he selected as his librarian the humanist Bartolommeo dei Sacchi, who was called Platina (1421-1487).[162] Platina was a prominent member of the Roman Academy. He

wrote on various moral and historical topics and was a sometime curialist. (He purchased one of the abbreviatorships under Pius II but lost it
under Paul II; this will be discussed below.) As librarian, Platina took
good care of his charges and tried to facilitate the orderly use of the
books; his loan books are a veritable register of Roman humanists.[163]
He also used his office to collect material on papal history and to produce his biographies of the popes.[164]

Among Platina's numerous humanist successors,[165] perhaps the best
representative of Roman humanism before the sack was Tommaso
Fedra Inghirami of Volterra (1470–1516).[166] Fedra, who acquired his
name as a result of his role in the production of Seneca's *Hippolytus*
staged by the humanists of the Roman Academy at the palace of Cardinal Raffaele Riario, worked his way up in the curial bureaucracy from
the post of scriptor. Evidence of his high position in the Curia was
his appointment as secretary to the Fifth Lateran Council. He established himself as a popular orator, poet, and commentator on classical
texts.[167] Julius II appointed him librarian in 1510, and Leo subsequently bestowed on him the position of professor of rhetoric at the
University of Rome (the *Sapienza*).[168] The Italian literary historian
Carlo Dionisotti has described Fedra, with his oratorical and literary
skills and his success in the Curia, as an excellent example of the assimilation of humanism socially and curially into Roman society.[169] Fedra's
oratorical talents made him a popular choice for funerals and other important curial events. Sensitive to his surroundings, Fedra proclaimed
the glories of the papacy and the advancement of humanist culture in
fine periods of Ciceronian Latin.[170]

The Vatican librarianship was certainly a humanist prize, and no less
a figure than the Florentine Angelo Poliziano expressed interest in
it.[171] Nevertheless, not all papal librarians were humanists. Alexander
VI, for example, appointed three Spanish ecclesiastics, Pietro Garcia,
Giovanni Fuensalida, and Gaspare Torrella, none of whom were humanists, and the last of whom was Alexander's private physician.[172] Garcia
(d. 1505)[173] held a doctorate in scholastic theology from the University
of Paris, and he is best remembered for his part in the condemnation of
Pico della Mirandola as a consequence of Pico's proposed debate of the
900 Conclusiones in Rome (1487), and for his treatise attacking Pico as
a heretic.[174] But Alexander's choices were essentially a departure from
the tradition of humanists on the staff of the library in the High Renaissance.

The office of librarian was a unique employment opportunity
within the Curia because it emphasized scholarly qualities. However,

scholarship was not always the determining element in the selection of the librarians and their assistants. In general, the Curia attracted and favored humanists who had secretarial skills and could faithfully execute the paper work that was the essence of the Curia as a governmental organization.

2

Curial Households and the Humanists

The numerous employment opportunities provided by the Curia Romana formed an essential element in humanist life in Rome. The bureaucracy assured many humanists of the necessary financial means to establish themselves in the city. There were, of course, limits to the Curia as an institution capable of providing for its members' needs. It did not contain all the possible positions open to humanists, nor did it define all the relationships humanists had among themselves or with the community at large. Curial offices were generally deficient in providing a broad social context for the humanists.[1] The Curia did not concentrate its energies on creating an ambience within which its officeholders could develop intellectually and socially, although it could limit any such development. To balance such deficiencies on the part of the Curia, the city of Rome offered other social and intellectual avenues of expression to humanists.

Among the most important of Rome's social organizations were the confraternities, which engaged in religious and charitable work.[2] They were often organized around the common professional or national background of their members. Even the Curia accommodated its structure to sponsor confraternities that enrolled as a group the members of curial colleges.[3] Although confraternities were popular with all segments of society, their attraction for the humanists was limited because they lacked an intellectual dimension.[4] Still, the confraternities had a certain value for the humanists insofar as they permitted them some social outlet within the general society.

The most important social institutions in Rome for the humanists were two: the various *familiae*, i.e., the official households or courts maintained by the pope, the cardinals and other prelates, and certain rich laymen; and the humanists' natural families. Like the confraternities, these institutions integrated humanists into society at large. The *familiae* provided the humanists with additional means of employment and points of admittance into Rome's peculiar society. These two bodies—the artificial *familia* and the natural family—shaped the social position of Rome's humanists in fundamental ways. This chapter will discuss the *familia* as it related to the humanists' needs, while the next chapter will investigate the role of the humanist families in Rome.

The curial *familia* consisted of those men, called *familiares* or familiars,[5] lay or cleric, Italian or non-Italian, who were employed to assist the lord in his religious, ceremonial, cultural, and personal duties.[6] This *familia* was an accurate reflection and extension of the Curia and of Roman society. Its members were exclusively male and at its higher levels celibate. Women were never mentioned as forming part of the staff, but they were in the secular households, as wet-nurses, seamstresses, and similar menials. The *familia* was arranged in strictly hierarchical order. The lord was the apex of power and he handed down authority to his subordinates. The *familia* even possessed a mechanism for enforcing obedience; its own courts punished infractions. Further, the *familia* organized and integrated cultural, domestic, religious, and administrative needs into a unity that served the good of its lord. In finding a place in a curial household, a humanist succeeded in establishing himself in a major institution of Rome's society, an institution with positive and negative aspects.

The familiars were primarily engaged in domestic management, although a limited number of clerics dealt with curial or episcopal administrative needs if the lord was also a bishop. These domestic requirements were broad, ranging from secretarial work to care of the stables. The *familia* attracted a wide variety of servants of different statuses, and a certain number of the employees were intellectuals. These courts were a continuation of the imperial-medieval secular court, which the clerics had adapted to fit their special needs.[7] According to Church law the clerical members of the *familia,* as assistants to bishops, had a certain canonical position. The *familia* was not an impersonal institution. In some ways the curial household could substitute as the natural family for those clerics who had no relatives in Rome. Lacking normal family bonds, such clerics, and those who assumed a clerical stance, found in the *familia* an institution that could respond to some personal needs. For those humanists in such a condition the *familia* could serve as a means of developing personal relationships, including intellectual ones.

This structured institution had a limited life span. It ceased to exist at the death or departure from Rome of the man who founded it. In this it differed from the courts of the feudal nobility in Rome. The courts of such Roman barons as Colonna and Orsini employed

humanists, but they offered limited opportunities. They were not reestablished periodically, and they did not employ new men regularly,
although they did grow and decrease with changes in family size. The
one exception to the temporary nature of the curial *familia* was the
papal household. Many of its lower functionaries continued to serve in
the papal palace for one pope after another. Within its life-time, the
familia bound together its members and endowed them with a continuous official status in Rome. Despite the brevity of its existence, the
familia helped to compartmentalize Roman social life. Men identified
themselves with their lord and his policies, and regarded as their enemies
their lord's enemies. As a group, however, these households displayed a
certain basic homogeneity in personnel, duties, and activities. This
uniformity allows us to treat them with a high degree of generalization,
although such a procedure does rob them of their distinctiveness.

The *familia* was directly and completely dependent on the will and
finances of its lord. While he obviously had to delegate most of his
housekeeping responsibilities to his various subordinates, he nevertheless set the tone of his court. Some high clerics who were noted for
their piety and learning, for example, sought out familiars of high moral
and intellectual worth and maintained well-ordered households; less
conscientious lords had courts with very different reputations. What
greatly affected the humanists in Rome was the number of learned
cardinals or bishops who directed their *familia*'s resources toward the
support and advancement of intellectuals. Lords with intellectual pretensions could hire humanists as secretaries or chaplains or could simply
open their houses to them as meeting places. This provided humanists
with a very definite and secure social position as the dependents of rich
and powerful lords, a situation they enjoyed as a consequence of their
learning.

II

In Rome's hierarchical society the papal *familia* naturally provided the
model for the other Roman households, both cleric and lay.[8] It was the
largest court in Rome by virtue of the special demands made on the
pope as the head of the Church's central government and by virtue of
the large number of liturgical, political, and personal needs of the pope
as bishop of Rome. The papal household consisted of certain cardinals,
other high clerics, and lowly, menial workers; it included those men
who actually lived in the Vatican palace and those who belonged to the
familia, enjoyed the privilege of eating at the papal table, but did not
reside in the papal palace. In this last group were a large number of

curialists, including the referendaries, the protonotaries, the auditors of the Rota, the papal secretaries, and the apostolic scriptors.[9]

As was true of the Curia Romana in general, the papal *familia* experienced significant growth in the later Middle Ages. Originally it consisted only of those men who were needed to assist the pope in his religious and domestic duties, and thus it had a practical though limited rationale. However, it grew both in size and in function during the papacy's residency in Avignon.[10] It increased in number from 192 members at the beginning of the Avignon period to 270 by the 1330s.[11] Assuming a more and more secular character, the Avignonese papal court even retained a large body of knights. In the Renaissance this expansion was at first halted by the Schism but soon began anew. In the pontificate of Eugenius IV, for example, the papal *familia* numbered a modest 130 members. Under Pius II it increased by approximately a third to 230 individuals, including the papal familiars' servants, who were housed at papal expense. At the beginning of the sixteenth century, Pius III's 370-member *familia* represented another increase of one third. By the reign of Leo X the papal *familia* had doubled to approximately 700 persons.[12] While Leo was especially active in creating offices for nonfunctionaries in the papal household, the increase in number from Eugenius's pontificate to Leo's corresponded to general changes in the Curia.

At the head of the papal court were those cardinals who enjoyed the privilege of maintaining rooms in the Vatican palace and housing their own servants there. They were called palatine cardinals. Some of these cardinals, such as the vice-chancellor, owed their position in the papal *familia* to their curial office, even though they did not always reside at the Vatican. Other palatine cardinals were close advisers of the pope and his personal friends or relatives, and their selection was completely an expression of free will on the part of the pope. The rest of the *familia* was divided between higher, or superior, officials and lower, or inferior, ones. In a list of the familiars of Pius III these officials are called, respectively, *primae sortis* and *secundae sortis*.[13] The first group, which in some cases enjoyed prelate status, constituted the intimate, or personal, *familia* of the pope. Its members were chosen to assist the pope in his most important duties and constituted the learned element in the household. The second group of lower functionaries or officers was in turn subdivided into two sections: the secret, or private, officials, who served the pope personally, and the common officers (*communes officiales*), who performed the same basic menial functions as the private officers but did so for the palace members as a whole.

In order to provide an accurate picture of the makeup of the papal household, it is useful to enumerate in some detail the *familia* of Leo X for the years 1514–1516.[14] The list, or *ruolo*, for Leo's court is extensive and clearly divided. It has received detailed study, so we have relatively full information on many of its higher members. In many ways Leo's court represented the high point of the Renaissance papal *familia*. With its 700 members, it was the largest of the Roman courts, and it reflected the great employment expectations that greeted Leo's pontificate.

The *ruolo* of Leo's household follows the division between superior and inferior functionaries. The superior officials were divided into a number of sections with titles that often referred to some domestic duty. The first group mentioned were the domestic prelates, including archbishops and bishops and those such as protonotaries and majordomos who enjoyed prelate status by virtue of their offices. There were twenty-eight domestic prelates (plus their servants) in Leo's court, among whom were the papal secretaries and papal librarians. The second group consisted of the *cameraii*, or chamberlains, i.e., those who had a position in the papal antechamber.[15] There were sixty-three chamberlains plus their servants, including two physicians and a surgeon. The third group included the *cubicularii*, a form of chamberlain. Like *camerarius*, *cubicularius* was a general term applied to a variety of men closely connected to the pope.[16] Included in the sixty-nine *cubicularii* were the papal singers. The fourth group consisted of the *scutiferi*, or heralds (another generic term), whom Leo organized into a venal college in 1515.[17] The ninety-three *scutiferi* included musicians, the master of the stable, personal assistants such as the *scalchus secretus* and *credentarius secretus* (titles referring to table duties),[18] an astrologer, and a *laicus qui facit ceram* (a laymen who makes wax). In addition to these four specific divisions there were other familiars: the chaplains and clerics of the chapel; the *forieri* (another type of chamberlain),[19] the assistants, or *custodes*, of the papal library; the supervisor of wax (as distinct from the previously mentioned wax-maker); the papal penholder (*pinnarius*, staffed by a Pole in Leo's court); the supervisor of supplications and the supervisor of the registry of supplications; a *scriptor*; and the papal buffoon, Fra Mariano, who was a *plumbator*, or sealer of bulls.

The inferior servants may be dealt with quickly for our purposes since the humanists were not found among their number. They included the various members of the kitchen staff, the gardeners, the stewards, the porters, and the stable hands. Information on these men is scanty and there is little that can be said about them. Certainly their labor must have been great, but this was compensated by a certain security in their posts and the honors and money that went with service to the pope and other powerful individuals in the papal household. Their number, together with the servants of the higher officials, accounts for the majority of the personnel in the papal court.

Although the *ruolo* provides some important details on the constitution of Leo's household, it says nothing about the financial demands of the *familia* made on the usually overextended papal fisc. As the director of his household, the pope had to feed, shelter, and pay for his familiars. In the case of the higher officers, the pope could avail himself of various avenues to supplement their salaries by appointing them to curial or ecclesiastical posts and rich benefices. Some of the inferior domestic officers may also have been rewarded in this manner. While the papal court was the largest such body in Rome, all contemporaries agreed that a grand manner of life befitted the papal office and was necessary for the performance of its duties. Yet the price for such lavishness could be great. It is not easy to determine how much the papal purse spent per year on the *familia* since bookkeeping techniques did not make clear or reliable divisions into income and expenditures. However, running the papal palace under Sixtus IV cost approximately 26,000 gold florins in 1480 (from a yearly income of almost 306,000 florins). The size of Sixtus's household, however, is uncertain. Under Clement VII, for a household approximately the size of Leo's in the years 1514–1516, the pope expended slightly over 40,000 gold florins (from a total papal expenditure of 476,000 gold florins).[20]

Two other important points should be made in reference to Leo's household. First, Leo staffed many of the superior offices with fellow Florentines and Tuscans. He was not the first or the last pope to favor his countrymen in this manner. However, he also advanced foreigners into his court; the names of Germans, Frenchmen, Spaniards, and one Pole appear in the *ruolo*. The name of only one Roman appears among the domestic prelates, and only four or five Romans served in all the superior posts.[21] This was in line with a non-Roman sentiment with regard to hiring in the Curia generally. The papal court thus reflected the cosmopolitanism of the Curia Romana.

The second important element in Leo's court was the prominence of humanists in its highest offices. Among the *familiares* whom we can definitely identify as humanists were the two papal secretaries Pietro Bembo and Jacopo Sadoleto, the orator and poet Raffaele Brandolini (who will be discussed below), the German Jacob Questenberg, and the librarians Lorenzo Parmenio and Romolo de Mammacino. In addition to these there was an added rubric entitled *scolares graeci,* although only one name is given, Constantinus Rale (Rhallus).[22] Leo supported the establishment of a college for Greek studies in Rome in the early years of his pontificate, and these individuals may periodically have been part of his court.[23] However, in order to determine the type of humanists Leo favored, we will look more closely at the careers of three of the men mentioned in the *ruolo:* Filippo Beroaldo the Younger, Giovanni Francesco Poggio, and Gentile Santesio.

Filippo Beroaldo the Younger (1477-1518)[24] came from a prominent Bolognese academic family and was the cousin of the famous philologist of the same name. He came to Rome about 1503 and entered the service of Cardinal Adriano Castellesi. His service with Castellesi may have been less than happy since in later years he attacked the character of his former patron in verse.[25] In about 1505 he passed to the service of Cardinal Giovanni de' Medici, the future Leo X. As pope, Leo rewarded Beroaldo's service by bestowing on him several rich benefices (yielding an annual income of 1,400 ducats) and making him a papal librarian. Beroaldo was a mordant poet, an accomplished Hellenist, and a professor of humanities at the University of Rome (his annual salary was 250 ducats), but his greatest contribution to scholarship was the *editio princeps* of the first six books of Tacitus's *Annales* (1515).

Giovanni Francesco Poggio (1447-1552)[26] was the son of the famous humanist and papal secretary Poggio Bracciolini. Born and educated in Florence, he took a degree in law. By 1496, he was in Rome, where he received an appointment as solicitor of papal letters. He was a strong opponent of Savonarola and used his legal training to defend the papacy against the Dominican friar. Julius II continued the papal favor begun by Alexander VI by appointing Poggio a scriptor of apostolic letters and an archivist of the Curia. As a Florentine exile he came to the notice of Cardinal Giovanni de' Medici, who patronized him and bestowed several benefices on him. Poggio was active in Roman intellectual circles, no doubt benefiting from his father's fame. Like some other Roman humanists, including Cardinal Castellesi, Poggio supported at the papal court the cause of the German Hebraist Johannes Reuchlin in his famous controversy with the Dominicans over the propriety of reading Talmudic texts. Giovanni Francesco did not rival his father's renown as a writer, however, although he did produce several legal and moral treatises.

The fact that Poggio and Beroaldo belonged to well-known humanist families aided their association with important figures in Rome and smoothed their way into important offices. Other members of Leo's *familia* came from obscure backgrounds and lacked such advantages. For these men a position in the papal court was an especially important honor and a proof of their ability to advance themselves. Such a figure was Gentile Santesio (1463-1526) of Subiaco, near Rome, who was known by his academic name, Pindarus.[27] Little is known about his entrance into the Curia. He must have demonstrated administrative talent, for he served as a curial diplomat in Hungary and Germany and as a governor of Rieti. In 1503 he entered the service of Cardinal de' Medici as his secretary. Leo provided him with several benefices and continued to employ him as a diplomat. His humanistic activities seem to have been confined to writing Latin poetry and attending the humanist assemblies in Rome.

The careers of these three humanists indicate the type of men who could exploit their literary talents and backgrounds to achieve employment in a papal household. Beroaldo was the most active in humanist production, while the other two intertwined their humanist studies and compositions with their curial and professional duties and service in the papal *familia*. What also bound these three men together was their connection to the pope while he was still a cardinal; they first came to Leo's attention because of their literary abilities or claims to the cardinal's political allegiance. They were fortunate in being able to move with their patron into the papal palace and enjoy rich rewards. Their careers thus highlight another aspect of Roman employment, the cardinal's *familia*.

❧ III ❧

A position in the papal household would have been a worthy goal for any careerist in Rome, including humanists. Apart from automatic membership accruing to a curial position such as abbreviator or scriptor, few humanists could hope to achieve a room in the Vatican. Even when a pope was favorably disposed to humanists, as was Leo, he had a limited number of posts to offer because political and familial responsibilities normally had to be satisfied before intellectual preferences. In compensation for the limits of papal patronage, Rome offered to the humanists positions in the *familiae* maintained by cardinals and other prelates.

The cardinal's *familia* was a smaller version of the papal household.[28] The cardinal's court was divided into superior and inferior officers for the performance of the same duties as their corresponding numbers performed in the papal palace, and life there could prove just as lucrative as a reward for faithful service. The cardinal had the duty of feeding, sheltering, and paying the salaries of his familiars. If also a bishop, the cardinal could appoint members of his staff to ecclesiastical posts. He was also in a position to further his favorites' curial careers. The cardinal's familiars shared many of the same privileges as their papal equivalents: they enjoyed certain prerogatives in obtaining benefices and had advantages in obtaining materials from the Curia.[29] Like the curial offices and the papal *familia*, the cardinal's court made Rome an attractive place to find employment.

The humanists realized the possible benefits of service in a cardinal's court. While secretarial posts were most appealing to them, they also had the opportunity of serving as chamberlains or chaplains. There was even the possibility of serving two cardinals simultaneously in some functions.[30] Some humanists were adept at using cardinalate service to advance their careers. They might serve several cardinals consecutively, moving to a new employer upon the death of their former patron or finding someone else more congenial. Such movement also served the purpose of opening up posts for newcomers. The humanist Scipione Forteguerra, called Cateromachus (1466-1515), served four different cardinals in Rome—Domenico Grimani, Alessandro Farnese, Franciotti della Rovere, and Francesco Alidosi—and also found employment in Cardinal Giulio de' Medici's entourage in Florence.[31] Similarly, Domizio Calderini (1446-1478), a noted classicist and papal secretary, served Cardinal Bessarion as a secretary and then passed to the employ of Cardinals Pietro Riario and Giuliano della Rovere; all three were powerful clerics.[32] Early service in a cardinal's household was an important step in the careers of many of Rome's most prominent humanists.

The cardinal's household had grown in the size of its staff and in importance during the Avignon period, mirroring the papal court's development.[33] While attention has been given to the Avignon period, the Renaissance cardinal's *familia* has not received equal attention.[34] Enough information is available to allow scholars to go beyond generalizations about the princely construction and extravagance of the cardinal's household and provide some statements on its constitution and relationship to humanists.

The vitality of the cardinals' *familiae* in Rome's social and intellectual life depended on the number of cardinals who were resident in Rome at any one time and on the frequency with which new cardinals were chosen and had to assemble their households in Rome. While the number varied, it has been estimated that between twenty-five and thirty cardinals lived in Rome at any one time during the High Renaissance.[35] Twenty cardinals seems to have been the minimum. Of course, these courts were not of equal size or importance. The variety of the cardinals' households demonstrates the great differences in social and financial position of the several members of the College of Cardinals.

A valuable enumeration of resident cardinals and the size of their households exists for the year of the sack of Rome.[36] This 1526/1527 census of Rome provides the membership figures for the households of twenty-one cardinals, all but one of whom were Italian. All of these cardinals were unfortunate enough to be in Rome when the imperial army entered and sacked the city. Although this census does not provide details on the individuals in the cardinals' *familiae,* it does furnish the best indications of the actual size and proportionate importance of these courts in Roman society.

The largest *familia* listed in the census belonged to Cardinal Alessandro Farnese, the future Paul III; it numbered 306 "bocchi" [*sic*], or persons. Farnese belonged to a rich noble family and could depend on his own considerable wealth rather than curial or ecclesiastical revenues to pay for his servants.[37] Only one other cardinal's court in this census was comparable to Farnese's, that of Cardinal Alessandro Cesarini. Cesarini came from a prominent Roman curial family that had benefited greatly from its service in the Church.[38] The smallest court mentioned belonged to Tommaso da Vio, Cajetan, and numbered only 45 familiars. Da Vio was a learned Dominican theologian, papal diplomat, and former general of his order; his years as a friar had not permitted him to amass a large personal income.[39] The average of these twenty-one cardinalate courts was 134 members. Individually, none of these courts could compare with the papal *familia*'s 700 members. Collectively, however, they accounted for over 2,800 positions in a city of approximately 55,000 adults.

As valuable as the list is, it does not tell the full story of the cardinals' courts. The census was not complete; it did not include those cardinals who, for whatever reason, were not present in Rome at the time of the census or were not in Rome at the time of the sack. Among those not mentioned were Cardinal Francesco Ponzetti, a physician and former member of Leo X's *familia* who had little wealth; and Giles of Viterbo, an Augustinian hermit and theologian who lived in a palace connected to the Augustinian Church of S. Agostino and was relatively poor. Also absent at the time of the sack were Giovanni Salviati, Agostino Trivulzio, and Pompeo Colonna.[40] All of these cardinals were rich and would have had large households. The inclusion of their courts would have significantly augmented the prominence of cardinals' courts in presack Roman society.

Even a small household of fewer than a hundred members would have been an expensive undertaking since the cardinal had to supply room and board as well as salary. Food alone could be a costly matter for a lord.[41] Only a few cardinals could call upon family wealth to supplement incomes derived from common cardinalate sources or from ecclesiastical or curial offices.[42] Without such independent sources a cardinal could experience great difficulty meeting his bills. Such a situation led to great indebtedness on the part of many cardinals. Consequently, excluding the pope himself, the College of Cardinals contained some of the greatest debtors in Rome. Despite the drawbacks of an extravagant life style, almost all contemporaries expected—indeed required—it of the entire college. A cardinal considered himself a religious prince entitled to the accouterments befitting such an exalted status. Any attempt to limit a princely life style could lead to criticism heaped upon the budget-conscious cardinal or one who wished to follow more closely an apostolic or ascetic life.

Although the case is not from Rome, a valuable instance of this attitude toward the propriety of display to the cardinalate is the rebuke administered by Julius II to Cardinal Francesco Ximenes de Cisneros, the devout reforming archbishop of Toledo. The cardinal was a Franciscan friar who wished to live a life of simplicity in accordance with his order's principles. However, when the pope (who also had been a Franciscan, but felt less strongly the need to live simply) learned of his modest life style in 1508, he wrote to the Spaniard. Julius admitted that he understood and even praised such a noble gesture *in interiori conscientia secundum Deum vivere,* but he nevertheless argued that *extrinsecus* the cardinal must forsake his modest habits as beneath his office's dignity.[43] In accordance with this attitude, the pope occasionally had to assist poorer cardinals in maintaining an appropriate life style or at least in giving a good impression to the people. If a cardinal in Rome could not afford a palace, the pope might lend him one belonging to the Holy See. This was especially necessary for some of the members of the religious orders who generally lacked private sources of income when created cardinals.

Papal support for cardinalate grandeur did not imply that the popes urged excesses on their cardinals. Magnificence did not mean excesses and personal aggrandizement; rather, it indicated, at least in theory, a properly modulated display for the sake of the office and its prestige. It was even argued that display had a role in controlling the revolutionary impulses of the people and guaranteeing political stability.[44] A happy medium was not always found. Popes since Avignon had urged the cardinals to avoid extravagant life styles, not to keep overly large staff or take part in excessively secular displays such as expensive dinner parties.[45] However, such papal remonstrances were weakened by the tendency of some popes to favor display by their favorites, especially relatives; by the amount of disposable income some cardinals controlled; and by the noble birth and pretensions of many of the cardinals. Certainly those cardinals who had powerful political connections could not easily be restrained from imitating rich secular lords. Thus luxurious living remained very much a reality in the Renaissance College of Cardinals.[46] Competition developed among cardinals who believed that the greater the household and its conspicuous consumption, the greater the reputation a cardinal would enjoy. Whatever the limits of these ideas in terms of finances and morals, they did have some positive effects on humanists and artists in Rome.

There is a lack of contemporary information on the construction and problems of the Renaissance cardinalate *familia* and its relationship to humanism. This paucity of material makes the discussion in the *De Cardinalatu,* published in 1510 by the Roman curial humanist and cleric Paolo Cortesi, especially valuable.[47] Although this text will be discussed in greater detail below,[48] it is useful to note at this point Cortesi's specific statements on the institution and governance of the cardinal's household. The *De Cardinalatu* is one of the very few treatises written as a handbook for a cleric by a humanist and from a humanist perspective. In it Cortesi explained the personal qualities and requirements of a cardinal, describing the *familia* from the master's perspective and invariably displaying his sympathies for the ruling powers. Cortesi established standards for the cardinal and his household which accurately reflected actual Roman practices and generally accepted ideals.

Cortesi's discussion of the *familia* occurs in the second book of his work, which bears the title *Liber oeconomicus.* This book details the cardinal's personal (as distinct from his moral and official) needs and duties, as well as his social and intellectual ambience. In conformity with his Roman environment, Cortesi presented the cardinal as an ecclesiastical prince requiring a great court. As a result, there are few differences between the type of household Cortesi prescribed for his cardinal and that which would have been proper for a secular lord. These differences can be seen in details such as the lack of any discussion of women or children, the need for a chapel, the number of clerical employees, and the use of ecclesiastical preferments as a form of payment, and in a general emphasis on the moral duties incumbent upon the cardinal. Cortesi's *familia,* therefore, was a manifestation of the cardinal's exalted social status and was only partly modified by the ecclesiastical nature of the household's director.

Since the *familia* constituted part of the cardinal's status as an ecclesiastical prince, Cortesi began his analysis with an outline of the finances a cardinal must command to perform his duties properly.[49] Cortesi argued that a cardinal must be paid 12,000 ducats per year from such general revenues of the college as the monies collected by the consistory

for approving episcopal advancements. If a cardinal fell short of this
amount, the pope should supply the necessary funds from his own
treasury. This sum was a large one and only a minority of contemporary cardinals actually disposed of that much money.[50] Cortesi probably was realistic in arguing that such a substantial amount would be
necessary to support the type of *familia* he considered proper to a
cardinal. His estimate of the size of the *familia* corresponded almost
exactly with the median of the 1526/1527 census discussed above—
140 members.[51]

Cortesi offered two justifications for such a large and expensive
household.[52] First, he felt that it corresponded to the general requirements of the time, *propter rationem temporum.* Since contemporaries
expected great display and a large *familia,* the cardinal should fulfill
those standards so that he might live in a modern manner and bring dignity to himself and his office. A modest life style or apostolic poverty
did not meet the requirement of modernity and, hence, did not suit a
cardinal. Second, Cortesi argued somewhat tautologically that a large
number of servants alone could assure that the cardinal's household
would be well run and that its members would live properly, *propter
perfectionem familiae.* In both of these cases, Cortesi displayed a practical attitude toward the society in which a cardinal had to function
and the special place he held in it.

In order to house such a large body of exclusively male familiars, the
cardinal required a great palace, and Cortesi gave much detailed advice
on this topic.[53] As befitted his princely status, a cardinal should have a
large palace built in accordance with the most modern architectural
theories and decorated in the latest styles of sculpture and painting.
The cardinal should build his home in a central area of town but away
from disturbing noises or noisome businesses. This was an important
precaution because some cardinals rented the lower floors of their
palaces to merchants or businessmen.[54] The palace should have a library,
an auditorium for lectures and discussions, guest rooms, an armory, an
audience chamber, bedrooms, music rooms, rooms for accountants and
secretaries, and an entire floor to house the *officiales secundae sortis.*
Cortesi further specified for his religious lord a chapel adorned with
paintings of the Virgin and the saints. In addition to sgraffito and paintings, the cardinal should also display gems and silver and gold vessels.
A garden should provide a pleasant ambience for dining. A large stable
should house a variety of horses and mules for the cardinal's personal
and ceremonial needs.[55] Although these specifications formed an ideal
structure, their essential validity was demonstrated by the great building boom in Rome which produced palaces similar to Cortesi's model.

In his exposition Cortesi specifically cited the palaces of Cardinals Raffaele Riario (1480s) and Adriano Castellesi (*ca.* 1503) as representing the most up-to-date Renaissance architectural theories.[56]

To the formation and governance of the *familia,* Cortesi devoted an entire chapter.[57] In keeping with the religious character of the lord, Cortesi stressed a moral dimension to the cardinal's relations with his familiars. The cardinal must follow the rule of nature which required him to lead his familiars to a virtuous life and to remove from their paths all impediments that could prevent their doing good. In staffing the household, the cardinal must select men who were naturally inclined toward service and who would be most susceptible to his direction. Cortesi excluded from this group the Romans, who, he felt, were not natural servants; the Neapolitans, who lacked an industrious disposition; the Florentines, who were too ambitious; and the Venetians, who were too haughty. Rather, the cardinal should turn to foreigners for his staff, especially Frenchmen, Germans, and Englishmen. These men valued the opportunity to serve a cardinal as a means of advancement. Among the non-Italians, Cortesi counseled against only the Spaniards, who in his view had defects similar to the Italians, being too ambitious to serve properly.[58] Such sentiments were not capricious on Cortesi's part; Julius II and Leo X both favored foreigners in staffing their *familiae.* Naturally, non-Italian cardinals favored their own countrymen in their households.[59] Interestingly, Cortesi seems not to have extended these reservations to Italian humanists as familiars, for his examples of humanist familiars were Italians.

Whatever the nationality of the servants, the cardinal must be prepared to pay them a fitting wage. Cortesi's rationale for this was a practical one. A well-paid *familia* redounded to the credit of its lord since its members would avoid fighting, gambling, and the other illicit acts that were a means of supplementing their small salaries. In providing for his servants, a cardinal defended his own good name, added to his own glory, and helped his retainers lead moral lives. Unfortunately, Cortesi did not detail what he considered the proper amount for each employee. Only in the case of major officials (*in maiorum gentium genere,* i.e., *primae sortis*) such as chaplains and heralds did he propose a set figure, 50 gold florins or ducats per year.[60] As for the clerical members of the *familia,* Cortesi recommended that they also have access to benefices without the care of souls, and in certain cases even be promoted to bishoprics. However, whoever received such preferments must possess the requisite abilities to perform his duties.[61]

In his discussion of the *familia,* Cortesi did not include a complete list of retainers. He mentioned variously secretaries, stable grooms, chaplains, a major-domo, a steward, accountants, heralds, artists, ushers, and physicians. Only the major-domo is described as performing a specific task, that of dispensing justice to the other members of the household.[62] The major-domo selected many of the menial servants and had the duty of supervising their work. Cortesi probably saw no need to list the members of the court for his audience since he did not plan to alter the established pattern. Rather, he contented himself with emphasizing the need for all the servants to obey their master faithfully.[63]

Cortesi realized the importance of the cardinals and their *familiae* in furthering the fortunes of humanists in Rome and the Curia. Patronage of learned men, and especially humanists, constituted a vital element in Cortesi's ideal household. His own circle of friends in Rome depended on cardinalate support; he mentioned several of his Roman friends who were in the service of wealthy cardinals.[64] In Cortesi's view, humanists and learned men generally made good familiars because they were more abstemious in their habits, more reserved, less ambitious, and more generally useful when it came to dealing with new problems than those who had not devoted their lives to study. The cardinal should seek out such men for his staff and patronage and favor learned men outside his household by opening his house and library to them.[65] Cortesi did not advocate indiscriminate patronage; there was a definite hierarchy to be followed in employing or supporting the learned. Cortesi urged the cardinal to select for special consideration men who engaged in humanistic studies and especially those who investigated the more recondite aspects of antiquity and the Latin language.[66] He also expected that the cardinal would be able to appreciate such erudition.

This emphasis upon the place of the humanists in the cardinal's *familia* highlights two aspects of the Roman humanist experience. The first was the dependence of many humanists on the type of support a cardinal could offer; the humanists' survival often depended upon their service to other men. The second centered on the cardinal as a major influence on the development of humanism in Rome through his direction of and participation in it. The cardinal was in a position to help bind humanism closely to the official needs and views of the Curia and the Church. As the second-most-powerful representative of the Church, he fitted this role perfectly since he had greater opportunities to mingle with humanists than had the pope. This allowed the cardinal to control which humanists should be advanced and which intellectual trends should receive greater attention.[67] It would be incorrect to overemphasize any sinister element in this power to manipulate; all patrons had some control over the content of their dependents' thought and writings.

As will be discussed in Chapter 4, there was a remarkable uniformity in Roman thought even without strong cardinalate direction. What Cortesi wished to underline was a mutuality of humanistic and curial-clerical needs.

In offering this idealized view of the relationship between the humanists and the cardinals, Cortesi drew upon recent history and contemporary events. In fifteenth-century Rome a number of cardinals had in fact used their *familiae* and palaces as centers for humanists. Some of these cardinals were especially devoted to specific aspects of humanism and used their position to help direct the interests of their dependents along particular avenues of research and composition. Others opened their palace libraries to the humanists generally and welcomed them into their homes for intellectual discussions. Whatever the depth of their own knowledge and appreciation of humanistic scholarship and literary production, these prelates made their courts into one of the major foci of humanist growth in Rome.

The man best remembered for making his home into a humanist center was Cardinal Bessarion (1403–1472).[68] As a Greek he was especially anxious to help his countrymen establish themselves in Italy and to advance the cause of Hellenic scholarship in Italy. To these ends he attracted men interested in Greek studies, especially Neo-Platonic writings, and urged both the Greeks and the Italian humanists to translate Greek texts into Latin. The authors Bessarion favored were theological, philosophical, and moral writers whom he believed would aid the cause of religion in the West. George of Trebizond, Theodore Gaza, Jacopo Gherardi, Giovanni Andrea Bussi, Niccolò Perotti, and Bessarion's secretary Domizio Calderini, all names we have encountered in other contexts, participated in the cardinal's "academy," as his contemporaries termed the gatherings at his palace.

Equally impressive in his contribution to humanism was Cardinal Francesco Todeschini-Piccolomini (d. 1503), a nephew of Pius II and later pope as Pius III.[69] Having inherited his uncle's humanistic leanings, he assembled in his palace in the center of Rome an excellent collection of Greek and Latin manuscripts and early printed books, as well as a number of fine antique sculptures. Like Bessarion he especially supported translations of Greek texts and patronized humanist theologians. Another of Pius II's cardinal-relatives, Jacopo Ammannati-Piccolomini (1422–1479), also exploited his *familia* and his cardinalate status to advance humanism.[70] Among those connected with Ammannati were the poet, grammarian, and classical commentator Giambattista Cantalico, the poet and historian Giannantonio Campano, and Jacopo

Gherardi. More selective in his patronage was Cardinal Rafaele Riario, who opened his palace to the presentation of classical theater by the Roman Academy. [71]

An insight into how these cardinalate *familiae* functioned as humanistic centers comes from the household of Cardinal Pietro Riario (d. 1474). [72] Riario maintained a large *familia* in his palace at SS. Apostoli, employing 500 persons and spending 150,000 scudi per year on this establishment. [73] Riario, however, should not be viewed as a typical cardinal; he was Sixtus IV's favorite nephew and held several very rich ecclesiastical and curial offices. Sixtus was immensely indulgent to his opportunistic relative and used him as a key figure in his policy of representing the papacy as a great secular power. Riario gave lavish banquets for visiting nobles and undertook an important building program. [74] This extravagance elicited criticism even from his contemporaries. As proof of his princely ambitions, Riario left a royal-sized debt at the time of his death.

We have a description of Cardinal Riario's *familia* from one of his humanist clients. In 1473 the humanist Ottavio Cleofilo of Fano (Francesco di Ottavio da Fano) [75] came to Rome to enter the employ of Cardinal Battista Zeno as a secretary. From Zeno Cleofilo passed to the service of Cardinal Riario. Cleofilo wrote to his friends in Fano telling them of his life in the palace of the rich and influential prelate. [76] Riario came to Cleofilo's attention, he told them, because of his fame as a great patron in a city that had, if not many, at least several outstanding ones. In Riario's palace Cleofilo heard lively literary discussions on poetry in which the cardinal himself occasionally participated. [77] All types of men found a home in such a grand court: architects, painters, singers, physicians, astrologers, philosophers, orators, and poets. [78] The high position accorded to poetry in the palace life was especially pleasing to Cleofilo since he himself was a poet. He willingly defended such a patron against those who attacked his employer's life style as too secular. But the glories of such a household were not to be long enjoyed, for the premature death of Riario left Cleofilo without a patron. He soon found a new supporter, however, in the rich cardinal Rodrigo Borgia.

Cleofilo's written description must not be accepted in all its particulars. He wrote it partly as a recruitment letter and partly as an advertisement of his own success in Rome; he did not intend it to be an objective appraisal of either Riario's or Rome's intellectual preferences. Certainly we may doubt the extent to which Riario personally could have debated a learned or poetic point with humanists, since his education had not been very distinguished. Yet even allowing for such exaggeration, there is an essential truth to Cleofilo's portrait of the cardinal's court as a meeting place for a variety of learned men and as an important link in the city's intellectual life and in humanists' fortunes.

As men like Cleofilo and Cortesi fully realized, the benefits of employment in a cardinal's *familia* could be substantial. A powerful cardinal-bishop could bestow rich ecclesiastical preferments on the clerics in his *familia*. He could play a decisive role in a man's entrance into the Curia, where powerful support also had great advantages. There were, however, negative sides to a close relationship with a particular cardinal. A cardinal often came to his station in middle age and could not be expected to live long. His death ended his court and required its members to seek new patrons, which was not a simple matter for everyone. In many ways a cardinal could do little better than Cardinal Bartolomeo Roverella, who petitioned Sixtus IV on January 1, 1484, to grant favors to his familiars, or Cardinal Raffaele Riario, who in his testament commended his familiars to the good will of the pope if he should die suddenly.[79] Further, a cardinal's personality could present grave problems. A patron could be indifferent or arbitrary in the treatment of his servants, who had little recourse to a just remedy since they were so greatly dependent on their lord's will. The curial humanist Benedetto Rizzoni (1454–*ca.* 1524), for example, belonged to the *familia* of Cardinal Domenico della Rovere, yet another of Sixtus's nephews who had been raised to the cardinalate.[80] Rizzoni served this powerful but intellectually mediocre prelate in the 1480s and 1490s. Over an unspecified argument with another member of the household, Rizzoni incurred his lord's displeasure and as a consequence was expelled by the cardinal from the *familia*. Despite Rizzoni's abject contrition, he could not regain his master's favor and finally resolved to find a more beneficent patron, which he did in another cardinal. When he discussed his fifteen years of service in the della Rovere household, Rizzoni complained that he had spent those years *non sine multis labore* [*sic*] *et vigiliis,* for which he felt he had received ill treatment. How common Rizzoni's lament might have been, or indeed how justified it was, cannot be determined, but such treatment was certainly a possibility.

The cardinal's *familia* carried one other major liability, and one that had consequences for the civil life of Rome. The unruly behavior of the cardinals' familiars caused much civil unrest in the city. Too often the familiars of one cardinal fought with those of their lord's enemies, taking into the streets a political, financial, or personal disagreement. Regional animosity and the political allegiance of cardinals produced much enmity and many occasions for brawling, especially as the French-Imperial conflicts intensified and turned Italy into their battleground. Contemporaries complained bitterly about the violence stemming from cardinals' households, and the pope's occasionally reprimanded the offending parties.[81] Humanists, no doubt, avoided the physical side of these encounters. They preferred to defend their patrons by producing satirical poems and orations against their enemies. They were not, however, immune to the consequences of conflicts between hostile cardinals. One cardinal's support could effectively exclude the good will of another cardinal and earn a humanist the long-lasting enmity of a powerful curial figure. A humanist at times had to display great agility to maintain amicable relations with as wide a circle of powerful men as possible.

It is unlikely that the life of a humanist was often endangered by his close adherence to one side or another. However, this was not always the case if the fate of the poet Jacopo Corsi (d. 1493) is any indication. The case is a bizarre one and not well documented, but it is worth relating as an extreme example. Corsi belonged to the *familia* or the Neapolitan cardinal Francesco Sanseverino in Rome. At a banquet attended by other cardinals, Corsi apparently sang some pieces that were critical of Cardinal Giuliano della Rovere. Della Rovere learned of this and decided to exact vengeance for this slight. He dispatched three men dressed as Spaniards to stab the poet to death.[82] Such acts of redress were exceptional, although contemporaries did not believe they were unusual.

When a humanist looked for employment in a cardinal's court, he probably ignored the negative elements, such as an unjust lord, or his future lord's enemies, or the possibility of the patron's early death. Rather, he realized that successful tenure in a cardinal's *familia* might well guarantee a financially secure future. Further, he would also have appreciated the value such courts played in encouraging contacts with other scholars and littérateurs, who could prove valuable in his humanistic career. While this attitude toward the *familia* was selective, it was accurate enough to be attractive and moderately realistic. Humanists were adept at seeing where their best interests lay and at exploiting them successfully, and they were naturally drawn to the cardinals' *familiae*.

❧ IV ❧

The papal, cardinalate, and other prelatic courts helped establish the social context of Roman humanists' lives by making them part of a multifaceted organism. These courts did not exhaust the picture of Roman courtly life, however. In addition to the clerical *familiae*, there were secular courts, which contributed to the integration of humanists into Roman society by providing them with opportunities to congregate.[83] The secular courts were less abundant and less powerful than the clerical households, but their presence was important as an alternative, and supplement, to the ecclesiastical variety. They need not be discussed in detail here since they performed many of the same functions as did the other *familiae* and employed similar individuals. Humanists used these courts in the same manner that they used the clerical *familiae* —as employment opportunities and as intellectual centers. The laymen who maintained these courts—notably papal relatives, bankers, and military leaders—depended on the Curia for their positions and wealth and stood apart from, if not in opposition to, the city's feudal nobility. As a result, their courts displayed many of the qualities of the clerical *familiae*—a close identification with papal incumbents and their policies, an uncertain life span, the arbitrariness of patrons, and possible disadvantages for those who were closely connected to one lord.

In some ways the secular lords competed with the clerics in their desire to display a magnificent life style, but they tended to define the elements of this magnificence differently. The lay lords preferred to surround themselves with other laymen, or clerics in minor orders, who shared their own interests; priests were usually chaplains and confessors, of course. As secular institutions, these courts included women and children and were, therefore, more like the courts found elsewhere in Italy. They formed an important exception to the clerical texture of Rome's ruling sectors.

Again, we lack many details on these secular courts. However, in 1540 the Florentine humanist-publisher Francesco Priscianese (1495–1549) produced a valuable description of the court of a secular lord in Rome.[84] Priscianese, a grammarian and scholar, was deeply interested in Italian court life. He spent several years in Rome and knew the needs of a secular court there. In many ways Priscianese's *Del governo della corte d'un signore in Roma* provides convenient parallels to the relevant sections of Cortesi's *De Cardinalatu* on the cardinal's *familia*. There were, of course, differences between the two: Priscianese's lord lacked a religious dimension and his court did not require clerics to assist him with his duties. In many ways, and especially in their menial functions, the two institutions were similar. Priscianese, however, was even more pragmatic in describing the needs of the secular court than Cortesi had been in his description of the clerical households. For example, he provided much specific information on the type of food the lord would need, and its price, while Cortesi gave only passing mention to such matters.[85]

The basic division of Priscianese's court corresponded to that of the clerical *familia:* higher officials (called gentlemen) and lower menials.

Humanists were included among the gentlemen, staffing such posts as secretaries and undersecretaries and, perhaps, chaplains. Like Cortesi, Priscianese believed that his lord had a special duty to patronize the learned. Priscianese expected that in addition to secretaries and chaplains, his ideal lord would employ at his court four learned men representing different fields of study.[86] These men would have no other duty than the intellectual advancement of their lord through learned intercourse and as ornaments at his court. For these services each was to receive 100 scudi a year (out of a total of 1,500 scudi in salaries paid to the entire 107-member household).[87] One of these four men would be expert in theology, another in philosophy, while the other two would specialize in areas that especially interested their lord. However, they all would possess knowledge of the four principal languages of the world, i.e., Hebrew, Greek, Latin, and Tuscan. Such linguistic requirements almost demanded humanistically trained occupants for these positions. In supplying such prominent positions for scholars, Priscianese emphasized the court as a major source of humanist patronage.

Of the secular lords who maintained important courts in High Renaissance Rome and who illustrate Priscianese's ideal, Agostino Chigi (1464–1520) stands out by virtue of his economic status and his support for humanist culture.[88] Chigi was a Sienese banker who established an important branch in Rome. He was especially successful and became one of the papacy's chief financial intermediaries. He came to Rome in 1494 and remained there till his death, serving four popes as a banker of the *Camera Apostolica* (one of the *mercatores sequentes Curiam Romanam*).[89] Much of his wealth stemmed from his control of the monopoly on the collection of the salt and sheep duties in Rome. By 1512 he was sufficiently wealthy to lend Julius II 40,000 ducats (with the papal tiara as collateral).[90] As an important papal financial officer, Chigi occasionally played a part in executing papal policies and diplomacy.[91] In 1520 Leo X rewarded his financial service to the Holy See with knighthood.

Although he was no scholar, Chigi was sensitive to new intellectual trends. He maintained close contact with prominent Roman humanists, for whom his home was a literary center. Among the members of his household was his chancellor, Cornelio Benigno (dates uncertain),[92] a prominent member of Rome's humanist assemblies. Benigno was especially devoted to Greek scholarship and seems to have persuaded Chigi to help fund a Greek press in Rome for a time.[93] Chigi's interest in new artistic forms made him one of the important secular patrons of art in Rome. He employed Raphael, Giulio Romano, Sebastiano del Piombo, and Baldassare Peruzzi to build and decorate his villa in Rome (the present Villa Farnesina), which the humanists and frequenters of Chigi's court Egidio Gallo and Blosio Palladio celebrated in verse.[94] Chigi's death deprived Rome of one of her outstanding and wealthiest secular patrons.

One household post which neither Cortesi nor Priscianese discussed, but which appertained especially to the secular court and attracted some humanists, was that of tutor. Teaching was a natural humanist activity. Humanists held some posts at the University of Rome (the *Sapienza*)[95] and also taught in the various preuniversity schools maintained in the *rioni* by the city's government.[96] The University of Rome, though, was not an illustrious institution and only a few humanists taught there at any one time; moreover, little information exists on the background and activities of the teachers in the *rioni*. Positions as private tutors were to be found in both clerical and secular courts. A cardinal might hire a humanist tutor to teach his illegitimate offspring, younger relatives living with him, the children of members of the *familia*, or poor boys from his hometown whom he educated as an act of charity; secular lords had their own children to educate. A tutor's position did not automatically entail membership in the *familia* or a permanent place in the palace. A humanist might simply visit the palace for a few hours daily in order to tutor in Latin composition or poetry. Although only a partial source of income, tutoring as a means of support was not disparaged or ill-regarded by the humanists.

An apt example of a humanist tutor in the Roman context is Raffaele Brandolini (d. 1517),[97] who followed his elder brother Aurelio, also an orator and poet, to Rome and by the 1490s had an established place there. Like his brother and other humanists, Brandolini used his humanist eloquence to make himself a free-lance orator. The abundance of official and quasi-official ceremonies in Rome provided many oratorical opportunities for humanist oratory, and Brandolini was particularly adept at funeral oratory.[98] He also found tutoring an acceptable profession. His students included Giovanni Maria del Monte, who later reigned as Pope Julius III (1550–1555), Prince Alfonso of Bisceglie, and the neo-Latin poet Marcantonio Flaminio. Del Monte was educated at the home of his uncle, a prominent jurist, *auditor causarum sacri palatii*, and later a cardinal, Antonio del Monte. Brandolini must have been a successful teacher, for his grateful student as pope had an inventory of his tutor's writings prepared as a means of preserving his mentor's fame.[99] This list shows that Brandolini was a loyal servant of his patrons, praised them in his writings, and was a keen student of Roman social life. Brandolini ended his career as a professor of rhetoric at the University of Rome (with an annual salary of 250 florins) and as a *cubicularius* in the *familia* of Leo X. Unfortunately, Brandolini had a falling out with the pope over a literary dispute with another poet and died in disgrace,[100] another victim of the whims of Rome's employers.

Whether as secretaries, undersecretaries, chaplains, tutors, or holders of any other post in the *familia*, humanists depended on the official court to help define and finance their social position. Humanists throughout Italy found courtly life, with its emphasis on service to a lord, compatible with their cultural interests and employment needs. In Rome the opportunities for courtly service were particularly extensive and potentially very rewarding. This was so because the leaders of the ecclesiastical courts, like those of the secular courts, had come to accept the patronage of humanistic learning as a proper function of their office, even though they did not always act appropriately. In providing humanists with an established place in Rome's social structure and the opportunity for upward mobility in the Curia, the *familia* contributed significantly to planting and nurturing humanist roots in Rome. While service as a familiar was less attractive than that of a curial officer, it was often a first step to professional advancement and security. A humanist could prove both his ability and his loyalty in personal service to a cardinal and thereby be more acceptable to the curial bureaucracy. Even if a man never succeeded in obtaining a curial post, the *familia* offered a viable alternative.

3
Humanist Families in Rome

Positions in the clerical hierarchy—the Curia Romana and curial *familiae,* ecclesiastical or secular—endowed humanists with the economic support they needed to remain and prosper in Rome and provided them with some form of social context. These were all official posts, which made the humanists part of larger institutions that directly reflected the religious and political needs of the theocratic government. The humanists' ability to function within these various organizations stemmed from their acknowledged literary and secretarial talents and their proven reliability as loyal functionaries. Whether as prelates, curialists, or familiars, many humanists found comfortable places in Rome's official, clerically directed society and more or less willingly accepted the constrictions of its hierarchical institutions.

As important as these institutional posts were to many humanists, they shared with other Italians a profound dependence on the bonds and security of the natural family. The family fostered the basic social, financial, and political ambitions of Renaissance Italians. Men accumulated large patrimonies so that they could glorify their family name and pass both on to their children. No element in Italian life was more central or more pervasive, and familial relations were as fundamental among the humanists as in any other group. In examining how the families of humanists functioned in Rome, our concern here is narrow. We are not interested in giving an exposition of the Italian Renaissance family. Rather, our goal is to consider the compromises required of the Roman humanist families in order for them to advance as economically and financially successful units. The special aspects of lineage and household organization which have interested recent scholars are discussed only insofar as they offer illustrations of how humanists functioned in Rome.[1]

❦ I ❦

The natural family as a force in humanist life in Rome encountered special problems. Three factors especially affected the way humanist families evolved. The first was the lack of important Roman familial traditions that could influence and promote humanism. Rome had had her entrepreneurial class and her feudal nobility, but they did not control the social and political destinies of the city.[2] The Schism and the reestablishment of papal hegemony throughout the papal states caused great economic and social dislocations and prevented the development of strong families that might have interested themselves in intellectual matters. The only families with any intellectual traditions that could foster humanism were those that depended on the Curia and were professional in background, such as the Valla family,[3] but their positions were definitely subordinate. The humanists therefore found in Rome no strong preexisting secular groups friendly to their intellectual interests and eager to exploit them as an element in establishing their identity or justifying their political and economic positions. This deprived Roman humanism of a natural arena of recruitment and weakened its attachment to the city.

In this deficiency Rome contrasted sharply with Florence.[4] In Florence humanism had early been co-opted by the ruling elite. Many of the prominent humanists in the early quattrocento in Florence were the sons of powerful ruling families. Florentine humanism in turn stressed topics that appealed to the merchant-based elite and defended their conceptions of themselves as a unique group and as the proper rulers of Florence. This made certain families fertile groups for humanism and helped to foster its value in other ruling and subordinate members of the society. In Rome wealthy families did not entertain these merchant ideals nor did they look to the classical learning of the humanists as a defense for their activities. The few Romans who did seek classical models usually did so for political, especially revolutionary, purposes in the tradition of Cola di Rienzo.[5] These, however, were exceptional cases. In Rome the humanists attached their hopes not to secular powers but to the clergy. At the beginning of the quattrocento, therefore, Roman humanists lacked that type of familial organization which proved so important to Florentine humanism's success.

Clerical dominance was the second factor that inhibited humanist familial development in Rome.[6] After 1420 the clergy reestablished its control over all aspects of Roman life and this coincided with the very period in which humanists made their way into Rome and the Curia in larger numbers. As the chief arbiters of Roman life, and officially celibate, the clergy displayed an ambivalent attitude toward the family as a constituent element in the city's society. Whatever the extent to which individuals followed their rule of celibacy, its requirement for entrance into the city's ruling class hindered the free growth of the family as a determining factor in Rome. Even in those cases where a cleric's family, such as that of the pope, acquired a certain importance in Roman society, there were limits to its future. Church lands could not be alienated, and unless the pope could acquire a patrimony for his children or nephews from other Italian rulers, another pope could deprive his family of its gains. Further, the possibilities for willing one's wealth to members of the family were limited by canon law for those curial clerics who died in or near Rome. This situation did not change until 1474.[7] The ruling class lacked familial traditions in Rome, and this affected all other groups, including humanists.

The dominance by the clergy, especially as it manifested itself in the requirement of clerical status for curial and courtly posts, affected the humanists in two ways. First, it prevented, or at least made more difficult, the advance of lay humanists in the bureaucracy. This tendency became even stronger as the Curia increasingly required clerical status for more and more offices, especially after the middle of the quattrocento. The second effect was to contribute to the general clericalization of humanism in Italy, especially in the second half of the century. Consequently, the clergy established both the general ambience in which humanists worked and also the manner in which they were to lead their own lives, including their relationship to the state of matrimony and the family.

The third factor blocking the development of a familial base for humanism in Rome was the impermanence of so many humanists there. Most humanists came to Rome from other parts of Italy or from other European lands. They often arrived in the city at the beginning of their careers, coming to serve in a cardinal's *familia* or seeking a teaching post or some curial office. They might stay for only a few years, until they had profited from the move or had decided that success lay in other quarters. Other humanists came when they had established literary careers in other parts of Italy and were seeking only to cap their careers by obtaining some lucrative post in Rome; these men did not intend to put down permanent roots there. Still others spent many years in Rome, established their families there for a time, and developed strong attachments to their offices and the city. These men did not commit their families' fortunes completely to Rome, however; they usually maintained homes in their ancestral cities or divided their time between Rome and other urban centers. This situation was very common. While it split a family's resources, such a division of loyalties did not prevent intellectual attachment to Rome and it has permitted the historian to consider such men as valid representatives of Roman humanism. The number of humanists who established permanent residence in Rome is less important than the humanism that came to be identified with the city's intellectual spirit and traditions. While the lack of permanence delayed close attachment between Rome and many humanists and contributed to a certain ambiguity in their relationship, it was not destructive to the growth of an intellectual uniformity.

These three agents were not effective in frustrating all humanist familial development. Counterbalancing factors allowed Rome to provide a certain social mobility to its inhabitants and thereby made the city more attractive to humanists. This mobility, however, was circumscribed. After 1400, social mobility in Italy was generally more difficult. This was as true for humanists as for others. Compared to other intellectual centers, however, Rome did offer certain advantages to humanists, for the layers of social stratification were less solidly established there than in other Italian cities.

In Naples, for example, the humanists proved useful to the kings as sources of secretarial expertise independent of the feudal nobility and were rewarded appropriately for their services. However, the feudal lords, both the great barons and the lesser ones (called the *seggi*), together with a strong lawyer class, prevented easy social access for non-aristocratic and non-Neapolitan humanists.[8] In Venice the humanists represented a social-political homogeneity. They were in great part members of a ruling elite whose scholarship did not form the basis for their social status. Those who were not part of the patriciate depended on it for support but could not enter it.[9] As a republic, Florence theoretically offered its citizens greater opportunities for upward movement, but this was to an extent illusory. From the end of the trecento certain rich families had moved to limit the openness of the city's ruling groups and blocked new families from advancing to the upper echelons of society.[10] As the Medici exerted increasing control in Florence after 1434, they displaced many of these older families and advanced their own supporters, but in great part the Medici continued the existing exclusionary system and limited the new groups' access to the ruling class. Compared to these cities, Rome actually appeared socially open and fluid.

❧ II ❧

The factors contributing to this relative openness were many. Rome was generally free of old civic traditions and a strong local aristocracy. The city's government was weak and completely dependent on the papacy after the latter's reestablishment.[11] The pope appointed its leaders and expected obedience, while the apostolic chamber controlled much of its economic activity. Civic policies consequently reflected papal and not municipal decisions. The last attempt of the city government to establish independence followed the expulsion of Eugenius IV from Rome in 1434. This experiment in republican rule ended in failure and in 1443 the pope returned in triumph and reintroduced papal hegemony. This lack of self-government enabled the humanists and other curialists to ignore the city government and either to withhold allegiance to it or to discount any exclusionary policy it might impose.

Rome's civic institutions were weak because of clerical control. This dominance had two important consequences: first, the social composition of the clergy as a group affected the constitution of Rome's society; and second, the clergy hurt the growth of local power groups. The clergy as a group displayed a varied social background. The higher clergy were rather more homogeneous, for aristocratic preferences were operative in their selection. This was less a specific reflection of the Church or of Roman conditions than it was a sign of the general advance of aristocratic government in Italy. Still, as a profession, the clergy since the Middle Ages had been relatively open to nonaristocrats, especially in its lower ranks, and thereby had provided some social mobility. The significance of this should not be overestimated, however,[12] for it did not automatically imply any familial consequences. The Roman curial-ecclesiastical structure followed this general tendency and permitted the movement of men from lower social groups or at least from undistinguished backgrounds. These parvenus were in a position to assist their families in improving their social statuses, a condition the humanists avidly exploited.

The clergy in Rome worked to prevent the growth of local traditions that could interfere with its rule. The papal states had always suffered from the ambitions of the nobles in and around Rome, and in the Middle Ages the pope often had to absent himself from Rome because of local aristocratic hostility. Since Avignon the papacy had spent large sums of money to destroy the local nobility and force it into submission. This produced a suspicion on the part of the clergy toward the Romans. Both Alexander VI and Julius II disliked the Romans, and the feeling was reciprocated.[13] Similarly, the bureaucracy showed a preference for hiring non-Romans. Humanists, who were usually non-Roman, benefited from this prejudice; they had the entire bureaucracy open to them.

Contributing to this receptivity to non-Romans within the bureaucracy were the experiences of the Great Schism and the population patterns of the Renaissance. The Great Schism and the claims of rival popes dislocated the Curia, broke its traditions, and opened its offices to an extent. While the Roman pope had to accept some officials from the ranks of the "antipopes" into his Curia, the continuity of families holding specific offices no doubt suffered. This meant that in the first decades after Martin's return, the bureaucracy encouraged qualified newcomers to enter its ranks.[14] The development of certain hereditary claims to curial offices and the introduction and spread of venality of offices would eventually end this institutional flexibility, but for most of the quattrocento the bureaucracy was marked by a certain openness.

The size of Rome's population also necessitated the admittance of immigrants, especially highly skilled individuals. Exact estimates of the population of Rome during the quattrocento are lacking, and the approximations that do exist must be used carefully. Still, a comparison with Florentine population statistics shows how underpopulated Rome was and how dependent it was on immigration. By the time of the Curia's return to Rome in 1420, the city's population had fallen below 20,000, while that of Florence was about 50,000. By the middle of the century, the two cities contained, respectively, about 33,000 and 54,000 inhabitants; the increase in Rome's population demonstrated the importance of immigration.[15] The most reliable estimate of Rome's population, however, appeared in the 1526/1527 census, which was discussed in Chapter 2.[16] Florence remained larger even after a century of rather rapid Roman growth; Rome's adult population of 55,000 still trailed Florence's 70,000. After the sack Rome's population again declined, as did Florence's as a consequence of plague. Because of Rome's relatively small population throughout most of the quattrocento, the Curia's posts had to be staffed by immigrants, a factor that contributed to social mobility.

All of these elements prevented the humanists' identification with Rome's civic traditions and contrasted with the civic humanism of Florence.[17] When the humanists in Rome wrote of the city, they referred not to her municipal government but to her glorious past as the center of the Roman Empire or to her position as the center of the Christian Church. Modern Rome was in some ways an embarrassment to them. In Florence the humanists exalted the city and its policies in modern and contemporary circumstances. But this civic humanism was in many respects a servant of the pretensions of the ruling elite. The Florentine humanists, who were to a great extent members and dependents of the ruling class, devoted their energies to exalting the status quo and defending the right of the oligarchy to rule. Roman humanists fulfilled similar functions, but instead of turning to the local government, they exalted the pope and the Church. Given the local traditions operative in their respective cities, Rome's curial humanists were effectively the mirror images of Florence's civic humanists.

Although the humanists participated in the mobility Rome offered,

their social backgrounds cannot be easily typified. Because the humanists were highly educated, they tended not to come from the lowest
elements in society, although some did. In general, humanists tended to
be sons of dispossessed nobles, the illegitimate sons of nobles, or the
sons of lawyers, notaries, merchants, or teachers. Usually they did not
belong to the ruling classes. The humanists who came to Rome did so
because they saw in the Curia opportunities for social and economic
advancement which they did not find in other places.

The careers of two successful humanists from modest circumstances,
the Tuscans Poggio Bracciolini and Leonardo Bruni, demonstrate the
mobility of humanists in Rome. Unlike many Florentine humanists of
their generation, they came from poor backgrounds, yet both became
wealthy and influential men outside the ecclesiastical hierarchy. Bruni
owed only part of his success to his years as papal secretary (1405–
1408), but it is significant that he had been encouraged to seek his fortune in the Curia by Coluccio Salutati, the leader of the Florentine
humanists.[18] Poggio, on the other hand, owed his social and financial
success directly to his long service in the Curia as a scriptor and papal
secretary. He established his family's subsequent social and economic
status in Florence on the basis of these curial offices.[19] He settled in
Florence in later years after his marriage (1453), and eventually became
the chancellor of the republic (as did Bruni) while still retaining his
curial posts. Whether or not these men could have been as successful
had they not entered the Curia is a moot question. What is important
is that they chose at some point in their careers to seek their fortunes in
Rome and depend on their literary abilities for their success in the
Curia. In Rome they did not have to belong to any economic or political
elite to achieve success as they might have had to do in other Italian
cities.

Others who imitated Poggio and Bruni in seeking better opportunities
in Rome were often equally successful. Many of these could not make
their fortunes in their native cities, or had not advanced as far as they
wished, or had been politically excluded from local political circles. Even
the growth of the clerical requirement for employment in the Curia did
not completely destroy Rome's appeal to lay humanists. Families and
individuals without strong clerical attachments continued to prosper
into the early cinquecento. This would change during the sixteenth
century, and a narrowing in social background would displace the openness of the quattrocento.

The exclusion of humanists (indeed all laymen) from political activity in Rome had one major benefit; it freed them from the political
liabilities that frequently accompanied citizenship in cities like Florence

and Venice. Since laymen took little or no part in the creation of policy unless they were related to the reigning pontiff, there existed little opportunity or temptation for the open political rivalry among families which could cause mutual destruction. Personal animosity never ceased, but it did not develop into a factionalism aimed at control of the government. Rather, Rome functioned as a refuge for those who had been excluded from their native cities for political trespasses. Giannozzo Manetti, for example, although rich and powerful, fled Florence because of the political hostility of other influential Florentine families. He lived his last years as an exile in Rome, where he was a papal secretary, and in Naples.[20] Similarly, Leon Battista Alberti suffered disabilities in Florence arising from his family's politics and for a time found a haven in Rome.[21] The struggles for political dominance that raged among wealthy and powerful families and social groups in other Italian cities did not develop in Rome, or at least did not become a major factor as long as the popes remained strong. (Again, the families of the popes were major exceptions.) This absence of internal turmoil permitted the families of humanists to concentrate on their own advancement.

Of course, the pope, as the ruler of the city, could affect the fortunes of humanists' families. While there was great continuity in the essentials of papal policy from one pontificate to another, a new pope could introduce a policy that favored certain parties, and this did, on occasion, help humanists. Those who came from the native city or country of the reigning pope obtained special support for posts; in the case of Pius II this indirectly benefited humanists.[22] Changes in papal policy could hurt some groups during periods of tension, but this was exceptional. Sixtus IV, for example, did not exclude all the Florentines or Tuscans from Rome when he declared war on the Florentine Republic in the aftermath of the Pazzi Conspiracy. Only those who were closely connected with the Florentine government or with the Medici—e.g., the Florentine bankers and individuals known for their pro-Medici sentiments—suffered, and then only temporarily.[23] As a group, humanists were usually spared the repercussions of such governmental conflicts. For the most part the limits of Roman life also insulated humanists from the excesses stemming from political rivalries.

❧ III ❧

Ironically, Rome's relative openness to new, upwardly mobile Italians and foreigners throughout most of the quattrocento was to end in part because of the actions of its very beneficiaries. In the last third of the century the parallel development of curial familial dynasties and of the venality of offices ultimately reinforced this tendency. Even the clerical members of a family participated in the former development. Indeed, an important mark of humanist life in Rome was this dynasticism, although the best-known dynasts were not humanists. Lawyers were especially adept in handing on their professional offices. Such families as the Accolti, the del Monte, and, earlier in the century, the Valla based their success on a legal dynasticism.[24] While the clerical requirement for many posts blunted this development by limiting the ability to inherit posts, fathers did seek to have their sons succeed to their posts when they resigned them. As an institution of competing careerists, the Curia was not always pleased with this procedure. Pope Calixtus III, for example, prevented George of Trebizond from resigning his secretaryship in favor of his son. The pope acted in response to the complaints of senior men who resented being ignored for promotion.[25] Still, the humanist families came to regard Rome and the Curia as the route, often denied them in their places of origin, by which to establish their families' fortunes. In turn, the Curia became the means by which to achieve high social and economic status in their native cities.

Marriage presented special problems in celibate Rome. As noted above, marriage could end a man's prospects for advancement. However, such negative elements were counterbalanced by the importance of intermarriage among curial families. Individuals found suitable mates in the children or relatives of their colleagues, although there was an equal tendency to seek a mate from one's native region; often, however, these patterns worked together. Children of curialists from the same region or town might marry. Such alliances could fully exploit connections in the Curia. Intermarriage became one means by which the families could overcome clerically imposed disadvantages and guarantee for themselves favorable treatment by the bureaucracy.

Another means of dealing with the clerical bias in Rome was to select careers for curialist children that would prove complementary. A curialist with several children could encourage one son to marry and succeed him while urging another to embrace the clerical life. If the clerical son succeeded in achieving a bishopric or cardinalate or some powerful curial post, and the married son produced children who could benefit from the clerical son's patronage, then the family's overall prospects would improve. A clerical family member could help his nephews secure curial or ecclesiastical posts. It was a convenient system, not unlike that employed by the feudal nobility and other wealthy families in Italy. The practice of resigning an ecclesiastical post in favor of a relative gave an almost hereditary character to many offices. It was an abuse that did not escape the criticisms of contemporaries.[26]

This dependence on having a clergyman in the family was greatly advanced by Sixtus IV. In his bull *Etsi universi Romanae Ecclesiae dominio temporali*, of January 1, 1474, the pope permitted curial clerics and laymen who died in Rome to will their real property to their families.[27] Prior to Sixtus's decree those clerics and laymen in the Curia who died in Rome or on missions for the Curia forfeited their property to the Holy See. This law even extended to papal and cardinalate familiars. In altering the law, Sixtus gave incentives to families to make Rome their permanent home and rendered clerical status an ally of family stability. He also gave a major impetus to clerical investment in new palaces in Rome.

Rome, therefore, compensated families for the political and social limits imposed on them by its clerical and hierarchical structure. It remained a place where a fortune could be made and a family's importance established if the city's opportunities were properly exploited. This did nothing to mitigate Rome's reputation as a center of moneychangers and opportunists who worked not for the good of the Church and the faithful but for their own personal welfare. This opportunistic attitude toward employment in Rome explains the migration of some curial families back to their hometowns, where they could enjoy and display their Rome-based prosperity while still maintaining their official positions in Rome.

❦ IV ❦

To test the patterns just described, as well as to illustrate the overall progress of familial dynasticism among humanists, specific examples of humanist families must be investigated. The groups chosen are to an extent arbitrary, reflecting what limited research has been done. The tendency of families to migrate back to their natal towns has scattered the type of documents needed. Still, an attempt has been made here to present families that represented both a certain degree of advancement in the Curia and some prominence in humanist circles in Rome. In order to establish the limits of the patterns sketched, two brief examples will be presented: one, a lay family with distinguished humanist credentials; the other, a clerical family of little humanist fame.

One of the most famous names in the history of Roman humanism was Flavio Biondo of Forlì (1388–1463).[28] Biondo elevated the study of ancient Roman history and antiquarianism to a high plane of sophistication in a series of histories of ancient Rome and medieval Italy.[29] Before coming to Rome he served as a secretary to Francesco Barbaro, governor of Vicenza (1425), and then as secretary to Giovanni Vitelleschi, governor of the March of Ancona. He came to Rome in 1432, was made a notary of the *Camera Apostolica,* and in 1434 became an apostolic secretary. Biondo married a woman from his native town and had ten children. The eldest, Gaspare (d. 1493), followed his father into the Curia, where he enjoyed a successful career. He succeeded his father as a notary in the *Camera* and then as papal secretary (both in January 1463). Three years later he became *magister registri Camerae Apostolicae.* Sixtus IV made him a papal scriptor (1466) and a *clericus* of the *Camera* (1476). He held both these posts while retaining his secretaryship and notaryship. [30] Alexander VI later used Gaspare on local diplomatic missions, and on one of these Gaspare was murdered. Gaspare married a woman of noble Roman birth, Lucrezia Margania (d. 1544), and had at least one son, Paolo. Gaspare seems to have devoted whatever scholarly talents he had to editing his father's writings and working for presses. His humanistic interests led him to take part in the meetings of the Roman Academy.

Biondo's third son, Francesco (dates uncertain), also entered the Curia as a notary of the *Camera,* succeeding his brother Gaspare in 1483. [31] He married, and his son, also named Paolo, became a scriptor and papal secretary (1503). Little is known of their other activities. Another of Biondo's sons, Gabriele (dates uncertain), belonged to the Roman Academy and became a priest. He composed religious works tinged with heretical ideas and spent most of his life outside the city. Of Biondo's seven other children, another son, Girolamo, is mentioned, but no information exists on his activities; two of Biondo's daughters married well, but outside Rome. [32]

Much less prominent in humanist circles was the Rizzoni family of Verona, but they illustrate another familial procedure. Giacomo Rizzoni (d. 1485) [33] came to Rome after studying Greek in the East as a tutor to Cardinal Pietro Barbo, the future Paul II. In 1463/1464 he was made an apostolic scriptor and an abbreviator *de parco maiori,* and shortly afterward he was selected *exactor et collector pecuniarum taxarum officii abbreviatorum.* At some point he took holy orders. His literary production was minor, being confined to translating Greek poetry into Latin. With his connections in the Curia, however, Giacomo helped his nephew Benedetto (1454–*ca.* 1523) gain entrance to the bureaucracy. [34] Benedetto became a papal scriptor in 1485 and joined the *familia* of Cardinal Domenico della Rovere, but following a dispute with the cardinal, he passed to the employ of Cardinal Giovanni Michele of Verona. In 1494 he was made an abbreviator, and in 1497 an *officialis collectoriae plumbi.* In 1505 he was created an apostolic chamberlain in the papal *familia,* and in 1506 he became an apostolic secretary. The wealth from his office allowed him to build a palace in Quinzano, near Verona.[35] He was a man of some religious sensibility and was probably a priest, for he joined the reform-minded Confraternity of Divine Love in Rome. He left no samples of humanistic work, although he belonged to prominent humanist circles. With Benedetto the family's curial presence ended.

The Biondo and Rizzoni families display the spectrum of humanists that were found in Renaissance Rome. The Biondo reached international prominence in the person of Flavio and established a highly successful curial tradition without entering the ranks of the clergy. The Rizzoni was a minor humanist family and had a relatively short association with the Curia. Unlike the Biondo, the Rizzoni based its success on clerical status. Between these two extreme types were most of the other humanist families in Rome. These others combined clerical and secular status with moderate amounts of humanistic production, some of which was of high quality and great influence. To demonstrate these more typical examples, two families, the Cortesi of San Gimignano and the Maffei of Volterra,[36] will be given special attention. These two families have been chosen because they had similar humanistic backgrounds and were closely connected in Rome and in their native Tuscany; they even intermarried. The time span of their curial history is almost exactly that of the period of this study. They encompassed both secular and clerical traditions, although increased clerical pressures are noticeable in their histories. Each family produced one humanist who in his writings helped define the special qualities of Roman humanism and who enjoyed an international reputation.

The origins of the Cortesi family are uncertain. The family came to San Gimignano from Pavia in the 1430s, although it may have been originally from Dalmatia.[37] The family moved to San Gimignano probably as a result of some criminal act on the part of a family member. The first Cortesi to transfer to Rome was Antonio Cortesi (d. 1474).[38] Antonio became a papal abbreviator *de parco maiori,* an apostolic scriptor, the head of the secretaries of the auditors, and a papal familiar.[39] This curriculum shows Antonio to have been a trusted member of the bureaucracy; he was highly regarded for his great skill in writing papal letters. Antonio based his family's future on two foundations. One was the Curia, where he enjoyed such success; the other was faithful support for Medici hegemony in Tuscany.[40] The latter allegiance was aided by

Antonio's marriage to Tita Aldobrandini, the daughter of an influential Florentine family. Antonio's marriage followed a not uncommon curial path; although in minor orders, he decided to marry and have a family. Despite his increasing curial activities, Antonio found time to compose two literary treatises. One, a discourse on moral philosophy, has not survived. The second, an attack on Lorenzo Valla's rejection of the Donation of Constantine, demonstrates his loyalty to curial policy.[41] Antonio and Tita had one daughter and three sons. The daughter, Caterina, married the son of another curial family, Antonio Maffei, and had one son, who also entered the Curia.[42]

Only one of Antonio's sons, Lattanzio (*ca.* 1462–1523),[43] did not follow his father into the Curia. Rather, he sought his fortune through military service, fought with the Duke of Calabria in the kingdom of Naples in the 1480s, and earned a knighthood. Despite his military accomplishments, Lattanzio had a humanist education and interests. He combined his profession and his avocation for classical studies by producing a paraphrase of Caesar's *Commentaries.* He also wrote the annotations for his brother Paolo's treatise *De Cardinalatu.*[44] In 1487 Lattanzio married Ippolita Saraceni of Siena, a relation of the papal Piccolomini family. No dowry was paid in this union; rather it was hoped that the girl's relative, Cardinal Francesco Todeschini-Piccolomini, the archbishop of Siena, would reward Lattanzio's brother Alessandro, who was a cleric, with some rich benefice or help him in his curial career.[45] From the late 1480s Lattanzio lived in the familial home in San Gimignano, where he cared for the family's affairs in Tuscany. He worked to obtain the abbacy of the Convent of San Girolamo of the Valambrosian order in San Gimignano for his mother's sister, a woman of between fifty and sixty years of age, who had been a nun at that convent for forty years.[46] Lattanzio had one son, Antonio, who continued the family name and inherited its wealth and seems to have passed his years in Tuscany.

Antonio's other sons, Alessandro and Paolo, followed him into the Curia. Both were clerics and had good prospects for advancement. Alessandro (*ca.* 1460–*ca.* 1490)[47] was born in Rome but was educated in San Gimignano and Pisa. While a student at the *studio fiorentino* at Pisa from 1476 to 1479, he identified himself with Florentine humanism and the Medici.[48] After his years in Pisa, he returned to Rome, where he began his curial career. His first post was as a papal scriptor.[49] Although Alessandro entered fully into Roman curial and intellectual life, he remained divided in his loyalties between Rome and Florence. In a letter of April 20, 1487, to his Florentine friend Francesco Baroni, he admitted that he had two fatherlands, Rome and Florence.[50] His

attachment to Florence and devotion to the Medici were well known to
his colleagues in Rome and caused him some trouble. In the same letter,
Alessandro gave proof of his steadfast devotion to the Medici. In his
youth he was such a known Medici partisan that Count Girolamo Riario,
a papal nephew, had him imprisoned in Castel Sant'Angelo in 1474 for
defending the good name of Lorenzo the Magnificent publicly. Later,
Sixtus IV, displeased with his nephew's deed, freed Alessandro from
prison. Such devotion, Alessandro believed, should be rewarded.[51]

Subsequently, in a series of letters to his friend Baroni written probably in 1488, Alessandro expressed himself candidly on his career and
his attitude toward the Medici. Alessandro informed his friend that he
wished to follow his father as an abbreviator *de parco maiori.*[52] He had
a clear idea of how to obtain such a post in Rome. He noted that there
were two possible roads to success. One would require him to serve some
prince. He rejected this route. He wrote that he enjoyed his life in Rome,
where his house was "un achademia [*sic*] di letterati," and that he had
no intention of abandoning his lifestyle to follow the whims of a lord.[53]
The second means was through ecclesiastical office with prelate status.
This route appealed to him, but he realized that to achieve his desired
goal he would need strong support from Lorenzo de' Medici.

In pursuit of this end Alessandro provided a realistic assessment of
advancement in the Curia. At the time of writing, he held three curial
offices; he was an apostolic scriptor, the *magister registri supplicationum,* and a solicitor of papal letters, called Janissaries in curial par-
lance.[54] While he admitted that these were all good posts, he realized
that a curialist must change offices in order to have a successful career.
Alessandro espoused the principle that advancement in the Curia requires movement since anyone who holds onto one office too long loses
his position (*conditione*)—an eternal rule for aspiring junior executives.
He planned to resign his scriptorship, which was worth 1,700 ducats,
and his solicitorship, which had been assessed at 700 ducats, in exchange
for either a bishopric or the desired abbreviatorship *de parco maiori,*
which was valued at 2,000 ducats. He was especially desirous of obtaining the abbreviatorship his father had held, because he had his father's
books and had been practicing writing supplications. Moreover, he
claimed a vague hereditary right of succession in noting *essem quasi
successor paterni regni.* Subsequently, he indicated that he would be
willing to accept a secretaryship and argued that his literary background
qualified him for that post.[55]

Alessandro made it clear to Baroni that he needed and expected
Lorenzo de' Medici's help in obtaining these offices. Certainly Lorenzo
was in a good position to aid him. Lorenzo's daughter had recently

married Innocent VIII's son, and so Lorenzo's relations with the Curia were warm. Alessandro hoped that Innocent would bend to Lorenzo's pressure on the matter of the abbreviatorship. This was important because, as Alessandro noted, Innocent reserved the abbreviatorships for his own people and could change its membership at will.[56] With his recently acquired relative, Lorenzo would therefore act as a guarantor for Cortesi.

Alessandro never received his abbreviatorship or a bishopric or a secretaryship. His dependence on Medici support in this instance proved misplaced. Indeed, his campaign for advancement in the Curia was a limited one. In addition to curial posts, Alessandro also sought ecclesiastical preferment through Medici support. Unfortunately, his wishes ran counter to Medici dynastic needs. Alessandro had earlier hoped to obtain the rich benefice of the abbacy of the Camaldolese Badia of Ss. Giusto and Clemente in Volterra. Again, Medici support would be crucial for a successful request. Alessandro expressed his desire for this aid through his contacts in Florence.[57] Lorenzo did in fact use his influence to determine the selection of the next abbot. However, Lorenzo's candidate was not Alessandro but his own son Giovanni. Alessandro accepted this setback philosophically, acknowledging that Lorenzo certainly had the duty to guarantee his own family's fortune. Nevertheless, Alessandro must have been bitter, especially since Giovanni also had recently received the rich abbacy of Monte Cassino. Alessandro felt that Lorenzo could well have afforded to allow the lesser abbacy in Volterra to go to his loyal supporter.

This and other events convinced Alessandro that he had to seek other patrons besides the Medici. The means he adopted in his new campaign were literary. He composed a long heroic poem in hexameters in honor of King Matthias Corvinus of Hungary, *Laudes bellicae Matthiae Corvini Hungariae Regis*. Corvinus was a noted patron of Italian humanists and Alessandro's method of presenting himself was a sound one. Alessandro may also have sought Spanish favor in a poem celebrating conquests in Spain against the Moors, *Silva de triumphata Bassa, Almeria, Granata* (published in 1492).[58] Nor did he ignore the French. He cultivated Cardinal de Foix and visited France in 1487. But in *ca.* 1490 Alessandro died, not having enjoyed any of the fruits of his labors.

Alessandro Cortesi was an accomplished poet and orator.[59] In addition to the poems in honor of the Hungarian and Spanish rulers, he had earlier composed a series of poems in honor of the king of France, Louis XI (1478). Another poetic series honored his close Roman friend Alessandro Farnese, the future Paul III.[60] His interest in Latin studies extended to philology and archaeology.[61] As a humanist he acted as a

conduit between Roman and Florentine humanists, especially Angelo
Poliziano. Alessandro informed his friend Poliziano of Roman dissatisfaction with the latter's translation of Herodianus, and Angelo replied
to these criticisms in a letter to Alessandro.[62] Among his close friends
connected with Florence were Giovanni Pico della Mirandola and the
Greek poet Michele Marullo. In Rome he belonged to the city's humanist circles and was especially close to his brother's in-law, Cardinal
Francesco Todeschini-Piccolomini.

Alessandro had the important task of guiding his brother Paolo's
education and early years in Rome. He took this responsibility seriously
and introduced the youth to the homes of the powerful in Rome, to
the city's intellectuals, and to the realities of curial life. Paolo admired
his brother, but also recognized certain negative sides to his personality.
He noted that Alessandro was fervid in temper, ambitious and shrewd,
proud and prolific, but gloomy in disposition, no doubt in part because
of his failure to advance in the Curia.[63] Paolo learned much from his
brother and perhaps as a consequence proved more successful in securing promotions. Although devoted to the Medici in his youth, Paolo
was more perspicacious than his brother in broadening his contacts with
other powerful men.

Like his two brothers, Paolo (1465–1510)[64] was born in Rome but
was educated in San Gimignano, Pisa, and Rome. One of his teachers in
San Gimignano may have been Michele Marullo, a close associate of the
Cortesi family. In Rome Paolo studied under Pomponio Leto, whom he
eventually succeeded as leader of the informal Roman academy.[65]
Young Paolo's most formative influences were his contacts with men
like Angelo Poliziano. He allied himself at first with the traditions of
Florentine humanism and Medici hegemony. He dedicated his first composition, the *De hominibus doctis dialogus* (written *ca.* 1490), to
Lorenzo de' Medici at the suggestion of Cardinal Todeschini-Piccolomini.[66] In it he judged the major Latin writers of the quattrocento
according to the standards of Ciceronian Latinity. The dialogue was
broadly patterned on Cicero's *Brutus,* and in this work Cortesi indicated
his movement away from Florentine eclectic literary theory toward the
severe classicism of Roman humanism.

Even though it was dedicated to a Florentine, the *De hominibus doctis*
reflected Cortesi's Roman ambience. There are three interlocutors in
the work, Paolo himself, Alessandro Farnese, and probably Giovanni
Sulpizio of Veroli.[67] Farnese was approximately Cortesi's age, and a
protégé of Alessandro and Paolo Cortesi. A member of a rich noble
family and destined for high Church office, Farnese belonged to the
humanist group surrounding the Cortesi. His humanistic interests were

broad, and he spent some time in Florence studying Greek.[68] Sulpizio (1450-1513) was one of Cortesi's Roman teachers.[69] After teaching in Veroli and Perugia, he established himself in Rome as a teacher and editor of classical texts. He professed a strict Ciceronian style in Latin composition and helped pass this preference on to his students.

Although never printed in its author's lifetime, the *De hominibus doctis* circulated among Cortesi's friends in Rome and Florence, where it was generally received with great enthusiasm. It showed Cortesi to be a keen and knowledgeable critic of contemporary writers. Some time before the dialogue was written, Cortesi collected a series of letters and organized them into a style manual, a popular form in the Renaissance. As he would do with the dialogue, Cortesi solicited the opinion of his friend Angelo Poliziano. Poliziano returned the work with severe criticisms. He denigrated Cortesi's slavish dependence on Ciceronian Latin. Poliziano's letter and Cortesi's defense of Ciceronian imitation became major statements of their respective literary philosophies in the Renaissance.[70] Although Cortesi's friendship with Poliziano survived this altercation, the controversy secured Cortesi's position among the Roman humanists and ended his early acceptance of Florentine literary concepts. However, Cortesi must have taken Poliziano's objections to heart, for the proposed manual never appeared. It is possible that the controversy turned Cortesi's mind from collections of other men's writings to original composition as a means of presenting his views.

Because of his literary reputation and his family's established place in the Curia, Cortesi rose in the Curia. Beginning as a papal scriptor in succession to Platina in 1481, he obtained the post of apostolic secretary in 1498, the position which had eluded his brother.[71] A further mark of his favor in the Curia was his appointment as apostolic protonotary. His position in Rome's intellectual life grew in the 1490s. He established an informal academy devoted to Italian poetry and Latin eloquence in about 1490. Cortesi's academy became the gathering place for other humanists in the Curia and in cardinalate *familiae*.[72] Through this academy he affected the development of Roman humanism and influenced its conception of literary art.

By the end of the 1490s Cortesi began to absent himself more and more from Rome and to seek a refuge in his home town. By 1503 Cortesi had left Rome and established his residence in San Gimignano.[73] This did not result from a desire to end his relations with the city or a rejection of its intellectual life. Rather, it was a calculated attempt to lay the foundations for his advancement to higher offices. Having learned from his brother's misfortunes the dangers of dependence on one man for support, Cortesi decided to secure his fortune by producing a series of literary pieces which would earn him what he desired. To do this, he could not chance the distractions of Roman life, and so he decided to return to San Gimignano, where he built a villa. There he devoted himself to writing, but he also entertained many of the cardinals and curial friends who took the time to visit him.

Extricating himself from his curial offices and establishing himself in San Gimignano, however, proved more difficult than he had expected. Paolo had decided to sell his secretaryship and to use the money to purchase some land from the monks of the Badia of Florence. [74] However, the pope interfered with his plans to sell the office, and Cortesi was unable to obtain the money in time to meet the commitment he had made to pay the monks by a fixed date. When he finally did complete the transaction, the monks complained that he had failed to meet the requirements of the contract and refused to fulfill their part of the agreement. Cortesi enlisted the help of his Roman friends Cardinal Adriano Castellesi and Mario Maffei to help settle the matter. [75] In the end Cortesi had to bring the case before the Rota in order to secure a favorable decision.

Once the case had been decided, Cortesi was able to devote himself to his literary pursuits. The first fruit of this period was his *In quattuor libros Sententiarum* (called both the *Liber Sententiarum* and *In Sententias*). [76] The treatise was a rewriting of traditional Christian theological topics in Ciceronian Latin. Formally it was based on the general outline of Peter Lombard's *Sententiae,* but it was essentially an independent treatise. The *Liber* expressed Cortesi's attitude toward the possibilities of the Latin language. As a devoted Ciceronian, Cortesi felt that all subjects, including Christian theology, could be successfully discussed in the words and style of the great Roman orator. Cortesi's work rehearsed the traditional theological opinions in a language that eschewed nonclassical vocabulary and syntax. He dedicated the treatise to Julius II and circulated copies among powerful individuals.

After publishing the *Liber,* Cortesi began work on his most important composition, the *De Cardinalatu.* [77] He wrote it while entertaining a variety of friends at his villa, holding mock gladiatorial games for the amusement of the local inhabitants and even helping less fortunate neighbors by offering them employment during a period of bad harvest. His experiences in San Gimignano, his memories of Roman friends and events, and the reminiscences of his acquaintances provided Cortesi with apposite anecdotes to support the views he expressed on all topics relating to a cardinal's life and duties. The *De Cardinalatu* contained stories about contemporary or near-contemporary popes, cardinals, bishops, secular rulers, and humanists whom Cortesi had known or whose fame he felt warranted their inclusion.

Cortesi had originally planned to compose a treatise on the prince, a common theme among quattrocento humanists. However, at the suggestion of his friend Cardinal Ascanio Sforza, Cortesi altered his plan and decided to write on papal authority. On further consideration, he again changed his mind and selected the cardinalate as his subject matter.[78] This was a particularly apt choice. The cardinalate represented an important force in Roman society and was especially influential in the city's intellectual life. Moreover, Cortesi aspired to high ecclesiastical office and in the treatise he could demonstrate his expertise in matters related to ecclesiastical polity. Although the *De Cardinalatu* constituted another element in Cortesi's plan to advance his career, it also presented a portrait of the cardinal recast in humanist manner in line with a humanist refashioning of the ideal prince and citizen.

While composing the *De Cardinalatu,* Cortesi occasionally circulated copies of completed sections to various cardinals, bishops, and secular rulers, as well as to the pope himself.[79] Usually the distributed selections praised either the recipient or some member of his family. In doing this Cortesi kept his name current among those men who could help advance his career. Unfortunately for Cortesi, the one person most important to his plans, the pope, did not bother to read the sections sent to him.[80] Nevertheless, the strategy was an intelligent one, and even began to have some positive results.[81]

In the *De Cardinalatu* Cortesi experimented with new forms in Latin composition. He moved away from his strict theory of Ciceronian imitation and substituted for it a style that remained equally classical but sought expression in unusual vocabulary and involved syntax, a style that required great erudition on the part of its author and its readers. Cortesi's close friend and one of the editors of the *De Cardinalatu,* Raffaele Maffei, complained to its author that the style was Apuleian.[82] By this Maffei meant that Cortesi had adopted a style and language that concentrated on obscure words, circumlocutions, and vocabulary based on Greek roots, all characteristics of the second-century North African writer Apuleius.[83] This technique often obscured the author's narrative. In his discussion of specifically Christian topics, for example, Cortesi had to resort to approximations, which often obscured his meaning. The rationale for Cortesi's procedure was the desire to prove that Latin could be used to discuss any topic in a form that was timeless, i.e., not bound to changing vocabulary or syntax. That this procedure would be confusing to the reader was recognized by Cortesi or his editors, or both, and a series of side notes explaining and outlining the content of the text was included. For the same reason, Lattanzio Cortesi added a series of annotations at the end of the text explaining the meaning of many of his brother's terms. Cortesi, however, mis-judged the patience of his audience, and the *De Cardinalatu* enjoyed only one printing. For the historian, however, the treatise provides valuable information on contemporary life and ideals as well as apposite and often entertaining anecdotes on the great and near-great of Renaissance Italy, especially Rome.

Cortesi did not live long enough to supervise the printing of the *De Cardinalatu*. The editing of the text was left to his brother Lattanzio, and his two close humanist friends Raffaele Maffei and the monk Severo Piacentino. A printing press was transported from Siena to Cortesi's villa to produce the text. Its appearance marked the post-humous culmination of Cortesi's literary career. He had succeeded both in producing a larger body of humanistic material and in advancing more successfully in the curial-ecclesiastical bureaucracy than had his brother. Only his early death prevented him from probably rising even higher and solidifying his reputation as a humanist.

While the curial presence of the Cortesi of San Gimignano ended with Paolo's death, one member of a cadet branch of the family did achieve what had eluded Paolo. Giovanni Andrea Cortesi (more commonly known as Gregorio, his name in religion) was born in Modena in 1483 and took a degree in law at the University of Padua in 1500.[84] Giovanni Andrea came to Rome after his university training and served as secretary to Cardinal Giovanni de' Medici. He must have been close to Paolo, for he wrote a poem praising his relative's theological and literary expertise which was printed in the 1504 edition of the *Liber Sententiarum*.[85] In 1507 Giovanni Andrea left Rome and entered the Benedictine monastery of Polirone, near Mantua. In the *De Cardinalatu* Paolo Cortesi praised his monkish relative for his learning.[86] Gregorio, as he was now called, devoted himself to reforming his order and re-storing its intellectual traditions. He became one of the major voices calling for a general reform of the Church, and participated in the reform commission that issued the famous *Consilium de emendanda ecclesia* (1537). He also distinguished himself as a literary opponent of Martin Luther. Pope Paul III, Paolo Cortesi's close friend, raised him to the cardinalate in 1542. With him the Cortesi family reached its highest curial-ecclesiastical position.

The career of the Cortesi in Rome demonstrates the close connection between humanistic activity and the careful careerism of most curialists. It also establishes a subsidiary point relevant to curial success. Men like the Cortesi could advance only so far in the Curia on the basis of their loyal service to the bureaucracy. For the higher offices, they depended on secular or high ecclesiastical patronage; in the case of the Cortesi, this patronage, in the form of the Medici, did not materialize. Paolo Cortesi's later concentration on his writing as a means of advancement was an acknowledgment that secular patronage was not always a dependable recourse. The use of his literary talents to find the necessary support from within the Curia and the Church was an affirmation of the value of humanist learning and an acknowledgment of his subordinate position, both of which required a careful balancing of and appeal to higher authorities. A family that had been closely connected to Florentine political and humanist traditions ended by abandoning those former loyalties and accepting the traditions and limitations of Rome.

VI

A similar experience typifies the Maffei of Volterra, a family with strong Tuscan loyalties which exploited its curial positions to obtain economic and social security. Also like the Cortesi of San Gimignano, they did not succeed in having a member achieve one of the highest ranks in the Curia. They could depend on neither strong secular support nor sufficient curial power to obtain a cardinalate. Still, they were generally adroit in using their offices as the basis for their family's wealth, and their number even included a humanist scholar with an international reputation.

The Maffei were a minor but economically solid Volterranean family. They came to Rome in the 1430s in the person of Gerardo di Giovanni Maffei, who obtained the post of notary in the *Camera Apostolica*.[87] Little is known of Gerardo, but he did rise steadily in the Curia. He was successively an apostolic scriptor (1444), *custos registri Camerae Apostolicae* (1455), the *magister registri Camerae Apostolicae*, and a papal familiar.[88] He was very active in his curial posts and produced an index of the *Camera*'s registers from the pontificate of Urban VI (1378–1389) to that of Eugenius IV.[89] His service in the *Camera* demonstrated his abilities and in 1457 Calixtus III made him a papal secretary. He remained a secretary under Pius II while still holding his other curial posts. His tenure as secretary is commemorated by an important register of papal briefs under Calixtus.[90] Gerardo was probably in minor orders from his first years in Rome, but sometime before 1451 he married Lucia di Giovanni Seghieri of Volterra.[91] He died in Rome in October 1466 leaving his wife with the care of their four sons. Upon his death his offices of *custos* and *magister registri* went to Gaspare Biondo.

Gerardo was not the only Maffei who sought his fortune in the Curia. Jacopo Gherardi, the papal secretary, was perhaps a relative. Also in the Curia was Gerardo's cousin Giuliano Maffei, a learned Franciscan (d. 1510).[92] He was favored by Pius II and by Sixtus IV, a fellow Franciscan, who made him bishop of Bertinoro (1477). While bishop of Bertinoro, Giuliano also served as *regens Poenitentiariae*. Julius II, another Franciscan, also furthered his career, making him papal librarian in 1504 and transferring him to the archbishopric of Ragusa in 1505. Upon Giuliano's death he was succeeded as librarian by Fedra Inghirami, also of Volterra.

Of Gerardo's four sons, three followed him into the Curia. The second-eldest, Giovanni Battista, a student of Guarino of Verona, died as a youth.[93] Gerardo's eldest son, Antonio (d. 1478), succeeded his father as an apostolic scriptor on November 6, 1466.[94] Although a cleric, Antonio married Caterina Cortesi, thereby uniting these two curial humanist families. Close association with the relatives of Sixtus IV led to his tragic end, however. Partly in revenge for the brutal sack of Volterra by the Medici forces in 1472, and partly in response to the policy of the Riario, his patrons, Antonio participated in the Pazzi Conspiracy to murder Lorenzo de' Medici and other members of his family. The plot failed and Antonio paid for his complicity with his life.[95] Despite this event the Maffei remained supporters of Medici hegemony in Tuscany. Antonio's only child, Giovanni Battista, entered the Curia. He and his uncle Mario purchased from Jacopo Gherardi a scriptorship in the penitentiary, indicating their intention to share its revenues if not its duties.[96] Giovanni Battista must have died at an early age since there is no further mention of him in the family records.

Gerardo's third son, Raffaele (1451–1522), commonly called *il Volterrano*, was born and educated in Rome, and was the most prominent of the brothers.[97] He entered the Curia as a papal scriptor in 1468 at seventeen years of age.[98] During the 1470s Raffaele shared with his brother Antonio a residence near the church of Sant'Eustachio where a printing press was housed that produced books meant for curial consumption.[99] He also joined the Confraternity of S. Spirito in Sassia in 1478.[100] In 1479, with the assistance of Jacopo Gherardi, Maffei entered the service of Cardinal Giovanni d'Aragona, the son of the King of Naples. As part of his duties Maffei accompanied the cardinal to Hungary to visit King Matthias Corvinus, the cardinal's brother-in-law.[101] The sojourn lasted through the winter and spring of 1479–1480 and was Maffei's sole excursion outside Italy. The trip had its exciting, even dangerous, moments, for the Turks were active in Hungary and the inhabitants proved to be hostile. Maffei returned to Italy with a negative impression of the Magyars. As a conscientious scholar, Maffei correlated his own experiences and readings in Eastern European history and used them in his large encyclopedia, the *Commentaria Urbana.* Maffei's account became a valuable source of Hungarian history in the early six-teenth century when the Turkish incursions into Eastern Europe turned the attention of the West to the Magyars. Upon his return to Italy Maffei resumed his curial post as papal scriptor. No doubt the service with Cardinal Giovanni and the trip outside Italy were calculated to ad-vance Maffei's career by providing him with some first-hand experience with non-Italian affairs.

Although Maffei was a cleric and as a scriptor a member of the papal *familia,* sometime before 1490 he decided to marry.[102] He chose as his wife Tita di Bartolomeo Minucci, the daughter of a prominent Volter-ranean family.[103] In view of Maffei's deep religious sentiments, which will be discussed below, and his favorable attitude toward monasticism, we may assume that he married out of a concern for the continuity of the family name and patrimony. With his two elder brothers dead and his younger brother, Mario, meant for the priesthood, Raffaele assumed the duty of preserving the family. He partly fulfilled these expectations, fathering two children, of whom a daughter, Lucilla, survived. Maffei was a very solicitous father; anxious for the girl's welfare when away from Volterra, he was especially concerned that her education progress properly.[104] Maffei never transferred either his wife or his child to Rome. Lucilla married the Volterranean curialist Paolo del Bava Ricco-baldi. Riccobaldi was a papal scriptor and eventually became the chief administrator of the family's property and in the end its inheritor. The couple had one surviving child, a son, Giulio.[105]

Throughout this period Raffaele maintained an active intellectual life in both Rome and Volterra. In Rome, despite his reservations about the moral character of the Roman academy, he probably attended at least once the annual humanist celebration commemorating the founding of the city of Rome.[106] It is also likely that he participated in Roman humanist archaeological activities, visiting Christian churches and mon-uments.[107] In Volterra, Maffei hosted an informal gathering of human-ists from as far away as Florence.[108] As a Tuscan, Maffei was especially anxious to maintain good relations with the rulers of Florence. Despite his brother's participation in the Pazzi Conspiracy, he corresponded with Lorenzo de' Medici.[109] After the Medici's exile, he cultivated good rela-tions with Piero Soderini. Maffei dedicated to him his translation of Procopius's history of the Gothic wars and wrote to him about historical and antiquarian matters. Maffei even exploited cordial relations with Soderini in favor of his relatives and friends.[110] Maffei also corresponded with Poliziano in Greek,[111] and was especially close to Michele Marullo (*ca.* 1450–1500). Marullo drowned when returning to Florence after visiting Maffei in Volterra.[112] Marullo and Poliziano were enemies, and Maffei's ability to maintain a friendship with both men attests to his diplomatic talents and the respect with which his contemporaries regarded him.

Unlike many other Roman humanists, Maffei was a devoted student of Greek, as well as Latin, civilization. In his early years in Rome he had studied for a time with George of Trebizond, the papal secretary, but George was old and Maffei did not gain much from his teaching.[113] Throughout his life Maffei worked to popularize Greek writings, especially those of Aristotle, and translated works by Homer, Xenophon, and Procopius.[114] His devotion to classical antiquity, philosophy, and history culminated in his encyclopedia, the *Commentariorum Urbanorum libri octo et triginta* (Rome, 1506).[115] Divided into three sections —*geographia, anthropologia,* and *philologia*—it was one of the first and most influential of the Renaissance encyclopedias and it earned Maffei a European-wide reputation as a scholar. Maffei collected information from writers of all ages to give his work as broad a scope as possible. The last section, the *philologia,* contains a book-by-book exposition of Aristotle's *corpus.* Significantly, the *Commentaria Urbana*'s appearance coincided with Maffei's departure from Rome after a period of slow withdrawal.

The decision to leave Rome had several causes. The low moral tone of Rome under Alexander VI disturbed Maffei. His advancing age made him sensitive to both his mortality and the need for peace in order to compose his thoughts and to produce worthwhile scholarship. In withdrawing from Rome Maffei followed a common curial procedure already seen in Paolo Cortesi. Although he was physically absent from the city, his thoughts continued to center on Rome. He kept in constant contact with Roman events and curial opinions through his brother Mario, an important humanist at the papal court, and his son-in-law, Paolo Riccobaldi, who was a resident of Rome for part of the second decade of the century. Maffei did not resign his scriptorship and continued to receive income from it.[116] The extent of his knowledge of and concern with Roman and curial affairs is demonstrated by two of his last writings (*ca.* 1519–1520), the *Brevis Historia* of the pontificates of Julius II and Leo X and an attack on Martin Luther, the *Nasi Romani in Martinum Lutherum Apologeticus.*[117] Both short works viewed their subjects from a curial perspective.

Maffei spent his last years in Volterra in religious exercises and scholarship. Despite his spiritual concerns, however, he continued to care for the physical and financial needs of his family. He was also solicitous for the religious and material welfare of his native city. He aided a group of nuns in Volterra, building for them an oratory and then a cloister at the Church of San Lino, at a cost of 8,000 scudi. He also served on a municipal commission to refurbish part of the cathedral of Volterra.[118]

During these years in Volterra Maffei produced his most important theological writings: a translation of several sermons and homilies of the Greek Father, Basil the Great (1515);[119] a theological textbook, the *De Institutione Christiana,* dedicated to Leo X (1519);[120] and the unfinished moral treatise, the *Stromata* (1518–1520).[121] These texts attest to Maffei's broad knowledge of classical antiquity and Christian history and theology, and to his deep concern with religious questions, especially as they relate to the individual's and society's moral responsibilities. His death, on January 22, 1522, came while he was still engaged in this religious work.[122]

As a historian, theologian, translator, and Latin poet, Maffei was a remarkably active and productive scholar and humanist.[123] He even pursued his scholarly interests while performing his duties in the Curia. His curial career was not remarkable, however. He never advanced beyond his papal scriptorship, no doubt because of his decision to marry and his own ambivalence toward the moral dangers implicit in curial life and service to the powerful. The possibilities for someone who shared Maffei's intellectual qualities and curial connections, but who was not burdened by these family and moral impediments, become clear in the career of Raffaele's younger brother, Mario. In many ways Mario Maffei epitomized both the positive and negative qualities of a High Renaissance humanist prelate.

Mario (1463–1537) followed the family tradition and entered the Curia.[124] After dividing his youth between Rome and Volterra, he acquired a scriptorship in the penitentiary (*ca.* 1493) and subsequently became an official in the office of the *plumbarius* in the chancery. He was active in the intellectual life of the city and frequented the home of Ermolao Barbaro.[125] Since he was in orders, he received appointments as a canon and sacristan of St. Peter's and as a canon of St. John Lateran.[126] He must have acquitted himself well in his posts, for in 1506 Julius II dispatched him to France on a diplomatic mission. In 1507, however, the pope recalled him to help supervise the building of the new St. Peter's.[127] His favor with Julius secured him an annual pension of 500 ducats.[128] Mario's position in the Curia further improved when Leo, a man who shared Mario's intellectual and artistic interests, succeeded to the Papal throne.[129] Leo made Mario secretary of the

College of Cardinals, abbot of the Badia of Ss. Giusto and Clemente in Volterra (the post Alessandro Cortesi had desired and which Leo had held), and in 1516 bishop of Aquino (in succession of Jacopo Gherardi).[130] Leo consulted Mario on literary and artistic matters and valued his friendship.[131] Mario's fortunes stagnated under Adrian VI, but his hopes for advancement in Clement VII's pontificate were partly realized. Clement did transfer Mario from Aquino to the richer see of Cavaillon in France in 1524,[132] but he never kept his repeated promise to provide Mario with lodgings in the papal palace and make him part of the *familia*, a concession Mario greatly desired.[133]

Despite his failure to secure quarters in the papal palace, Mario did well in Rome. He inherited a home in the district of Parione from his father and one in Sant'Eustachio from Raffaele, to which he added houses in Campo Marzo, Trastevere, a second in Parione, and two *vigne* on the Aventine.[134] Mario owned several properties in Volterra, building a large palace in town, for which he acted as architect, and San Donnino, a villa in the countryside.[135] His wealth, which was based on curial and ecclesiastical revenues, allowed him to live in lordly fashion in Volterra after his departure from Rome in 1526.[136] His withdrawal from Rome might have been caused in part by his failure to advance beyond his episcopal rank. However, he resisted pressure from friends to take up residence in his diocese of Cavaillon and personally oversee its direction, preferring instead to delegate his duties to a vicar and to devote his time to personal and family matters.[137]

As a humanist, Mario never rivaled his elder brother Raffaele, but he was a prominent figure in Roman humanist circles in the first quarter of the sixteenth century and was generally respected for his learning. He knew classical philosophy well, especially Aristotelian philosophy, and displayed a fine artistic sensitivity. In his youth he composed a dialogue on literary topics and a series of poems (all unpublished).[138] His major contribution to scholarship was his collaboration with the Roman publisher and classicist Jacopo Mazzochio in compiling the important collection the *Epigrammata Antiquae Urbis* (1520).[139] His interest in classical antiquities led him to collect inscriptions and to host an informal academy in Rome devoted to their study.[140] Maffei was known for his genial personality and ready wit, factors that made him popular with other humanists. He was especially close to the papal secretary Jacopo Sadoleto, who dedicated his dialogue *Phaedra* to him,[141] and to Blosio Palladio, the poet, orator, and later papal secretary. Mario took an interest in Blosio's career and obtained for him a benefice in Volterra.[142] Mario's greatest achievement in Rome was probably artistic. As already mentioned, he helped supervise early work on the rebuilding of St. Peter's. In 1520 Cardinal Giulio de' Medici, later Clement VII, asked him to supervise the completion of the Villa Madama following the death of Raphael Sanzio, its principal architect.[143]

Despite his personal and curial success in Rome, however, Mario remained dissatisfied. Following his promotion to the see of Cavaillon, he failed to obtain a cardinal's hat. Neither Leo nor Clement would readily bestow a red hat on a friend who was dependent on them and had little support to offer when they could obtain financial or political advantages by bartering with wealthy rulers. This disappointment probably led to Mario's resolve to quit Rome and live in Volterra, from which he made frequent trips to other Tuscan cities. Mario's hopes were renewed when his old friend Alessandro Farnese was elected pope (Paul III) in 1534. Mario returned to Rome to deliver his personal congratulations and to forward his own cause.[144] The unresponsiveness of the pope, however, finally forced him to abandon all hope of obtaining a red hat. He spent his last years securing his family's social and financial position. In pursuit of this end, he adopted his brother's son-in-law Paolo Riccobaldi and made him his heir. He entrusted to Paolo the general direction of his rich holdings. Mario supervised the education of Paolo's son, Giulio, who was born in 1518 and bore Clement VII's given name at Mario's insistence. Mario also purchased for the boy a papal scriptorship.[145] At one point Mario intended to pass on his ecclesiastical posts to Giulio, but when it was decided that the boy would not take holy orders, Mario disposed of the posts to his own profit.[146] Content with having secured the continuation of the family fortune, Mario died in Volterra on June 24, 1537.

Mario's career brought together all the elements that characterized humanist careerism in the Curia. His family was well established and he naturally continued the family tradition of service in the Curia. His humanist education allowed him to move easily through the best humanist circles in Rome and contributed to his success with Leo and Clement. Using the sizable fortune he extracted from his curial and ecclesiastical offices, he was able to advance his family. Because he combined holy orders with his humanist and curial talents, he advanced to positions that were denied his married brother. The contrast between Mario and Raffaele is illustrative. Raffaele remained suspicious of the glamor of the Curia and Rome, although he was captivated by it. Mario fully accepted the moral ambiguities of Rome, indeed thrived on them, and used them to his benefit.[147] Ultimately, the very advantages Mario enjoyed because of his humanist and curial connections prevented him from obtaining higher rank. Mario lacked an independent power base to support his climb to the curial apex. His complete dedication to the bureaucracy made him essentially dependent on the Curia and a victim of the papacy's greater political needs. He had been defeated by a basic rule of the Curia and the Church: hierarchy means dependence. He was unable to establish an independent foundation from which to maneuver. The game of careerism could not be played with halfway measures. What the Curia offered by way of enticement and preferments, it offset with its manipulative use of subordinates. The Curia gave Mario much, but always within limits.

Mario's lack of success, like that of Alessandro Cortesi, must be kept in perspective. If these men did not obtain all they sought, they did achieve much. Further, they had the advantage of building on the successful work of their relatives in the Curia. Like all curialists, humanists such as the Maffei and Cortesi viewed the Curia from a professional perspective. They did not deny to it a certain religious dimension, but day-to-day experiences with its rules, duties, and petty jealousies emphasized its mechanical, bureaucratic side. The spirit of its employees was that of other governmental functionaries; ultimately the curialists, including the humanists, displayed a pragmatic and proprietary attitude toward the Curia. It offered jobs that could provide financial security and social prominence for themselves and their families. They exploited it and its satellite courts selfishly and created as best they could around them social and intellectual institutions to serve their own needs. With skillful handling, the Curia could be made the social and financial servant of its employees provided they did not attempt to break its rules and traditions or aspire too high.

4

The Roman Academies

Rome's appeal to the humanists went beyond its value as an employment center. The city represented an ideal, and thus inspired men's imaginations with its classical ruins and associations.[1] This sense of the ideal attracted many humanists to Rome, and employment opportunities allowed them to stay, even though the time available for exploring the city would as a result be limited. To realize fully the possibilities of Rome as a source of intellectual inspiration, however, humanists required associations with other men who had similar interests. This need was not satisfied within the curial bureaucracy, although some humanists did take advantage of their proximity at work to discuss literary questions as well as to engage in scholarly and personal arguments.[2] Such encounters were only passing and irregular and could not fulfill the humanists' desire for mutually interesting and long-term intercourse. Consequently, other institutions developed to meet these needs. As already discussed, the various households of cardinals and rich laymen constituted one type of cultural center for humanists, but these courts had their disadvantages. They were essentially part of Rome's official structure and imposed duties on their members. Further, the cardinal or lord hosting them could direct the topics discussed. Humanists, therefore, sought other means of expressing their interests outside any official confines.[3]

The forum that humanists developed to provide intellectual companionship was the informal academy, and the academic movement in Renaissance Italy contributed to the development and consolidation of humanist thought.[4] Academies defined safe areas for intellectual expression in an Italy that was becoming more and more hostile to certain types of intellectual and political discussions. Whether as a scholarly or political oasis, these academies lacked regularized organizations or well-established lines of authority. They were informal and usually met at the home of a senior or generally respected or wealthy individual who could provide some form of leadership and a pleasant environment. These meetings were loosely organized and probably irregularly attended. The term *academy* has been applied freely to all such gatherings in the

Renaissance. While it is often inexact, representing many variations on a theme, it remains a useful designation for humanist associations in Rome and elsewhere as long as the limits are kept in mind.

Despite their informality and lack of hierarchy, the humanist academies provided enough uniformity for those who attended to conceive of themselves as belonging to a particular group with certain general lines of orientation. The existence of academies in three major Italian humanist centers—Florence, Rome, and Naples—in the last quarter of the quattrocento indicates that some form of academic organization was a generally accepted solution to a real need. Each of these academies differed in its emphasis, partly reflecting the political situation of its location, partly mirroring the interests of its leaders. All responded to the humanist desire to associate together for mutual support and enlightenment.

The Roman academy covered here—more accurately the several Roman academies, since there was more than one continuous group in the Renaissance—differed from the other Italian academies. It contrasted most clearly with the Platonic academy of Marsilio Ficino in Florence.[5] The Roman group was unofficial in its origins and structure (with the exception of the years of Sixtus IV's pontificate), while Ficino's academy had the patronage of the *de facto* rulers of Florence, the Medici. The Medici provided Ficino with his house, encouraged his translations of Plato, and even took part in some of the academy's sessions. Furthermore, the Roman academies lacked any set philosophical commitment. Despite the Neo-Platonic tendencies of Bessarion's circle, until the sack of Rome the Roman academies had no philosophical preferences. Unlike Ficino's academicians, the Romans were not fascinated by Plato. Indeed, the Romans tended specifically to ignore philosophical speculation in favor of literary composition, history, and archaeology.

The Roman academies bore closer resemblance to the Neapolitan academy of Giovanni Pontano (1429-1503).[6] Pontano and his disciples had the same basic orientation toward Latin classicism that marked the Roman academicians. Pontano was a poet, orator, philologist, and literary critic, as well as secretary to the king of Naples. Both the Roman and Neapolitan academies had to develop within the limits imposed by a curial ambience. However, these courts were very different. The kingdom of Naples was the center of a feudal society and its values differed from those of other parts of Italy. Neapolitan humanists tried to reform an essentially feudal culture by recourse to classical *exempla*. The Roman court resembled the medieval feudal one of Naples, but it did not value the military profession and the code of honor which the Neapolitan lords did. Still, similarities were strong since both courts favored certain types of literary composition, especially poetry and oratory.

The Roman academies therefore formed a unique, if not unparalleled, movement in Renaissance Italy. They also had a continuity that did not depend on the fortunes of one man, although they were greatly influenced in their development by the interests of their various leaders. While their loose, unofficial character limits our knowledge of many details of their meetings, what we do know indicates that the various academies were extremely important in providing an intellectual unity to Roman humanism and in helping to define its specific character. They did so partly because they functioned as arbiters of taste, or at least their leaders did. Whether the major impetus of an academy was literary, historical, or archaeological in nature, or a combination of these, it allowed for the airing of diverse opinions and the formation of acceptable standards. The academies acted as both the regulators of opinion and the disseminators of opinion among the Roman humanists.

I

The first and most important group centered on the person and interests of Pomponio Leto (1427–1498).[7] From the 1460s Leto hosted humanist meetings in his home on the Quirinal Hill. Leto, the illegitimate son of the noble southern Italian family of Sanseverino, felt himself an outcast because of his birth. He assumed a classical name, left the kingdom of Naples, and emigrated to Rome in the late 1450s to study Latin with Lorenzo Valla. Valla's death in 1457 caused Leto to seek another teacher, the poet Pietro Odi da Montopoli (d. *ca.* 1463).[8] Leto had chosen Rome as a scholarly locale because his interests centered on the study of Latin literature and history. Unlike other humanists in Rome, Leto did not avail himself of the Curia as a means of livelihood, but rather chose to teach, eventually rising to the professorship of rhetoric at the University of Rome.

Leto devoted his attention almost exclusively to Roman studies, concentrating on Roman classical culture to the point of eccentricity. He tried to live according to the examples of classical writers, even gardening according to the precepts of Columella and other Roman authors. This was, however, a pursuit that appealed to many of his fellow Roman humanists. The members of his academy took classical names and referred to Leto as their Pontifex Maximus.[9] They discussed various aspects of classical history and civilization, engaged in archaeological investigations, and criticized the original Latin compositions of their friends. Leto set a standard in classical studies which his disciples willingly followed and made a central component of Roman humanism.

The history of Leto's academy falls into two distinct periods: the early years of the academy until 1468; and the refounding of the academy as a religious *sodalitas* in 1478. The dividing point in this history was the suppression of the Roman academy by Pope Paul II in 1468.[10] Details on this suppression remain vague, but the general course of events is sufficiently clear, and the suppression has come to influence the various interpretations of Roman humanism and its relationship to the Church and to Christianity generally. Vital to our understanding of it are the personalities of its main participants, since there is little reason to believe that Paul's actions against the academy represented the response of the clerical establishment to a grave, widespread dissatisfaction with Roman humanism; rather, it expressed one man's, or at most a small group's, views.

The immediate occasion for Paul's attack on the academy was his reform of the Curia.[11] One of the posts Pius II had expanded and made venal was the College of Abbreviators. As has been seen, the office of abbreviator was one of the chancery posts the humanists found especially congenial to their interests and talents. Among those who purchased an abbreviatorship during Pius's reign was Bartolomeo dei Sacchi, called Platina,[12] who had paid a substantial sum for the post and had placed his hopes for a secure future in it. Partly as a reform to limit the venality of offices and partly as a sign of ill will toward his predecessor and the men he appointed, Paul abolished Pius's expansion of the office but did not return the money invested by the abbreviators.

Deprived of both his post and his money, Platina vented his anger in bitter letters to Paul demanding satisfaction. In one of these letters he threatened to appeal to a general council over the head of the pope if he were not compensated for his loss. This threat was ill-advised. Pius II had forbidden all appeal to a council against the decision of a pope as part of his policy against conciliar claims. Platina's recklessness provided Paul with justification for his action against the humanists. At the same time Platina was challenging the pope, Paul received information that some members of the Academy planned to revolt against papal authority and to establish a republic in Rome. Paul acted swiftly. He ordered the arrest of Platina and several other academicians, accusing them of sodomy, republicanism, irreligion, neopaganism, and heresy.[13] What had begun as a personal problem for Platina had become the concern of the entire Roman humanist community.

The incarcerated academicians did not lack defenders in Rome, and a number of cardinals appealed to the pope to temper his actions, most notably, Bessarion, Francesco Gonzaga (to whom Platina had been tutor and secretary), and Ammannati-Piccolomini.[14] The cardinals were a natural constituency for the humanists in prison since many of the accused were secretaries of cardinals.[15] The pleas of these cardinals for leniency were, however, ignored. Paul intensified his actions against the academicians by securing the extradition of Pomponio Leto back to Rome from Venice, where he had gone earlier to prepare for a voyage to the East in order to master Greek and Arabic.[16] Nor was Paul's imprisonment of the academicians a light one.[17] Platina was first imprisoned in Paul's Palazzo Venezia (San Marco) and then transferred to Castel Sant'Angelo, where he remained for a year and was subjected to periodic torture, as were other academicians.[18]

Paul's own personality provides an important criterion by which to judge the truth of his accusations.[19] He could be a testy individual and was not universally liked. His uncle Eugenius IV had helped him advance in the ecclesiastical establishment and he seems to have developed some of the arrogance of the well placed. Supremely confident of his own views, he brooked no opposition from any quarter. While intelligent and well educated (partly by humanists such as George of Trebizond), his special interests were narrowly focused on aspects of ancient history and the collection of ancient gems. The presence of humanists among Paul's secretaries indicates that he did not oppose all humanists and realized the benefits of humanism.[20] He did, however, display an antipathy to some forms of ancient Latin poetry. Such a hostile attitude had been evident in the first years of the quattrocento in Rome and had elicited a response from the humanist Francesco da Fiano (*ca.* 1350–*ca.* 1425), who defended the morality of ancient poetry.[21] The strictures that Fiano had encountered and that Paul echoed were meant narrowly to include poets like Martial but not writers like Cicero and Seneca. Nevertheless, the rhetoric that accompanied this position easily allowed for a broader condemnation of all classical studies.

Paul's charges must be dealt with indirectly since the little information available is biased in some manner. Even the statements of the humanists themselves must be used with care since they were usually made under pressure or torture. There was, however, some basis for the charge of sodomy. Leto was thought to harbor more than pedagogical interest in his students while in Venice and was under arrest for sodomy when Paul secured Leto's extradition from Venice.[22] Homosexual poetry was produced by some members of the academy.[23] There were, no doubt, some practicing homosexuals among the humanists and other curialists in Rome. For some the imposed celibacy of the clerical state may have exacerbated individual tendencies. The mimicking of ancient practices so common in the academy also may have extended to the

homosexuality of Greek pedagogy (certainly the accusations against
Leto were of this type since he was under arrest in Venice on sodomy
charges when extradited to Rome). Socrates was a byword for more
than wisdom in the Renaissance. It is unlikely that the academy was a
homosexual demimonde or that Paul had any proof of its being so.
Furthermore, homosexuality was too easy an accusation to cast at men
who had forfeited marriage for reasons of career.

The recent history of the papacy lent credibility to the pope's fears
of a republican revolt. Eugenius IV had been expelled from Rome in
1434 by the city government with cries of reestablishing the Roman
Republic.[24] The last years of Nicholas V's reign were clouded by the
poorly conceived and executed but classically inspired revolt of Stefano
Porcari to expel the clerics and introduce a republic.[25] The papacy and
the Curia were therefore sensitive to any vaguely republican sentiments
in Rome. Consequently, it was dangerous to hold or express republican
ambitions. While there was probably no real republican movement in
Rome which could have threatened the papacy after Nicholas's reign,
memories of the decades of papal weakness were very real to Paul and
his contemporaries. Further, Platina's appeal to a council against the
pope reinforced the suspicion of the academy's republicanism. The
councils were associated in the curial mind with antipapal attitudes,
especially those expressed against the Church's monarchical organization.

In their defenses both Platina and Leto maintained that the humanist
Filippo Buonaccorsi of San Gimignano (1437-1496), who was called
Callimachus Experiens in the academy, a close friend of Leto and secretary to Cardinal Bartolomeo Roverella, was the one who had proclaimed
republican and anticlerical sentiments in the academy.[26] If true, as it
seems to have been, then it justified Leto's and Platina's bitterness over
their fate since Callimachus had escaped from Rome when the suppression began and eventually found a safe and successful exile at the royal
court in Poland. Callimachus's sentiments gave some substance to
Paul's claims that there was republican agitation within the academy.
Moreover, this republicanism bore a close connection to anticlericalism.
Callimachus specifically called for the overthrow of the priests and their
expulsion from Rome. However, there is little reason to believe that
anything more than talk was involved. The desire to expel the priests
and return to an ancient Roman republic mixed idealism and a dissatisfaction with the clerical power that could thwart the ambitions of a lay-
man. Since so many of the academicians were clerics, or were in the
direct employ of clerics, a certain bitterness toward some clerical
superiors or employers may help to account for this anticlericalism. The
Roman academy lacked the political means to implement any republican

or anticlerical scheme, and there were no indications that men like Leto and Platina were especially interested in politics of any variety. Republicanism was, at best, a historical escape from political and social realities—a vague dreamworld.

The final charges of irreligion, neopaganism, and heresy were historically the most influential of the accusations. Leto's first academy was characterized by religious indifference. Leto himself may even have been hostile to religion, depending on how we take Marco Antonio Sabellico's (1436–1506/1508) characterization of Leto as *contemptor religionis*.[27] Sabellico had been Leto's student and spoke with some authority. Religious discussions had no place in the first academy and there was no religious quality to its meetings. But this indifference must not be confused with an anti-Christian attitude; even the anticlerical sentiments of Callimachus should not be interpreted as necessarily antireligious. In support of his attacks Paul pointed to the choice of classicized names by the academicians and their reading of "obscene" classical poetry. But neither accusation is proof of irreligion or heresy in itself. Indeed, Paul's accusations lacked real substance. Rather than a hostility toward religion, Leto and his disciples can be faulted only for a lack of interest in it. Even this was to change in time, and the later members of the academy, including Leto, showed greater sensitivity toward the religious aspects of their society. In their religious attitudes, as in their morality, the academicians probably differed little from contemporary nonhumanist curialists.

Paul's accusations found some echo in his own day. An undated letter written to Platina by Battista dei Giudici da Finale, bishop of Ventimiglia (d. 1484), is an important testimony to this. Dei Giudici was a respected scholastic theologian with a history of opposition to elements of humanism, especially humanist attempts to reinterpret Aristotle.[28] In his letter the bishop repeated charges of paganism and antireligion against Platina which he said he had heard expressed by others in Rome, but he firmly dissociated himself from those views.[29] Although he eventually became Platina's friend and said the mass at his memorial service in 1484, there was tension between the bishop and the humanist at the time concerning the bishop's curial activities.[30] Whatever the personal element, dei Giudici's statement indicates that Paul had his supporters in a group of conservative clerics which included the bishop. Similarly, the humanist Raffaele Maffei in 1506 accused Leto and his disciples of antireligious activities, and in this he may have been influenced by Paul's accusations.[31]

The pope's hostility toward the academicians has also affected the way subsequent historians have treated Leto and his group. Nineteenth-

century historians interpreted the academy along the antireligious lines
indicated by Paul. The academicians' various activities provided "proof"
for these views. Their visits to the Roman catacombs, where they had
written their names on the walls, became instances of the desecration of
Christian holy places.[32] The arguments have often been restated to
demonstrate the pervasiveness of antireligion at the very center of
Christendom.[33]

Paul's actions succeeded in tempering for a time the enthusiasm of
some Roman humanists and reinforced the need for accommodation
on their part to the Curia and the city's religious establishment. The
opportunity for such an accommodation came in the pontificate of
Sixtus IV. Sixtus showed none of his predecessor's hostility toward
the Roman humanist community or those whom Paul had persecuted.
Despite Sixtus's traditional Scholastic education and his deep interest
in religious orthodoxy, he was not offended by the neoclassical leanings Paul had found so objectionable. The suppression did not long
outlast its initiator. During Sixtus's reign the academy was re-formed
under Leto's direction, although some changes were made in its organization.[34]

As an indication that the academicians had learned something from
their recent experiences, they reorganized the academy into a religious
sodalitas of Sts. Victor, Fortunato, and Genesio in 1478 and placed it
under the protection of Cardinal Domenico della Rovere, one of Sixtus's
nephews. The patronage of these saints was chosen since their feast day
coincided with the birthday of Rome, the Palilia, April 20, and the
academy was especially dedicated to celebrating the founding of the
city. The religious and secular concerns of the academicians and their
need for official support conveniently coincided in this instance.

Certainly the official curial bureaucracy displayed no prejudice toward the humanists who had been imprisoned. Leto was readmitted to
his post at the University of Rome even while Paul was alive. He was a
popular teacher, and later students found his propagation of neoclassicism as inspiring as earlier ones had.[35] Sixtus IV appointed Platina
the first librarian of the reconstituted Vatican Library, and Platina produced the first modern, large-scale history of the popes.[36] Platina's
assistant at the library, Demetrio Guazzelli (d. 1511) also had been imprisoned.[37] Guazzelli also became a canon of St. Peter's and accrued the
revenues from a large number of benefices. Of the other imprisoned
academicians, Agostino Maffei (d. 1496) continued to enjoy a successful
curial career, becoming *taxator* of papal letters; Marco Lucido Fazzini
Fosforo (d. 1503) was created bishop of Segni by Sixtus; and Pietro
Demetrio (d. 1488) taught at the University of Rome.[38] Official Rome,

therefore, essentially ignored Paul's accusations and rewarded the academicians for their loyal service with high curial positions.

❧ II ❧

Under Leto's direction the renewed academy continued to cultivate the major theme that came to delineate humanism in Rome, i.e., an almost exclusive dedication to Latin studies. The study of Greek had never ceased in Rome, and the city had housed a large number of humanists who translated Greek texts. Especially during the lifetime of Cardinal Bessarion, Rome had a tradition of Greek scholarship, although it did not extend far beyond the cardinal's circle. Later in the Renaissance, Hebrew and other Eastern languages received attention in Roman humanist circles. However, Latin was the language of the Roman humanists, and Roman civilization inspired them. Alessandro Farnese, the young Roman aristocratic member of the academy who eventually became Pope Paul III, for example, decided to go to Florence in his youth in order to study Greek.[39] Vernacular studies were generally ignored by Leto's academicians (with the notable exception of Marc'Antonio Altiere),[40] although later academies did devote their attention to vernacular poetry.

Leto's first academy had been indifferent to philosophical and theological or religious subjects, even in their classical forms. In this, his academy contrasted with the interests of Bessarion's contemporary group. In the second academy this situation changed. Although Leto himself and the academy as a group remained essentially disinterested in religion and philosophy, many members devoted themselves to these areas. Platina, for example, wrote dialogues on moral philosophy and under Sixtus issued his history of the popes. Other poets and orators produced a large body of Neo-Latin religious works. It would be too simple to argue that this was merely a response to Paul's suppression. Rather, one sees the blending of the classical and religious character of Rome. This change, while foreshadowed in humanists like Valla, received its greatest impetus under Sixtus IV. The humanists came to feel they had obtained papal approval for their introduction of classicism into religious topics, and in time an ideology developed that expressed this blending.

This Latin classicism exhibited itself in many forms. Leto wrote on Roman history, and other members of the academy were especially active in commenting on classical Latin authors.[41] The academicians revived classical theater as part of their studies.[42] Even their handwriting was influenced by Leto's desire to recover as much of the Latin past, or what he thought was the classical past, as he could and integrate it into his daily life.[43] However, two forms in particular came to represent this interest in Latin. The first was the production of original neo-Latin poetry and oratory, both secular and religious. The second was the study of Roman archaeological remains. Together they monopolized the major energies of the academicians and represent their greatest contributions.

As a center for Neo-Latin poetry and oratory the academy found that its preferences conveniently coincided with those of the papal court. Rome offered a variety of opportunities for formal orations and poetic displays.[44] Official ceremonies, religious and secular, required orations; funeral services for important persons usually included an oration or a poetic collection; and the dedication of a new building or merely the need for pleasant entertainment could be turned into a literary occasion. Both poetry and oratory were acceptable to the papal court since they could be used to praise the pope or a rich cardinal and proclaim the glories of the Church and its representatives in the most fashionable literary forms. This tendency to praise and glorify the subject of a poem or an oration limits the value of these works as historical sources, but occasionally they do provide interesting sidelights of contemporary events. They were careful presentations of the canons of classical forms—Ciceronian in the case of the orations, Vergilian or elegiac in poetry—to an audience that took great pleasure from finely formed classical phrases and verses. For the humanists these occasions also had the added feature of providing needed supplements to their incomes.

Occasionally a group of poets came together to commemorate an event. From Leto's academy three collections of funeral poetry demonstrate both the ability of the academicians and the place their poetry held in the social and political world of Renaissance Rome. The first was a collection of poetry in honor of Alessandro Cinuzzi (a page to the pope's nephew Count Girolamo Riario), who died in 1474.[45] The second, of 1484, consists of poems read at a memorial service for Platina by his fellow academicians.[46] The third, of 1488, memorializes the son of the Florentine representative to Rome, Orsini Lanfredini.[47] The poems offer the proper lugubrious sentiments expected of a funeral piece, praising the deceased in excessive hyperbole and drawing on a variety of classical associations and precedents. Their content is unexceptional and of little lasting literary value, like most occasional neo-Latin poetry produced at the papal court.[48] However, they do indicate the important position of neo-Latin poetry in Roman courtly social life. The death of a high official or of a familiar of a Roman aristocrat was seen as a proper occasion for the display of classicized verse.

Any number of individuals could be chosen to demonstrate the caliber of the poets and orators of Leto's academy.[49] Sigismondo dei Conti, for example, was the only humanist to contribute to all three collections.[50] Despite his busy curial career, dei Conti was an active member of Rome's humanist circles. One of the more colorful characters from the academy was the cleric Giovanni Battista Capranica (1450–1484), who had the academic name Flavius Panthagathus and was a member of both the first and second academies.[51] Capranica belonged to a distinguished curial family that produced the learned cardinal Domenico Capranica (1400–1458).[52] He probably had a degree in law since he taught that subject at the University of Rome (1473), and probably held other curial posts. He had a prominent place in the academy, holding the title of *sacerdos Academiae Romanae*. At the request of Sixtus IV Capranica accompanied Leto on a trip to Germany in 1478 in search of manuscripts for the new papal library. Also in 1478 Sixtus appointed Capranica bishop of Fermo; however, Capranica quarreled with the city officials and had to absent himself from his diocese. When he did return to Fermo in 1484, his presence and actions (seemingly morally compromising) resulted in his death by defenestration at the hands of an angry populace. As a poet he was respected and his death was deeply felt by the academy.[53]

A good example of a new member of Leto's academy is the humanist Aurelio Lippo Brandolini (1454–1497).[54] Born in Florence but raised in Naples, where he belonged to Pontano's academy, Brandolini left Naples in 1480 to seek his fortune in Rome. Like many other humanists, Brandolini as a mature writer had decided his future lay in Rome. His first writing there was a series of poems, *De laudibus beatissimi Sixti IIII* (*ca.* 1481), which praised the pope, his virtues, and his court, and was dedicated to Sixtus's nephew, Cardinal Giuliano della Rovere.[55] Brandolini cast his poems in epic proportions, with scenes set in heaven showing divine favor to the pope's election and with comparisons of Sixtus's rule to that of the Roman emperors. More mundanely, the poems sang the praises of Sixtus as the restorer of Rome, concentrating on the pope's building program. While not great works of literature, the poems are good representations of the classicizing motifs and procedures favored by the academicians. Brandolini was equally prized for his ability to produce extemporaneous verse and to accompany himself on the lyre.[56]

Brandolini did not enter the Curia but maintained himself through teaching and oratory, which depended on his contacts with powerful prelates. He was especially close to Cardinal Francesco Todeschini-Piccolomini. He dedicated his most important religious work, the *In*

sacram historiam Hebraeorum Epithoma, to that prelate.[57] Only a few
of his orations survive. Perhaps his most important is that in honor of
St. Thomas Aquinas, which he delivered on the saint's feast day (March
15, year uncertain). In it Brandolini presented the Scholastic theologian
in particularly humanistic fashion by emphasizing the saint's background in the liberal arts and his study of the Church Fathers.[58] Different talents were required for his defense of the Venetian ambassador
to Rome, Antonio Loredan, who was recalled to Venice in 1487 to
answer charges of misconduct in office.[59] Brandolini wrote this oration
in a properly Ciceronian form, which fitted its subject matter.

Among the humanists of the Roman academy Brandolini was held in
high regard. He contributed to Platina's memorial collection.[60] As a
scholar he subscribed to the academy's concentration on Latin culture,
and under Leto's influence he wrote a commentary on Vergil's *Geor-
gics.*[61] Perhaps his closest friend in the academy was Demetrio Guazzelli.
Guazzelli transcribed some of Brandolini's writings and Brandolini
recommended his friend to Angelo Poliziano.[62] Despite his close friend-
ships in Rome and the high esteem he enjoyed, however, Brandolini
left Italy in 1489.

In an attempt to establish his fortunes more securely Brandolini emigrated to Hungary to the court of Matthias Corvinus. Although he spent
only a year in Hungary, he produced there his best-known work, a
dialogue in defense of human dignity which included the king, his
Italian wife, and the bishop of Nocera, Pietro Ransano, as interlocutors.[63]
In 1490 Brandolini returned to Italy and entered the Augustinian
Hermits. Despite his failing eyesight, he continued to be an active
preacher, dividing his time between Florence and Rome. He died in
Rome in 1497.[64] His name was kept alive in Rome by his younger
brother Raffaele, who was equally famous as an orator. Brandolini was
a facile poet and orator whose skills were greatly appreciated by the
papal court. His success was an index of his ability to respond to the
forms favored by both the curial and humanist establishments of Rome.

Leto's second academy attracted not only mature humanists like
Brandolini but also young men who were just beginning their humanist
careers. Further, it displayed the same cosmopolitanism that characterized Roman society as a whole by including some non-Italians, e.g., the
poet Elio Lampridio Cerva of Ragusa in Dalmatia (1462–1520).[65]
Cerva's success as a poet led to his crowning as poet laureate during
ceremonies accompanying the celebrations for the birthday of Rome,
the Palilia, in 1481.[66] The festivities of the Palilia blended the academy's
devotion to poetic composition with the revival of classical antiquity,
the academy's *raison d'être.*

The other aspect of classical antiquity favored by the second academy was archaeology. Here again Leto led the way, although he was building on a foundation laid by Flavio Biondo, the papal secretary and historian.[67] Biondo had begun the task of locating and identifying the places mentioned in the ancient histories of Rome, but this was not an easy undertaking. Debris had accumulated over the centuries and ancient monuments had been destroyed or transformed into popular dwellings; the exact location and outlines of the ancient buildings and monuments could not be determined. Through imagination and careful scholarship, however, Leto, like Biondo, had some success in reconstructing the ancient city.[68] Leto's identifications of many places were faulty, but they inspired an archaeological consciousness that was to have artistic fruits in subsequent years in the work of men like Raphael[69] and a scholarly continuation in the work of Leto's disciples. The academicians' trips to the catacombs also reflected their archaeological curiosity.

Among Leto's immediate successors in archaeological studies, two deserve special attention for their continuation of their master's work, Andrea Fulvio and Pietro Sabino. Fulvio (*ca.* 1470–1527)[70] came from the city of Palestrina to study with Leto. In order to support himself he taught privately and later served as one of the city's *rioni* teachers. Like his master, Fulvio displayed little interest in Greek studies and devoted himself to Latin literature and archaeology.[71] Part of his work consisted in collecting ancient inscriptions and details from ancient monuments. This meticulous labor yielded in 1514 his most important work, the *Antiquaria Urbis,* followed in 1517 by his *Illustrium Imagines,* which depicted the ancient emperors.[72] His knowledge of ancient art, numismatics, and architecture made him a valuable adviser to artists and other antiquarians such as Francesco Albertini.[73]

Both Leto and Fulvio devoted their major attention to pagan antiquities. The Christian monuments of Rome were less cultivated but were not ignored, as the academy's trips to the catacombs demonstrate.[74] Leto's chief successor in the study of Christian antiquities was Pietro Sabino (dates uncertain).[75] Sabino was a pioneer in the study of Christian inscriptions in Rome and made a collection of them which he dedicated to King Charles VIII of France. Sabino was also an accomplished Latin philologist and assisted Ermolao Barbaro with his *Castigationes Plinianae.*[76] Like Leto and Fulvio, Sabino became a teacher and taught Latin and Greek at the University of Rome.

Leto ignored few elements of the ancient Latin heritage. History, philology, and archaeology were the bases of his own scholarly work, while other members of the academy either followed his lead or used his principles in oratorical and poetic composition. Whatever the specific form the academicians used to apply their talents and learning, they never strayed far from the concentration on Roman antiquity which inspired Leto's life. He bequeathed to Roman humanism values that formed the basis for its unique position in the intellectual history of the Italian Renaissance. Leto's strengths generally became the strengths of Roman humanism, his weaknesses its weaknesses.

❧ III ❧

Leto's academic activities were continued by a series of smaller groups. The organization and even the time periods of these academies are obscure, and they were probably even less cohesive than Leto's. Only a few present any definite contours. They depended on the hospitality of a wealthy curialist who provided a place to meet and perhaps some intellectual direction. One of these loose associations was the academy of Mario Maffei.[77] We lack specific information on its members or its period. It consisted of friends who met occasionally at Maffei's home in Parione to discuss their mutual interest in antiquities. Maffei owned a collection of ancient inscriptions and thus provided the raw material for discussion. It is likely that groups that left so little information were minor influences in Rome, and that they represented established interests rather than new ones. More important, however, was the academy of Leto's immediate successor, Paolo Cortesi.[78]

Cortesi maintained his academy in Rome from the early 1490s until his departure from Rome in 1503. Our major source of information concerning the academy is one of its most illustrious members, Vincenzo Calmeta (d. 1508), who briefly described it in his biography of the Italian poet Serafino Ciminelli Aquilano (1466–1500).[79] Serafino had come to Rome in 1499 in the entourage of Cardinal Ascanio Sforza. During Serafino's period in Rome, Calmeta noted,

> there flourished likewise . . . our academy in the home of Paolo Cortesi, a young man much respected in the Curia for his learning, position, and affability: one could have called this not a house of a courtier but a shop of eloquence and a meeting place of every noble virtue. There came together every day a great multitude of men of high ability: Giovanni Lorenzi of Venice, Pietro Gravina, the bishop of Montepiloso,[80] Agapito Geraldini, Manilio Rhallo, Cornelio,[81] and many other learned men, under whose shadow younger ones who were still desirous of broadening their virtue brought themselves to spend their days there and took delight in it. The ardors of Aretino[82] were greatly esteemed among the vernacular poets, nor was there little estimation of our fragments. Serafino,[83] therefore, who had

closer relations with me than with any other living person, determined to frequent this academy.[84]

To those humanists mentioned by Calmeta may be added Battista Orsino of Foligno, who served as the secretary of Cardinal Giovanni Borgia; Francesco Sperulo of Camerino and Piero Francesco Giustolo, both of whom served Cesare Borgia; the poet Jacopo Corsi; and others.[85]

The list of members of Cortesi's academy mentioned by Calmeta and in other sources provides us with a good cross section of the types of humanists who were found in Rome in the early sixteenth century. The pattern of career advancement sketched in the previous chapters holds true for these men as well. Perhaps the most successful of these humanists was the Venetian Giovanni Lorenzi (1440–1505).[86] After studying at the University of Padua, Lorenzi came to Rome in 1474 in the *familia* of Cardinal Marco Barbo, a fellow Venetian. In Rome he entered the Curia as a papal scriptor and was a familiar of Sixtus IV (1470). In 1484 he received an appointment as apostolic secretary and as an abbreviator *de prima visione*. Innocent VIII made him papal librarian in succession to the humanist Cristoforo Persona in 1487.[87] In about 1490 he was appointed *magister registri supplicationum* (in succession to Alessandro Cortesi),[88] and in October of the same year he became *taxator litterarum apostolicarum*. The pontificate of Alexander VI ended his advancement, however, as a consequence of his close association with Borgia's predecessors. Papal retribution against a predecessor's favorites was not unusual. Lorenzi remained financially solvent because, in addition to his curial posts, he continued to hold several benefices. This allowed him to act as a minor humanist patron, and he employed the German humanist Jacob Questenberg as his secretary. Lorenzi's membership in Cortesi's academy testifies to his interest in Latin and vernacular poetry. Cortesi considered Lorenzi a learned, well-spoken, open, and humorous man.[89] He was a Hellenist of ability and he translated selections from the writings of Sextus Empiricus and Plutarch into Latin.[90]

While the coming of the Borgias to power ended Lorenzi's curial career, it benefited most other members of Cortesi's academy. Agapito Geraldini (1450–1515),[91] for example, depended on the Borgias for his advancement. Agapito came from a noble Amelian family that had connections to the Court of Naples. His father was a jurist and served both in Rome and in the kingdom of Naples. Two of Agapito's uncles were bishops and helped enlist the support of the Borgias for their young relative. Agapito first came to Rome as a cleric in 1480, perhaps in the *familia* of Cardinal Filippo Ungetti. In 1482 he was appointed an abbreviator of papal letters and a familiar of the pope; at some later date he was also made an apostolic protonotary. He might also have served as a secretary to Alexander VI.[92] In 1497 he passed to the service of Cardinal Giovanni Borgia and then in 1498 to Cesare Borgia's employ as a secretary. His service to Cesare continued until Borgia's fall after Alexander's death. His secretarial duties were heavy and Cesare depended on his abilities as negotiator, diplomat, and administrator during his campaign in the Romagna.[93] His loyalty to the Borgias was rewarded with the archbishopric of Siponto (1498) and several other benefices. After Alexander's death and Cesare's flight to France, Agapito divided his time between his native Amelia and his home in Rome. He belonged to both Leto's and Cortesi's group. Cortesi praised Agapito as an urbane and mordant poet.[94] Like other members of Cortesi's academy, Agapito composed popular Italian lyrics called *strambotti*.

Agapito's career shows that the Borgias found it useful to employ humanists. This was not necessarily a reflection of their own intellectual interests, but rather a desire to follow the current fashion and to exploit learned men as propagandists. This was especially true in the case of Pier Francesco Giustolo (d. 1515).[95] Giustolo came to Rome from Spoleto, where he had served the commune as a notary. He spent some time in Leto's academy and probably studied with him. He betrayed a disinterest in Greek studies which was characteristic of Leto's followers. Giustolo, who was deficient in Greek, compared Vergil with Homer and attacked the latter for a lack of decorum in his poetry. Concern with decorum in literature was an important theme of the Cortesi academy and reflected the academy's devotion to the canons of classical eloquence.[96] Giustolo's appointment as one of Cesare Borgia's secretaries marked a major advance in his career and he repaid it by writing panegyrics in honor of his employer's military campaigns.[97]

Cortesi's academy had its cosmopolitan elements. Manilio Cabacio Rhallo of Sparta (*ca.* 1447–*ca.* 1521)[98] came to Italy with his family in 1459 as a result of the Turkish conquests in Greece. He was a member of the *familia* of Cardinal Giovanni d'Aragona, the son of the king of Naples. He divided his time between Rome and Naples, where he attended the academy of Giovanni Pontano.[99] In Rome he also served in the *familia* of Cardinal Marco Barbo, a prelate who employed many humanists.[100] He was an accomplished poet; he was held in high esteem by Paolo Cortesi for his eloquence and he composed an epitaph in honor of Alessandro Cortesi.[101] The dedication of one collection of his poems, the *Juveniles ingenii ludus*, to Cardinal Galeotto Riario, seems to indicate some contact with that prelate. In addition to his poetry he gave his attention to Latin philology and discovered Festus's *Collectanea priscorum verborum*.[102] He remained a prominent member of Rome's intellectual community and was favored by Leo X with the archbishopric of Monemvasia and the bishopric of Hieropetra in Crete. His inclusion in the humanist collection the *Coryciana* of 1524 attests his continued esteem as a poet.

It is significant that several representatives of southern Italian humanism who had contacts with Giovanni Pontano's academy in Naples also attended Cortesi's gatherings. As stated above, both academies shared a devotion to classical civilization and classical poetry which suited their respective courtly surroundings. A further example of this Neapolitan connection is Pietro Gravina (*ca.* 1453-1528).[103] Gravina was born in Palermo in Sicily but spent his life in Rome and Naples. His poetic abilities made him a prized member of Pontano's academy.[104] There is little information about his presence in Rome at the time the Cortesi academy met. However, there does exist a sermon Gravina delivered before Pope Alexander VI at the feast of the Ascension in 1493.[105] Such a prestigious circumstance probably means that his oratorical talents were as substantial as his poetic ones. He represented that type of humanist who passed through Rome for a time without establishing any lasting roots but who easily fit into its intellectual circles.

This summary of the academicians' careers demonstrates their central place in the intellectual life of Rome. Their poetic, secretarial, and philological skills provided them with vital elements for success in Rome. Calmeta's discussion further indicates that these men conceived of their academy as a means of disseminating their literary theories to younger humanists who were just beginning their climb up through the curial bureaucracy. Like Leto's academy, Cortesi's group sought to establish norms, in its case literary and especially poetic ones, and to promulgate them among younger men as rules to be followed.

The meetings at Cortesi's home centered on two literary themes. The first was the search for eloquence, which must be understood to refer to Latin prose style. As a leader of the strict school of Ciceronian imitation in Rome, Cortesi naturally used his academy as a conduit to develop and expand his ideas on a Latin style that was dependent on imitation, a view which would have been seconded by so many professional secretaries. The other, younger, academicians would have realized the value of conforming to the dominant Latin style of the Curia. In emphasizing Latin style Cortesi's group exhibited another facet of the classicism Leto advocated.

The second concern of Cortesi's academy, vernacular poetry, occupied Calmeta's attention. This was natural since Calmeta and the subject of his biography were vernacular poets. This devotion to vernacular poetry was natural to men who were connected with courts that in general found poetry a congenial literary form. Cortesi himself wrote Italian poems called *strambotti,* originally a popular poetic style that was refined by learned associations.[106] Such an interest in vernacular poetry did not conflict with the academy's devotion to Latin eloquence, for both were inspired by the humanist theory of imitation.

Serafino Aquilano and his contemporaries evolved a form of poetry which depended on the imitation of Petrarch's verses.[107] This Petrarchism consisted in the copying of Petrarch's conceits and forms, especially those of the *canzoniere.* These poems were sung to musical accompaniment and were especially popular as court entertainment. Cortesi in his *De Cardinalatu* commented on the origin and importance of Serafino's poetry:

> Finally, those forms of poetry usually are numbered which consist of of eight lines [*strambotti*] or three lines [elegies], which type Francesco Petrarch is said to have first established among us as he sang his exalted poems with a lute. But of late Serafino Aquilano was the originator of the renewal of this genre, by whom such a controlled conjunction of words and songs was woven that there could be nothing sweeter than the manner of his modes [of singing]. And so such a multitude of imitative court singers emanated from him that whatever is seen to be sung in this genre in all Italy appears to be born out of the model of sung poems and melodies.[108]

Cortesi's statement makes it clear that the vernacular poetry represented by Serafino appealed to humanists both as a continuation of a literary, imitative form and as a proper response to the needs of humanists dependent on courts for their livelihood.

A view of how Cortesi's academy might have functioned is provided by Calmeta in his description of a discussion of decorum in literature, especially vernacular poetry, held between Cortesi and a group of *literati* on the portico of Cortesi's home.[109] In this passage Cortesi provides his listeners with a series of examples taken from Dante and Petrarch to demonstrate the principle of decorum. To emphasize his point Cortesi also refers to the work of the artist Pisanello.[110] Cortesi's argument is that style must fit the subject being described. It is probable that the members of the academy would discuss the ideas set forth and the examples used to support them, and that some general principle would emerge which they could use in their own writing. If Calmeta's narrative is representative, then it shows the normative nature of the discussions held at the academies. Further, it demonstrates that the topics under consideration were closely related to both the humanists' desire to apply classical standards to contemporary literature and the requirements a court-oriented society placed on literary humanism in Rome.

❧ IV ❧

The Roman academy movement continued to shape the literary and archaeological activities of humanists after Leto's death and Cortesi's departure from Rome. The center of the academy in the first two decades of the cinquecento passed into the *horti* (so named because the gatherings were held in gardens) of two well-established curial humanists, Angelo Colocci and Johannes Goritz.[111] Like Cortesi, these men were sensitive to the needs of the official courts and the desires of the humanists for companionship. Together their academies marked the highpoint of the Roman academy movement as well as the beginning of its decline.

Angelo Colocci (1484–1549)[112] came from a family with connections to both the kingdom of Naples and the Curia. Colocci's great-grandfather had served as an auditor of the Rota and papal chaplain in 1378.[113] Angelo spent his early years in Naples, where he participated in Pontano's academy. For career purposes he emigrated to Rome before 1499, by which date he had purchased the post of abbreviator for 2,500 ducats,[114] thus initiating a highly successful and profitable curial career. Besides the abbreviatorship, Colocci held the post of procurator of the penitentiary (purchased for 700 ducats), the *magister registri litterarum,* and *sollicitor litterarum apostolicarum* (purchased for 800 ducats). In 1510 he became an apostolic secretary and subsequently a notary in the *Camera Apostolica,* the governor of Ascoli, and finally the treasurer-general of the Church in 1538.[115] Although Colocci married in 1505, his wife's death in 1518 allowed him to take holy orders and become a candidate for ecclesiastical preferment. In 1520 he became a canon in the cathedral in Jesi, his ancestral home, and in 1537 he was created bishop of Nocera.[116] Colocci's various offices made him a rich and influential man in the Curia and in Roman humanistic circles, and he used his income to further literary and archaeological studies. His devotion to classical antiquity led to his formation of an important collection of archaeological and classical artistic monuments in his home, which had once belonged to Leto.[117] His study of ancient classical civilization led to his concentrating on scientific topics; unfortunately he never completed a planned monograph on ancient weights and measures.[118] Although he was an accomplished Latin poet, he also studied Italian, Spanish, and Portuguese literature.[119] Greek scholarship interested him as well, and he supported the printing of Greek books in Rome.[120]

Our information on Colocci's academy is indirect. The academy did not produce a unique literary collection, as did Goritz's, nor does any particular event in its history provide us with a clear picture of its contours or of the men who gathered at Colocci's home. If Colocci's group followed his own general intellectual interests, then it discussed a remarkably broad spectrum of subjects. In a letter written to Colocci in 1529, a member of Colocci's and Goritz's assemblies, Jacopo Sadoleto, nostalgically recalled the meetings of the Roman humanists in his youth at Colocci's and others' *horti*.[121] Sadoleto noted that these *horti* were places where all the arts and sciences, but especially eloquence, were discussed, and that members came to read their own writings and expound a great variety of topics openly.[122] Sadoleto indicated that Colocci's academy was similar to the other Roman groups in providing a clearing house for intellectual opinions and the formation of general principles in conformity with the dominant classicism.

Colocci's academy has been overshadowed by the group patronized by Johannes Goritz, even though both academies were similarly constituted and were frequented by the same group of humanists. Goritz's academy was particularly active during the pontificate of Leo X and continued until the sack of Rome. Goritz (mid-quattrocento to 1527),[123] who was called Coricius by the humanists, is a further example of a successful curial careerist who turned his attention to advancing humanism. He was born in present-day Luxembourg and obtained a law degree before moving to Rome in the reign of Alexander VI. He became a registrar of supplications under Alexander and eventually an apostolic protonotary.[124] His position allowed him to purchase a villa between the Forum of Trajan and the Campidoglio, and there his academy met.[125] His villa, however, was seized by the invading forces during the sack and Goritz fled to Verona, where he soon died.

Goritz's academy attracted many prominent humanists and clerics, including the two papal domestic secretaries, Jacopo Sadoleto and Pietro Bembo, the future pope Alessandro Farnese, the future cardinal Giles of Viterbo, Bishop Mario Maffei, Raffaele Brandolini, Fedra Inghirami, Blosio Palladio, and Baldassare Castiglione.[126] The common devotion of these men to Neo-Latin poetry brought them to Goritz's academy. It was Goritz's good fortune to be able to supply his poets with an occasion to practice their art and he thereby guaranteed his own immortality.

In 1512 Goritz began the decoration of an altar in the Augustinian Church of Sant'Agostino.[127] He secured the services of Raphael to paint above the altar a fresco of the prophet Elijah flanked by two angels and he commissioned the sculptor Andrea Sansovino to do a grouping of the Virgin, Saint Ann, and the Christ Child. Saint Ann was Goritz's patron saint and he was greatly devoted to her cult, which was popular in the lower Rhineland. The statue became a meeting point for the humanists of the academy, who annually gathered at the church to celebrate Saint Ann's feast on July 26. Part of the festivities consisted of the humanists' affixing to the statue their Latin poems in honor of Goritz, Saint Ann, or other members of the academy. The poems from a decade of these festivities were collected and published by Blosio Palladio in 1524 in a book entitled *Coryciana.* [128]

The *Coryciana* is divided into several sections, including the *epigrammata, icones, hymni,* and *annales,* and also contains a long poem on the poets of Rome by Francesco Arsilli, *De poetis urbanis,* which is dedicated to Paolo Giovio. [129] In these poems the humanists celebrated their own talents and intellectual position as well as the talents and piety of their patron. The more than four hundred poems are of varying value in quality and historical interest, but they are good examples of the classicism that inspired Roman humanists and the literary conceits that attracted them. A particularly striking feature of the poems is the classical form in which religious subjects are discussed. Christ and the Virgin are transformed into classical gods who inhabit Olympus. [130] The poems sing the praises of a humanist culture as the central element in a reclassicized society. The *De poetis urbanis* specifically identifies the Rome of Leo X with the glories of Augustan Rome. [131]

Goritz's academy marked a major plateau in the development of Roman humanism. All these academicians demonstrated the unified nature of Roman humanism, its dedication to neo-Latin classicism and to the search for absolute models with which to implement it. There were, however, severe limits to the humanism these academies nurtured. While the assembling of so many men who were interested in similar ideas had its obvious value, it also tended to enforce a uniformity which had an ultimately deleterious effect on the vitality of Roman humanism by making it inbred; the same men met at the same places to discuss the same questions within the same general strictures and with the same results. The academies institutionalized the defects as well as the positive elements of Roman humanism. The debilitating effects of such a uniformity became evident as the quality of Roman humanists declined, partly as a result of the change in political circumstances which limited patronage in the last years of Leo's reign. While the sack of Rome completed the destruction of Roman humanism, the seeds of its internal decay were evident almost a decade earlier when a certain sterility and inbreeding began to characterize the Roman academies.

❧ V ❧

This change in the character of Roman humanism is best illustrated by the controversy that centered on the Belgian humanist Christophe de Longueil (Longolius) (1488–1522),[132] a controversy which divided the humanists in Rome. Longueil was one of those Northern European humanists who considered their education incomplete without a period of study and travel in Italy. A somewhat exuberant but also unstable personality, he fell completely under the influence of humanists, especially those in Rome, who advocated strict imitation of Ciceronian Latin. His devotion was so complete that his friends in Rome succeeded in obtaining for him a grant of honorary Roman citizenship in January 1519. However, before it could be bestowed, a group from the Roman academy attacked him for *laesa majestas* against Rome. The accusation stemmed from a youthful oration Longueil had delivered in France praising the virtues of the ancient Franks at the expense of the ancient Romans. Roman humanists split over the question of Longueil's guilt. Longueil's supporters, who included Bembo and Sadoleto, defended their young protégé, but while the attacks of the Roman extremists were silly enough in themselves, Longueil's response was even more extraordinary. Longueil agreed to participate in a public debate arranged by members of the academy for June 16, 1519, on the question of his "treason." The debate was to be held on the Campidoglio before the government of Rome and all interested listeners, and his opponent was to be the young humanist Celso Mellini (d. 1519),[133] a scion of an old Roman family and a member of Goritz's academy. Before the debate could be held, however, Longueil fled Rome in fear of his life. The debate was never held and Longueil lived the rest of his life in Padua in the household of the young English noble Reginald Pole.[134]

The Longueil affair underscored the limitations of the Roman humanist community. The hostility toward Longueil as a foreigner, a posture which also inspired some of the Roman humanist opposition to Erasmus a few years later,[135] reflected a narrow chauvinism at work against the intellectual caliber of Roman humanism and its tradition of cosmopolitanism. Although the Roman humanists were divided over the question of Longueil's guilt, it seems that those who opposed Longueil foreshadowed future developments in Rome while his supporters belonged to the passing, much broader humanist world of Julian and Leonine Rome. Infighting had always been a characteristic of humanism, but the nationalistic antagonism that surfaced in the Longueil affair was of a different, more serious, and ultimately destructive nature.

Even before the sack of Rome, however, the élan of Roman humanism was declining. The problem implicit in the Longueil affair becomes clearer when we investigate specific humanists. The careers of some humanists show that they became intellectually barren in the Roman environment. For some, sterility resulted from the responsibilities imposed by curial posts; there was little time for scholarly or literary enterprises. But this had always been a problem with curial humanism. Furthermore, patronage contracted. Leo emptied his treasury fighting ill-advised wars, Adrian VI was uninterested in humanistic patronage, and Clement VII was in a poor financial position through most of his pontificate. Uncertainty plagued the future of Roman humanism financially, politically, and religiously as Rome went on the defensive in response to the religious turmoil in Germany and the Franco-Spanish threats to Italy. These events had a psychological effect on Roman humanists, as two examples will demonstrate.

Blosio Palladio (d. 1547)[136] was a prominent humanist and had a successful career in Rome. His literary production, however, was not indicative of his talents or of his central position in Rome's intellectual life. Only a few orations and poems attest to his literary abilities, and the work most often associated with his name, the *Coryciana,* was a text he edited.[137] He was a favored curial humanist and served as secretary to both Clement VII and Paul III. As a cleric he held several benefices and eventually received a bishopric. These posts made him a wealthy man and he used his monies for charitable work. Still, the absence of any major humanistic work by Blosio is significant. One is left with the definite impression that he belonged to an intellectual world that had passed, and that he could not find the justification or strength to commit himself to the new one he served. Perhaps he sensed that Roman humanism, with its optimistic devotion to neoclassicism, was not the proper response to the new problems facing the Curia and Italian intellectuals.

A similar impression emerges from the latter part of the career of Mario Maffei, Blosio's close friend.[138] Maffei's expertise in ancient philosophy, art, and archaeology, as well as his talent as a Neo-Latin poet, placed him in the center of the Roman humanistic tradition. He enjoyed papal support and a large income from his benefices. Yet, unlike his elder brother Raffaele, Mario produced only a youthful dialogue, a few poems, and some contributions to the *Epigrammata Urbis Romae* (1521), a collection of Latin inscriptions. Perhaps Mario's trouble related to his success as a courtier at the papal court, a position which did not permit him time for scholarship or literary composition. However, unlike Palladio, Maffei left Rome in the mid-1520s and spent his time in his palace and villa in and near Volterra. There he did have time for humanistic enterprises, but instead he spent his energies in managing his estates and doing some minor curial politicking from afar. Perhaps Maffei's withdrawal from the city indicates that he sensed that the world he had known in Julian and Leonine Rome had ended and that he no longer belonged to the world that was taking its place, and this realization enervated him. Whatever the exact reasons, Mario had the ability and time to follow his brother in scholarship, but lacked the internal strength to undertake any large literary schemes. Courtiership absorbed his youth, and his mature years found him alienated from the intellectual companionship and support necessary to undertake and sustain important literary work.

Even though intellectual stagnation overtook the Roman academies and Roman humanism generally in the 1520s, earlier the academicians did endow Roman humanism with a sense of unity and a dynamic quality. The limits of the academies were those of Roman humanism generally: an excessive concern for authority, a certain monotony in personnel and topics, and a general subjection of intellectual life and interests to the needs and concerns of court life. The academies were in part a response to the curial demands made on humanists, but they also functioned as a supplement to court culture rather than as an antithesis to it. They allowed the humanists a privileged and safe area in which to take refuge from occupational problems and to develop those skills and interests, especially in poetry and oratory, which would enable them to meet the requirements of the Roman courts. That humanists both inside and outside the academies were successful in blending their classical culture with the strong religious and political requirements of the Curia and the papacy becomes clear when we turn to a consideration of the particular ideology humanists expounded in the years before the Reformation and the sack changed Rome's intellectual life.

PART II
HUMANIST THEOLOGIANS IN ROME

5

The Idiom of Roman Humanism

The later history of the Roman academies demonstrates the increased interest shown by humanists in the pervasive religious ambience of Renaissance Rome. While Leto's first academy was marked by an indifference toward religion and a certain antipathy to the all-pervasive clerical atmosphere, the members of the second academy produced works that had obvious religious content and incorporated classical forms. In the *Coryciana,* Goritz's poets integrated religious themes into their neoclassical poetry. The change from religious indifference on the part of many humanists to an increased acceptance of Christian topics for poetic, oratorical, and scholarly compositions represented an important alteration in the direction of Roman humanism as well as acceptance of humanism by the religious establishment.

The integration of religion and classical culture was not, however, unique to Rome or to the last years of the quattrocento. Since Petrarch some humanists had made it their aim to produce a body of literature which fully integrated the Christian beliefs of the writer with the classical forms and ideals of antiquity.[1] Roman examples of this procedure exist, but there was no consistent expression of the idea until the middle of the century, and it did not become the standard view until the last quarter of the century. Early quattrocento Roman humanists like Poggio Bracciolini had done little to contribute to a uniquely Roman view of humanistic culture and its relationship to Rome's religious position. The reasons for the shift in Roman humanism after mid-century have already been discussed in part. With the accession of Sixtus IV, the papal court's receptivity to the literary talents of the humanists made the latter eager to please ecclesiastical patrons with their poems, orations, and other writings, and so religion became a more prominent theme in their writings. This change coincided with changes in the overall nature of Roman humanism. The men who produced these poems and orations on religious themes were more closely identified with Rome and its ecclesiastical inhabitants, often because they themselves were clerics, unlike many of their humanist predecessors. They saw in Rome their primary home and in the Curia Romana their chief center of activity. Even if they did not spend all their lives in Rome, they looked to the city and the Curia as their intellectual and financial bases. As a consequence, uniquely Roman elements came to define their attitude toward their scholarship, their ideals, and their means of expressing themselves.

In all of this, Roman humanists followed broader trends in Renaissance intellectual life in the second half of the quattrocento.[2] A good representative of these new elements among Renaissance intellectuals was the Florentine academy of Marsilio Ficino.[3] Although Ficino was not a humanist in the strict sense, but was a Platonic philosopher, his academy did attract humanists, especially those who were interested in Greek thought. Ficino and his associates sought in Plato a guide not to civic life but to mystical-religious experience. While members of this academy did not desert politics completely, there was evident in Florence a definite turning to metaphysical and religious questions. Ficino's academy was formed through the good will and patronage of the Medici and was, to a degree, an extension of Medici dominance in Florence. Florentine humanism adapted itself to fit the limits of political expression imposed by the Medici and substituted for political discussions metaphysical ones. Since Rome never enjoyed the political life Florence once had, its humanists did not seek political refuge in metaphysical speculations but rather increased their attention to religious and related questions as a means of expressing their acceptance of political reality in a society dominated by clerics. When Roman humanists chose to deal with religious topics, they were giving their assent, even if in modified form, to the religious and political world they knew.

The potential for tension to develop between humanistic pursuits and the Christian content the humanists wished to express did exist.[4] Humanism was an essentially secular movement, however, and only the humanists' interest in moral philosophy encroached on the areas usually relegated to clerical writers.[5] Thus acceptance and accommodation, not tension, marked the experience of humanists as religious writers in Rome. What made this transition from classical to religious expression possible within Roman humanism was the close connection between the Church, the Curia, and the papacy on the one hand and the classicism that characterized Roman humanism on the other. To articulate such a relationship, the humanists developed what may be termed an ideology that cast the Curia with the pope at its head as an ally of their new classically based culture. This was achieved by a special reading of history and by ignoring the differences between ancient culture and medieval Christianity. The humanists expressed this ideology in a variety of contexts, and their success with it lay in their use of it as a general statement rather than as a detailed proof of their views. As a set of governing principles, this ideology did not necessarily reflect objective reality, but it was the means humanists used to integrate possibly conflicting elements and produce a functional unity. This ideology had limits both as an acceptable expression of the views of a large body of intellectuals and as an ultimately defensible conception; still, it served the needs of the Roman humanists until the Reformation and the sack of Rome. Once this ideology was formed, the humanists could move to religious questions—and in some cases to technically theological ones—in a more systematic manner. The humanists easily transferred language and ideas used in the secular cultural sphere to the religious one.

The first, tentative, expression of a special relationship between the Curia Romana and the papacy and the new humanist culture came from the Florentine-born humanist Lapo da Castiglionchio (1405-1438).[6] Lapo's family background was in law and he taught humanities at the University of Bologna before entering curial service in 1436. In the Curia, Lapo belonged to the humanist group patronized by Cardinal Giordano Orsini.[7] After the cardinal's death in May 1438, Lapo composed a short treatise, *Dialogus super excellentia et dignitate Curiae Romanae*,[8] in which he and Bishop Angelo of Recanati, a curialist who had helped bring Lapo into papal service, discuss the moral probity and religious nature of the Curia and its personnel. The dialogue is not easy to interpret. Although Lapo presented certain basic arguments in favor of the Curia as a home for humanists, it is likely that he had grave reservations about his statements and wished to contrast an ideal with the imperfect reality of life in the Curia. Whatever his own personal reaction to these arguments, he presented views that circulated in humanist circles in the Curia and that he had probably accepted at one time.[9] In the dialogue, therefore, we have the first systematic, even if a hostile, exposition of the Curia as a center for humanist culture.

The dialogue stresses the relationship between the Curia Romana as the center of Christianity and the great cultural and political capitals of antiquity. The Curia is described as the focal point of a Christian monarchy that enjoys, indeed surpasses, the glories of ancient Athens and Rome.[10] As a religious center the Curia brings a variety of men together to devote their lives to God. Many men who are prominent for their religious as well as literary abilities, Lapo argues, find a home in the

Curia; Ambrogio Traversari, the Florentine humanist-monk, receives special praise as an exemplar of such men.[11] Religion, however, is not the only element that attracts men to the Curia. The Curia also offers the perfect ambience for scholarship since there is always the opportunity for intellectual intercourse and time for study. As a diplomatic center the Curia entertains a variety of men who are unfamiliar with one another yet who find a common means of expression in the Latin language: "What will we say of our men, that is, these who are now involved in the Curia Romana, the French, Germans, Hungarians, Scots, Britons, Slavs, who are made intimate by the communion of the Latin language and by daily commerce with us."[12] Furthermore, the Curia has the riches to support this magnificence. Lapo spends much space defending the riches of the Church, and it is here that his attitude toward the limitations of the Curia is most obvious.[13] His immoderate language in defense of the wealth of the Curia seems to indicate a skepticism toward it.

Lapo's dialogue set before the reader a series of views of the Curia as an employment center for humanists, views that he probably had once accepted.[14] The comparison of the Curia to the great cultural centers of antiquity was a theme that humanists would continue to use in the future.[15] For our purposes, the most important element in the dialogue was the stress given to the Latin language as a unifying force in the Curia. Although Lapo did not make the cultural connections between the Latin language and the Curia which other Roman humanists would, he did note that Latin was an essential ingredient in the connection between the Curia and the men who frequented it. For all of Lapo's disillusionment and dissatisfaction with the Curia, he did present the opposite claims clearly.

A more positive evaluation of the Curia as a humanistic and cultural center is found in the work of Lorenzo Valla. Valla's treatment of the Curia stemmed from his views on the continuity and eternity of the culture of ancient Rome. He portrayed the Curia and the pope as the new inheritors of the ancient past and its major representatives in modern life.

Valla developed his views on the Curia in his *Oratio in principio sui studii* (1455),[16] which he delivered as an inaugural lecture at the University of Rome. It might at first seem ironic that Valla, the great enemy of papal temporal claims, should propose to make the papacy and the Curia the center of the renaissance of Latin culture. Yet in his criticisms of the papacy Valla had sought not to destroy the institution but rather to reform it; he had worked to make it more sensitive to its theological and religious duties and less preoccupied with political and financial matters.[17] In the *Oratio* Valla developed a cultural construct, not a political manifesto. His assertions were embedded in his theory of language as the means of cultural transmission. Valla's great desire was to reshape culture on the basis of a close investigation of antiquity, and he appreciated the possibilities of the Curia as a center for humanists.

Valla first enunciated the basic principle of the *Oratio* in his *Elegantiae,* a major discussion of the Latin language. In his analysis of Latin style in the latter work he treated the Latin language and the Roman Empire as a cultural unit. The empire was guaranteed continuity and expansion because the Latin language continued to be spoken and written by more and more people who had never known the old political empire. Valla proclaimed the eternity of the Roman Empire through its language: "Romanum Imperium ibi esse, ubi Roman lingua dominatur" ("There is the Roman Empire, where the Roman language rules").[18] A cultural phenomenon assumed the position once occupied by a political institution. In the *Oratio* Valla took this equation of language with culture and applied it to a new setting. For him the Roman Empire, where good letters and arts once had flourished, lived on in the Christian religion and more specifically in the Curia Romana and its head, the pope. Christianity and Latin were coextensive and eternal. The popes acknowledged this connection by supporting Latin, which in turn was a bulwark to the Christian faith.

Valla's oration stated the basic elements of the ideology developed by humanists in the Curia throughout the second half of the quattrocento. The unity of ancient Roman culture, the Latin language, and the Christian religion as represented by the pope and the Curia was emphasized in the strongest terms. Of course, Valla was not the first writer to connect the Roman Empire and the Church; using the idea of the *translatio imperii,* which was based on the Donation of Constantine, medieval writers, especially lawyers, called the Church empire and the pope emperor, an identification that was accepted by curial humanists despite Valla's attack on the Donation.[19] However, by stressing the linguistic basis of the identification and by concentrating their attention on the Curia and its seat in Rome, Valla and the humanists who followed him imparted greater specificity to the equation than the medieval thinkers had. Furthermore, the medieval writers did not see this Roman culture in the same terms as did the humanists, who were experimenting with new expressions and more exact information about antiquity. Thus, while there was some historical precedence for what Valla attempted, there was no exact parallel.

❧ II ❧

Valla's oration was general in its presentation and argument; it lacked extended discussion of historical detail. It stated rather than demonstrated its case. The task of providing a more detailed and historically based discussion of the identification of the Curia and the papacy with humanist culture was taken up by the Florentine humanist Giannozzo Manetti (1396–1459).[20] In his biography of Pope Nicholas V Manetti further developed the constituent elements of the humanistic identification of classical culture with the Church. Although Valla had made language his central theme, Manetti emphasized the essential value of humanistic scholarship to the Church in general and especially to the Curia and the papacy. In his biography of Nicholas V Manetti paid tribute to an old friend and benefactor, proposing the pope as a model for the union of classical and Christian culture. By centering on the person of Nicholas, Manetti demonstrated the propriety of humanistic learning at the highest point in the curial and ecclesiastical bureaucracies, thereby making the pope a standard for all others. Manetti, like Valla, emphasized the importance of the head, the papal office, as the means of continuing the identification of Latin humanist culture with Christianity.

Although Manetti spent only a short time in Rome, he contributed significantly to the luster of its humanism. Born and raised in Florence, he was one of the most active humanists in the service of his home government. His political activity was matched by an enormous breadth of scholarship and learning. He was especially interested in theology, and he studied Hebrew as well as Greek so that he could more fully investigate the sources of Christianity.[21] Because of his interest in the linguistic basis of theological studies, Manetti, again like Valla, was a major representative of Italian humanist pursuits in theology, especially in Biblical studies. His devotion to his government and his fame as a scholar, however, did not prevent adverse fortune from plaguing the last years of his life. As a result of a foreign-policy disagreement with Cosimo de' Medici, he left Florence. Fortunately, he found a home in Rome under the patronage of his old friend Nicholas, who made him an apostolic secretary. His refuge in Rome ended with Nicholas's death and he retired to Naples and the court of King Alfonso, where he died in 1459.

In his biography of Nicholas, Manetti presented the pope as the ideal humanist cleric. Manetti envisioned a clergy whose education incorporated the new humanist culture and traditional Christian theology. In detailing his portrait, Manetti dwelt on many topics that are only tangential to our interests here but that do contribute to a comprehensive view of the new humanist-clerical culture that he believed was valid for the Curia and the Church at large. For example, he gave extensive attention to Nicholas as a builder, as a man who used architecture to express the glories of the Church. The importance of this section of the biography for us lies in Manetti's comparison of Nicholas's building program with the great architectural enterprises of the ancient Jewish and pagan rulers. In rebuilding St. Peter's and other churches in Rome as well as the city's fortifications and surrounding towns, Manetti's Nicholas acted on a classical scale and model.[22]

The first element in Manetti's picture of the perfect humanist cleric was Nicholas's education. Here Manetti brought together three elements: the traditional Scholastic theological tradition, patristic studies, and the new humanistic learning. To him Nicholas represented the integration of the various sources of Western culture. Manetti was especially anxious that Nicholas's humanistic learning be interpreted as encyclopedic in scope, covering all elements of Rome's ancient heritage, and thus as a path open to all clerics.[23] The result of such broad learning in Nicholas's case was a man who was expert in both secular and divine eloquence, a man who demonstrated his value to the Church in his success as a diplomat, peacemaker, and reformer of Church ceremonies. This educational background, therefore, showed its full potential only in the highest office of the Church.

In discussing the deeds of Nicholas as pope, Manetti stressed three great acts. The first was the building scheme for Rome and the surrounding areas. The second was the commissioning of the translation of ancient and patristic Greek texts. To accomplish this second task, the pope employed many learned men and rewarded them well, occasionally with offices in the Curia.[24] This established the propriety of humanistic scholarship both as a justification for patronage and as an undertaking befitting the Curia. Finally, the pope founded a great library. Again Manetti compared this with ancient precedents, specifically the library founded by Ptolemy II Philadelphus in Alexandria.[25] To add luster to this library, Nicholas dispatched scholars throughout Western and Eastern Europe in search of new manuscripts by ancient writers in an effort to bring them to Rome. In recounting this enterprise Manetti stressed the breadth of writings collected, linking the undertaking with Nicholas's own encyclopedic interests and education.[26] The result of highlighting these three papal acts was to render Nicholas the prototypical patron of arts and letters and to bind the humanist culture closely with the religious world of the papacy as a means of advancement within the bureaucracy.

Manetti concluded his biography with the death-bed oration Nicholas delivered to the assembled cardinals.[27] In this long speech the pope defended the various programs he had undertaken and urged the prelates to follow his example by supporting arts and learning for the good of the Church. At one point he specifically proclaimed the humanities as an essential element in the education of the clergy: he argued that humanistic learning makes men free and offered himself as an example of one who was learned in human and divine matters.[28] Nicholas thus bound humanistic studies closely with the religious mission of the priest and the Church. Manetti's successors in Rome had little difficulty in expanding this equation until there was a virtual identification between humanism and religion.

Manetti's life of Nicholas initiated a minor genre of humanist papal biography. Despite these several imitators, his work remains the most impressive of all in its unity of conception and is the most important for identifying elements in the Roman humanist ideology. Manetti's example in papal biography was followed throughout the quattrocento and into the first years of the cinquecento.[29] In addition to Nicholas, Pius II, Paul II, Sixtus IV, Julius II, and Leo X all received special treatment, while the entire line of popes was described by the humanists Platina and Jacopo Zeno (1418-1481).[30] The merit of these biographies rests in their identification of the cultural and intellectual dimensions of the papacy and the Curia Romana. For example, Michele Canensi (d. 1480), a biographer of Paul II, maintained that the Curia was in the process of cultural transition to humanistic values during the reign of Nicholas V.[31] Even when a pontiff such as Paul II showed little sympathy for humanistic studies, the historians centered their attention on members of the College of Cardinals or the Curia who did meet the requirements of humanistic culture and patronage. Humanism was an integral part of these histories, not simply in their literary style, but also insofar as humanism was a living part of their subject's ambience.

The humanists' interpretation of the papacy and the Curia depended on the connection between the Roman Empire as a cultural concept expressed through its language and the papacy and the Curia as the inheritors of the prerogatives of the Roman Empire. In assuming a Roman imperial attitude, the humanists believed that the popes and the curial bureaucracy accepted the protection and propagation of the humanist culture, especially the Latin language. This argument was aided by the general acceptance of Roman imperial characteristics in papal circles. The pope's master of ceremonies defined the papal office by reference to ancient Roman precedents,[32] and Julius II styled himself Caesar.[33] Among the humanist historians Platina, in his collected biographies of the popes, argued that one could not discuss papal history without discussing imperial history, and therefore he balanced papal and Roman history. Raffaele Maffei, writing at the end of the humanist papal biographical tradition, compared Julius II to Tiberius (although to make a negative point) and Leo X to the religious Numa the second king of Rome.[34] The pope as the new emperor, the Church as the new empire, the cardinals as new senators, the Curia as a new forum of government—these were not unknown comparisons among curialists; however, the humanists gave to all this a more immediate meaning by stressing language as the medium of culture. It was therefore especially on the basis of the humanist ideal of language that they could effect the final connections made between their culture and the Curia and the papacy. The major means by which to express this ideal was Ciceronianism.

❧ III ☙

In his life of Pope Paul II (1474), the humanist Gaspare of Verona (1400–1474), a well-known educator in Rome, selected for special praise those curialists who he felt represented the more learned traditions in the Curia. Among those discussed are two whose claims to inclusion rested with their ability to write Ciceronian Latin. The first mentioned is Raffaele Brugnoli, whom Gaspare calls "Ciceronis imitatorem egregium ut eius epistolae ad filium vel apertissime declarant" ("an outstanding imitator of Cicero as his letters to his son clearly show").[35] Brugnoli enjoyed a successful career in the Curia, eventually serving as secretary to Alexander VI. The second figure commended for his Ciceronian abilities was the lawyer Niccolò Gallo, a canon of St. Peter's and a professor at the University of Rome. Gaspare described Gallo as a companion to Cicero, as a man "cuius lingua latina Ciceronis videbatur, adeoque compte scribebat (de orationis ornatu loquor) ut qui diceret melius ignorarem" ("whose speech seemed to be the Latin of Cicero, and indeed he wrote elegantly (I am speaking about the ornament of speech) so that I do not know who spoke better").[36] In these men Gaspare traced the advance of Ciceronian Latin in the Curia Romana. The emphasis on the progress of Ciceronian Latin attests to the development of humanist culture in the curial bureaucracy. While the standards of Ciceronian style were accepted by most Italian humanists, they were most prominent in Rome. Roman humanists gave to Ciceronian style not only a preeminence but a superior place in the history of the Latin language. Although they used this language to express their cultural and religious views, it, in turn, had definite characteristics which rendered it the appropriate vehicle by which to present the Roman humanist ideology.

Cicero's importance in the history of Italian humanism cannot be overestimated.[37] His writings defined the fundamental concept of *humanitas,* i.e., the knowledge of how to live as a cultivated, educated member of society, as the cultural ideal of the Romans.[38] For Cicero language played an essential role in this ideal. Rhetoric or eloquence not only expressed *humanitas* but also came to be identified with it; the perfect representative of *humanitas* was the orator, the man who spoke and wrote elegantly and thus was truly human. The cultivation of a fine Latin style to a great extent defined culture, and this language could conciliate a variety of ideas and traditions to form a cultural unity. The patristic Latin writers generally accepted this Roman ideal and occasionally cultivated a Ciceronian literary style in their writings. In the Middle Ages, however, this vision of language disappeared. Medieval writers developed a technical, scientific language that ignored the rhetorical and cultural associations of classical Latin. The humanists reacted against this medieval technicalism and sought to recapture the ethical and cultural values of the Ciceronian orator by restudying ancient writings. Beginning with Petrarch, this Roman linguistic ideal acquired a nationalistic component. The Italian humanists considered Cicero's language their own national tongue, *nostra lingua latina* as they termed it. While such an identification gave fuller meaning to the re-creation of classical Latin and prevented it from becoming an empty formalism or affectation in the quattrocento, in time it would cause a narrowing of the universal claims of Latin, as seen in the Longueil case. In looking to the orator as a spokesman for and arbiter of culture, the humanists turned to Cicero for both the ideal and the means to implement it, i.e., style. Humanist linguistic ideology differed from the ancient Ciceronian formula insofar as it incorporated Christianity.

In Rome Cicero played a vital role in both defining classical antiquity and providing humanists with a means of expressing their cultural-religious views. Roman humanists gave Cicero a special place in accordance with their tendency to choose a single authority to follow in both literary and nonliterary enterprises.[39] The authorities chosen were classical authors who were felt to exemplify best the finest characteristics of ancient Rome, especially the Rome that had conquered the world. Classical models became infallible authorities who proclaimed the glories of rulership, or *imperium;* it was an authoritarianism that paralleled the authoritarian structure of the papal government. The classical models selected as authorities were representatives of the Golden Age of the late republic and early empire, a time the humanists felt they were reestablishing in modern Rome at the cultural level. Interwoven with this authoritarian classicism was an imperialism according to which Rome still held some form of world domination. In this instance, as defined by Valla, it was a cultural domination. The rhetoric of imperialism was not alien to the papacy's political aims, and the humanists realized the practical value of singing the praises of this new empire. However, even when praising an individual pope for his imperial deeds, the humanists were always anxious to portray a revivified Roman culture firmly established in Rome and the Curia and independent of any individual pope.

The use of Cicero as an authority in Roman humanism had one major limitation. Cicero's ideal of *humanitas* included the political duties of the orator. It was precisely this feature that had attracted earlier Florentine humanists to Cicero as a representative of the republicans' rejection of tyranny, an attitude that was impossible in Rome, where only praise and defense of the government were acceptable.[40] Consequently, Roman humanists neglected the political side of Cicero's life and teachings. Certainly they knew of his work in the Senate, but they preferred to look to Cicero as the great Latin stylist rather than as a politician and defender of the republic. Cicero the literary theorist replaced Cicero the political actor. His language was used no longer to defend the rights of the private citizen in a republican environment or to urge the hearer to defend his republic, but rather to praise a new Roman imperialism, or more accurately an imperial Church.

While Cicero provided the model for prose composition, the humanists turned to Vergil as their authority on poetry.[41] Especially under Leo X they cultivated the forms of the Vergilian epic. The most famous example of Roman Vergilianism was Girolamo Vida's *Christiad,* a retelling of Christ's life in Vergilian hexameters. Although completed and published in the late 1530s, the work was an outgrowth of Vida's years in Rome under Julius and Leo, and was awaited by the Roman humanists as the final expression of their culture. Just as Vergil's *Aeneid* was as much about the glories of Augustan Rome as it was about the deeds of the pious Trojan, so Vida's *Christiad* was meant to reflect the cultural glories of papally supported humanism. This Vergilianism could be used for similar if less exalted themes, as Vida's lost *Juliad* showed.

The search for authorities also dominated nonliterary fields. Parallel to Ciceronianism and Vergilianism was Vitruvianism.[42] The humanists accepted Vitruvius's *De architectura* (first century A.D.) as the fundamental text on classical architecture and propagandized its importance among the practicing architects, who in turn accepted Vitruvius's pronouncements and descriptions as authoritative even while they altered them to fit their needs. When Raphael turned his attention to architecture, he enlisted the aid of the humanist archaeologist Marco Fabio

Calvo in reading the difficult Vitruvian text.[43] Calvo shared with Raphael an avid interest in the archaeological remains of classical Rome, and published a defective representation of the ancient city in 1527. To help Raphael, Calvo translated the *De architectura* into Italian. The buildings of High Renaissance Rome demonstrate Vitruvianism's hold on the Roman humanistic and artistic imagination.

The chief means of expressing Roman humanism's authoritarian and imperial associations was, however, Ciceronianism. A study of this movement can clarify much of the intellectual ambience of humanist Rome, for Ciceronianism acquired a quasi-religious dimension that corresponded to the Roman humanists' view of the religious establishment. Language was more than a means of communication for the Roman humanists; it represented culture itself. Something so essential touched every aspect of life, including religion. While it must always be remembered that not all humanists in Rome were avowedly Ciceronian in their writings, the movement did express the essential ideals and forms that gave Roman humanism its unique definition.

Ciceronianism sprang from the desire to have the best possible Latin serve as a fundamental element for renewing culture. In Rome it was the form of Ciceronianism which became the focus of attention rather than the *content* of Cicero's writings, even though humanists generally accepted the writings as expressions of ancient thought. The form of Latin was vital to the humanists' idea of the rebirth of Latin and was especially important to the humanists' role in the Curia Romana. As a Roman movement, therefore, Ciceronianism responded both to the humanists' practical needs and to a particular view of the history of Latin.

Although Latin had ceased to be the general language of discourse in the West except among the intellectual elite, in the Renaissance it was not simply a language of the past; it still displayed qualities of a living speech. The Church in particular supported Latin as the universal language, although it was generally indifferent to Latin's literary qualities. As part of their return to the values of antiquity, the Roman humanists sought to reestablish a language that functioned according to the rhetorical standards of classical authors so that they could write like the ancients. Such a goal was not easily achieved since texts were lacking and elementary education remained medieval in many ways. Ciceronianism appealed to humanists as the vehicle for achieving a classical Latin. In its simplest form Ciceronianism argued that the language of Cicero—especially that of the orations with their balanced periods—was the best Latin prose style.[44] It could be used in all nonpoetic compositions and could be employed to explain any subject matter. Imitation was the means by which humanists could recapture Cicero's style and write a purified Latin.

The Ciceronians were essentially a self-defining group. A humanist proclaimed himself to be a Ciceronian or anti-Ciceronian according to the style and vocabulary he used or professed to use. In general, periodic sentence-structure and the exclusive use of words found in Cicero's extant writings defined what the humanists meant by *Ciceronian,* although the degree of the writer's adherence to these two principles depended on his learning and patience. The use of strictly Ciceronian vocabulary was probably the greatest common denominator of the movement and the weakest element in the theory of Ciceronian imitation. However, the fidelity of a Ciceronian to the principles was less important than his espousal of those principles as the standards for all prose compositions. Even the most expert of the Ciceronians were fallible in their own writings since they did not possess the entire corpus of Cicero's writings and could not definitively state what word was or was not used by Cicero. This underlines the importance of Ciceronianism in Rome as a cultural rather than a technical touchstone.

As proponents of Cicero's Latin and as self-appointed exponents of the unity of classical culture and Christianity in Rome, humanists had to contend with a mixed legacy, for Ciceronianism had had an ambiguous relationship with Christianity since late antiquity. Hostility toward Ciceronianism was not unknown. An early expression of possible conflict between Christian and Ciceronian principles was presented by Jerome. According to Jerome he had devoted years to developing his Latin style in accordance with the canons of Ciceronian imitation and was proud of his accomplishments. However, one evening in an alleged dream Christ appeared as his judge and asked him who he was; Jerome responded, "Christianus sum," to which Christ rejoined, "Non Christianus, sed Ciceronianus."[45] Jerome took the hint and abandoned his literary pursuits (although not for good) and devoted himself to religious and Biblical studies. Jerome's dream demonstrates not only the great appeal of Cicero's language to ancient as well as Renaissance writers but also the ability of Ciceronian Latin to dominate a man's mind and govern his priorities.

Jerome's ambivalence, however, should not be taken as the representative response of the Church Fathers to Cicero.[46] Lactantius, in contrast, was called the "Christian Cicero" for his fidelity to Ciceronian compositional principles. Augustine, who was well educated in late Roman rhetorical theory, praised Cicero for both his philosophical writings and his style.[47] Even in the Middle Ages some scholars acknowledged Cicero's uniqueness and turned to his writings for stylistic models.[48] However, it was the Italian Renaissance that revived the cult of Cicero and made it the cornerstone of a renewed rhetorical theory, and it was Renaissance Rome that witnessed the full development of Ciceronianism.

Roman humanists gave eloquent expression to the values of Ciceronian rhetoric. While they were not unique in this, they were more thorough and propagandistic than others. Ciceronianism was a literary form that naturally appealed to men employed as curialists, teachers, and secretaries to cardinals, activities that depended on the best and most impressive style. In addition, this style became dominant at the very time when humanists had accepted the need to bind humanism more closely to the papal and curial bureaucracy on which they depended. Ciceronianism became not only an acceptable Latin literary style but the preferred form for expressing the ideals of Roman humanism and those of the Curia, the papacy, and the Church.

The first curial humanist to stress and defend the importance of Cicero to Latin composition was Poggio Bracciolini. In a feud with Lorenzo Valla prior to the latter's return to Rome, Poggio argued for the uniqueness of Cicero's style against Valla's preference for a more eclectic Latin eloquence based on Quintilian.[49] While Poggio represented the increasing dominance of Ciceronian Latin among the humanists in the Curia, his position was not well developed and did not carry any ideological component; he did not connect the means of expressing an idea with the idea. For Poggio Ciceronianism was simply the best Latin style and had no particular value as a means of presenting a Roman point of view.

Valla and Poggio defined the terms of the controversy as a choice between eclecticism and Ciceronianism. Imitation as a literary procedure as such was not in question; both sides agreed that the only way to perfect Latin was to follow the lead of the great ancient Latin writers. The debate between them centered on how strictly one particular writer should be imitated. In Rome this dichotomy was given fuller expression by Paolo Cortesi, both in his own original composition and in a controversy with Angelo Poliziano. Cortesi argued that Cicero was simply the best of all Latin stylists, but he grafted this view onto a more sophisticated theory of literature and imitation.

Cortesi offered his basic defense of the literary underpinnings of Ciceronianism in his dialogue *De hominibus doctis* (*ca.* 1490), which he dedicated to Lorenzo il Magnifico.[50] In it Cortesi proposed a moderate idea of imitation. The achievement of an elegant style, he emphasized, requires practice in imitation; practice allows the writer to develop the constituent elements of elegance.[51] Imitation, however, functions along with the ability of the writer to judge for himself; it is never mindless copying. Judgment and imitation form the art of eloquence, which can rectify any inadequacy in a writer's natural skill. The art of eloquence is, therefore, essentially the ability to examine and make critical judgments and to put those judgments into practice through imitation. Cortesi willingly admitted the place of individuality in literature. As he put it, nature has not made all men the same; all are different, and some are more adept at one thing than another. Imitation, however, can supplement these differences and make eloquence available to all. In Cortesi's view acquired skill and practice were essential to literary art. Imitation was part of the process of perfecting.

In this theory of literature and imitation Cicero provided the essential elements. Ciceronian oratorical ideals underlay the entire dialogue and provided the basis for judging the style of other writers. In the *De hominibus doctis* periodic sentence-structure (*numerus*) set the standard for all prose writing.[52] Cortesi, however, mentioned Cicero by name only occasionally, but when he did it was significant. Cortesi called Andrea Contrario (dates uncertain) a *simia Ciceronis* (ape of Cicero) rather than an *alumnus Ciceronis* because of his unsuccessful attempt to imitate Cicero.[53] Obviously Cortesi did not conceive of Ciceronian imitation in a mechanical fashion; he believed it could be mastered only through hard work. In the dialogue, however, Cortesi did not specifically advocate the exclusive imitation of Cicero. He had accepted the elements of Ciceronian style, but did not use the dialogue to proclaim Cicero the sole source of the best Latin, for he had done that previously.

Cortesi made the transition from a general theory of imitation to a specific Ciceronianism in a controversy with Angelo Poliziano, his youthful companion, just prior to completion of the *De hominibus doctis*.[54] Although Poliziano accepted the ideas expounded in the *De hominibus doctis* and had praised Cortesi's work earlier,[55] when Cortesi sent Poliziano a copy of a collection of letters to be used as a style book, the latter rejected the effort as worthless because of its sole dependence on Ciceronian style. Poliziano cautioned Cortesi against relying on one stylist, no matter how great, as the sole writer to be imitated.[56] Rather, he advised, Cortesi should read Cicero and other great Roman writers and develop his own unique style. In Poliziano's view strict imitation weakened language and left the imitator without any ability to portray his own views. He advocated self-expression within the form of eclectic imitation.[57]

Cortesi's response to Poliziano's attack was a moderate, intelligent defense of imitation in general and of Ciceronianism in particular. Cortesi defended the naturalness of imitation and the propriety of Ciceronian imitation as the means of restoring eloquence to the literary culture of his day. Cortesi argued that "no one can at present speak with eloquence and variety unless he places before himself a model to imitate."[58] Without this model a writer is like a traveler in a foreign land without command of its native language; he is in a sense speechless. Imitation can give him the gift of speech by enabling him to read and speak proper Latin; and the best author to imitate is Cicero.[59] In Cicero's time the method of imitation was fixed; literary laws saved the student from slavish copying. But these laws were later lost, and Cortesi maintained that imitation remained the sole means by which to cultivate a proper style. For Cortesi, individuality was not endangered by literary imitation, because the true imitator "reproduces the face, gait, posture, carriage, form, voice, and figure and yet he keeps something individual, something natural, something different."[60]

Cortesi based his theory of imitation on Aristotle. He supported his argument for the necessity of imitation in all the arts on two standard Aristotelian-Scholastic formulas: "I maintain that imitation is necessary, not only in eloquence but in all other arts as well; for all knowledge is obtained from antecedent knowledge and nothing is in the mind that is not before perceived in the senses."[61] In accordance with this Aristotelian emphasis, Cortesi considered imitation a natural act. Just as in nature, which art imitates, there are degrees of perfection, so likewise in pursuing eloquence there are degrees: the greater the time expended in imitating, the better the product. "So eloquence has one art, one form, and one image, and those who turn aside from it are found to be distorted and lame."[62] Cortesi joined Horace and Aristotle in arguing that imitation of nature leads logically to the imitation of the best model—Cicero, of course.

Cortesi's response to Poliziano marked an important development in a particular Roman form of humanism. In addition to basing imitation more firmly on a philosophical foundation than had the earlier Roman humanists, the advocates of this theory of imitation followed more closely the archaeological-authoritarian rules of Roman classicism. Cortesi made Ciceronianism a model for the expression of all topics. Cortesi in many ways articulated and defended what was a fact of intellectual life in Rome—the great and often exclusive dependence on Ciceronian Latin in all nonpoetic composition, especially oratory. He provided this linguistic form with greater authority, however, by placing it more fully within a theory of nature and literary art. He even attempted to put his theory into practice by writing a theological treatise according to Ciceronian principles; his attempt is discussed in Chapter 6.

The controversy between Poliziano and Cortesi highlights a major difference between Florence and Rome as humanist centers. Poliziano and his followers in Florence advocated the eclectic school of imitation, while most Roman humanists, led by Cortesi, proposed the strict Ciceronian school. These differences were fundamental and led to some bad relations between individuals.[63] The differences between these two centers continued in a controversy over imitation between Gianfrancesco Pico della Mirandola and Pietro Bembo in 1512. Neither man was specifically identified with either city when the two entered into their controversy, but they did present the theories of the two competing literary ideals. Pico's connection to Florence was through his uncle, the famous Giovanni Pico, while Bembo had only recently arrived in Rome when the controversy erupted. Bembo had already established a reputation as a literary theorist and would soon be appointed a papal secretary in recognition of his accomplishments as a Ciceronian stylist.

In their letters these two humanists made explicit the ideas sketched in the Poliziano-Cortesi correspondence. Pico's attack on the idea of literary imitation and on Ciceronian imitation in particular formed part of his general critique of antiquity.[64] Pico differed from Poliziano, indeed from all humanists, in his view of imitation as a danger to man's natural instincts. Basing himself on Platonic philosophy, Pico argued that style is innate in every man and that no one person is so perfect that an imitation of him alone is justified. Antiquity does not enjoy a monopoly on genius, he wrote; rather, modern man has surpassed his classical predecessors in such fields as art.[65] In Pico's view imitation was essentially a flawed technique since no one can imitate a writer in every way; a variety of styles is more natural and preferable.

In his reply Bembo defended what he felt was a moderate theory of imitation.[66] He distinguished between borrowing and imitation. To borrow some element from an ancient writer is acceptable as long as it is done in moderation, but this is not imitation. Imitation, he argued, concerns the entire body and structure of style. By imitating the totality of the best model, the student can in time surpass the imitated. Bembo's law of imitation was threefold: "First, to place the best before us for imitating; second, to imitate in such a way that we strive to attain [the perfect]; and finally to try to surpass [the model]."[67] Perfection results from contact with the best, and the best, of course, is Cicero.

In his second letter, which specifically attacked Cortesi's ideas, Pico reasserted the Platonic base of his theory of style: In every man there exists a particular, distinct idea of style; a writer must follow his innate sense of style and not try to imitate another.[68] The imitator is in Pico's estimation a thief who pays for his crime with his own strength and spirit. Furthermore, imitation harms a writer because different intellectual activities require different styles. Art indeed imitates nature, but nature is diverse.[69] Pico concluded his letter by changing the terms of the debate in a significant manner. He contrasted the imitation of Cicero, a false imitation, with the imitation of the Apostle Paul, a true imitation.[70] Pico made explicit a relationship between language and religion which recalls Jerome's dream. He sensed an idolatrous character in the Roman humanistic emphasis upon Ciceronian imitation. His criticism foreshadowed the particular attack on Roman humanism as religiously suspect advanced by Erasmus in the 1520s.

Roman humanists based their selection of Cicero as the perfect model on a particular reading of the history of the Latin language. Cardinal Adriano Castellesi provided a succinct sketch of this historical view in his short discussion of the Latin language, *De sermone latino,* which was published in 1516.[71] Castellesi enjoyed a reputation as an imitator and propagator of Ciceronian Latin style. In his tract he analyzed the defects of contemporary Latinity from a historical perspective and provided standards for Latin usage which sought to correct the evil effects of the abandonment of the best Latin following the fall of the Roman Empire.

Castellesi viewed the history of Latin as a continuum with certain definite subdivisions, and this allowed him to select the perfect period of Latin style. He divided the history of the Latin language into four periods. The first, *antiquissimum,* extended from the beginnings of Latin to the time of Livius Andronicus (*ca.* 285–204 B.C.), but Castellesi could not provide details on this Latin since so little of it remained. The second, *antiquum,* which extended from the time of Livius Andronicus to the time of Cicero, was a period of building which never developed one, unitary, polished style. The third, *perfectum,* was the time of Cicero, a period of pure, eloquent Latin.[72] Cicero was not alone in reaching this perfection, although he was the central figure in Castellesi's analysis. The fourth period, *imperfectum,* was one of decline from eloquence and proper Latinity; it extended to the writer's own day and was characterized by a lack of discrimination. Writers such as Apuleius (second century A.D.) introduced improper words, an aberration that continued to Castellesi's day.[73]

According to Castellesi, the age of Cicero was a *fundamentum quoddam eloquentiae* ("a certain foundation of eloquence") which must be imitated. Eloquence in writing is proper to all studies. To be eloquent an aspirant must avoid the new and archaic words advocated by semi-learned men and follow only the best. Castellesi essentially advocated a balance between novelty and archaism. For him the perfect Ciceronian mean was a model that everyone could follow and perfect. The avoidance of novelty and archaism opened Ciceronian eloquence to all students; hard work and close observation were required to imitate Cicero, and these qualities could be cultivated by all. In Castellesi's view Cicero's language defined proper Latinity because it avoided the extremes of the old and the new. Castellesi repeated the battle cry of the Roman Ciceronians: Imitate the best, and the best is Cicero. Although Castellesi realized that Cicero's language was not the only great production of the perfect period, he considered it to be the only example of perfection worth following.

The exponents of Ciceronianism worked to create a literary tradition with which writers could identify.[74] They did this by establishing canons of literary criticism by which to judge all styles of writing. After a period of "barbaric" decline, the Ciceronians argued, the only way to find purity of style and expression was through Ciceronian imitation. The establishment of this model would enable a writer to place himself within a literary tradition with laws and canonical writings. For the Ciceronians imitation did not destroy individuality or ability but regulated it and used it to create new cultural forms. To the subjective dependence on individuality the Ciceronians added the objectivity of tradition. A great respect, indeed veneration, for authority and tradition informed Ciceronianism.

Ciceronianism was important for the humanists because it provided them with a critical literary theory. In following a perfect model, writers not only identified themselves with the best, but they also permitted themselves the scope within which to make innovations that could be judged by others. Ciceronians felt that without a model there could be no judgment of writers based (at least in part) on objective criteria. Since Latin was a language that had to be re-created, this objectivity was all the more important to the humanists. How could one judge a writer using an essentially learned language unless objective standards were available to all?

Once an authority has been established, however, it is easy for it to become oppressive; form can too easily pre-empt content. This was the ultimate fate of Renaissance Ciceronianism in Rome and elsewhere; spontaneity succumbed to an essentially scholastic search for unusual words in Ciceronian texts and the use of mechanical periodic sentence-structure to express all subject matter. Ciceronianism's appeal was that it allowed any writer to perfect his style by observing the rules and using the correct vocabulary, but these requirements themselves became confining. The objectivity provided to the movement by an accepted authority led to an orthodoxy that developed into a strait jacket.

This outline of the development and meaning of Ciceronianism explains its importance to Roman humanism and to Renaissance humanism generally. By embracing the new orthodoxy of Ciceronianism, Roman humanists reinforced their essentially classical view of culture and satisfied their need for a language that could also express their approval of the curial and papal establishment. The literary theory did not require the expression of an ideology, but the historical circumstances in Rome allowed for its union with such an ideology. In time Ciceronianism would become a European-wide phenomenon, but its ideological components would remain essentially Roman.

❧ IV ❧

In the hands of the Roman humanists Ciceronianism allowed an authoritative expression of the imperial political and religious ideals of the papacy and the Curia within a humanistic cultural context. Even though Ciceronianism was not embraced by all Roman humanists, it is nevertheless the best indicator of how the Roman humanists wished to express their relationship to the religious complexion of the Curia and Rome. Ciceronian Latin was the instrument most often employed by Roman humanists to express their cultural ideals and the imperial view of the Curia Romana and the papacy. This resulted partly from the important place in curial and humanist life given to oratory. Through the Ciceronian style of oratory the humanists could stress their imperial and triumphant attitudes in a religious and ecclesiastical context. While there was some moral indignation in humanist rhetoric, the most successful practitioners of Ciceronianism were those who expressed the triumphal union of humanist classicism and Roman Christianity within the context of Rome and the Curia.

Fedra Inghirami is a good example of this use of rhetoric to praise established ideals. For Inghirami, Cicero's imperial language had a *magnitudinem quae par quidem romano imperio fuit eloquendi* ("a magnitude of eloquence which certainly was equal to the Roman Empire"),[75] a sentiment in which Cicero himself would have concurred.[76] But for Inghirami the Roman Empire was no longer the political empire of history but the papacy and the Curia Romana. The new empire was defined by the extent of the pope's authority, which even surpassed that of the old Roman emperors.[77] The language of Cicero was a natural form for expressing Inghirami's view of the Christian-papal empire as the continuation of the Roman Empire.

A further example of how Ciceronianism was utilized to express the Roman humanist ideals of religion and culture, as well as the intrinsic limits of this form which was so concerned with praise and beauty, decorum and glory, is an oration delivered by Blosio Palladio.[78] Blosio's position in the Roman academies of Goritz and Colocci, his posts in the city's officialdom and the Curia, and his ability to write good neo-Latin poetry and prose made him a natural spokesman for the ideals that bound Roman humanism to the ecclesiastical and religious traditions of Rome. Palladio expressed his ideas in an oration in honor of Leo X (*ca.* 1518) in which he recapitulated Roman history from a Christian-humanist perspective. He argued for the central position of the papacy in the union of Christianity and classical culture. The oration was written to celebrate the dedication of a statue in honor of Leo which had been commissioned by the Roman city government, and Palladio took the occasion to paint Roman and Christian history on a vast canvas.[79] The oration was never delivered, however, for Leo died before the dedication ceremonies could take place.

Blosio concentrated on two topics in his oration: the first was the story of the Roman Empire from its beginnings through its greatest achievements to the period of its decline; the second was the continuity of the Roman Empire in the Christian era. Blosio posited the existence of two parallel and complementary kingdoms, one heavenly, the other terrestrial. He saw no incongruity between these two empires as Saint Augustine had in his two cities.[80] He began his narrative with the Ovidian myth of the Golden Age, a time when men lived in peace and mutual harmony.[81] This idyllic period of peace was destroyed, however, by the introduction of cupidity and the desire for riches. From these defects war and domination resulted and with them the first empires appeared, beginning with the Assyrians.[82] These early empires were evil and made unjust war and propagated nefarious religions.

This period of evil empires ended with the establishment of the Roman Empire. Throughout his oration Blosio made it very clear that God consistently favored the Romans. Their empire was God's chosen instrument, first for the establishment of peace and concord among men, and subsequently for the propagation of his religion.[83] Rome's wars were just and spread peace and civilization; the empire's rule was mild. Governed by a wise Senate and supported by a virtuous army, the Roman Empire grew to an unprecedented extent and adorned itself with beautiful buildings. An essential element of this glorious empire was the cultivation of good letters.[84] If the Romans were not the abstract thinkers that the Greeks were, they nevertheless prized learned men and knew how to reward the worthy. The true glory of the empire was to be found not in its military success but in its contributions to culture, which outlasted the political and military features of the empire. Blosio joined Livy in proclaiming that there had never been a more righteous or greater empire than that of Rome.[85] Even the barbarians could not withstand the advance of Roman culture and accepted its laws and letters.

Such a glorious picture of Rome made it difficult for Blosio to provide a cogent explanation of its decline. He acknowledged the bad emperors and the corruption of the army and the Senate, but he assigned the destruction of the empire to *fortuna*.[86] Since Blosio was not a historian, he lacked the tools and the will to provide a searching analysis of the breakdown of the empire. Further, his theme was the glory and continuity of the empire, not its downfall; it did not suit his purposes to emphasize the negative side of the history of Rome.

The end of the empire as a political unit was only the beginning of the tale, however. Blosio went on to emphasize the religious dimension of the Roman Empire, which allowed him to connect it closely with the Church and the pope. *Fortuna* had destroyed the empire, but God in his mercy had selected Rome as the site for the establishment of his new church.[87] An eternal celestial kingdom developed parallel to a terrestrial one. God had chosen the period of the Roman Empire as the time when Christ would appear in the world. Blosio then drew a number of comparisons between Rome and Christianity: both were originally founded by poor men; twelve apostles went forth to convert the world, just as twelve prefects governed the provinces.[88] He passed over the persecution of the Christians quickly since the Romans embraced the new religion. Once the new religion had been established, he continued, the Roman Empire oversaw its propagation throughout the world.[89]

Blosio argued that God ordained the Church as the successor to the Roman Empire. On the ruins of the Roman Empire he had established his Church and watched it grow and become strong. The new Christian empire had even surpassed its predecessors in extent with the additions of the New World and the Indies.[90] Blosio realized that there were differences between the Christian religion and the Roman Empire, that a break had indeed occurred, and that Christianity was not simply another empire like Rome's. However, he was eager to present the similarities between the two rather than to emphasize the dissimilarities. In Blosio's view the Roman Empire and the Roman Church formed a unit.

In Blosio's oration the popes are presented as new emperors performing great deeds: Leo I turned back the Huns from the gates of Rome, a series of popes organized crusades to fight the Church's external enemies and summoned councils to deal with internal ones.[91] All the popes sought to maintain and increase religion, Blosio claimed. He placed Leo X in this line of illustrious popes. He listed the good deeds the pope had performed for Rome and the Church and added a few that he did not do.[92] Leo was the great benefactor of the city in Blosio's rhetoric;

he displayed all the virtues befitting a great ruler, a new emperor. Because of his wisdom and care Leo had even been able to deal effectively with the Lutheran threat![93] Fittingly he brought to Rome religion and peace after the arms of Julius II.[94] Once again the city was adorned with great architectural monuments as it had been a millennium and a half earlier.

Blosio concluded his oration by describing the statue of Leo that had been commissioned by the city council.[95] It attested to the pope's popularity among the people of Rome. Because of it Leo's memory would last forever. Significantly, Blosio drew attention to the imperial aspect of the statue by emphasizing its placement on the Campidoglio, the center of Imperial Rome.[96] He invoked the Virgin to witness the truth of his statements. However, he described her not as the humble mother of God or as the grieving mother of a dead son, but as the successor to the proud Jupiter: "You, now, not Jupiter, but the Capitoline Virgin, the Parent of God, who presides over the hills of the city, you protect Rome and the Capitol."[97] The Campidoglio represented the civic and religious center of the old Roman Empire, but it also symbolized the transformation from ancient to new, Christian empire. The Virgin replaced the pagan deity but retained Jupiter's classical and imperial significance.

Blosio's Ciceronian oration epitomized the High Roman Renaissance humanist view of Christian and ancient history. In his hands the classical and Christian pasts were given a singular interpretation that blended the various aspects into a new cultural unit. Blosio did not simply equate Christ or the Virgin with Jupiter; he used this rhetorical device to express the essential unity he saw between the pagan culture of Rome as revived by the humanists and the Christian culture of his day. The rules of Ciceronian rhetoric allowed him to proclaim this unitary view without requiring that he explain those elements which simply did not fit it well. For Blosio and his contemporaries the unity of Christian and pagan Rome at the cultural level was not a matter for discussion but a reality to be broadcast as strongly and as felicitously as possible.

As Blosio's oration shows, Ciceronianism was eminently suited for the portrayal of religious ideals in a triumphant rhetoric. The Ciceronians preferred to praise rather than to condemn; they did not debate a topic but offered a world view to be accepted by all. Their literary ideal fit the imperial and orthodox worlds of Rome perfectly. However, there was a serious deficiency in the Ciceronianism of the Roman humanists;

it was not a proper instrument of defense against attacks on its conception of religion and language. Its practitioners found it more practical for restating doctrine than for arguing for or against alternatives. This limitation was the fault not of Ciceronianism itself but rather of those who used it. The Ciceronians were capable of expressing the Roman humanist ideology but not of defending it successfully.

The final expression of this ideology and its limits came in the criticisms of Roman humanism made by Desiderius Erasmus.[98] Erasmus had spent several months in Rome during his visit to Italy in 1509–1511. Although he met many famous individuals there, he was not positively impressed by the humanism he encountered. The Roman humanists' dependence on Cicero caused Erasmus, among others, great concern. His own literary ideas were analogous to the eclecticism preached by Poliziano and his Florentine school. Further, in Erasmus's mind the literary excesses of the Ciceronians were paralleled by the political excesses of Julius II and by the religious indifference and anti-Christian attitudes he felt accompanied excessive classicism in literature.[99]

Erasmus's doubts about the nature of Roman humanism became more explicit upon his return to Northern Europe in 1512. Although he admitted his admiration of and indebtedness to certain individual Italian scholars, he allowed his distaste for the Roman variety of humanism to become more and more strident, and he broadcast his feelings freely in many of his widely circulating letters.[100] This negative assessment of the Romans was reinforced by the troubles Erasmus encountered with the curial hierarchy, including some humanists, who accused him of secretly favoring and supporting Lutheran opinions.[101] Although Erasmus made an effort to maintain good relations with powerful curial prelates such as the learned cardinal Tommaso Campeggio and Jacopo Sadoleto,[102] the Curia grew more and more suspicious of his religious attitudes throughout the 1520s. Erasmus's views on the proper function of language, his distaste for the religious tendencies of Roman humanism, and his personal problems with the curial bureaucracy contributed both to his condemnation of Roman Ciceronianism and to his opponents' growing animosity toward him.

A clash between Erasmus and the Roman humanists was inevitable. The first indication of this was an oration delivered by the Roman humanist Giovanni Battista Casali. Casali (1473–1525)[103] was an examplary representative and natural defender of Roman humanism. A Roman by birth, he had studied with Pomponio Leto, had belonged to the Roman academy, and eventually taught Latin at the University of Rome. As a cleric he received a canonry in the church of St. John Lateran from Julius (1508) and subsequently one in St. Peter's from

Leo (1517). He was a popular preacher in Rome and was respected by other humanists. In 1524 he defended the ideology of Roman humanism and its Ciceronianism in his diatribe *In Desiderium Erasmum Roterdamnum invectiva.* [104]

It is not known what specific events caused Casali to write the *Invectiva.* He was probably aware of Erasmus's general opinion of Roman humanism, and this would have been a sufficient stimulus to move him to attack the Dutch humanist. Since the *Invectiva* was never published, we cannot determine how his fellow Roman humanists reacted to his arguments; nevertheless, later events indicate that Casali captured accurately his contemporaries' attitudes toward Erasmus and their general estimation of the place Ciceronianism held within the Roman ambience. No clearer expression of Roman humanist views exists.

Casali began his attack by berating Erasmus for ingratitude toward the Roman humanists who had given him a warm reception during his visit to the city over a decade earlier. He knew of Erasmus's attacks on the Latinity practiced in the Roman academy and intended to defend its purity; indeed, he maintained that the academy included the *principes assertatoresque linguae latinae* ("the leaders and protectors of the Latin language"). [105] Casali differed from his predecessors in citing the academy as the center of the new linguistic purity. In Casali's view the academy brought all men together and thereby shared in the universality of Rome and the Church. [106] Contrasting Erasmus's views with this universal culture, Casali labeled Erasmus *barbarus.* He even attacked Erasmus's command of Greek and compared it unfavorably with Italians' expertise in that language. [107] He provided an extended defense of Cicero and Ciceronian imitation along lines that by then were traditional in Roman Ciceronian literary theory. [108] Because of Erasmus's attacks on Roman humanists and their literary principles, Casali labeled Erasmus a *dux stultorum,* a charge he claimed was supported by Erasmus's *Praise of Folly.* [109]

Casali then moved from a consideration of Erasmus's literary production to an attack on his religious position. Denying that Erasmus was an interpreter of Sacred Scripture, Casali damned Erasmus as an apostate who simulated religious poetry while destroying its doctrines. [110] Casali castigated Erasmus as a *pseudochristianus* who spread his evil teachings among all other Christians and led them away from the true faith. [111] It was significant, he noted, that the man who attacked the orthodox Roman linguistic theory was equally guilty of denying the orthodox faith. In his *Invectiva* Casali declared the general Roman dissatisfaction with Erasmus's literary and religious positions. A clear statement of Erasmus's views was soon to follow.

Erasmus gave full and final expression of his attitude toward Ciceronianism as practiced in Rome and its academies in his *Ciceronianus* (1528).[112] The *Ciceronianus* can be read on many levels. Linguistically it contains Erasmus's comprehensive view of pedagogy, an effective defense of literary eclecticism, and a superb satire of his Ciceronian opponents. In it Erasmus argued that Ciceronian style and vocabulary were not valid for all topics and especially not for describing modern problems; language was dynamic and had to change to accommodate new ideas and circumstances.[113] Further, in the *Ciceronianus* Erasmus made one of his strongest statements on the religious crisis of his day. The attacks made in the *Ciceronianus* on the religious excesses of the Italian, especially Roman, Ciceronians balanced Erasmus's parallel criticisms of Lutheranism.[114] It was at this religious level that the *Ciceronianus* assumed a critical importance with reference to Roman Ciceronianism.

From the Roman perspective the *Ciceronianus* was significant because it appeared only a year after the disastrous sack of Rome; it constituted yet another attack on the beleaguered city and its intellectuals. In addition to the literary arguments he presented in the *Ciceronianus,* Erasmus specifically criticized the religion of the Roman Ciceronians. At one point he complained that these men eschewed Christian symbols in favor of "monuments of heathenism." Included in this group were paintings with classical, mythological topics, which Erasmus contended received greater attention than works with Christian themes. However, the classicizing form Erasmus condemned most vehemently was Ciceronianism. One of the Ciceronian interlocutors in the dialogue explains the reason for this:

> These are mysteries hidden under the veil of the Ciceronian name. Under the show of a beautiful name, I assure you, snares are held out to simple-minded and credulous youths. We do not dare to profess paganism. We plead as an excuse Ciceronianism. But how much better it would be to be silent![115]

In Erasmus's view, even when the Ciceronians did speak of Christian themes their aim was sinister; they covered all Christian things with pagan names so that they might spread their pagan views more effectively.[116]

Toward the conclusion of his dialogue, Erasmus recalled the fate of Christophe de Longueil. Lamenting Longueil's early death and his excessive devotion to Ciceronian canons, Erasmus discussed his writings. In his orations Longueil applied the terminology of ancient Rome to present-day Rome even though the institutions and persons he mentioned no longer existed. Indeed, Erasmus ridiculed Longueil's and the Roman humanists' view of contemporary Rome as a continuation of ancient Rome:

> Take away the pope, the cardinals, the bishops, the Curia and its officials, the ambassadors, the churches, colleges and abbeys, and the rabble . . . and what will Rome be? You answer that the authority of the Pope handed down by Christ is greater than was formerly the rule of the Senate and the Roman People, or even, if you please, of Octavius Caesar. Suppose it is, only acknowledge that the kind of rule is different. Then you see that the same language will not fit if we decide that it is Ciceronian to fit the language to the present theme.[117]

Erasmus denied the cultural unity of the Roman and the Christian empires which formed a basic element of the Roman humanist ideology. For all his desire to use classical learning in the service of Christianity, Erasmus viewed the Church and the Roman Empire as two very different constructs. Therefore, for Erasmus, in writings on Christian affairs the language of the ancients was not an acceptable standard.[118]

By advocating a Poliziano-like eclecticism,[119] Erasmus denied both the literary basis of Ciceronianism and the cultural basis of the unity of Christian and classical antiquity as conceived by the Roman humanists. To Erasmus Roman Ciceronianism was a form of sterile pedantry and had no value in the defense and propagation of Christianity.[120] Fundamentally, however, Erasmus saw in Roman Ciceronianism a threat to Christianity: A dependence on Ciceronian style would lead to a formalism in thought which Erasmus labeled paganism. Like the Judaizers of old and the factionalistic Scholastics, the neopaganism of the Roman Ciceronians was a threat to Erasmus's *philosophia Christi,* to the evangelical reading of Christianity.[121] Erasmus argued that all things, cultural as well as literary, require a specifically Christian standard.[122] As Pico had done, Erasmus contrasted a true, Christian imitation to a false, literary, Ciceronian imitation.

For Casali, his Roman contemporaries, and Erasmus, language and religion were bound together.[123] Both Erasmus and his Roman opponents posited a unity between culture (as represented by or expressed in a literary form) and religion. The Romans found in classicism and its acceptance by the important elements in the Curia justification for advocating their cultural norms in a classical Latinity that had almost hieratic qualities; this language, they argued, was the proper companion to the traditional Christianity of papal Rome. Erasmus opposed this view by denying the close relationship between culture and religion. He did not see himself as a high priest serving a religious formalism; he accused the Roman Ciceronians of doing that. Neither group could separate its religious ideals from its literary and cultural ideals.

❧ VI ☙

The relationship between language, culture, and religion posited by the Roman humanists was a historical phenomenon. In Rome in the later quattrocento and the beginning of the cinquecento, literary and scholarly ideals, religious forms, and political needs coincided to allow a group of intellectuals to construct an ideology that unified all these elements. In other places, where these predilections were lacking, Ciceronian imitation did not support such an ideology. But in the Roman setting, where the papacy was seeking new defenders, where the Curia was willing to accept certain types of literary expression, where classical values were invading every expression of life, and where the humanists wished to secure for themselves an accepted place in the power structure, this unique integration of culture and religion was possible.

An interesting afterglow of the ideology of High Renaissance Roman humanism came in the middle of the seventeenth century when political, religious, and literary elements assumed a similar configuration and permitted the development of a new Ciceronian ideology.[124] The Rome of Pope Urban VIII (1623–1644) boasted of producing a "Second Roman Renaissance," the worthy successor of Julian and Leonine Rome. Its intellectuals sought the proper Latin style to express the universal claims of Rome and its *arcana imperii.* Not surprisingly, Cicero supplied this need. The humanists of Barberini's Rome looked to the humanists of the Roman academy under Leo X for their models. They praised the pope, Rome, and Christianity in the same periods and terms that would have been familiar to Inghirami, Palladio, and Casali. However, instead of the humanists of the academy, the Jesuits and their disciples now expounded Cicero, and their orations proclaimed the glories of Rome and the empire in the baroque surroundings of the Gesù. This latter-day Ciceronianism differed from its cinquecento predecessor in being associated with the religious orders, especially the Jesuits, and hence more official, and in expressing the needs of a religious revival, the Counter Reformation. The Church and Rome had changed, but Cicero, appealing to both the literary and erudite-archaeological tendencies of Roman intellectuals, remained their leader.

This new phase of Roman Ciceronianism highlights the importance of Ciceronianism to an understanding of the Roman humanist ideology of the High Renaissance. Ciceronianism was not coextensive with the

Roman humanist ideology, but it did enjoy a special relationship to it which was generally acknowledged. The humanists of the early cinquecento had successfully combined classical and Christian elements to fit their special requirements. Ciceronianism's viability lasted as long as there were no major attacks on the equation between religion and classical culture. When these attacks did come, from Luther and Erasmus, the ideology experienced a crisis it did not survive. Until then, however, Ciceronianism was perfectly suited to express the Roman humanist ideology. It even permitted the clear presentation of this ideology in the nonhumanist, indeed potentially hostile, world of theology, as will be seen in the next chapter.

6

Classicism in Humanist Theology

The classicism that characterized Roman humanist attitudes toward scholarship, oratory, poetry, and art also influenced the way many humanists in Rome viewed theology and religious questions. Through the use of classical motifs, *exempla,* and language, these humanists reinterpreted traditional Christian theological ideas. The result was a new expression of theology, one that rejected the forms (but not consequently the content) of traditional Scholasticism and looked back to the writers of antiquity, Christian and pagan, for models.[1] Roman humanist theological writings depended on a series of nuances and reformulations rather than the introduction of new doctrines. Theology, therefore, was yet another aspect of life which the humanists felt themselves capable of reinterpreting for their Roman audience in accordance with the standards they had established for all literary composition. Humanist confidence in this endeavor took time to develop. The increasing body of neo-Latin poetry which incorporated theological and religious themes dedicated to popes and cardinals by humanists, and the beginning of a fuller exposition of Christian thought and history inspired by humanistic studies of antiquity, were important steps in this process of incorporating classicism and religious thought in the second half of the quattrocento. The humanists' entrance into the theological arena was neither automatic nor without clerical opposition, however. Humanist writers on theology had to contend with the hostility of some professional theologians in Rome. This opposition reinforced the desire of some humanists to emphasize the agreement between their new formulations and established teachings. The theological tradition had to be altered in this scheme, although its substance was essentially accepted. It was a procedure several humanists employed with success.

Rome was well stocked with professional Scholastic theologians, the majority of whom belonged to the mendicant orders. They taught at the *studia generalia* of their orders and the University of Rome (*Sapienza*) and supplied the Curia Romana and the papal household with theological expertise.[2] Although most Scholastics probably had little direct contact with the humanists, there was a history of antipathy be-

tween members of the orders and curial humanists in the early quattrocento.[3] However, this early antipathy was moral in nature; the humanists criticized the hypocrisy of many of the religious orders, and the
orders were suspicious of classical studies. The hostility was not based
on the orders' opposition to humanism's encroachment on their selected
preserve of theological exposition, but as the humanists entered the field
of theological composition, they had to deal with this hostility. Especially at the beginning of the cinquecento, however, some prominent
mendicants such as Giles of Viterbo and Cajetan (Tommaso da Vio)—
an Augustinian and a Dominican respectively[4]—were open to humanistic influences and maintained close contact with humanistic circles.
These men utilized humanistic techniques and would have been willing
to accept serious theological works composed by humanists in humanistic forms.

The mendicants were not the sole defenders of the claims of traditional Scholasticism to a theological monopoly. Some important conservative prelates in the Curia held theological degrees, usually from
Northern European universities, and were especially vigilant in policing
the orthodoxy of theological expression in Rome.[5] Although the educational formation of these Scholastics was alien to the literary and classicizing views of the Roman humanists, their contact with humanists was
probably more frequent than that of the mendicants because they were
not bound by cloister and encountered humanists on official and social
occasions. Still, these prelates were jealous of their position and did not
look kindly on men without theological degrees usurping their special
position in the Curia. While in general the Scholastics, whether mendicant or secular, remained essentially indifferent to the unitary view of
Christianity and classical culture expressed in humanist orations and
poems, humanist theological compositions elicited their opposition.
Their professional pride and passion for orthodoxy bristled at the
temerity of orators and littérateurs presuming to teach the theological
establishment in their domain.

The hostility of the Scholastics in Rome had to be neutralized, and
so confrontation and compromise defined the religious production of
Roman humanists. On the one hand, humanist theologians claimed for
themselves the right to deal with every type of theological and religious
question (especially those that dealt with morality) in their own manner; on the other hand, they had to defend their procedures against the
constantly suspicious scholastics. They were therefore anxious to place
themselves within a religiously orthodox tradition (usually a patristic
one, but occasionally a truncated Scholasticism) which their opponents
could not easily impeach.

Humanists did on occasion take the offensive, however. Lorenzo Valla's attack on Scholasticism in his oration in honor of Thomas Aquinas (March 7, 1457) was the most significant theological argument from any Roman (or other) humanistic perspective.[6] While Valla praised Aquinas for his sanctity of life and his orthodoxy, he rejected the metaphysical underpinnings of Aquinas's theology. Valla denied that the philosophical theology and dialectical methods that characterized Scholastic thought had value for the Christian in his effort to lead a good life. He compared the theology of Aquinas and his followers to the rhetorically influenced and humanistically more acceptable theology of the Church Fathers, and found Aquinas's thought greatly wanting. The Church Fathers conveyed God's word without an elaborate metaphysics and in a manner more in keeping with the spirit of Scripture. These criticisms struck at the very foundation of Scholastic thought and provided a rationale for constructing a new base for theology. The radical nature of Valla's oration assured it few followers among the Roman humanists. The latter were willing to accept scholasticism within limits and did not intend to propose a completely new form of theology, but like Valla they sought a theology that would utilize the rhetorical foundations of their own culture and present theology in a new and to them more acceptable manner.

Generally, however, the Scholastics attacked and the humanists defended. The basic arguments in support of humanist theological writings were conveniently summarized in the preface to Aurelio Brandolini's *Epitome of the Old Testament* [*In sacram Hebreorum historiam Epithoma*], which was composed in the 1480s.[7] As has been noted, Brandolini was a popular orator and poet in Sixtine Rome. He was also an important humanist theologian. A rewriting of the Old Testament in the elegant Latin favored by Roman humanists, the *Epithoma* was aimed at a wider audience than professional theologians. Brandolini ignored doctrinal issues and subtler points in Biblical interpretation, but he nevertheless elicited strong criticism from some Scholastic theologians for tampering with the Sacred Scriptures. In his defense Brandolini outlined certain basic humanist attitudes toward theology and Scholasticism which were to characterize the humanists who wrote after him.

Brandolini began by arguing that the humanists' expression of Christian truth was as valid as that of the degree-holding Scholastics. In support of this proposition he cited contemporary Roman practice and early Christian history. In Rome the pope willingly listened to learned men without degrees disputing theological topics.[8] Papal approbation proved that university training was not essential for theological discourse. Furthermore, Brandolini argued, the Church Fathers lacked academic degrees, yet they were the founders of Christian theology. Brandolini maintained that only the ability to teach should determine a man's competence in expounding theology; learning must have some practical result, preferably to communicate and help an audience.[9] If teaching was the essential function of a theologian, then the best preparation for this task was the rhetorical training that distinguished the humanists. The orator brought to theology a breadth and communicability that was lacking in the *doctores theologiae.*[10] This rhetorical foundation revived the tradition of the Church Fathers. In language less radical than Valla's, Brandolini argued for the priority of rhetoric over professional theological training. He proposed a functional definition of the theologian: anyone who actually writes on theology.[11] For Brandolini a Christian had a definite right to deal with the tenets of his faith in whatever form he thought proper and had no need for a conferred degree.

In Brandolini's second argument he advanced the propriety of humanist language in theological discourse. He denied the Scholastics' charge that in providing a new form to the Scriptures or other traditional theological works the humanists were corrupting their meaning. Rather than harming the truth, he argued, humanist language made Christian teachings more appealing to the believer.[12] It persuaded and moved the reader to accept such doctrines as the Trinity and the Virgin Birth, which reason cannot grasp. The emotive-voluntarist aspects of rhetoric moved the believer more directly than the intellectualist philosophy of the Scholastics. Again, he noted, Christian history showed that the Apostles themselves altered the language of Christ in their preaching in order to fit the needs of their audiences. Jerome, for example, actually changed the language of Scripture itself.[13] In his translation Jerome responded to the heretical threats of his day; Brandolini argued that in order to meet the needs of their day and audience contemporary humanists had to be as free as their predecessors to adjust the language of theology.

Finally, Brandolini criticized the procedures of Scholastic theologians as expounders of Scripture. Their dependence on outdated commentaries written in barbaric Latin prevented Scripture from addressing new problems and the present needs of Christians. This resulted from the Scholastics' exaltation of speculative philosophy over Biblical theology. The Scholastics had invented a complicated terminology that obfuscated Scripture's meaning rather than clarifying it.[14] The sacred texts of the faith lost their power and immediacy through the Scholastics' use of dialectics and ambiguous language. Brandolini cast the language of Scholasticism as an impediment to the proper understanding of Christian doctrine.

❧ I ❧

Other humanist theologians developed Brandolini's major points within an orthodox and conservative reading of the Christian faith. These writers took the elements that Brandolini emphasized and expanded and altered them to the degree they found necessary. They all sensed the need to deal with the challenge of Scholasticism either by rejecting the basis for it or by incorporating Scholastic ideas into their work. They realized the need to maintain the sympathy of their audience in order to integrate theology and humanist culture. In Rome this meant allaying the fears of the religious establishment regarding any hint of heresy and persuading both the Scholastic theologians and the humanists that theology could be expressed in a literary style. One of the first Roman humanist theologians to undertake this dual task was the Ciceronian, papal secretary, and apostolic protonotary Paolo Cortesi.[15]

Cortesi presented his ideas on theological composition in his *In quattuor libros Sententiarum* (also called *Liber Sententiarum* and *In Sententias*) (1504). He wrote it according to the rules of strict classical Latin, or as he termed it, *eloquium romanum.*[16] Cortesi chose to present his ideas in the form of a commentary on Peter Lombard's *Libri quattuor Sententiarum,*[17] although he used the genre in a very free manner. The choice was significant. In his work Peter Lombard had compiled different scriptural, patristic, and early medieval theological statements. The *Sententiae* served as a manual of theology which presented the student with a systematic exposition of the major theological questions and their subdivisions. It contained a body of authoritative statements from the past, a guide through major controversies, and the necessary tools to explicate Sacred Scripture. Peter's collection was the means by which a Scholastic could develop his own views and express them within the established scholarly tradition. Its suitability for teaching made it the standard theological text in the Middle Ages.

Although Peter tried to avoid the extremes of both fideism and philosophical speculation, the *Sententiae* became the primary text to which later theologians applied their dialectical abilities in attempts to solve disagreements and express their own ideas. Ironically, the *Sententiae* enjoyed a limited popularity among some humanists, for its encyclopedic and conciliatory presentation of scriptural, patristic, and medieval opinions avoided the greater complexities of late medieval theology.[18] However, the humanists also believed that in its adaptability to the dialectical approach, the *Sententiae* helped corrupt the theological method.

In using this standard text, Cortesi placed himself formally in the medieval theological tradition, but separated himself from it in both his organization and linguistic style. The organization of his commentary did not follow Lombard's subdivision of topics into questions, articles, and smaller questions (*quaestiunculae*), which had permitted dialectical expositions of the *Sententiae*. Rather, he maintained an essentially literary form, avoiding external division in the narrative and analyzing topics without giving specific quotes from authorities and without explicating the text in any literal fashion. The language of Cortesi's commentary was the highly classicized Ciceronian Latin of Roman humanism, which differed radically from the Scholastic Latin of other commentaries on the *Sententiae*. Despite these differences, however, by relying on this text Cortesi was able to discuss a variety of theological matters without fear of Scholastic criticism of his choice of issues. In a sense he joined battle on the enemy's ground.

Besides favoring the *Sententiae* because it was the standard theological text of his day, Cortesi was attracted to it by its conciliatory character. To unite opinions rather than to stress differences generally appealed to humanists; they sought to propose positions that would be acceptable to believers. In order to accomplish this they avoided protracted controversies and the use of dialectics. Cortesi followed this basic approach in his treatise. He presented the various opinions of the theologians and stressed an acceptable catholic view whenever possible. If any tendency characterized humanist theology, it was the search for agreement among a variety of religious and philosophical sources.[19] Cortesi provided a Roman humanist example of this approach to theological truth.

Cortesi dedicated the *Liber* to Julius II shortly after his election to the papacy (1503). In the *prooemium* to the first book, which is a general introduction to the entire text, he expounded the value of humanist eloquence to philosophical and theological discourse in a manner reminiscent of Brandolini's *Epithoma*.[20] The *prooemium* offered a justification for Cortesi's views of language and the relationship between language and religion. His arguments reflected the views he had formulated in his defense of Ciceronianism against Angelo Poliziano.[21]

In the body of the *prooemium*, however, Cortesi had a more specific target in mind when he discussed language and theology. He wished to respond especially to Giovanni Pico della Mirandola's letter to Ermolao Barbaro of 1485 which attacked humanist linguistic theory and defended the integrity and validity of Scholastic Latin.[22] Cortesi never mentioned Pico or Barbaro by name in the *prooemium*, but a comparison of Pico's and Cortesi's positions establishes the latter's dependence for major themes on the former's letter. In his letter Pico (speaking through a fictitious Scholastic) sharply distinguished between reality (*res*) and language (*verba*), between philosophy and rhetoric, or, as he called them, wisdom and eloquence. He argued for the exclusiveness of philosophical terminology and, by extension, philosophy itself. Philosophical Latin may have been rude and ugly, but it fit its subject matter admirably, Pico argued, because it kept away the unlearned.[23] Pico's scheme contrasted the mendacity of eloquence with the truth of philosophy. Philosophy builds while eloquence destroys. The rudeness of philosophical speech resembles Scripture, and like Scripture, philosophy does not need the embellishment of elegant Latin. Wisdom comes not from eloquence but from philosophical speculation.

Pico attacked the very foundation of the Latin classicism of Rome, especially Ciceronianism, by denying the existence of a standard Latin based on perfect classical models. His argument was that words were established either by convention (*arbitrium*) or by nature.[24] If they were established by convention, then no single language could claim superiority, for men determine what language is and what words mean. There would be no absolute meaning or value to any particular language or indeed to language in general. This "nominalism" dispensed with the claims of eloquence. If words were established by nature, then philosophers should decide what language is, for they are trained to deal with such questions. The humanists would thereby lose all claim to being the arbiters of meaning and the guardians of language.[25] Pico specifically rejected Roman Latinity—the imitation of the Latin of Rome's Golden Age—as of no special worth. An Arab or an Egyptian could speak as appositely as a Roman on a philosophical subject, Pico proclaimed.[26] A Spanish, British, or Parisian Latin—in essence any Scholastic Latin—holds as much power and authority as did Roman Latin, with its search for classical models and its careful imitation of the best.

Cortesi in the *prooemium* followed the issues Pico had outlined in his dispute with Barbaro—the arbitrary nature of language, the distinction between eloquence and wisdom, the exclusive claim of philosophy, the acceptability of any literary form to express ideas, the uniqueness of a classicized Latinity—and tried to answer Pico's arguments in a programmatic fashion. He chose to respond to Pico because of Pico's fame and influence as a philosopher and theologian, and because of their own friendship.[27] In answering Pico, Cortesi dealt with the most pervasive arguments that had been made against the cultural ideal he was trying to establish through his literary enterprises.

In the body of the *prooemium* Cortesi argued the propriety of uniting eloquence with philosophy and theology (he did not distinguish between the two in his discussion). To do this he set forth a series of arguments against propositions drawn from Pico's letter. Some philosophers, he began, create their own words, claiming this as their right since words are arbitrary, a matter of will (*voluntariam esse opinentur*). Other philosophers argue that philosophy is sufficiently beautiful in itself, that it does not need externals such as beautiful words. Still others argue that philosophy should be kept ugly and rude so that the common people and those without degrees will be discouraged from investigating its teachings.[28]

Cortesi rejected as foolish the opinion that every philosopher should have the right to form his own words. Such license would bring an end to philosophy, for by adding its own new and unknown words each generation would destroy all intelligibility. In dealing with those who rejected the ornamentation of philosophy, Cortesi asked if the beauty of philosophy was a natural quality inherent in it or if it was artificial, something added to it. If it was natural, then either it existed in the mind as a concept (*in mente et cogitatione*) or it was expressed externally by some gesture (*nutu*). If this natural beauty existed in the mind as a concept, then there was no possible basis for discussion, for it was the literary quality which concerned Cortesi, not metaphysics. No literary criterion was valid for judging a concept. If, however, philosophy's beauty was presented through gesture, then certainly language was the means men used to express themselves. Literary art, therefore, determined the beauty of philosophy.[29] The natural and artificial aspects of beauty were one in philosophy, Cortesi argued, since whether natural or artificial it was language that was at issue.

Literary art—skillfully crafted eloquence—increased the pleasure of a study and encouraged better judgment, Cortesi continued.[30] Eloquence was part of wisdom, and not opposed to it as Pico had argued; it moved men to study and respond to the good. Philosophically, therefore, it was related to the very nature of any discipline, and by extension it was especially necessary for Christian theology since it made Christian truth acceptable to all believers and moved them to engage in its study. But eloquence was not merely the adornment of ideas. It was a natural quality. It did not use appealing means to hide pretense or false opinions. Rather than accuse eloquence of meaningless ostentation, Cortesi argued, philosophers should look to their own horrid style, which was a form of display. They used their bad style as a means of keeping their discipline from the people rather than making it accessible to the learned nontheologians and nonphilosophers. Envy and avarice motivated them to segregate their discipline from believers.

Equally false was the condemnation of eloquence as unsuitable for Christian teachings because of its pagan origins. Those who proposed such an argument, Cortesi noted, had forgotten that the ancient Christian writers were learned in the literary arts. Jerome and Augustine wrote eloquently without damaging their teachings or succumbing to pride.[31] The enemies of eloquence were ignoring the sources of their own discipline. Philosophy also had pagan origins, yet philosophers employed its teachings in their writings. Just as these men accepted only part of the pagan classical heritage, so also they followed their own philosophical authorities selectively. Plato, Xenophon, and above all Aristotle were praised for their literary accomplishments as well as for their learning.[32] Anyone who was devoted to these thinkers logically should strive for an elegant style as well as for fidelity to their philosophical ideals. For Cortesi the classical heritage was a unity and one could not arbitrarily reject only one section on the basis of arguments that were valid against all of it.

The essential element in Cortesi's defense of an eloquent philosophy and theology in the *prooemium* was the naturalness of eloquence for all disciplines. Cortesi proposed an analogy to nature: ". . . in my opinion . . . nature always joins beauty with utility as by its own certain alliance."[33] As a natural element in philosophy and theology, eloquence affected the way men responded to these disciplines. What possible advantage could these studies have to men if they were repulsive in their style? To further emphasize this naturalness, Cortesi compared beauty of style to good health in a man. Just as a good complexion was a proof of general health, so a beautiful style indicated a well-rounded composition.[34] Proof that modern philosophy and theology were not healthy was found in the attitude of contemporary humanists to them.[35] Studies that the humanists should have cultivated were being ignored by them. Cortesi believed that humanist literary art could correct this perversion and return these disciplines to the general audience that required them.

In writing the *Liber Sententiarum*, therefore, Cortesi had two objectives: to defend the union of eloquence with philosophy and theology against the Scholastics, and to convince the humanists and other non-professional theologians and philosophers to devote their attention to these disciplines.[36] There was obviously some criticism of contemporary humanism and its pedagogy in this dual approach. However, Cortesi did not place the blame primarily on the humanists for their misguided aversion to theology and philosophy. In Cortesi's eyes, the humanists had been forced to slight theology and philosophy in their educational framework by the opposition of the professionals and their insistence on bad style.[37] Still, Cortesi wished to reform the humanist curriculum, at least at the textbook level, through the introduction of an eloquent theology. Such a curriculum reform would bring the humanists into more frequent and deeper contact with theological and philosophical studies and in particular it would respond to the needs of Cortesi's clerical-humanist Roman audience. If Cortesi was in the process of clericalizing humanism by making elements of Scholastic theology compatible with it, he was equally anxious to make the clerics and theologians more humanistic. The *Liber Sententiarum* was the first step in this two-part process.

The defects of both the philosophers and theologians and the humanists that Cortesi specified in the *prooemium* of the *Liber* also occupied his attention several years later when he was composing his final work, the *De Cardinalatu* (published in 1510). In the *De Cardinalatu* Cortesi discussed the limits of both theologians and humanists in their preoccupation with only select elements of their disciplines. Before turning to the body of the *Liber,* where Cortesi put his ideals into practice, it will be valuable to complete the review of his thoughts on this problem as he developed them in the *De Cardinalatu.* [38]

In a discussion of preachers' belonging to religious orders, Cortesi condemned the mendicants' excessive concern for philosophy, especially for the natural sciences, which he believed provided only doubt and misinformation. Rather than spend their time studying such uncertain philosophical topics, Cortesi argued the preachers should direct their attention to Sacred Scripture, which contained certitude and truth. [39] In order to make their preaching more effective, however, they needed to turn to the rhetorical arts. Preachers had to know the *artificium dicendi* in order to make men hear and thereby follow their teachings. Indeed, God made use of the art of speaking as an ally in moving men to embrace the good. [40] Cortesi thus implied that there was a divine mandate for Christian preachers to learn and make use of rhetoric.

Cortesi was even-handed in his criticisms, however. Just as the preachers erred in their devotion to philosophy and their rejection of rhetoric, so the humanists displayed a similar narrowness. Cortesi went so far as to consider as heretics those humanists who shunned all theology and devoted themselves exclusively to letters. [41] He specifically complained of those in Rome who upset his stomach because they knew only a page or two of Cicero yet thought that this was enough learning for life. The humanists could not consider themselves learned without theological knowledge, especially knowledge of the writings of Aquinas. [42] Cortesi's desire to join humanist eloquence with theological truth was central to both the *Liber Sententiarum* and the *De Cardinalatu* and formed the rationale for the literary productions of his last years.

Cortesi provided in the body of the *Liber Sententiarum* a resolution of the concern with the dangerous separation of theological and humanist learning he had set forth in the *prooemium*. He did not propose any new doctrines, but rather used certain forms and stratagems to make theology an acceptable field of study to the humanists, especially those who were active in Rome. In analyzing the *Liber,* therefore, it is necessary to note how Cortesi made theology humanistic in form, and how he tried to provide in his exposition the material he believed his audience should possess. Cortesi intended for the *Liber* to be polemical; he addressed it to two different groups, and his aim was the reconciliation of opposite intellectual attitudes.

❦ II ❦

The organization of the *Liber Sententiarum,* or *Theologumenon omnium sententiarum typus* as Cortesi also termed it, follows the fourfold division established by Peter Lombard.[43] The first book discusses God, the Trinity, God's powers and attributes. The second deals with the Creation, the angels, demons, man, Original Sin, and the Fall of Man. Book III considers Christ as the savior of mankind, his attributes as God-man, his Passion, and concludes with a section on moral and theological virtues. The last book discusses the means of grace available to man, the sacraments as well as the Last Judgment, the Beatitudes, hell, and the resurrection of men. All these topics are central to Christian theology and are discussed at least summarily in the *Liber.* Although Cortesi made his work comprehensive in scope, covering all the topics outlined above, he avoided detailed expositions. Rather than lengthy discussions, the *Liber* provides the basic questions and arguments on each topic in as concise a form as possible. Naturally, some questions do receive greater attention than others because they are more fundamental to faith than others, but Cortesi made no attempt to treat all the problems equally. The importance of a question and the need for conciseness of presentation determined the *Liber*'s relatively small size (forty-six folios).

Cortesi accepted medieval opionion on the content and major aim of theology, and thus he devoted the first question in the *Liber* to the nature and material of theology itself. He commented that theology is a science with three subjects: God as creator of all, Christ as the perfect summation of all, and the sacraments, which concern all matters relating to man. As a science, theology deals with God and is, therefore, superior to all other sciences. It shares in both the contemplative and the active life. However, being primarily concerned with heavenly matters, theology is more properly contemplative than active or practical.[44] Cortesi concluded, as did the Scholastic theologians, by describing theology as a science primarily involved in contemplation, but he did so in language which was not that of the other scholastics.

The basic procedure Cortesi followed in the *Liber Sententiarum* was first to introduce a subject, such as the *De scientia Dei* (Distinction III of Book I), and then to deal with the important questions related to it: e.g., whether there is knowledge in God, whether God knows singulars, whether God knows things outside himself—all standard medieval formulations.[45] A series of marginal headings supplied the reader with the more traditional theological and philosophical terminology since the strict rules of classical word order and choice prevented Cortesi from using them. Each article moves systematically to consider each of the questions mentioned and does so without breaking up the body of any question. The views of ancient philosophers such as Plato and Aristotle and other non-Christian writers such as Averroës are summarized, as are those of a series of Christian theologians beginning with the Church Fathers, Latin and Greek. There is little direct citation of Scripture. Occasionally Cortesi uses his authorities dialectically. In the section on God's knowledge of singulars, he contrasts Aristotle's negative view with Aquinas's positive one, and then Aquinas with the Scotists, and finally Averroës's negative opinion with Algazel's and Avicenna's positive one. Cortesi concludes by giving the accepted opinion among Christians, that God does know singulars.[46]

Central to Cortesi's method was the blending of classical language and Christian meaning, as seen in Distinction III of Book IV, *De sacramento poenitentiae.*[47] In this distinction Cortesi organized under one heading not only penance and its subdivisions but also indulgences, thereby conforming to late medieval practice and especially to that of Aquinas.[48] However, in Cortesi the tripartite division of penance into *contritio, confessio,* and *satisfactio* becomes *contusio, confessio,* and *persolutio.*[49] Cortesi felt required to use the word *indulgentia,* but apologized for doing so (". . . eam indulgentiam [audeamus enim hoc verbo uti]"), no doubt because its connotation of remission of punishment was postclassical. He presented the opinion of Aquinas that indulgences have power "non modo in senatus foro sed etiam in ipso Dei iudicio," giving *senatus* here the meaning of "Church."[50] Similarly, he used such words as *eucharistia,* which had patristic warrant.

Cortesi's Latin in the *Liber* was neither Scholastic nor traditional Christian. The Latin of the Scholastics was a technical language with specific formulas and simplified syntax. It was essentially a nonliterary language which sought to express the abstractions of Greek philosophy with scientific precision. It avoided the metaphorical and rhetorical language of classical Latin, which the humanists prized and accepted as standard. Scholastic Latin developed closely from the translation of Greek philosophical, especially Aristotelian, vocabulary and ideas. New words were invented and old ones made to carry new meaning. It was a language invented for metaphysical speculation. All these qualities— formalistic, technical, nonliterary, and metaphysical—alienated humanists and caused them to reject centuries of scholastic learning at a pedagogical and methodological level. Humanists took the highroad linguistically and employed rhetorical devices, strict classical vocabulary, highly involved syntax; theirs was an aristocratic, or elitist, language as opposed to the technical, functional idiom of the Scholastics.[51] Cortesi's sentences are classical in form, relying on periodic sentence-structure, rhetorical questions and balances, and indirect discourse. The ideal is literary rather than technical—i.e., literary canons rather than the theological tradition of previous generations determine language. A comparison of Cortesi's sentences with any Scholastic, e.g., Aquinas, will show that Cortesi was actually more concise in his statements although not necessarily clearer.[52]

But style was only one way in which Cortesi followed his classical models. His choice of vocabulary, as noted above, especially separated him from his Christian predecessors. Behind this was Cortesi's desire to make the Christian Church and theology more harmonious with his classicism. A few examples will indicate his procedure. When discussing the power of the keys held by the pope and extended to priests Cortesi wrote:

> However, we say that a certain highest type of rule [*imperium*] was constituted in the Senate [the Church] to which the remaining [priests] submit [and] from which they obtain circumscribed rule [*dominatum*] over certain persons. However, since it would seem that the use of the heavenly keys requires some right of rule [*imperium*], for this reason we say that he who has the power of the highest rule [*imperium*] can use the same keys over everyone.[53]

The comparison of the indulgences to the treasury of the Church was common, but Cortesi's language was nontraditional:

> And so for this reason we speak of the sacrifice of Christ and the saints [*divorum*] as a certain treasury [*aerarium*] of the Church [*Reipublicae*], in that as in a vessel each one generally throws in revenue until it is filled. Nor do we say that there will be a completion, except in the funeral pyre of the burnt and ashen world. Wherefore, we say that a multitudinous supply of indulgences has come about.[54]

Cortesi translated discussions and controversies over these problems into spectacles, and the theologians into Christian gladiators:

> And many tunic-clad theologians [i.e., members of the religious orders], who like helmeted gladiators [*mirmillones*] or armed Thracians [*Thraces*] produced gladiatorial shows [*questiones disputatae?*] in the midst of the people, reject this gift of indulgences as useless, affirming that they seem to be striving for a useless gift.[55]

While Cortesi's conclusion affirming the value of indulgences was perfectly orthodox, his means of expressing this view separated him from the body of Scholastic theologians and joined him to humanist contemporaries and their classical models.

An instructive example of Cortesi's classicizing of a Scholastic opinion occurs in his discussion of the right of the state to baptize non-Christian children against the will of their parents. This question divided the Thomists and the Scotists. The Thomists argued that the parents' rights over their children should not be compromised by the state, while the Scotists favored the ultimate power of the government over its citizens. Cortesi followed Scotus's commentary on the *Sententiae* in supporting the power of the state.[56] Both argued that the civil authority had ultimate power to deal with its citizens' welfare. Scotus in his commentary made use of classical terminology in expounding a view that was consonant with the Roman judicial elements in the case. Cortesi, even though he partly accepted Scotus's reasoning, did not accept his specific formulation and changed the language of the opinion. In restating the arguments, Cortesi substituted a more classicized vocabulary. For him the rules of classical purity could be ignored only for the gravest reasons.

Cortesi's classicism had the effect of emphasizing the Roman quality of the Christian religion. Through Cortesi's language Christianity exhibited close ties with the culture of the ancient Roman world, especially Imperial Rome. Cortesi did not express concern for any danger that might result from such an equation of Christianity with pagan Rome. The union of Roman classicism and Christian beliefs so common to Renaissance Rome was given unique expression in the *Liber Sententiarum,* where the break between ancient culture and Christian teachings was reduced if not completely resolved. Language was Cortesi's device for uniting Christianity and classical culture.

In Cortesi's language Christ as man is portrayed as *sospitator quatenus chalmyde humana amictus* ("a savior wrapped in a human cloak") (f. 28r), and his mother, the *Dea mater* (ff. 11r, 29r), and her Immaculate Conception, as *absolutissimus conciliandi actus* ("the most perfect act of conciliation") (f. 11v). The opinions of the saints are rendered *sententiae heroum* (f. 35r). Aquinas, Cortesi's favorite Scholastic, is typified as the *Apollo Christianorum* (f. 17v), and is compared to the painter Apelles: *Divus Thomas qui ut in pictura Apelles praeclare sentit quid sit in dicendo satis* ("Saint Thomas, who as in a picture by Apelles outstandingly declares what is enough in speaking about a question") (f. 39v). Scotus is *Argus theologorum* (Argus was a hundred-eyed classical figure) (f. 28v); Augustine is *phyticus theologiae vates* ("the fruitful prophet of theology") (f. 33v). Priests become *flamen dialis* ("a priest of Jupiter") (f. 34v) and *flamen piator* ("a sacrificing priest") (f. 35v). A decree of the Church is *senatusconsultum* (f. 34v). A sacrament is *sacrum* (f. 33r). A church building is a *publicum delubrum* ("public temple" (f. 35v). Hell is *Orcus* (f. 36v) and *Stygius et Cocytus* (rivers of the Underworld) (f. 30v). Heresies are *perduelliones* ("treasons"), venial sin is *ignoscobilis tabes* ("forgivable sin"), and mortal sin is *capitalis tabes* ("deadly sin") (f. 35v). Specific theological terms are also altered: *divina patefatio* is "revelation" (f. 30v), *collatio* is "analogy" (f. 11r), *praesignatio* is "predestination" (f. 9v). *Sors,* which has mercantile connotations, denotes indulgences (f. 35r). Adam is called the *Phaëthon humani generis* (f. 21r), and Paris is transferred into the *Athenae Christianorum* (f. 24v).

Such phrases and circumlocutions have been judged by scholars as either a paganization or a trivialization of Christian thought.[57] But such scholars refuse to accept Cortesi's theological exposition on its own terms and to admit that it belongs to an ancient tendency in Christian literature. Cortesi's aim was to make theology part of the humanist classical culture. He chose the language of the Roman humanists, which he had helped to form, and applied it to a new discipline. He belonged to the Roman humanist tradition of transforming Christian topics and personages into their classical equivalents. We have already seen, in the poetic compositions of the *Coryciana,* how common this was. Analogous to Cortesi in procedure was Paolo Pompilio (d. 1490), a poet and member of Leto's academy who rewrote the Nicene Creed in classical verse and spoke of God as the *parens rerum* who created the world from Olympus.[58] Such classicizing was not without its critics in Renaissance Rome, but the humanists were willing to defend this procedure. Consider, for example, the short treatise by an unknown Roman humanist called Nicomachus from the 1460s. When speaking of the pagan gods Jove, Phoebus, and Mars in his writings, Nicomachus claimed that he was really referring to the saints Peter, Paul, and Jerome.[59]

Cortesi was optimistic about the Latin language as reconstructed by humanist theory. He believed that Latin, especially Ciceronian Latin, could express any idea or set of ideas without impairing comprehension.

Such an optimism underlay his belief that he could construct an elegant theology that would appeal to theologians and humanists. Cortesi applied his highly erudite knowledge of classical forms and vocabulary to Christian topics in the belief that such a classicizing could make Christian doctrines clear to their readers, and that those readers would take great pleasure in the erudition displayed in such writings. This humanist optimism made theology no different, at least formally, from any other discipline or topic.

In a broader historical context the archaizing employed by Cortesi and his fellow Roman humanists was neither unique to them nor opposed to the older traditions of Christian writers. Early Greek Christians had attempted to write on religious topics in good but archaic Greek.[60] In pursuing this aim they had found it necessary to use the terminology of Thucydides rather than specifically Christian, and later, vocabulary. Ironically, ancient pagan Greek writers used more specifically Christian terms in their writings than did some of their Christian contemporaries. The ancient Latin Christians, though somewhat less extremely, concurred with their Greek co-religionists in presenting Christian thought in the language of the pagan writers.[61] Behind these activities was the desire to write theology according to the best literary standards of the day and thereby make it acceptable to secular culture and appealing to the learned. Antitheses were glossed over through language. Christian history therefore supported Cortesi's method, as he himself noted in the *prooemium.*

Cortesi's aim and procedure can be compared to the classicizing of religious topics undertaken by artists in Rome in the High Renaissance. The tendency to present Christ and the saints as newly classicized heroes takes linguistic expression in Cortesi. His language and the pictorial language of Raphael, for example,[62] present Christ and the saints not as humble figures but as classicized, idealized persons with perfect human forms. Inspiring both Cortesi and Raphael was an archaeological attitude toward the past, the desire to find the best and reinterpret it in contemporary circumstances. Like humanist rhetoric, Raphael's images exalted and glorified. They sought not the model of the man of sorrows but Christ the king and glorified leader. Classical proportions and concepts of physical beauty removed the Virgin, Christ, and the saints from the iconic world of the Middle Ages and presented them as individualized classical heroes.[63] The juxtaposition of Raphael's *School of Athens* and the *Disputà* in the Vatican *Stanze della Segnatura* is a close parallel to Cortesi's *Liber.* While pagan and Christian are distinct in the pictorial cycle, their form is one and the same, and the unity between them is thereby expressly stated. Raphael and Cortesi shared the desire to reconcile not only classical and Christian culture but also differing philosophies in order to present a unique unity to their audiences.[64] The pictorial and literary languages these men utilized appealed to the cultivated elite of Rome.

❧ III ❧

The reform of theological language was only part of Cortesi's aim in writing the *Liber Sententiarum;* he was equally concerned with spreading Scholastic theological views among the humanists. This was part of a procedure of "popularization," insofar as Scholastic ideas, transferred into classical Latin, would become common among the humanists and used by them in their work. The attention paid to the Scholastic writers, most notably Aquinas, sets the *Liber* off from other humanist theological compositions, which either condemned Scholastic theology in general or ignored it altogether.[65] In the *Liber* Cortesi summarized the ideas of the major Scholastics and translated them into humanist Latin, thereby creating a form the humanists could easily assimilate and use. Cortesi established a set of standard scholastic formulations that would appeal to his readers because of their conciseness. The selectivity in his discussions of Scholastic writers was gauged to the sensibilities of his humanist readers. He chose those Scholastics whose ideas he felt a humanist must know in order to be fully educated.

The first method Cortesi used in the *Liber* to acquaint its audience with the Scholastic writers was the citation of a number of theologians followed by short designations of their party or order. Occasionally the religious orders are designated by the color of their garments: Franciscans are denoted as *ex caesia disciplina* ("from the gray order") (f. 8r). A similar form, short epithets, is used to characterize a theologian's major characteristics. Cortesi's judgment of Aquinas as a great conciliator and authority is seen in his references to him as he who *phisiologiam cum theologia coniunxit* ("joined natural philosophy with theology") (f. 18r); he who is *maturus et sanus theologus* (f. 12v); the *theologorum parcissimus* ("most economical of theologians") (f. 25r); he who *orthodoxeo senatui tantum authoritatis impertit* ("shares so much authority in the Orthodox Church") (f. 34r); he who is *homo in omni theologia tardigradus* ("a man slow-paced [i.e., careful?] in all theology") (f. 42r); *Divus Thomas lunensi marmore candidior* ("Saint Thomas brighter than the marble of Luna") (f. 25v); and *Divus Thomas ut musicus inter obstrepentium voces nihilo minus recte canit* ("Saint Thomas, like a musician among the voices of the noisemakers, sings correctly") (f. 38v). Scotus is called *doctissimus omnium* (f. 21v), *pugnacissimus omnium*

(f. 25r), *acerrimus bellator* (f. 12v), and *theologici principatus avidus et capax* (f. 34r), indicating modified respect for the Franciscan and a general preference for Aquinas. Durandus of Saint-Pourçain (a fourteenth-century Dominican theologian) becomes *in theologia magnus mediator* (f. 21v), *pseudo-Aquinas* (f. 41v), and *maturius et verius theologus* (f. 25v). Ockham is described as *distinctus et tunicatus thorocato Scoto* ("distinguished and covered with the Scotist cuirass") (f. 25r) and *egregie versutus scriptor* ("an exceptionally clever writer") (f. 25v). Not improperly, Peter Lombard is styled *dux sententiarum* (f. 38r); Anselm of Canterbury is labeled *locuples* ("rich") (f. 25r); Ambrose is *litteratissimus theologorum* (an important identification since he was a Church Father) (f. 22v); Alexander of Hales is *in theologia sincerus et sanus* (f. 21v); and Richard of Media Villa is *locuples et fusus theologus* (f. 33v) and *theologiae polyhistor* (f. 43r).

Similar treatment is extended to the pagan philosophers. Aristotle is *princeps philosophorum* (f. 28v), *in omnium natura vaferrimus auctor* (f. 6v), and *syllogismorum Daedalus* (probably indicating some reserve—his metaphysics could not reach its final end) (f. 18v). Cortesi also provides a brief outline of the major Greek philosophical schools: *id quod Platoni placet, vehementer Aristoteli displicere, et quod a Stoicis prebetum, a Peripateticorum familia refelli* ("that which pleases Plato greatly displeases Aristotle, and what is approved by the Stoics is rejected by the family of the Peripatetics") (f. 12r). Most charming of all, Cortesi refers to Epicurus as the philosopher *quem ego Paridem philosophorum voco* ("whom I call the Paris of philosophers") (f. 6v).

Cortesi's greatest energies, however, were devoted not to naming and finding clever characterizing epithets for the Scholastic and pagan writers, but to presenting their varying views, analyzing them briefly, and supplying a critical evaluation of their opinions and their orthodoxy. Apart from the sections on such questions as the Trinity and the Person of Christ, which had been settled by the early Church Fathers and to which later theologians added little, Cortesi's major emphasis was on the great Scholastic thinkers. In accordance with the medieval formula of *philosophia ancilla theologiae*, he elevated theology above the sciences because of its superior subject matter.[66] Aquinas and Scotus, therefore, can properly be compared to the ancient philosophers Plato and Aristotle.[67] Indeed, in Cortesi's view Christian thinkers surpassed all the pagans in every matter save eloquence.[68]

In judging the acceptability of various opinions, Cortesi advocated the following principle: *Nos vero qui non argumentorum numerum sed electum quaerimus* ("We seek not the number of arguments but the best").[69] He did not fully explain in the *Liber* how this principle operated, but a few years later, in the *De Cardinalatu,* he expanded his discussion of it. When explaining the popularity of Averroë's views on the unity of the intellect, Cortesi argued that those learned men who had shown exemplary morals should be followed more closely than those who had been merely learned. In particular, the saints should not be opposed lightly.[70] Furthermore, Cortesi advised that consideration of both the morals and the number of followers a saint had should be taken as the rule by which to judge the acceptability of his opinion. Cortesi's general idea seems to have been some form of *consensus doctorum* or *consensus doctorum sanctorum.* Such a consensus did not remove the need to judge critically among the varying views but it did give a basis for making a decision.[71] However, Cortesi believed that the judgment of the Church on any topic must be accepted as final; to oppose it was heresy.[72] Theological discussion must always develop in submission to the authority of the Church.

In dealing with specific doctrines in the *Liber* Cortesi primarily divided opinion along a Thomist-Scotist axis, although he gave attention to a variety of other Scholastic thinkers as well.[73] He canvassed Aquinas's and Scotus's views and those of their followers and often stated his preference. While Aquinas's opinions were not in themselves sufficient to elicit Cortesi's automatic assent, they did carry great weight with him. He was especially drawn to Aquinas because of what he termed Aquinas's lucid treatment of topics. He lamented, for example, that Aquinas's clear explanation of God's omnipotence, which avoided excesses in speculation, had been ignored or corrupted by others seeking complicated theories.[74]

The differences between Aquinas and Scotus described in the *Liber* revolved not on fundamental doctrines of the Christian faith but rather on details. Neither Aquinas nor Scotus denied the Last Judgment, but they did disagree on whether the damned would see Christ during it. Scotus and his followers rejected Aquinas's argument that seeing God was a joy that must be denied the damned. Cortesi, following the lead of the majority of Scholastic theologians, accepted Aquinas's view.[75] He judged Aquinas to be generally in accord with the teachings of the Church on this matter. On the question whether any good results from sexual relations in marriage, Cortesi found Aquinas's positive view more in keeping with the teachings of the Church than Scotus's negative response.[76]

Cortesi's general preference for Thomism extended even to its intellectualistic tenets. In discussing the locus of happiness, Cortesi accepted Aquinas's arguments for the intellect and rejected Scotus's voluntaristic view.[77] Cortesi argued similarly in the *De Cardinalatu* when he defined contemplation in essentially intellectual terms as learning and study.[78] Despite the voluntaristic emphasis of humanist rhetorical theory, Cortesi's dependence on a highly literate, indeed erudite, Latin as displayed in the *Liber* and the *De Cardinalatu* appealed essentially to the intellect. Similarly, Cortesi accepted the intellectualistic tenets of Aristotelian psychology.[79] However, Cortesi did not detail his views on the power of the intellect or the role of the will.

Occasionally Cortesi set off Aquinas's and Scotus's views on an unsettled point. He discussed the important question of the Immaculate Conception, for example, which severely divided the Franciscan and Dominican schools of theology and had been a source of much contention throughout the quattrocento. Sixtus IV, a Franciscan, supported the doctrine, as did his nephew, Julius II, also a Franciscan. It was a topic of much debate in Rome in Cortesi's youth.[80] In discussing it Cortesi canvassed the various opinions offered by Aquinas, Scotus, and their followers but left the question open since the Church had not given a final statement.[81] Occasionally, different views were judged to be acceptable.[82] When Cortesi lacked the final decision of the Church, he preferred to provide no definitive statement and merely to indicate where there was agreement or divergence so that his readers might judge.[83]

Cortesi's treatment of the Scholastic theologians was analogous to the *viri illustres* tradition used by ancient writers and humanists to describe intellectual and literary developments. Jerome had employed the form in describing Christian writers in the fifth century.[84] It allowed the author to provide a short series of biographies and critical estimates of his subjects. Cortesi himself had followed this procedure in the *De hominibus doctis,* in which he judged Renaissance literary figures. The Scholastics he discussed in the *Liber* functioned as the clerical or theological equivalents to the writers he had judged in the *De hominibus doctis;* however, in the *Liber,* orthodoxy and clarity rather than fidelity to Ciceronian style determined his choices.

❧ IV ❧

Cortesi generally ignored contemporary theological questions and writers in the *Liber,* just as he had ignored living writers in the *De hominibus doctis.* This lack of contemporary representatives stemmed from the humanist annoyance with the excesses and controversies of modern theologians. The one major exception was Cortesi's treatment of Pico della Mirandola. We have already seen how Cortesi cast the *prooemium* and the ultimate justification for the *Liber* as a response to

Pico's attacks on humanist Latin. Cortesi gave some consideration to Pico's views in the *Liber* and used him as an important model in his *De Cardinalatu*. Moreover, Cortesi was in the process of rehabilitating Pico's reputation among the Roman humanists and clerics, and this procedure required an investigation of Pico's theological views. [85]

Cortesi's treatment of Pico in the *Liber* centered on Innocent VIII's condemnation of the *900 Conclusiones* Pico planned to debate in Rome in 1489. His aim, therefore, was limited; he did not intend to offer a general defense of the various components of Pico's theology. The men who condemned Pico were Scholastic theologians and they censured him on specifically Scholastic questions. [86] Consequently, Cortesi treated Pico as a Scholastic theologian and not as an exponent of humanist theology. Close friendship with Pico and great esteem for him as a learned and holy man motivated Cortesi, not a feeling that humanist theology was somehow included in the condemnation of Pico.

The portrait of Pico which emerges from the *Liber* is a positive one despite the pope's censure of him. Although Cortesi rejected Pico's criticism of humanist literary theories, he did consider Pico a more stylistically elegant theologian (*litteratior*) than the Scholastics. Compared with the writings of the Scholastics, Pico's style was superior. [87] Cortesi discussed three of Pico's thirteen condemned propositions. All three concerned divergences from standard Scholastic formulas. In his discussion Cortesi supported the Thomistic or commonly held Scholastic views challenged by Pico, but he did not discuss them in detail. He stated the accepted opinion and tried to show that Pico's refusal to follow it did not betray any heterodox tendencies.

The first of Pico's condemned theses discussed by Cortesi was whether God could have assumed whatever nature he wished in the Incarnation. Pico had challenged as contrary to God's rationalism the general Scholastic opinion that God could have assumed any form, even that of the devil or an inanimate object, and still have saved man. Cortesi attributed Pico's unacceptable view to his age at the time of the disputation (he was only twenty-three years old then) and to his excessive reliance on dialectics. [88] In Cortesi's judgment, Pico's own learning and pride had seduced him to propose novel ideas.

Cortesi explained the second disputed point in a similar manner. Pico had denied that Christ actually descended into hell physically after the Crucifixion, a view which contradicted Aquinas and most Scholastic writers. In his defense Cortesi maintained that Pico's intention was not to preach heresy but to enhance his fame. [89] Cortesi mentioned without comment the third of Pico's condemned theses included in the *Liber;* it dealt with the type of veneration which should be rendered to the cross.[90] Since only three of the thirteen condemned *conclusiones* appear in the *Liber,* we may assume that Cortesi did not believe that the others seriously compromised Pico's orthodoxy.

Cortesi's clearest statement in defense of Pico's orthodoxy came in his discussion of the Spanish prelate Pedro Garcia's attack on Pico in his work the *Determinationes magistrales* (1489).[91] A doctor of theology from the Sorbonne, Garcia, a close associate of Cardinal Rodrigo Borgia and subsequently Vatican librarian, represented the conservative Scholastic theologians in Rome who opposed Pico's syncretistic theological tendencies. Cortesi's answer to Garcia's charges concentrated on Pico's personal rehabilitation and did not offer a general defense of Pico's system. Certainly Cortesi did not find Garcia's work a threat to his own procedures in the *Liber* or in any way antihumanistic in intent.

Cortesi conceded that Garcia had made some good points against Pico in his text, but denied that the bishop was correct in assigning heresy to Pico.[92] Cortesi disassociated himself from Garcia and official Rome's condemnation. In his final judgment on Pico, Cortesi denied that he was in any way heterodox, as his Roman Scholastic enemies had charged, and argued that he had been led by excessive dependence on dialectics, the tool of the Scholastics, to propose unacceptable opinions. In no sense did Cortesi perceive in Pico's troubles any danger to humanist theological activity. To Cortesi personally, Pico's fame and position were in no way compromised by his condemnation, and Pico remained for him the *doctissimus Italorum* who was exemplary in learning and holiness.

Cortesi's defense of Pico also reflected his essential sympathy with his friend's aims. The type of syncretizing and conciliating which Pico had practiced in his *Oratio* and the *900 Conclusiones* and which humanist theological and philosophical writers favored resembled Cortesi's own approach in the *Liber.*[93] As did Pico, Cortesi felt the need to reconcile ancient and Christian ideals as well as the various theological schools' views. Both dealt with a variety of theological and philosophical opinions in the hope of arriving at some norm which could be accepted and used by others. Obviously, Cortesi's and Pico's approaches differed in both depth and comprehensiveness. Lacking any interest in the esoteric or Eastern and cabalistic wisdom that Pico felt to be important, Cortesi subscribed to what may be termed traditional currents and ideas. He was always aware of the limits imposed by his clerical-humanist audience in Rome, where conservative theological views were strong and, for career purposes, safer. Still, the conciliatory tendencies of the two men were marked; they ignored differences among various authorities or explained them away in order to arrive at the most acceptable norm.

By blending Christian theology and humanistic Latin, Cortesi fought
the common humanistic disinterest in theological and philosophical
questions and the professionals' hermetic approach to their disciplines.
He was both an apologist for Christian theology to the humanists and a
propagandist for humanist values against the technical barbarisms and
dissensions of the theologians. He judged theology a study that should
be appreciated by all Christians, and he tried to establish that theological language could be made appealing to the humanists. The *Liber Sententiarum* was intended to prove that humanists could embrace the
values of theology without fatally compromising their literary and historical ideals. Further, Cortesi's new theological language was an admonition to the philosophers and theologians that they had a duty to
make their subjects more up-to-date and acceptable to the nonprofes-
sionals. He believed that a need existed for a new presentation of theology
and philosophy which, while offering no new doctrines, would give
these disciplines a new voice: a voice of erudite, pleasing Latinity free
of extended disputation.

Cortesi wrote his theological text primarily for the humanists and
clerics of Rome. With ever more humanists taking holy orders for
career purposes and clerics wishing to absorb humanist culture for the
same reason, theology offered itself as the point of contact and opposition. By classicizing Christian, and especially Scholastic, theological
thought, Cortesi demonstrated that one need not reject humanism to
express the essential teachings of the Church nor discard elements of
Scholastic thought and orthodoxy to speak and write like a humanist.
Moreover, Cortesi's *Liber Sententiarum* could make the humanists'
task of incorporation into the Church's establishment much easier.
However, the humanist focus on morality and practical action which
characterized other contemporary writings was lacking in the *Liber*.
Cortesi accepted the centrality of morality in learning but he discussed
it in the *De Cardinalatu* rather than the *Liber*. As an introduction to
the *De Cardinalatu*, the *Liber* offered the theological ideals which would
provide a basis for action. How they were implemented in the *De
Cardinalatu* will be discussed in a subsequent chapter;[94] here we must
note that the *Liber* and the *De Cardinalatu* were united by a dependence
on broad learning as the basis for moral action. Cortesi emphasized the
practical aspects of virtue and learning; they permit a man to judge a
situation and make a morally correct choice. Consequently, in the *De
Cardinalatu* Cortesi defined contemplation as study and religious duty—
essentially practical matters. Through his learning the humanist-cleric

who is the hero of the *De Cardinalatu* understands the reasons for acting well and develops the means to do so. While this is essentially an intellectualistic approach, with the will following the intellect, the imperative for action remains foremost.

Cortesi believed that his work had to have a moral effect, but by defining morality along essentially rationalist lines he compromised his aim. Cortesi's theology is less a matter of beauty providing the impetus to moral action than of erudition impressing by its breadth and ingenuity. This is a *theologia erudita* or *docta* rather than a *theologia rhetorica*. [95] Cortesi's theology was meant for an elite audience and he hoped that his works would respond to the needs of that audience. The spirituality that could arise from his theology, or that it could aid, was erudite, aristocratic, and essentially formal—an approximate mirror of Rome itself. The danger in this theological outlook was that it could lose itself in its own cleverness and conceits; such a theology could be reduced to a series of short, elegant aphorisms and such a spirituality could be transformed into the general advice to act in accordance with reason and decorum. This was a danger many Roman humanists and clerics did not escape.

❦ VI ❦

The *Liber Sententiarum* was applicable to more than the particular problems and needs of Rome; it had perhaps even more readers outside Rome and north of the Alps. Northern humanists, in the midst of their struggle with the established Scholasticism of the universities over the nature of theology and their right to discuss theological topics, found the *Liber* a convenient support for their goals. Of the four editions of the *Liber*, one was Italian (Rome, 1504), and three were non-Italian (Paris, 1513; Basel, 1513 and 1540). In introductory letters[96] to the Basel editions, the German humanists Konrad Peutinger and Beatus Rhenanus praised Cortesi for his elegant theology, which they argued recalled the writings of the Church Fathers, and advocated Cortesi's method as a model for all those who wished to unite eloquence with theology.

Peutinger's and Beatus's enthusiasm for the *Liber*, however, was expressed before they came under the influence of Desiderius Erasmus, who would have had a very different view of the value of Cortesi's theological tract.[97] Although Erasmus did not specifically cite the *Liber* in any of his writings, there are indications that he knew it and did not approve of it. In the *Ciceronianus*, where Cortesi is condemned for his strict adherence to Ciceronian imitation, Erasmus cites a series

of classical renderings of Christian terms which might have been extracted from the *Liber* or based on it.[98] For Erasmus the type of classicizing Cortesi represented was simply neopaganism and was therefore
a danger to the Christian faith. He portrayed it as an unacceptable procedure for Christians and as dangerous as the contentiousness of the
Scholastics.

Erasmus's judgment, like that of modern commentators who have accused Cortesi of trivializing, underestimated Cortesi's historical context.
Cortesi responded to the theological and humanistic needs of High
Renaissance Rome and its humanist and clerical inhabitants. The *Liber*
was the culmination of one aspect of the linguistic theories of Renaissance humanism. Cortesi had succeeded in making the Christian theologian speak elegant Latin, no mean accomplishment. There was a
great deal of intellectual agility in Cortesi's work which characterized
one element of humanist Christian thought in Rome in the years before
the advent of Luther.[99]

Cortesi's *Liber Sententiarum* represented the high point of humanist
theological classicizing and an essential acceptance on the part of humanists of certain elements in medieval theology, but there were other
writers from the same humanist circles in Rome who would accept
neither classicizing nor dependence on Scholastic writers in theological
discussions. Roman humanism betrayed a greater diversity in its theological thought than in other scholarly topics. Acting as a seemingly
polar opposite to the *Liber Sententiarum* was Adriano Castellesi's *De
Vera Philosophia,* one of the more problematic texts originating in
Roman humanist circles.

7

Scriptural Skepticism

Cortesi's *Liber Sententiarum* provided a clear statement of the classical tradition of Roman humanism in a theological context. It furnished an aristocratic, learned audience with an aristocratic, learned theology that avoided controversies and subtleties and expounded the glories of its subject. In its classicizing and in its willingness to accept, at least in a pragmatic and modified fashion, elements of High Scholasticism, it represented one pole in Roman humanist thought. In the very humanist circles frequented by Cortesi, however, a radically different approach to religion was proposed by Cardinal Adriano Castellesi, one of the few humanist members of the Renaissance College of Cardinals, in his *De Vera Philosophia* (1507).[1] Castellesi implicitly rejected Cortesi's accommodation with Scholasticism as well as his concentration on the use of essentially literary principles in his presentation of theology. Castellesi did not follow the classicizing trend in theology, but he developed his ideas from humanist elements, especially the revival of patristic studies and a suspicion of the value of human speculation in religious matters. To these he joined strong emphasis on Sacred Scripture and faith as the sole sources of truth. The appearance of *De Vera Philosophia* demonstrated the variety of intellectual stratagems employed by Roman humanists in their theological thought on the eve of the Reformation.

Castellesi's *De Vera Philosophia* belongs to a tradition of anti-intellectualism, antirationalism and antiphilosophy which appeared periodically among Christian writers, especially during times of great philosophical and literary acitivity. From Tertullian through Bernard of Clairvaux to Castellesi's contemporary Girolamo Savonarola, a variety of Christian thinkers exhibited a suspicion of secular learning and exalted the uniqueness of faith and revelation over all human knowledge.[2] Humanists since the time of Petrarch had echoed these themes in their controversies with professional philosophers and theologians. The last decades of the quattrocento and the first of the cinquecento contributed a new element to this antirationalism, partly as a response to the political and social breakdown of Italy. Thinkers began to question the ability of human reason to comprehend and solve contemporary problems. They turned to astrology and prophecy and away from rational calculation as a means of discovering answers to the insecurities of the world.[3] In religion this attitude manifested itself in a rejection of the religious establishment with its philosophical theology and in an emphasis on a direct, nonintellectual approach to faith. A skeptical attitude toward all human knowledge and an absolute certainty through belief rather than a carefully developed rational theology attracted many. In the Renaissance, skepticism was a weapon of religion.[4] Even intellectuals opposed reason and learning.[5] The fideistic and antiphilosophical diatribes of Girolamo Savonarola in Florence, for example, attracted the adherence of humanists and philosophers.[6]

Castellesi subscribed to many of these fideistic and antirational trends. However, in expressing his doubts about the value of human reason and in defending the autonomy of faith, he relied on the antiphilosophical traditions of humanism and the study of patristics. In accordance with general humanist tendencies, Roman humanists distrusted the ability of human philosophy, especially metaphysics and natural philosophy, to aid men in leading moral lives. In their deep commitment to classical antiquity they developed an antipathy toward those elements in philosophy which stressed metaphysical speculation that concentrated on literary and philological studies.[7] The humanists found in the *studia humaniora* a better guide for leading a moral life than could be found in philosophy, an attitude which was no doubt bolstered by the excesses perpetrated by some Scholastic philosophers and theologians in Rome. The entire tradition of the Roman academies centered on literature and archaeology and shunned philosophical speculation.

The second humanist tradition in Rome which Castellesi used in developing his fideistic and scriptural ideas was the study of patristics.[8] The early Church Fathers played an important part in humanist spirituality and in criticisms of contemporary theology. It was a logical extension of the humanists' study of pagan antiquity to move to consider the exponents of early Christian thought. The strong rhetorical flavor of the early Christian writers also made them a natural object of humanist investigation. In Rome, patristic studies even included translations of Greek texts, which had been inaugurated by Nicholas V.[9] By the beginning of the cinquecento the Vatican Library was offering to the humanist community a large number of patristic writings and they were being borrowed by many, including Castellesi.[10] In Castellesi's case the reading of the Fathers had a profound effect on his religious attitudes.

The *De Vera Philosophia* is really a patristic primer containing excerpts from the writings of the four Latin Doctors of the Church—Augustine, Ambrose, Jerome, and Gregory the Great. Castellesi arranged these selections as an attack on Scholasticism and, to a lesser extent, the humanists' exaltation of eloquence. The cardinal took from his sources several key ideas, including a reliance on Sacred Scripture as the sole source of religious truth, skepticism toward the value of human learning and reason, and an emphasis on the primacy of the will over the intellect. It was an idiosyncratic and unbalanced approach to the Church Fathers, but it served Castellesi's ultimate purposes of the glorification of Scripture, the affirmation of the priority and independence of faith, and the requirement of moral action as confirmation of faith. Castellesi's patristic thinking was conservative insofar as it relied on the most common Fathers and did not seek out less well-known Latin or Greek writers.

Other influences in Rome might have moved Castellesi to construct an attack on human reason and a defense of faith. As a Hebrew scholar of some note, Castellesi would have been familiar with the circle of men, including Giles of Viterbo and the Franciscan Pietro Galatino (1464-1540), in which a variety of religious traditions intermingled.[11] This group manifested strong mystical and Biblical tendencies, especially the study of the Cabala, which worked against the claims of rationalism.[12] While these studies did not lead to any organized break with Scholasticism, they did instill a critical attitude toward many of the excesses of philosophical theology. Castellesi's dependence on such activities must remain conjectural, however, for we have no direct proof of his attitudes toward mysticism or radical Biblicism.

Similarly, Castellesi's mastery of Ciceronian style, which had accounted for his succcess in the Curia, would have provided him with an important source of ancient skeptical thought. Recent scholarship has established the importance of Cicero in transmitting elements of Academic Skepticism to Renaissance readers before the discovery of the Pyrrhonian texts of Sextus Empiricus.[13] Although Castellesi's skepticism and scripturalism had essentially Christian roots, his sources, especially Augustine, had in their turn been significantly influenced by Cicero and his writings. Either directly or indirectly Castellesi must have been influenced by the skeptical elements in Cicero's works.

Another possible influence on Castellesi was the rhetorical skepticism of writers like Lorenzo Valla.[14] This form of skeptical argumentation derived from the Fathers, especially Lactantius, who in his *Divine Institutes* developed this technique after the pattern of Academic Skepticism. Lactantius used skepticism in a highly rhetorical manner to deny the pretensions of philosophy. The opinions and arguments of the various philosophers were turned against them to prove their insecurity and falsehood. Philosophy was used to destroy philosophy, reason to obliterate reason; only faith and Scripture could provide truth. The elements that constituted the opposing philosophical systems were analyzed and systematically exposed as untrue. The rhetorical skeptics' approach to philosophical teachings and their refutation was much more careful than Castellesi's, which relied simply on denying the value of human reason rather than on proving the statements made. Nevertheless, there were definite similarities between Castellesi's and the rhetorical skeptic's aims and approaches.

❦ I ❦

The little information that is available on the genesis of *De Vera Philosophia* comes from Castellesi himself. The treatise was first published in Bologna in 1507 and was dedicated to Castellesi's major benefactor, King Henry VII of England.[15] In the dedication Castellesi related the events that caused him to compile the *De Vera Philosophia*. Since his youth, he commented, he had heard learned Christians proclaim that in order to understand Scripture a man needed the philosophy of Aristotle and that Aristotle and the other philosophers were in heaven. These same men had claimed that those theologians who were ignorant of Aristotle and did not use human reason in their theological studies could not understand Sacred Scripture. In his own experience Castellesi had found theological students and members of the religious orders to be more learned in human philosophy than in Scripture itself.[16] Dissatisfied with this situation, Castellesi said he turned to the Latin Doctors of the Church and scrutinized their writings for guidance in matters of faith and salvation. From their books he extracted certain statements which he believed were needed by a Christian to develop a proper understanding of Scripture.[17]

Although specifics are lacking in this prologue, some general points do emerge. First, Castellesi was recalling not a recent event but something he had experienced over a long period of time, and this indicated that the cardinal had given much thought to his response. Second, Castellesi probably framed the statements he reported in an extreme form that allowed him the freedom to stress his opposite position with greater vehemence. Further, his specific references to Aristotle and his mention of the religious orders point to the Scholastic theologians and philosophers as his major opponents as those against whom he had developed his readings. Plato and other Greek and Roman thinkers are condemned in the body of the *De Vera Philosophia,* but it is Aristotle who elicits Castellesi's primary attention.

In a subsequent edition, the Dominican Cyprianus Benetus of Aragon (d. 1522) wrote a letter of support which was published as a second introduction. Benetus was a Parisian doctor of theology and Castellesi's chaplain.[18] He taught at the University of Rome and in later years wrote a defense of the Eucharist against Martin Luther.[19] Like his patron, Benetus was a student of the Church Fathers. He had edited a collection of writings by Athanasius, Cassiodorus, Cyprian, and other early Christians (1500),[20] a fact which indicated not only his essential sympathy for Castellesi's undertaking but perhaps also his help in producing the *De Vera Philosophia.*[21] In his introduction, Benetus echoed the position that only "true philosophy," i.e., the teachings of Scripture, can lead a Christian to grace and salvation. He praised Castellesi's short work as an ornate, learned, and practical compendium which could prove valuable in leading the reader to the truth.[22] He noted that he had demonstrated the work's utility in his courses at the University of Rome, where he used the *De Vera Philosophia* as a tool to attack Plato, Aristotle, and the other philosophers. His teaching had met with such success that his students had requested that he sponsor a new edition of the work, a task he willingly undertook.[23]

Benetus's short statements are instructive. The mention of his teaching at the University of Rome with the aid of the *De Vera Philosophia* is an indication that the suspicions Castellesi had expressed about philosophical theology could be found even among the most outstanding representatives of Scholasticism, the Dominicans. As a writer and theologian, Benetus was manifestly traditional and conservative, yet even he must have been tried by the excessive philosophical speculations that accompanied much contemporary Scholastic thought. His introduction indicates that there was a ready audience in Rome, and in religious circles, for Castellesi's strictures.

Castellesi's method in the *De Vera Philosophia* was a simple one. He selected passages from the writings of the four Latin Doctors of the Church that expressed the exaltation of Scripture, the supremacy of faith, and the denigration of human reason and learning. In order to give order to these selections, he organized them into a series of interlocking statements or introductions. As noted above, the choice of the four Latin Doctors was a conservative one. Castellesi ignored the Greek Fathers, whose works he could read in the original, as well as other Latin writers such as Tertullian and Lactantius, who could have served his purposes well. This selectivity may indicate that he believed that the views expressed would be more acceptable and stronger if bolstered by the most common and authoritative sources. Castellesi arranged these excerpts along specific themes—e.g., what faith is, what its place in man's life is, what ought to be believed, the idea that all philosophers are in hell, and praise of Sacred Scripture.

Castellesi favored the use of short excerpts to express an opinion. In his brief rewriting of canon law, the *De Romanae Ecclesiae potestate* (*ca.* 1492,) he brought together a series of propositions from canon law organized along lines similar to the *De Vera Philosophia* and written in humanistic Latin.[24] In his popular history of the Latin language, the *De sermone latino,* he quoted heavily from ancient authors, and in the *De modo loquendi,* he collected classical quotations, especially from Cicero, as a textbook of Latin style.[25] In the case of the *De Vera Philosophia* Castellesi favored this procedure because it allowed him to base his statements on authorities rather than argumentation and thereby to gain maximum acceptance.

While few of the words in the *De Vera Philosophia* are Castellesi's, the organization of the treatise presents his own views; he made the Latin Doctors speak for him.[26] Certainly, complete fidelity to his sources was not Castellesi's primary intention. Since he no doubt felt that he was expressing their theological essence, he saw no need to provide a complete, impartial exposition of the full theology of his various authorities. Nor was he anxious to establish an impartial balance within the text. While a variety of the works of the four Doctors are represented, they are not evenly distributed. Of the approximately 582 selections in the *De Vera Philosophia,* no less than 394 are taken from Augustine's writings or from works attributed to him. Ambrose is represented by 73 selections, while Jerome, with 66 selections, and Gregory, with 49, receive less attention. The *De Vera Philosophia* expresses an essentially Augustinian conception of faith and knowledge.

Castellesi's approach to Augustine was solidly humanistic. Despite the African bishop's popularity in the Middle Ages, the humanists in a sense rediscovered him. His rhetorical education and his non-Aristotelian and nondialectical approach to theological questions supplied a model to the humanists in their attempt to construct a new *theologia rhetorica.* The humanists, for their part, tended to interpret him to fit their specific needs. They ignored his dogmatic writings in favor of his defense of secular learning in the *De Doctrina Christiana* and in his autobiography. The humanists ignored Augustine's polemical writings because they addressed questions that did not interest them. The humanists' Augustine was a very different saint and teacher from the chief dogmatic theologian of the Scholastics.

A one-sided interpretation of Augustine emerges from the *De Vera*

Philosophia. In Castellesi's work Augustine expresses the central position of faith in all aspects of life, the essential priority of the will over the intellect, and the ultimate importance of Sacred Scripture over all other forms of knowledge.[27] Castellesi approaches Augustine in a nondogmatic and nonphilosophical manner. Neo-Platonic vocabulary and ideas do appear occasionally in the *De Vera Philosophia,* but their metaphysical implications are ignored. The doctrinal character of much of Augustine's theology, such as the nature of grace, remained outside Castellesi's purview. While Pelagianism and Arianism do appear in the text, it is not their doctrines that are discussed but their impudence toward Sacred Scripture. All of this underlines the hortatory and moral nature of the *De Vera Philosophia.*

❧ II ❧

The four books of the *De Vera Philosophia* progress from a general treatment of faith to a final praise of Sacred Scripture and are connected by a continual denigration of human reason and secular learning. The first book establishes what faith is and how man attains it, and details the various relationships between intellect, faith, and authority. It has the most theoretical cast of the four books. The second emphasizes the results of sin, especially its deleterious effect on the human intellect, and discusses how man can overcome the limits of a flawed nature; in general this book displays a greater concern for the dynamics of faith than does the first. The third book discusses how Sacred Scripture should be studied, in what spirit it should be approached, and its proper use. The last book consists of a systematic attack on all human knowledge, especially philosophy, and a presentation of the true philosophy, i.e., Sacred Scripture. It concludes with a section devoted to the praise of Scripture. Throughout its sections the treatise presents faith and Scripture as the unique sources of Christian life and moral action.

Castellesi begins the *De Vera Philosophia* in Augustinian fashion by noting that man's fear of his mortality leads him to have faith in God.[28] This faith is central to all Christians since it is belief in Christ. It stands apart from and above all human knowledge and reason. Indeed, all understanding flows from faith since it opens the intellect to divine matters. Faith is central to man and permeates every aspect of life. Castellesi follows Augustine in specifying three types of faith. The first governs matters believed but never known, such as the events of past history; the second, things understood as soon as they are believed; and the third, those matters believed and then understood, such as the divine mysteries.[29] This final, religious, faith depends on God's inspiration of a man's will and is thus independent of the intellect; its divine origin accounts for faith's superiority to all human things.

Although human reason can provide a knowledge of inferior matters, Castellesi judges it worthless for understanding the spiritual truths a Christian needs.[30] Only Scripture can provide the believer with the means to achieve salvation. Reason for Castellesi is a severely limited instrument, incapable of understanding or contributing to man's spiritual needs since it can grasp only the transitory and not the eternal, which is God. Its complex operations produce nothing of value and contrast with the simplicity of faith, which offers truth. The history of Christian heresies proves that reason's defects render it a danger to the believer and the Church, causing men to prefer their own opinions to the truth contained in Sacred Scripture.[31] Reason gives men false pride in their abilities and turns them away from God. It therefore stands opposed to the truth of Scripture, which comes from God and is expressed independently of human reason.

The first book concludes with another important Augustinian theme, the position of the Catholic Church in a Christian's faith. The authority of the Catholic Church guarantees and nurtures faith. It does so through expounding the Scripture, through the universal traditions of the Church, and through the particular instructions given the Church by God.[32] While Scripture teaches man what he must do in order to be saved, it is on the authority of the Catholic Church that he accepts Scripture as authoritative. The Church is the final guarantor of faith and the truth of Scripture.[33] This dependence on the Church provides an objective check to faith by excluding a subjective reading of Scripture and an individual interpretation of its teachings. What one Christian believes must be what all Christians believe, and the Catholic Church defines the content of this belief. The correctness of a Christian's faith is measurable against a perfect standard.

Book II of the *De Vera Philosophia* shifts from a discussion of faith in general to the moral good that results from faith and Scripture. Castellesi relies on Augustine's Neo-Platonic views for the moral criterion used in evaluating knowledge: All knowledge must assist man in doing good.[34] To live virtuously man must purge his soul of the filth of this world and turn his attention to God.[35] The accumulation of riches, the search for nobility, and the striving for eloquence blind man to the simplicity of the Scripture and cause him to reject its truth. Purged of these worldly desires, the Christian soul rises to a new level, that of knowing God.[36] This purgation allows the soul to behold God, which is the ultimate gift of faith. But faith leads to and requires purity of the soul since sin prevents the proper comprehension of what faith teaches.

Castellesi follows Augustine's Neo-Platonism in arguing that the human soul (*anima rationalis*) is near God when it has purged itself of sin and is infused with charity.[37] Purgation enables the soul to perceive the highest good and to follow it.[38] The evils of this world disturb the clear vision of the soul, which must be at peace and un-disturbed by earthly chaos in order to choose the good. Castellesi combines Augustine, Ambrose, and Jerome to show man's progression to purity:

> The order of proceeding rightly [to purity] is described by Augustine: "When they [i.e., the faithful Christians] believe in the Scripture unshakably, they act by praying, seeking, and living well so that they will understand." Ambrose in *De Officiis* explains what occurs to him who prays and reads, saying, "We speak to Christ when we pray, but we hear him speaking to us when we read the divine oracles." Jerome tells us what to read "[The Psalms] . . . lead us through ethics to theology and make us pass from the elements of the killing letter . . . to the life-giving spirit."[39]

Scripture must be read continually with care, attention, and zeal. This constant meditative process enables man to understand the teachings of Scripture and become familiar with them. Divine reading feeds man's soul and controls his senses.[40]

Castellesi stresses Scripture's effects on the will and through the will on the intellect. Faith brings man to Scripture and with God's help and his own zeal he comprehends God's words and follows them, but to put this procedure into effect direct contact with Scripture is essential. *Sapientia* (understood as "piety") flows from meditation on and knowledge of Scripture. This familiarity with God's word must be matched on man's part with good acts.[41] Castellesi presents a fourfold scheme of man's movement to God, a progression dependent on the will. First, there is reading (*lectio*). This reading is the diligent scrutiny of the contents of Scripture and is proper to beginners. It leads to meditation (*meditatio*) upon Scripture, which involves the interior intellect and is an activity of the more proficient. Third, there is prayer (*oratio*), which enables man to communicate with God. Prayer belongs to the devout and permits the Christian to move to the final stage, contemplation (*contemplatio*). Contemplation is above the senses and can be undertaken only by the blessed.[42] Human understanding is limited to the first step, but it is stirred by the will's desire to know revelation. All these stages must follow in their proper order so that the Christian may reach God.

If contemplation is the final product of a cooperative effort between God and man, it has important external manifestations. The wise man, i.e., the Christian who has come to know God, can never be passive. His wisdom and knowledge of God's teachings require him to perform good works and to please God in this life. Contemplation does not turn the Christian away from the world but rather makes him an interpreter of God's teachings in the world. Good works are not the cause of faith but are its manifestations in the world.[43]

Book III expands on the proper utilization of Scripture. The Christian knows that a careful reading of Scripture will always unveil the truth since God and the Catholic Church would never deceive him; nevertheless, some aspects of Scripture are clearer than others.[44] The teachings of Scripture always agree, and the Christian must firmly believe those which agree with the Catholic faith.[45] In this interpretative process the Holy Spirit aids the Christian in understanding the more difficult parts of Scripture. If more than one explanation is possible, the believing reader must have confidence that the Holy Spirit will provide the correct meaning.

The Christian must approach the Scripture in humility and should not attempt to inflict human reason on it. Scripture is self-explanatory and has no need of human reason. Indeed, the seeming contradictions and obscurities of Scripture really prove reason's limits.[46] God has hidden secrets in Scripture which are meant to frustrate the foolish, who rely on reason, and to encourage the wise, who accept human limits. When reason is applied to Scripture, contention rather than clarification results. Both the obscure and the clear passages of Scripture demonstrate the need for God's revelation.

> It is obvious, therefore, that neither in the obscure places nor in the clear ones in Sacred Scripture ought either human conjecture or opinion, which is the philosophy of the world, determine anything rashly, but in all these things revelation is necessary.[47]

This correct understanding of scriptural teachings allows man to be wise and to act justly. Revelation, however, acts in union with charity. Charity makes even human knowledge (*scientia*) useful.[48] Although all human knowledge is worthy of damnation, charity can vivify it and make it productive.

Castellesi granted to human knowledge only a severely circumscribed value in interpreting revelation. Essentially, he believed, human knowledge threatens wisdom by undermining humility and inciting contention. He was especially anxious to discourage disputation over such mysteries of the faith as the Trinity. The Christian need not argue with the unbeliever and the philosopher about the cross and Christ's teachings, for faith does not require human reason's defense. Against those who attack faith the Christian need only counter with the authority of Scripture.[49]

Book IV both extends the criticisms developed against reason and resolves all questions posed in the treatise. Castellesi first contrasts Scripture with dialectics and philosophy. The anti-Aristotelian nature of this attack is made clear when Aristotle is called "Prince of the dialecticians."[50] Logic is cunning; it uses man's opinions against himself. Logic offers mere probability, while Scripture provides the Christian with secure truth. Dialectics causes contention and destruction by attempting to refute truth rather than helping to establish it.[51] Besides being a source of vanity and opinion, dialectics is used by the heretics to advance their teachings and to attack the authority of the Church; hence, dialectics is God's enemy.[52] The traditions of man stand opposed to divine revelation.

From dialectics Castellesi passes to rhetoric, for which, he maintains, the Fathers of the Church had little use: "We reject the charm of rhetoric and the beauty of childish and ostentatious eloquence, and take refuge in Scripture."[53] The rhetorical arts produce an eloquence that fosters only vanity and ostentation. When applied to Scripture's truth, they hide its simplicity and beauty. Although eloquence can be joined to the Christian's language, there is always the danger that those who do so act from a love of the speech of the pagan poets and orators rather than from their concern for Christian revelation.[54] The other sciences—geometry, mathematics, and music—provide the Christian with nothing necessary for his salvation, and astrology spreads only error and superstition.[55] Whatever their marginal utility to the believer, these sciences lead to error and are completely worthless in man's search for salvation. The desire to understand the physical universe is especially valueless, indeed dangerous. Those who dispute what Scripture teaches regarding the composition of this world discover nothing that relates to the future life. Knowledge of the stars cannot help in interpreting Scripture; all man needs to know is that the cosmos has been created by God.[56] Ignorance of this truth moves man away from God by concentrating his attention on the creatures rather than their maker.

Similarly, Castellesi argues that the liberal arts must be judged by their agreement with revelation; they are vain unless employed with God's grace.[57] Since the saints did not know them, these arts are superfluous to the Christian. This is even more true of philosophy than of the other disciplines. Philosophers are foolish in their search for knowledge because they produce nothing but error and contention. Even those philosophers who do try to know God are impious and stupid since they act not according to God's will (*secundum Deum*) but from human motivations (*secundum hominem*). Lacking grace, they become the servants of the devil.[58] What has Aristotle to do with Paul or Plato with Peter? asks Castellesi.[59] All philosophical speculation undertaken without God becomes stupid and false. Castellesi concludes that the philosophers are without faith, that they are the enemies of the Christian faith and the minions of the devil. Since they have no faith in Christ, they will receive their just reward in hell.[60]

Castellesi moderates this blanket condemnation by admitting that the believing Christian can study philosophy validly if it has some practical value and if it can help refute the philosophers. He accepts Augustine's analogy from the *De Doctrina Christiana* of the Jews taking the Egyptians' gold and silver during the Exodus as proof of the Christian's right to use pagan philosophy and arts, but he contends that this must be done within limits.[61] The Christian must always realize that the philosophers are the patriarchs of the heretics.[62] The true philosopher is not one who strives for the secrets of this world but is a lover of God and is guided by grace.[63] Whatever Castellesi grants to secular knowledge, he immediately nullifies.

Castellesi concludes the *De Vera Philosophia* with an extended tribute to Scripture, *de laudibus Sacrae Scripturae,* i.e., the true philosophy.[64] In this section he recapitulates and expands his previous themes. Scripture stands above all creation; it is simple, proclaims the truth, and is medicine for the soul.[65] All the Church's preachers and doctors have based their teachings on it. Frequent reading of Scripture illumines the heart, rectifies speech, sanctifies the soul, strengthens the faith, rejects the devil, and counters sin.[66] It contains all knowledge and is beyond the ingenuity of man to comprehend. Scripture gives all human knowledge a new meaning by relating everything to God and our neighbor: "Physics is God the creator of all things; ethics is a good and honest life formed by loving what ought to be loved, i.e., God and our neighbor; logic, which is the truth and light of the rational soul, is nothing but God."[67] Scripture leads man to act morally through the love it engenders for God and other men.

❧ III ❧

The basic themes of the *De Vera Philosophia* reappear constantly in a variety of often repetitious forms. This pattern stemmed from the essentially rhetorical nature of the treatise, which was aimed at moving the reader to act. Moreover, the rhetorical form was natural, considering that Castellesi had chosen to use the writings of the four Latin Doctors, who were themselves dependent on rhetorical principles; it was especially true of Augustine. Despite Castellesi's attacks on rhetoric, he used it both to exalt the truth of Scripture and to deny the value of other sciences, including rhetoric. Castellesi's procedure was to establish a formula in an extreme form, then to modify it, and finally to return to the original argument with full force. The procedure had the effect of reinforcing the primary (more extreme but simpler) meaning of statements and of limiting the value of rational explanation. It made acceptance of the bald condemnation clearer and more secure than the modifications. All of this was directed at emphasizing the centralizing of morality in the search for truth. Moral action flows from faith, which is a function of the will and humility. All human action and thought must be gauged by the demands of morality. Castellesi used rhetoric as a natural ally to morality. Man acts with intentions that respond to the will; man's disposition makes his acts either good or bad.

The rhetorical presentation of Castellesi's themes flowed from his acceptance of Augustinian voluntarism; the will is the source of knowledge and action. While the intellect follows the will in accepting faith and its teachings, it can also act as a hindrance to implementing the truth. The depreciation of the intellect and all human reason and knowledge results in the exaltation of the will. No exercise of rationality can aid the soul in its search for God. This acceptance of patristic voluntarism denied the intellectualistic underpinnings of Aristotelian Scholasticism.

Castellesi's theology was strongly scriptural. His aim was to provide a secure scriptural foundation for theology and Christian life in opposition to the philosophical speculation that characterized Scholasticism. But he modified this scripturalism with a strong patristic and ecclesiological control over the interpretation of revelation. The Christian must turn to the Church and the Church Fathers for his guidance in understanding Scripture and in implementing its teachings. These limits upon any type of individualistic or private interpretation of Scripture also derived from Augustine. Castellesi's scripturalism functioned within the context of the Church as the guarantor of truth.

Similarly, Castellesi believed that a Christian's faith is never sufficient in itself, but receives its strength from its agreement with the
beliefs of the Catholic Church as a whole. The tradition of the Church
and patristic teachings ultimately determine the meaning of revelation. Castellesi's emphasis on faith and Scripture is never a justification
for subjectivity; there is always the objective authority of the Church
which defines and limits both faith and the intrepretation of God's
word.

Castellesi's rejection of Aristotle followed a form common to medieval and humanist religious thought. Although Aristotle contributed
greatly to the systematization of Western thought, and especially
theology, in the Middle Ages, he was considered by conservative theologians, especially those influenced by Augustinian Neo-Platonism, to
be an opponent of Christian morality because of his deterministic
natural philosophy.[68] Furthermore, Aristotle's development and use
of dialectics made him the natural enemy of all who felt that too much
effort had been expended on fruitless discussions of unimportant or
incomprehensible questions and not enough in expounding topics
that related to man's moral needs. Castellesi attacked Aristotle and his
Christian followers on both counts. His anti-Aristotelianism formed
part of his general desire for a theology that addressed more practical
questions, questions reminiscent of an older, nondialectical theological
tradition. Augustine remained the major alternative for those who
were dissatisfied with a theology based on Aristotelian philosophy.

Castellesi criticized philosophical theology as a threat to Christian
morality. In his treatise he did not attempt to sketch a broad theological system but concentrated instead on those elements which respond to the imperative of moral action. He read Scripture and the
works of the four Latin Doctors with this aim always foremost in his
mind. He believed that the directives of theology and moral action
became clearer to the believer when they were free of philosophical
exposition. Like other humanists, Castellesi defined theology as the
ability to move men to do good rather than as a science that produced
theories and elaborate explanations. He probably felt free to avoid
discussing the doctrinal content of Christianity since the Church would
always act as its official guardian.

Skepticism and fideism dominated the *De Vera Philosophia,* but they
were employed in a limited fashion. Castellesi's skepticism differed
from the skeptical teachings of certain philosophical schools of antiquity that were being revived in the early cinquecento.[69] There was
none of the rigid philosophical treatment of questions which character-

ized the work of other Christian exponents of skepticism, such as Gianfrancesco Pico della Mirandola. Rather, Castellesi simply denied that philosophy and human knowledge can provide truth; there was no need for proof because he was relying on authorities. His fideism was equally qualified. Faith in his view must always work within an ecclesiological framework that prevents any radical break from the generally accepted religious traditions. For all his extreme statements, Castellesi's message was ultimately very conservative.

❧ IV ❧

Although Castellesi made no claim to originality in discussing perennial problems in Christian thought in the *De Vera Philosophia,* the treatise did represent an important, or at least noteworthy, indication of the growth of skeptical and fideistic sentiments among humanists in the late quattro and early cinquecento. It was especially significant because Castellesi came from a humanist center that was not prone to fideistic theology. Yet in comparison with other contemporary writers who discussed the same themes, Castellesi was moderate and responsive to both religious concerns and certain secular humanist doubts concerning the role of philosophy in religious and intellectual life.

A useful bench mark in judging Castellesi's place in his own day is the short treatise *De studio divinae et humanae philosophiae* (1496), by Gianfrancesco Pico della Mirandola (1469–1533).[70] We have already encountered Pico in the discussion on Ciceronianism, but he was also a major advocate of the skeptical-fideistic approach to theology in the early cinquecento. Gianfrancesco had been greatly influenced by his uncle Giovanni Pico in his youth. The elder Pico had devoted his early years to the search for a unifying knowledge based upon the study of all forms of ancient wisdom. Gianfrancesco Pico's years of study of secular philosophy ended in Florence, where he came under the influence of Savonarola. He was especially taken with the Dominican monk and came to reject the syncretistic tendencies of his uncle in favor of a fideistic approach to Christianity and a skeptical attitude toward all human knowledge.[71] He helped reintroduce the skeptical writings of Sextus Empiricus and wrote a major attack on Aristotelian philosophy and human science, the *Examen vanitatum doctrinae gentium* (1515).[72] As an exponent of skepticism Pico was a more extreme and effective advocate than Castellesi.

The *De studio* originated from Pico's years in Florence with Savonarola. It differs from the later *Examen* in being a theological investigation of philosophy rather than a philosophical exposition of the faults of philosophy. In the *De studio* Pico limits himself to the more traditional topics and bases his criticisms on the tenets of fideism. His conclusions dovetail in many respects with Castellesi's. While it is impossible to determine if Castellesi knew of the *De studio* when he composed the *De Vera Philosophia,* the general ideas and procedures of both indicate their common Augustine origins.

In the *De studio* Pico divides knowledge or philosophy (*scientia*) into two types: human and divine.[73] Human philosophy functions through sensory knowledge. Even when attempting to approach God, it relies on an indirect approach through sensible creatures. Its reliance on knowledge through the senses makes it dangerous to the Christian because it substitutes human for divine matters. Divine philosophy, which is the Sacred Scripture, approaches God directly and ignores the senses.[74] Pico accuses the proponents of human philosophy of rejecting the teachings of Scripture in favor of the falsehoods acquired through the senses, of forgetting that all human acts receive their validation only through God.

While human knowledge can have a limited value for the Christian, it always remains potentially dangerous. All the various disciplines humans have developed are valuable only insofar as they can help a man act morally, but to act morally a man must have faith.[75] Since human philosophy can lead a man away from the truth, Pico cautions that a Christian must always hold fast to his faith and follow the teachings of the Church. Like Castellesi, Pico offers the Church as the natural complement to a man's faith.

In the *De studio* Pico contrasted Scripture and human knowledge as strongly as Castellesi would in the *De Vera Philosophia.* Human knowledge can offer the Christian nothing that is necessary for salvation; Scripture suffices to provide the truth. Whenever a Christian attempts to introduce philosophy into scriptural studies, for whatever reason, he is in danger of losing hold of Christ's precepts.[76] Pico exalts the importance of the unlearned man in the Church, citing the Apostles, who were uneducated in human philosophy. A true theologian is learned in Scripture and knows, loves, and venerates God alone.[77] Pico proposes Francis of Assisi as the perfect model for the believing Christian. Educated in divine letters rather than the commentaries of the Scholastics, Francis was secure in his faith.[78] The simple man of faith excels all the philosophers and learned theologians.

The *De studio* was as direct as Castellesi's treatise in its approach. Both limited human knowledge to a minor, ancillary position in relation to faith, but emphasized it as a danger rather than as a limited aid. Scripture and faith alone provide the truth a Christian requires for salvation. But this absolute dependence on faith and Scripture is modified by the magisterial authority of the Church. Pico did not provide any detailed arguments for his rejection of human philosophy, but like Castellesi he accepted the essential dichotomy between any knowledge arising from the human sphere and coming from the divine. The effect was to render faith essentially independent of all human comprehension.

The essentially religious condemnation of philosophy displayed by Pico and Castellesi had secular humanist echoes. A few years after Castellesi compiled the *De Vera Philosophia,* Jacopo Sadoleto presented the basic humanistic suspicions of philosophy in the first half of his dialogue *De laudibus philosophiae,* the *Phaedra (ca.* 1517).[79] Dedicated to Mario Maffei, the *Phaedra* features Tommaso Fedra Inghirami, a former friend of Castellesi's, as the spokesman for the *studia humaniora* against the claims of philosophy. The statements made in the *Phaedra* closely parallel the views expressed by Castellesi, although they arose from a different attitude toward the value of secular learning in man's life.

In the dialogue, speaking through Fedra, Sadoleto discusses three topics that Castellesi had developed. First, philosophy loses itself in worthless disputation. Philosophers fight among themselves with the whore dialectics as their ally and provide no true wisdom.[80] Despite their self-aggrandizing name, "lovers of wisdom," they show themselves to be the very opposite. Second, human knowledge is greatly circumscribed by God so that there are things men do not and can not know. The natural sciences and the occult arts in their different ways attempt to know the unknowable and succeed only in deceiving men.[81] Finally, philosophy fails to provide a viable ethics.[82] Moral virtue alone defines the good man. Rather than look to such vague definitions as Aristotle's principle of the happy means, *mediocritas,* for guidance to the virtuous life, men should look to the history of the Romans for models. Fedra concludes that humanistic studies, with their concern for man in society and his moral needs, are superior to the pretensions of the philosophers.

Fedra's attacks on philosophy differed fundamentally from those expounded by Castellesi. Fedra's suspicions of philosophy, especially Aristotle, stemmed from secular values and lacked reference to theological problems, while Castellesi's work was solely religious in inspiration and argument. The skeptical attitude toward the values of philosophy and especially the natural sciences formed only a part of Castellesi's treatise. Finally, and most significantly, Castellesi did not advocate humanistic studies as the answer to man's search for moral guides.

One final comparison with the *De Vera Philosophia* helps to establish the currency of Castellesi's views. The *Libellus ad Leonem X,* by the Venetian monks Paolo Giustiniani and Pietro Quirini, expresses a suspicion of classical studies and philosophy on religious grounds that disturbed the intellectual community in Venice.[83] Although the two monks directed the *Libellus* to Leo as part of a reform program, they gave some consideration to the education of the clergy.[84] In their estimation secular learning was dangerous, and could be pursued only under the close control of religion. Classical languages, in their estimation, could contribute to the necessary linguistic expertise needed for scriptural and theological study but had no independent value. Like Castellesi, these monks emptied secular learning of its value save as an adjunct to religion.

As expressed in the *De Vera Philosophia,* Castellesi's attitude toward philosophy, Scholastic theology, and secular learning was very much in accord with one intellectual trend of his day. Compared with Pico, Fedra, and the two Camoldelese monks from Venice, his thought was both moderate and representative. While all these writers could easily be placed within a long tradition of Christian or classical skeptical thought, their appearance in Italian intellectual circles in the late quattro- and early cinquecento points to a widespread dissatisfaction with contemporary religious thought as a guide to the moral life and to a proper understanding of Christian revelation.

Although Castellesi's treatise expressed ideas that belonged to an old Christian tradition and that reflowered throughout Europe in the High Renaissance, one encounters specific problems in interpreting the *De Vera Philosophia.* These relate to the major thrust of Roman humanist thought. Castellesi's denial of philosophy and eloquence, of Scholasticism and the classical tradition of Roman humanism, leads naturally to a comparison between the *De Vera Philosophia* and the *Liber Sententiarum* of Paolo Cortesi and the values of his school of classicizing. Some nineteenth-century historians argued that Castellesi actually conceived of the *De Vera Philosophia* as a calculated response to Cortesi's *Liber Sententiarum,* and that he represented a group of "Christian" (as opposed to "pagan") humanists who found the work of Cortesi's school of classicizing unacceptable.[85] Certainly the proximity of the dates of the two works (1504 and 1507) gives a certain conjectural support to this argument. Ultimately, however, it must be rejected, for it is based on the conception of humanism as either "pagan" or "Christian," and misrepresents the major thrust of Castellesi's treatise. Castellesi was not retreating from the humanist learning and values that his other writings represented; rather, he was seeking to modify certain elements within Christian thought, and this was an indication of the diversity of humanist religious expression in Rome.

Castellesi presented the *De Vera Philosophia,* as he himself tells us, in response to the excesses of the contemporary theologians and philosophers. It was directed against the Scholastic's pride and the false teachings of the philosophers and proclaimed the uniqueness and sufficiency of Christian revelation and faith. Literary studies were indeed criticized in it, but they were not Castellesi's major concern. The *De Vera Philosophia,* like the *Liber Sententiarum,* was born of dissatisfaction with Scholastic philosophy and theology and the desire to return to the roots of Christian thought and moral action: the Scriptures and the Church Fathers in particular. The two authors differed, however, in their attitudes toward what was acceptable in the exposition of Christian truth. Cortesi accepted both Roman classicizing as a means of theological expression and certain elements of High Scholasticism, while Castellesi rejected precisely these elements within a fideistic theological context. The statements Castellesi made were radical for the thinkers of Rome and must give us pause when we identify the Roman classicism represented by Cortesi as the standard within humanist circles, yet Castellesi's strictures had a specific application and were not meant to refer to all humanist learning.

Castellesi's literary career proves that he took his own prohibitions not as a rejection of humanist and philosophical studies in themselves but rather as an abridgement of their value to theology. Castellesi was aware of the deficiencies in the way Christian theology was presented and taught to believers and he tried to respond to consequent dissatisfaction in a sharp manner. It is impossible to estimate how many of the Roman humanists, generally clerics, would have subscribed to Castellesi's statements. His stand was a unique expression from Roman humanist circles, although certainly not unknown at that time outside Rome, and hence it cannot be accepted as a standard view with broad applicability.

Castellesi was himself capable of blending the Christian and the classical. In his poem the *Venatio* (1505) he concludes his description of a boar hunt with the presentation of the pagan gods rising from their strongholds and witnessing their coming destruction before the Christian God.[86] This was as thorough a blending of Christian and classical idioms as any Cortesi ever made, but it was one which established the antithesis between things Christian and classical.[87]

Whatever Castellesi's ultimate belief in his own prohibitions, they are important indications from within Rome's humanist circles of the limits of Cortesi's type of classicizing. A more moderate but equally effective modification of Cortesi's views came from Castellesi's and Cortesi's old Roman friend the humanist Raffaele Maffei.

8

A Moderate Classicism

Cortesi's intellectualism, classicism, and moderate Scholasticism and Castellesi's voluntarism, fideism, and antiphilosophical theology defined two poles in Roman humanist theology. A third, more moderate position, however, originated from the same humanist circle and was addressed to the same audience. Raffael Maffei, in two theological tracts, the *De Institutione Christiana* (1518) and the *Stromata* (ca. 1519–21), proposed a moderate classicism that avoided the extremes of Cortesi and Castellesi.[1] Maffei was as optimistic as Cortesi concerning the value of classical learning in a Christian context, but he avoided Cortesi's rigid formalism. While essentially an intellectualist in his approach, Maffei realized the importance of the will in producing moral acts. Further, he accepted elements of High Scholasticism while still maintaining a critical stance toward Scholastic excesses. Like Castellesi's, Maffei's theology was inspired by the Church Fathers and can be understood only by specific reference to his extensive patristic studies. Maffei's approach to the Church Fathers, however, was less idiosyncratic than had been the cardinal's. The greatest difference between Maffei and his two contemporaries and friends stemmed from his strong historical and scholarly background, which awakened in him the desire both to place his work within a secure tradition and to deal more systematically and even-handedly with that tradition. As a result of this attitude, Maffei's theological writings exhibit a breadth that is lacking in both the *Liber Sententiarum* and the *De Vera Philosophia*. Maffei described basic theological concepts in a broader and more precise manner than either Cortesi or Castellesi.

Maffei spent the last decade and a half of his life away from Rome, in residence in his ancestral home, Volterra. Despite this long period of absence, he remained essentially a Roman humanist in his attitudes toward theology and contemporary culture and in his sense of affiliation. His views always centered on Rome and the preoccupations of its intellectuals. Withdrawal from Rome, however, did provide him with a certain sense of detachment that allowed him to avoid the tensions and excesses of those humanists who remained in the city. Especially in his classicism, Maffei's writings display the Roman humanist ideals of Julian Rome (Maffei left in 1506), but they are ideals that have been modified by almost two decades of religious study and meditation.

Maffei dedicated his broad classical scholarship to essentially religious ends. This orientation marks even his most secular composition, the *Commentaria Urbana* (1506).[2] The *Commentaria Urbana* was one of the earliest humanist encyclopedias. It covered all forms of secular knowledge—geography, biography, history, the natural sciences, philosophy—but did so from a particularly Christian perspective. In his dedicatory letter to Julius II, Maffei argued that universal knowledge can illumine the human mind and aid the Church.[3] Morality must at all times define the value of scholarship, he wrote. In its provision of abundant examples of the actions of good and evil men, the *Commentaria Urbana* could help the reader to follow the good and avoid the evil.[4] Whether taken from sacred or profane history, its teachings and examples could profit the Christian. From the beginning of his literary career, Maffei maintained that a close relationship exists between all forms of scholarship and morality.

The publication of the *Commentaria Urbana* coincided with Maffei's return to Volterra, and there his concern with religious questions began to dominate his life. Maffei took up a religious retreat and devoted his time to spiritual exercises and religious study; he remained, however, very much concerned with his family's temporal welfare.[5] He delved deeply into the sources of Christian thought and decided to devote the rest of his life to a program of religious composition. This, he believed, would allow him to relate his theological scholarship to contemporary religious and moral problems. Maffei believed that his own religious study and meditation could assist other Christians in their search for moral guides.

For his own religious mentors Maffei turned to the Fathers of the Church. In his patristic research he followed the established Roman tradition of translating the writings of the Greek Fathers.[6] It is indicative of Maffei's broad intellectual scope that he did turn to the Greek Fathers for his models rather than limit himself to the Latin Fathers as Castellesi had done. Maffei's first contribution to theological studies was a patristic translation. Unlike Valla, Maffei conceived of his patristic study as being fundamentally complementary to Scholastic theology, not opposed to it; he wished to utilize all the sources of Christian thought available to him. His acceptance of all Christian writers paralleled his openness to the classical heritage; his one criterion for a writer was his value in aiding man to lead a moral life. A practical, morally based, but encyclopedic theology resulted from this receptiveness,

a theology which avoided speculative debate and allowed Maffei to concentrate on producing a coherent theological exposition directed toward the needs of leading a moral life.

The Church Father who provided Maffei with his most satisfactory
model of the moral man was the Greek Basil the Great (330-379).[7]
Basil had been educated in classical and Christian learning, became a
monk, participated in the active administration of the Church as a
bishop, wrote in defense of the faith, and offered a moral ideal for
Christians. He also played an important role in supporting the humanists' claims to being pedagogical and moral reformers. Since Leonardo
Bruni's translation of Basil's defense of classical literature, *On Reading
Gentile Writers,* humanists had made constant appeal to that text in
explaining their own attraction to the dependence on classical authors.[8]
Maffei echoed Basil's view that a Christian can read with benefit those
pagan writers who teach moral lessons, and was naturally attracted to
this Father.

Maffei had devoted much attention to Basil before he began to
translate his writings. As early as 1501, while in Volterra, he had informed the humanist and papal secretary Sigismondo dei Conti of his
intention to translate Basil's writings.[9] To further his plan, he had
enlisted the secretary's aid in an ultimately futile attempt to obtain
one of Basil's manuscripts from the Vatican. Maffei had also requested
the assistance of the ruler of Florence, Piero Soderini, to secure a copy
of Basil's sermons from the Badia of Florence.[10] The register of bor-
rowers of the Vatican Library shows Maffei's continuing interest in
the Greek texts of Basil and the other Greek Fathers, Gregory of Nyssa,
Gregory of Nazianzus, and John Chrysostom. The first results of this
research were Maffei's short portrait of Basil in the *Commentaria
Urbana*[11] and the previously discussed dedication to Julius II.

By 1515 Maffei had completed an extensive study of Basil's teachings and had published his own translations of a series of Basil's writings.[12] In the dedication of the translations to his brother Mario,
Maffei explained that old age had caused him to leave Rome and seek
time for spiritual reflection in Volterra.[13] He had turned first to Aristotle, his companion since youth, and in particular to Book X of the
Ethics, for guidance in preparing for his end. However, he was dissatisfied since the Philosopher merely notes what must be done and not
how it can be accomplished.[14] In turning to Scripture, *sacra volumina,*
he discovered what must be done but faltered before the magnitude of
the requirements. Realizing that he must prepare himself, Maffei
settled on a program of composition which would enable him to explain these matters to himself as well as to others. The first step in this

process was translating Basil, for Basil's sermons offered the knowledge
Maffei was seeking.[15] Maffei noted that the cultivated style and singular
eloquence of Basil's writings made him particularly well suited for the
role of moral leader; he called him the *morum ac disciplinae christianae novus et inexorabilis censor* ("the new and relentless judge of
morals and Christian learning").[16]

Maffei's prefatory remarks expressed the basic structure underlying
his theological thought. Aristotle, whose writings Maffei knew well
and had helped to popularize among humanists in the *Commentaria
Urbana*,[17] had not supplied Maffei with the means of leading a holy
life, but Maffei did not reject the Philosopher completely. Aristotle's
philosophy, and by extension all classical learning, could aid Christians
by providing a starting point in their search for truth, but they must
soon pass to Scripture and other sacred writings. Basil and the other
Church Fathers would guide them in acting morally. Maffei's patristics
was not a matter of pure scholarship, but a spur to leading a Christian
life. Accordingly, Basil's life and writings offered a model for imitation.
As a great systematizer of Christian and secular learning, a master of
spirituality, and a model of moral action, Basil functioned as Maffei's
principal mentor.

The Basil translations were a crucial component of Maffei's theological development. They connected his early career as a classical scholar
and translator of Xenophon and Homer[18] with his later life as a moral
theologian. Basil's effect on Maffei was profound; he supplied Maffei
with the basic rationale for his other theological compositions. Although Basil appears only occasionally in the *De Institutione Christiana*
and the *Stromata,* those references show Maffei's primary interest in
Basil as a teacher of morality.[19] After translating many of Basil's
writings Maffei felt himself prepared to produce his own statements
on theology and the moral life.

❦ I ❦

The first original publication resulting from Maffei's devotion to
theology was the *De Institutione Christiana.* The treatise was accompanied by two shorter pieces: the *De Prima Philosophia,* a Scotist
discussion of metaphysics; and translations of devotional sermons by
John of Damascus and Andrew of Jerusalem.[20] In selecting his title
Maffei again turned to a patristic source, this time Lactantius, whose
Divine Institutes was one of the earliest systematic expositions of
Christian doctrine in Latin.[21] In his dedicatory letter to Leo X Maffei
justified his work by repeating what he had written in the preface to

the Basil translations, that he was not satisfied merely with study but felt that he must also compose in order to relate what he had learned to the Christian life.[22] He wished to expound the teachings of Scripture and to show others what the holy books taught. In this Maffei emphasized an active rather than a contemplative attitude toward Christian revelation.

Maffei offered his work as an exposition of the essential scriptural truth and as an aid to others in their search for salvation. Throughout antiquity, he maintained, learned men had sought this very end but had failed to attain it because they did not know Christ. Maffei supported his own theological formulations by arguing that the exposition of truth is not limited to one particular form. Claiming the same right as had the ancient Christians and the Scholastics to express the meaning of Scripture, he felt free to examine previous writers and to use and adapt them as his needs required. Maffei portrayed himself as a continuator of the Christian tradition of theological exposition:

> I have tried especially in my work to shun the ornaments and balsam of the leaders of this art as much as will be fitting with my simplicity and to collect those soldiers wandering about through the land into one battlefield and at the same time to dress them up in another style, [and] finally I have tried to add something of a new offspring to the parts of the ancients.[23]

Maffei, like other humanists, had a dynamic view of theology and morality which required constant reformation.

As his model in the *De Institutione Christiana* Maffei selected Aquinas. Aquinas had blended philosophy and Christian truth so well that he was a worthy successor to the followers of Socrates.[24] In Maffei's eyes Aquinas was justly termed *noster dux*. This favorable attitude toward Aquinas did not commit Maffei unconditionally to Thomistic teachings, however. In metaphysics, for example, Maffei used elements of Scotus's philosophy.[25] Nor did Maffei display any preference for the followers of Aquinas in his evaluation of the excesses of the contemporary Scholastics. Rather, like many other humanists, including Cortesi, he viewed the Dominican as the most dependable of the Scholastics and the clearest in his exposition of Christian truth.[26] Finally, in choosing Aquinas rather than Peter Lombard as his guide, Maffei showed himself to be more sensitive to theological changes than Cortesi, who followed the older writer. In the cinquecento Aquinas's *Summa Theologiae* would replace the *Sententiae* as the standard theological text.

Despite his utilization of Aquinas in the *De Institutione Christiana,*

Maffei's procedure differed radically from that of his Scholas ic predecessors. He imbued his work with a much broader cultural perspective
than did the Scholastics in their writings. Naturally this reflected Maffei's extensive study of classical civilization. He cited numerous classical
writers, and the comparison he made between Aquinas and Socrates
was more than a rhetorical device. Maffei's theological writings portrayed a unified view of culture, combining Christian (patristic and
Scholastic) and classical in one form.

The *De Institutione Christiana,* like Cortesi's *Liber Sententiarum,*
is a theological textbook. It reviews classical, patristic, and Scholastic
opinions on a variety of theological topics and presents its subjects in a
format that is useful to a nonphilosophical and nontheological audience. There is also an autobiographical element, in Maffei's concern
with monastic topics. Maffei was greatly attracted to the religious life
and tried to integrate its ideals into his daily activities. Despite this
personal feature, the *De Institutione Christiana* has a theoretical aim,
to discuss a variety of Christian doctrines and explain their significance. As a theoretical exposition it was conceived of as an introduction to the moral teachings of the *Stromata.*

Maffei often made explicit use of Aquinas's *Summa Theologiae.*
Some sections of the *De Institutione Christiana,* such as the chapter on
angels, depend on Aquinas for their arguments and the authorities
cited.[27] The extensive discussions and refutations of classical and Mos-
lem writers on a variety of technical questions, such as the nature of
the soul, probably stemmed from the same source.[28] In his presentation
Maffei followed a basic Aristotelian-Thomistic approach. The *De Institutione Christiana* discusses the major Scholastic schools and how they
differed on specific issues; thereby it functions as a theological primer
analogous to Cortesi's *Liber Sententiarum.* Maffei's object was not to
consider every problem in all its parts but to sketch general lines of
filiation among thinkers which could be used by the reader to understand the issue at hand. The *De Institutione Christiana* is not another
Summa Theologiae, however, either in bulk or in comprehensiveness.
Rather, it is a short-cut by which the nonexpert can acquire the basic
arguments, ideas, and technical theological vocabulary that help form
the basis for a Christian life.

Despite the similar goals of the *De Institutione Christiana* and the
Liber Sententiarum, there were important differences between Maffei's
and Cortesi's procedures in discussing the same topics. Maffei was more
interested in the technical aspects of metaphysics and psychology than
was Cortesi, although certainly even Maffei's discussions of these topics
was moderate compared with those of contemporary Scholastics. The

two Roman humanists also differed in their language. Maffei eschewed Cortesi's Ciceronianism, although his language was also based on humanistic principles and displayed a broad knowledge of Greek and Latin classical writers. He used traditional Scholastic terminology, but his syntax and general vocabulary were humanistic. Both writers displayed the same suspicion of the plodding nature of Scholasticism and its indifference to the lay reader.

There are also similarities and obvious differences between the *De Institutione Christiana* and the *De Vera Philosophia.* Maffei's theology responded to the same scriptural imperatives Castellesi outlined in his treatise. Maffei, however, approached problems in a more moderate manner than did the cardinal. Whereas Castellesi was suspicious of all philosophical theologians, Maffei willingly used those writers who he felt were both orthodox and moderate in their arguments. In essentials such as the primacy of faith, morality, and the ecclesiological tradition supporting the faith, the two men agreed.

Maffei's *Stromata* completes the teachings of the *De Institutione Christiana.* Specific details on its composition are unknown; from references within the work we know that it was begun after the completion of the *De Institutione Christiana.*[29] Since the *De Institutione Christiana* went to press in 1518, we may date its composition from that year. Although Maffei did not live to put the finishing touches on the *Stromata,* its composition dominated the last years of his life. Its pages contain his final opinions on the place of the Christian in the world and the means available to him to act morally and guarantee his salvation.

Maffei did not claim any guide for the *Stromata,* as he had for the *De Institutione Christiana.* Nevertheless, a candidate is available, Clement of Alexandria (second century A.D.). Clement's *Stromateis* [*Miscellanies*] were partly available in medieval *florilegia,* and a Greek text was in Florence by the end of the quattrocento.[30] Moreover, Maffei's choice of title for this work seems to be an obvious reference to the writings of the Alexandrian Father. Structurally, the two works are similar. The manner in which Maffei integrated his discussions of a variety of subjects, such as the best forms of historical composition, philological and linguistic topics, and events in his own life, parallels the loose structure that characterizes Clement's treatise.[31] This fluid form could have been inspired by such humanist treatises as Poliziano's *Miscellanies* and Pietro Crinito's (*ca.* 1465-*ca.* 1507) *De Honesta Disciplina* (1508);[32] however, the religious intent of Maffei's work and his devotion to patristic writers, especially the Greek Fathers, makes Clement a more likely source for the structure of the *Stromata.*

❧ II ❧

The *De Institutione Christiana* and the *Stromata* together form a theological encyclopedia. The former provides the theoretical basis for moral theology, while the latter completes the structure with a fuller exposition of moral principles and how to apply them. Technical discussions are more prominent in the *De Institutione Christiana* and its companion the *De Prima Philosophia,* which are essentially repetitions and summaries of established Aristotelian-Scholastic philosophical and orthodox theological views. Apart from these technical matters, certain themes unite the *De Institutione Christiana* and the *Stromata* and display Maffei's orientation toward theology as the basis of moral action. These are the areas on which this chapter will concentrate, for they show Maffei as a humanist theologian comparable to his Roman and Florentine contemporaries. In view of Maffei's basic acceptance of Scholastic theology, his attitude toward the Scholastic theologians will be discussed first.

Maffei willingly appropriated any source of truth available to him. He betrayed no absolute preference for any theological or philosophical school. Echoing the arguments presented in the introduction to the Basil translations, Maffei proclaimed the variety of paths men can follow to find God:

> Just as in the Catholic faith, in which all the equally good and faithful meet together in the same spirit to embrace the one God and Father of all, truth is often thought out by different people in different ways and means so that each one lives more or less according to his own nature, humors, fortune, and grace, and likewise often the teachings of all the best learned men are different but all concur in the investigation of the one good and true, which we read sometimes happened to the most holy men and to the Apostles themselves.[33]

Only the revelation of Sacred Scripture limits this diversity of theological opinion and personal positions. All Christians must believe what Scripture teaches and adhere to the unity of the faith. In some matters later writers had a clearer idea of Scripture's teachings than did their predecessors; hence the work of theology is never finished.[34] Any Christian who seeks God sincerely in his own fashion will reach him.[35] Maffei followed other humanist theologians in arguing that he and his contemporaries could contribute meaningfully to the exposition of religious truth. From the observation that diversity characterizes the world[36] he concluded that God had left contingencies in it so that there would be a variety in creation. In accordance with this principle Scholastic theology became only one more element in religious diversity; it held no monopoly of theological or religious truth.

Maffei displayed no doctrinaire attitude toward the contending theological schools that characterized late Scholasticism. Like Cortesi, he sought to establish a balance between Scotus and Aquinas by using them to define the general theological problems and arguments and the limits of acceptable opinion. Although Maffei owed to Aquinas the general outline of the *De Institutione Christiana,* he did not follow the Dominican in all matters. On specific questions of metaphysics, for example, he preferred Scotus. Maffei considered metaphysics a useful instrument in raising the human mind to higher levels of thought, but he did not deal extensively with all its elements. While familiar with contemporary writers, Maffei's aim was to treat Aquinas and Scotus and their respective schools as he did Plato and Aristotle, as a basis for discussion, and not as the sole sources of truth.

Maffei cites the differing views of Aquinas and Scotus on a number of topics: potency and act,[37] the scope of the intellect,[38] the power of sin,[39] the fall of the angels,[40] grace,[41] the Eucharist,[42] cognition,[43] predestination,[44] and Christ's blood.[45] In canvassing arguments on these various theological and philosophical topics, Maffei did not always offer answers to the problems raised. He accepted these questions as unsettled since he was not interested in advancing new theological opinions. Maffei's approach to disputed points was to avoid areas of great polemical disagreement or to treat them summarily and concentrate on what help the Christian could use in leading a moral life. When he did discuss an involved matter, his only reason for doing so was to aid the Christian in his search for salvation. He believed that a proper understanding of the significance of specific doctrines could inspire hope and joy in the Christian.[46] For example, Maffei cited Scotus's view that predestination is contingent and that no one can ever be certain of his own salvation. He did so in order to argue that God's foreknowledge should not undermine the Christian's striving for salvation.[47] Maffei dismissed extensive discussion of the subtleties related to predestination as useless to the Christian in leading a good life.

Maffei expressed grave reservations about the theological arguments that characterized late medieval Scholasticism. He admitted that dialectics could be useful against heretics,[48] but he condemned the tendency to debate foolish questions, which, he believed, had no value or real importance.[49] Questions such as what the fate of man would have been had Adam not sinned or whether the Virgin was born free of Original Sin, which the Scholastics believed were important, were dismissed by Maffei as of no value to the Christian. Rather, they were the weapons of sophists and ostentatious men.[50] Maffei stated that to investigate too deeply the mysteries of the faith was to become crazed with reason (*cum ratione insanire*).[51] His discussion of the Eucharist (Book IV, Chapter 9, of the *De Institutione Christiana*) included a reference to the bitter debate between the Dominicans and the Franciscans over the nature and present location of the blood Christ had shed on the cross. He lamented that religious men wasted their talents in such pointless disputes when they could be devoting their abilities to the search for truth.[52] Maffei presented an incisive comparison between the factionalism of the religious orders in his own day and the dissension that arose among the early Christians in the time of the Apostle Paul:

> And as these contenders assert repeatedly from the very beginning that I am of Apollo, I of Paul [1 Cor. 1:12], so likewise today I am a Thomist, I a Scotist, I am an assertor of my opinion, you of yours, whatever kind it is. Surely they bring the pestilential poison of ambition in place of religion to the holy meetings, while some are more concerned with a reputation for ingenuity than with the truth of the matter [discussed].[53]

In Maffei's judgment scholastic disputation, especially abstract metaphysical speculation, depresses the truth and threatens the peace of the Church and the spiritual health of the Christians.

In the *Stromata* Maffei provided a more detailed analysis of the abuses of the Scotists. He compared the absurd men of his own era to former times when Platonists and Aristotelians fought with each other. This zeal for contention was the special fault of the Scotists. They always found the ideas of other theologians erroneous. They opposed their opinions to those commonly accepted by other religious orders. Worse, they portrayed their teachings as oracles to the people, thereby corrupting and confusing the believers. Maffei enumerated four persistent evils caused by the contentions of the Scotists:

> First, they scoticize [*scotizant*] themselves and their souls, that is, they darken, . . . although they say that they illumine, others. Then such men never come to the perfect knowledge and taste of theology since they have the part of the metaphysician rather than that of the perfect theologian. Third, as we see by experience, it happens rarely that they bear the desired fruit for the listeners. Finally, they excite the greatest contentions and sects among the faithful, especially the schools of theologians.[54]

Addicted to their own master, the Scotists scorn all others and spread sedition and tumult instead of knowledge of the good. As had Cortesi, Maffei blamed the contentions of the theologians for causing other learned men to abandon the study of religion.[55]

As a contemporary example of the danger that arises from these theological and philosophical excesses, Maffei selected Pico della Mirandola. His analysis of Pico's theology followed the same lines that Cortesi's had. Maffei admitted that Pico was a man of exceptional ability but noted that he was also seriously flawed. His youth deprived him of the prudence needed to deal with complicated questions and led him into error. In the case of the *900 Conclusiones,* Maffei explained, Pico had taken a series of false propositions and used his subtle abilities to make them appear true. In time, however, Pico realized his mistakes and with advancing age and the prudence it brings devoted his last years to a proper Christian life.[56] For Maffei, Pico's excesses reflected the evil influence of the contentious Scholastic theologians.

Maffei, again like Cortesi, believed that in concentrating on Aquinas and Scotus he obtained the best of Scholastic thought. Both men felt that they could use Scholasticism in a nonpolemical fashion. To do this they wished to separate Aquinas and Scotus from their followers and their orders' near adoration of them in order to make them classic spokesmen for Christian truth. In a sense Maffei and Cortesi separated Aquinas and Scotus from their Scholastic ambience and isolated their views. In so doing, these humanists could safely cite and exploit them without having to deal with their followers and the interpretations and conflicts that had arisen from their theories. Humanists, indeed all Christians, could accept the views of Aquinas and Scotus on issues they agreed upon as essentially orthodox and representative without becoming involved in subtle distinctions. In the case of questions on which these two theologians differed with each other and on which the Church had not issued a final decision, Christians could simply place the opinions side by side and judge themselves. These two great Scholastics thereby became authoritative spokesmen, holding a position immediately below the Scriptures and the Church Fathers as expounders of the truth. One could exploit them as required without making any commitment to their entire intellectual system. Although this approach had ahistorical elements, it did allow the humanists to excerpt the nondisputative sections from their thought and propagate them as standard.

Analogous to Maffei's treatment of the Scotists and the Thomists was the work of the Carmelite humanist and poet Battista Mantovano Spagnoli (1447–1516), *Opus Aureum in Thomistas.*[57] The *Opus* attacked the excessive claims made by the Thomists for the theology of Aquinas. Both Maffei and Mantovano acknowledged Aquinas and Scotus as important teachers in the Church, but neither accepted the schools that grew up around them as faithful representatives of their views or as sole claimants to truth. Instead, both emphasized the contingent nature of human knowledge and the need to strive constantly for truth rather than rely on one man's authority.

🦴 III 🦴

Maffei's condemnation of Scholasticism's excesses reflected his concentration on morality and the Christian's struggle for salvation. The same perspective forced him to reject certain tendencies in contemporary humanism. Maffei demanded that the civilization of eloquence meet the same standards of balance and moral utility as theology; the excessive pursuit of eloquence can be as threatening to the moral imperatives of religion as theological contentiousness, he argued. The analogies between theology and eloquence are clear: Theology is a good, but can be misused unless it is related to the moral life; eloquence is a good, but is subject to similar misapplication. In the fashion of Gianfrancesco Pico and Castellesi, Maffei separated eloquence from truth: *nulla enim eloquentia major quam dictorum factorumque veritas* ("for no eloquence is greater than the truth of words and deeds").[58] Maffei criticized certain forms of oratory that were popular in his day, claiming that they betrayed more concern for beauty than for content.[59] Eloquence becomes arrogant when its attraction consumes its practitioners and offers no end outside itself. Maffei singled out certain extemporaneous orators who were famous in Rome, especially Pietro Marsi, a cleric and professor of rhetoric at the University of Rome who had studied with Pomponio Leto, Bishop Giannantonio Campano, and the very popular Aurelio and Raffaele Brandolini.[60] Such orators receive much praise for their work, but unfortunately too often they lack content and produce merely pleasant phrases. Maffei concurred with Plato's condemnation of the poets who lack *doctrina.*[61] Similarly, he argued that something inelegantly written may contain important teachings.[62]

Such a generic attack on rhetoric can be found in the writings of other humanists as well as nonhumanists. Castellesi, for example, was stronger in his condemnation, but paradoxically he is better known than Maffei as an advocate of eloquent Latin style. Maffei did not deny the values of rhetoric, but rather warned that its use could conceal a lack of content. His own writings indicate that his concern for eloquence had a personal component. Before his retirement to Volterra Maffei had written a poem on the founding of Rome.[63] His later works, the *Brevis Historia* and the *Apologeticus* against Luther, reflect his knowledge and use of classical rhetorical principles.[64] His attack on eloquence became specific when he turned to the question of the relationship between eloquence and theology. His general rule was that Christian studies do not require eloquence. Indeed, language should be fitted to the Holy Scriptures;[65] to prefer one's own style, no matter how beautiful, to that of the saints and Apostles was to betray a disdain for Christianity.[66]

The use of non-Christian vocabulary to express Christian ideals elicited Maffei's particular censure. He admitted that he himself had been guilty of such excesses and he criticized those members of the religious orders who engaged in this abuse. In his later life Maffei rejected the introduction of pagan classical terms into the Christian themes so popular in Rome, just as he condemned archaisms in literary compositions.[67] As an example of this excess Maffei cited the well-known Franciscan preacher Jacopo della Marca:

> Again, certain profane, although Latin, [words] ought to be avoided, such as *divus* for saint and *concinnator* or *orator* for preacher, which I gladly retract if I ever carelessly used them in my writings, and I am amazed that this [is done] by certain grave and very religious men, among whom is Blessed Jacobus Picens.[68]

There are obvious analogies between Maffei's views and those expressed by the Scholastic opponents of such humanist theologians as Brandolini. However, Maffei was devoted to humanist learning and culture and he wished to establish rules that he believed would lead others along the correct path. He did not intend to exclude humanists from theological activity as some Scholastics did.

Certainly the type of literary composition which Maffei condemned in Jacopo della Marca was most perfectly represented by Paolo Cortesi. Yet Maffei never mentioned his old friend, even though there are indications that he felt that Cortesi's type of classicizing was all too prevalent among the Roman curial humanists.[69] Perhaps his long friendship with Cortesi prevented him from criticizing him publicly. Maffei's general attitude toward such literary theologians was clear; their activities were excessive, and by wasting time and energy on unimportant matters, they could impede the moral life. In contrast to Cortesi's Latinity, Maffei advocated a language with an evangelical basis:

Therefore, the Apostles were able to persuade more by the naked speech [*sermo*] without the splendor of words and the acuteness of dialectics or the tragic facility of the voice than all the schools of the philosophers or all the sages or prophets of the Indians or Egyptians.[70]

Maffei and Castellesi contrasted Scripture with both Scholastic dialectics and humanist eloquence to prove the authority of God's word. Neither rhetoric nor dialectics nor any form of philosophy or ancient wisdom was equivalent to the pure speech of Scripture. However, Maffei never forced his criticisms to the extremes Castellesi did.

Maffei's position was more balanced than either Cortesi's or Castellesi's. Moreover, there are obvious similarities between Maffei's position and Erasmus's double attack on Scholasticism and Ciceronianism. Maffei's analysis of the theological and moral problems of his day paralleled Erasmus's: The excesses of Scholastic theology frustrated the Christian by enticing him into worthless digressions, while humanist excesses belittled the uniqueness of the Christian message; the solution was a return to the moral teachings of Scripture with the aid of the Church fathers. Neither man questioned the essential value of ancient learning. Although Maffei was not a Biblical scholar, he was aware of the need for critical textual studies of Christian writings in order to arrive at the truth, a procedure that depended upon humanist study of the ancient texts.[71] While Maffei and Erasmus differed in their attitudes toward monastic spirituality, Erasmus being much more critical of its worth, they shared the same evaluation of the basic problems of their day and the means of solving them.

IV

The problem of the propriety of Latin eloquence in theological discussions led naturally to the question of the use of pagan authorities in similar contexts. Maffei cited classical writers almost as often as Scripture and Christian authors in the *Stromata,* and the pagan Greeks and Romans contributed importantly to the *De Institutione Christiana.* Maffei found the ancients especially appropriate as exponents of morality. The place and function of pagan authors in Christian writings and teachings had been a major preoccupation of his patristic sources. In translating Basil the Great and in giving his final theological work a title reminiscent of Clement of Alexandria, Maffei paid homage to two of the greatest exponents of the incorporation of pagan learning into Christian teachings. They had aimed at producing a new cultural construct. The Greek Fathers had been more concerned with this problem than had the Latin Fathers, and as a result of his readings, Maffei must have been very sensitive to this difference. In a sense, Maffei recapitulated the procedure of the Greek Fathers, arriving at an amalgam of Christian and classical elements like that which had inspired so many other humanists.

Although Maffei emphasized that pagan writers and their teachings could have no value for the Christian if he did not remain true to the tenets of the faith,[72] he nevertheless claimed that they could aid the believer in living well. Some ancients had been able to overcome, at least to an extent, the limits imposed by their superstitious religions and their ignorance of Christ's teachings.[73] The Christian may choose from the pagan *exempla* those who support the moral life and Christian principles (a formulation first developed by Basil the Great).[74] Maffei freely cited the Apostle Paul and Cicero side by side in order to stress a moral point.[75] He judged Plato's view of providence compatible with the Christian one.[76] Seneca, he noted, advocated the need for honesty in public and private life as well as the value of patriotism and respect for neighbor and religion.[77] Pagan philosophers approached the truth but always fell short of reaching it because they mistook separate substances as the ends in themselves rather than as means to the good. Maffei implied that the good pagans were saved, however, and he stressed that the Christian, in order to act morally, may use the entire body of classical Latin and Greek thought as a support.[78] Maffei never lost the balance between Christian and classical elements which he had inherited from Basil the Great.

As a student of ancient philosophy and culture, Maffei held strongly Aristotelian views. The discussions of philosophical topics and metaphysics in the *Commentaria Urbana* and the *De Prima Philosophia* followed Aristotle's teachings on most matters. His summaries of the writings of Aristotle which formed the last sections of the *Commentaria Urbana* became popular and were reprinted separately by others as introductions to translations of Aristotle. His devotion to Aquinas was a further example of his general philosophical orientation. As an Aristotelian, Maffei displayed a suspicion of Platonism or at least of certain developments in Neo-Platonism. He argued in the *Stromata* that many Christians had gone astray in following Platonic doctrines too closely. Origen, for example, had erroneously argued that the souls of men had been created from all eternity, a false teaching that was attributable to Platonic influences.[79] Maffei felt that Platonism's threat to orthodoxy continued into his own day. He complained that many men in Italy defended Platonic theories and carried them into the churches, where they taught them to the faithful. Men come together in *conciliabula* or *sodalitates* to discuss only Platonic writings and glory in being called Platonists rather than Christians, he lamented.[80] The obvious referent of these statements was the circle of Marsilio Ficino of Florence, whom Maffei never cited in his later theological writings. Although the Ficinian Platonic academy was only a memory when Maffei wrote this admonition, he had enjoyed close relations with Florentine humanist circles in his youth, when the academy flourished, and would have been aware of Ficino's teachings. Maffei's suspicion of Platonism probably developed in his later years, but the hostility he directed against an interpretation of Christianity through Platonic philosophy perhaps represented a growing feeling among some groups in sixteenth-century Italy.

This aversion to Plato and his followers did not extend to Socrates, however. Maffei followed his patristic predecessors and humanist contemporaries in advancing Socrates as the prime ancient example of the moral man.[81] Socrates overcame the limits of nature and strove to act morally. He was the first to speak of the moral aspects of life,[82] and he exemplified one of Maffei's favorite virtues, parsimony of speech.[83] Socrates was more than simply another example of a good man; he had helped give morality a universal claim and therefore was closer to Christianity than other philosophers. Socrates' philosophical importance in Maffei's eyes heightened his role as a moral teacher.

By emphasizing Socrates and similar classical thinkers and personages, Maffei implied that man possessed the ability to regulate his acts and in some manner his search for salvation. The ancients showed what could be accomplished within human limits and talents, and Maffei wrote the *De Institutione Christiana* and the *Stromata* in great part to broadcast this message. This conception of man's place in the salvific process flowed naturally from the general concepts Maffei had taken from his patristic and classical sources. In dealing with these questions Maffei was concerned not with creating a new theology but with demonstrating that man had the ability to overcome his limits and to cooperate with God's grace to earn salvation.

❧ V ❧

In Maffei's moral theology man is the image of God, endowed with intellect and will, but flawed through sin.[84] Maffei used as his starting point the Socratic admonition to "know thyself," a teaching which Basil the Great had echoed and which had inspired other Renaissance philosophers and theologians, e.g., Marsilio Ficino.[85] Self-knowledge helps man to realize his flaws and conquer them. Man can appreciate that he is corruptible and vile but also that he has a soul which is immortal. The themes of dignity and sinfulness emphasized the ambivalent nature of humanity. Through both his free will and God's grace man can reach beyond his limits.[86] Salvation is a cooperative effort between God and man; man helps to advance the process of reaching for God through his realization of both his limits and his abilities.

The Christian in overcoming his limitations is an active agent in achieving salvation. He must strive to act morally. Morality is not simply a function of the intellect.[87] Maffei subscribed to a voluntarism that was common among humanists.[88] All praise results from action,[89] and proper use of the will (*bene velle*) is superior to knowledge (*bene intelligere*).[90] This stress on the will did not prevent Maffei from accepting certain intellectual tendencies implicit in his Aristotelianism, however. Man has the power to develop the intellectual virtues,[91] but he must do so with humility.[92] The Christian follows reason,[93] which should mediate his entire life as a balance to the will;[94] God's grace combines with a man's intellect and will to insure his salvation. God saves man through man's own abilities, merits, and free will.[95] Man's hope in God's grace rests upon his own merits.[96] Maffei strove to establish a balance between man's intellect and will and between God's grace and man's freedom to act.

Maffei outlined certain general rules and principles which he believed could serve as guides in man's search to act morally. A Christian can find support in imitating those who have succeeded in living morally. Maffei related the general need to imitate great men with the need to imitate religious models.[97] Such imitation is a product of nature itself:

> Since it has been established by nature and often happens that below the excellence of the archetype a copy [*apographum*] exists and is less [than the archetype] the more imperfect the former is, and sometimes it falls [so far short] that it has absolutely no merit. Wherefore, we are exhorted to raise up our eyes to the mountains [Psalm 121:1], and to come near to the wisdom of the Maker as far as is permitted by imitation.[98]

Imitation becomes a moral principle vital to the Christian in his struggle for salvation. In Augustinian Neo-Platonic fashion Maffei argued that God has established certain archetypes in nature which man through diligent observation can use to bring forth good. The greatest models for moral action are the Christian saints,[99] but even contemporaries can be copied profitably.[100] Imitation forms a natural part of human activity and builds a man's confidence to do what he must. Of course, there will always be deviations from any exemplar, and Maffei realized that one must have a practical attitude toward imitation.[101] It works within the confines of a man's nature and God's grace.[102] The search for the spiritual life is guided by man's abilities and the grace God gives him.

Simply to place a model before the Christian does not in itself suffice to elicit a fitting response; the process requires great diligence. Indeed, the exhortation to persevere and be diligent is a trademark of Maffei's moral writings. No Pelagian tint threatens this balance, for man's striving for salvation always proceeds under God's direction.[103] Maffei expected man to utilize his own powers even though religion supplemented his limits.[104] A man's desire to follow the good, and the diligence needed to achieve this end, can overcome the defects of his intellect and give him strength in other aspects of life.[105] In all matters natural ability (*ingenium*) requires zeal and diligence if it is to bear fruit.[106] A Christian makes use of both reason and acquired skill (*ars*) to correct his weak and faulty nature. This acquired skill imbues the mind with discipline and habit (*mos*), which should be practiced without ostentation.[107] Diligence, which is "the zeal and application of the soul in doing something" (*studium applicatioque animi ad aliquod agendum*), supports a man's hope and natural abilities.[108]

The moral rules Maffei developed betrayed his strong monastic tendencies. In certain points in the *Stromata* he attempted to justify his own preference for monastic spirituality as represented by his religious retreat after years of activity in Rome; the problem of the active life versus the contemplative one was very real for him.[109] He tried to solve the dilemma by writing about it. His discussion of marriage betrays this ambivalence. He argued that marriage can pose an impediment to virtue but not an absolute one.[110] He included Basil the Great's monastic writings in his translations as a patristic base for monastic practices.[111] But these ideals did not always dominate. Maffei did not present poverty, an essential element in all monasticism, as a constant good; indeed, he warned that it could endanger the moral life rather than spur man to virtue. Maffei never resolved this ambivalence between the secular life and his respect, indeed preference, for monastic life. The overt monastic elements in the *Stromata* did not alter his aim to establish principles that would be applicable to all Christians.

An example of Maffei's monastic attitude was his concern for quiet and solitude. The admonition to be silent and parsimonious of speech particularly addressed monasticism, which depended on silence for contemplation.[112] A strong suspicion of needless talk and lightheartedness is evident in Maffei's writings. He had stated his reservations about excessive speech and his preference for silence in the *Commentaria Urbana.*[113] In the *Stromata,* citing Seneca, he warned against those people who laugh too much and too easily.[114] However, he did not cast this admonition in narrowly monastic terms; he gave it wider application by offering Socrates as a model of the man who speaks only when necessary and hence displays the proper gravity.[115]

Significantly, Maffei's discussion of silence led him to consider the relationship between the Church and society and thereby to reveal the limits of his monastic attitudes. While he accepted the importance of silence, he acknowledged that the Church was essentially a civic organization and that sermons and good examples must have an audience; sermons produce nothing if practiced in an empty field.[116] Certainly Christ sought solitude in the desert on occasion, but this did not imply an anticivic stance.[117] Maffei's realization that the Church must guide man in secular society and not in hermetic isolation modified his disposition to universalize monastic virtues and practices. This attitude brought him close to the quattrocento humanists' concentration on civic life. For Maffei the Church remained actively involved in man's daily experiences and not an ideal segregated from the world.

The theme of the social aspect of the Church led easily to a consideration of the role of the Church as the regulator of Christian belief, and the place the Church holds in the Christian's struggle for salvation. Maffei believed in the existence of an *ecclesiae consuetudo* which remains undivided despite diversifying pressures.[118] This tradition preserves the teachings of the faith as passed down from its originators through the writings of the Greek and Latin Fathers and continued in the bishops and the holy men of the religious orders.[119] Maffei knew well that this was not the story of continuous enlightenment, but he felt that despite the abuses of some bishops, the teaching of Christian doctrine and moral castigation always remained available to the believers. While Maffei did not believe that change in the Church was always for the good, he realized that it was natural and that the Church of his day was not necessarily inferior to that of the past.[120] Indeed, his own writing proves the continuity of the tradition of theological exposition that is essential to the faith. In support of the practices of his own day, Maffei cited a sermon by Pope Leo I (440–461) which was very popular with contemporary Roman humanists and preachers; in it the pope defended Christian Rome against claims of pagan Rome's superiority. In Maffei's estimation, what was true of Leo I's Rome was equally true of Leo X's city.[121]

In agreement with his Roman humanist background Maffei conceived of the Church in terms of the continuation of the Roman Empire. While he was sometimes critical of the pretensions of the Curia Romana and complained about its imperial claims and its self-aggrandizement,[122] he believed that a direct connection did exist between the empire of the Caesars and the contemporary Church:

> Finally Gaius Caesar destroyed everything by rebellion, confounded divine and human things, invaded the fatherland, and snatched the empire by force for himself and left it to his heirs until Constantine, who handed it over with his own hands to his successors along with the finally accepted faith and yielded the city of Rome to the pope. Therefore, the Church makes the empire, once the [source] of so much injury and obtained by tyranny, now a holy and just thing.[123]

Maffei accepted the curial view of history and of the Donation of Constantine, at least in some modified form.[124] He did not, however, believe that there were not important differences between the ancient empire and the new Christian one. In assuming the rule of the West, the Church cleansed the empire of the crimes the pagan Caesars had committed and made it holy. Maffei's conception of empire implied not only a continuous entity but a radical change in the nature of the empire. The Christian empire did not succeed to the pagan one in all areas; there were essential differences that reflected the moral superiority of Christianity. Maffei provided a middle ground between Erasmus on the one hand and Cortesi or Palladio on the other.

❧ VI ❧

Unlike his Roman friends Cortesi and Castellesi, Maffei lived to react to Martin Luther. His *Nasi Romani in Martinum Lutherum Apologeticus,* written in 1520,[125] answered Luther's early attacks on Rome and the papacy. In the *Apologeticus* Maffei used basic humanist and theological concepts to defend the Church and Western culture generally. In this treatise he summarized his essential views as well as the basic presuppositions of curial humanism. Although his knowledge of Luther's teachings was second-hand, obtained probably through the writings of the papal *magister sacri palatii,* the Dominican Silvester Prierias,[126] and although he did not understand all of Luther's criticisms correctly, Maffei clearly realized that Luther was attacking the foundations of a classicized view of culture which had been advanced by the Roman humanists.

Using an effective rhetorical device, Maffei had Rome, as the *nasus romanus,* speak in the first person singular.[127] Maffei's Rome personified Western culture, and had provided peace and law to the world. Again Maffei postulated a continuous development from ancient Rome to Christian Rome. As Rome proclaimed, "After the faith had been received, I gave forth *exempla* no less than before.[128] In this polemical context, however, Maffei preferred to state the relationship between ancient and Christian Rome more boldly. Rome has taught the same moral lessons throughout her history. Rome has both conquered the barbarians and defeated the enemies of the faith; its victories have made its rites and teachings universal. Maffei's unitary view of Roman history provided him with the basis for his defense of Western culture in the body of the *Apologeticus.*

In detailing the criticisms and teachings of the German reformer, Maffei laid special stress on Luther's rejection of the Christian tradition. Rather than humbly accepting the tradition of Christian teachers, Luther demonstrated his pride by denying the authority of centuries of the Christian magisterium. He arbitrarily excluded all post-Augustinian theologians from an authoritative place in the Church, thereby destroying the continuity of Christian doctrine.[129] To counter Luther's attacks, Maffei emphasized the position the Scholastic theologians held in the teaching tradition of the Church and their value as expounders of Christian truth; he thereby implicitly defended his own right to contribute to the understanding of Christianity.[130] It should be remembered that Maffei's criticisms of contemporary Scholasticism centered on its excesses and not on its fundamentals.

In reply to Luther's attacks and in accordance with Maffei's strongly pro-papal feelings, the papacy is given a central place in the *Apologeticus.* Maffei argues that no one should seek to find faults in a reigning pope; rather, the good Christian must leave to God a papal sinner's final judgment.[131] The pope guards the Christian tradition and the truth of Scripture and to attack him is to side with the heretics. As the leader of the Church, he interprets the Christian tradition authoritatively. No interpretation of Scripture, therefore, can be independent of the tradition of the Church; private interpretation endangers the unity of the Church and threatens orthodoxy.[132] Thus, all contemporary practices rested on the integrity of the Christian tradition as interpreted by the pope.

The *Apologeticus* concludes with a defense of Aristotle and the classical authors used by Christian writers throughout the centuries. Luther, Maffei concedes, rightly condemns those who wander from the truth in their pursuit of pagan learning, but he himself has gone astray in extending this condemnation to all who have given attention to the ancients. Ancient philosophy and classical learning can be a

source of strength to the Christian as well as a danger. Maffei understood Luther's criticisms as being directed not merely at the excesses
of contemporary Scholasticism and certain practices of the Church
(all of which would have elicited Maffei's agreement), but at the very
essence of the Christian tradition. To make this point, Maffei invoked
his favorite, Basil the Great. Philosophy, poetry, history—all classical
literature—can be used by the Christian when it teaches moral truths;
this was the common argument of Basil and Maffei, as proved by men
like Jerome and Augustine. Ulysses is as valuable a model of patience
as Job. The wisdom of God is great and can use all things, even evil
ones, to bring forth good.[133] A Christian's use of classical learning is
not an aberration for Maffei but an essential element in the Christian
tradition. In this, one of his last writings, Maffei reiterated the message
of the *Commentaria Urbana,* his first work, thereby indicating the
essential unity and continuity of his thought.

The *Apologeticus* summarized the moderate strand of Roman
humanism which Maffei represented. Maffei avoided the extremes of
Cortesi's language and the shrillness of Castellesi's deprecation of
secular knowledge. He was able to incorporate a variety of humanist
and medieval traditions and use them to create a complete theological and cultural scheme. He tried to rationalize the secular and Christian
cultures by emphasizing the points they had in common. For a model
he turned to the Church Fathers, especially the Greeks. Like Cortesi,
Maffei accepted the teachings of Scholasticism as part of the deposit
of truth, but like Castellesi he felt the need to censure the Scholastics'
excesses strongly and to constantly warn of the limits of reason. His
success in holding to a middle ground between his two friends allowed
him to form a more balanced theology and to try to avoid an improper
emphasis on one element over another.

Maffei was a Roman humanist and his cultural and theological ideas
revolved on the presuppositions expressed by Roman humanism. To
provide a cover and unifying force in his conceptions of culture and
theology, Maffei viewed the Church and the papacy as the continuators
and guardians of Roman secular and religious values. Maffei's writings
proved that the Roman curial humanist conception of the Church and
its place in culture could incorporate the entire theological structure
of the Fathers and the Scholastics to form a moderately phrased
synthesis. He believed that his classical and Christian authorities taught
the same message, but that they did not have to speak in exactly the
same terms in expressing their essential unity. Fundamental to this
projection of unity was Rome, which he viewed as the symbolic and
actual center of Western culture. Maffei's Rome embraced all learning

and used it to aid the Christian in his struggle for salvation. This high-minded view of the place of Rome in the cultural and religious life of his day accounts for Maffei's concern with Rome's abuses and his place in the reform tradition of Renaissance Rome which formed a logical conclusion to the moral and intellectual concerns of so many contemporary thinkers.

9

Roman Humanism and Curial Reform

No topic so fully occupied the minds of religious thinkers in the quattro- and early cinquecento as the state of the Church and the need for its reformation.[1] Although reform of the Church was an ancient theme built into Christianity by its views of sin, decline, and regeneration,[2] quattrocento Christians saw in the dislocations and scandals of the Great Schism and in the tendency of the clergy to become ever more involved in political and financial affairs proof of the vital need for reform at all levels. In their analyses of the causes of decay, all quattrocento reformers centered their attention on the defects of the papacy and the Curia Romana. No matter how unfamiliar they might have been with the actual workings of the Curia, they saw in the financial exactions of the bureaucracy, the irregularities of Roman clerical life, and the papal power of dispensation the roots of a general decay in Christendom which required immediate attention.[3] The number and variety of men who produced reform literature proved the seriousness of the reform crisis.

Within the body of reformers the humanists formed a small though influential group. Their reform plans were logical extensions of the moral emphasis in humanism's rhetoric.[4] Those humanists who considered the defects of contemporary religious life followed the secular procedure of seeking ancient models for reform; the only difference was that the Fathers of the Church replaced the ancient pagans. Using their knowledge of the Christian past and the ideals of patristic thinkers, many humanists condemned the luxury, religious indifference, and irregular lives of their contemporaries, especially the clergy.[5] The humanists shifted the foundation of reform away from the theological and legal bases that had inspired medieval reform thought and substituted general moral propositions and a historical dimension. In keeping with rhetorical theory, they approached reform from the perspective of the individual in society. Church reform thought complemented the individualistic moral interests of Renaissance humanists, although the two were not necessarily the same or always connected. While not all humanists moved from the proclamation of personal moral improvement to the reform of Christian society in general, a substantial number did.

Like their non-Roman contemporaries, Roman humanist reform writers emphasized morality, but they differed from them in their familiarity with the roots of dissatisfaction in the Curia and in their greater sensitivity to the institutional dimensions of reform.[6] Roman humanists were more conscious of the need to move from personal, or individual, reform to general, or institutional, reform, but they were not always successful in devising mechanisms by which to pass from one level to the other. As moral critics Roman humanists found much material for complaint and castigation in the city.[7] As members of the Curia and the ecclesiastical establishment, they were more precise in their criticisms but less able to analyze the problems in any radical fashion. Roman humanist reform thought always betrayed both the real desire for amelioration on the part of Roman intellectuals and their inability to propose any efficient solutions.

The bureaucratic nature of the Curia and the humanists' position within its various offices resulted in an essentially mechanistic view of curial and, ultimately, Church reform. This resulted in part from a defect in humanist reform rhetoric, which lacked tools for a critical assessment of institutional and societal abuses. This deficiency was especially evident when reformers dealt with the Curia and the papal household. Since a series of laws and regulations defined the Curia in terms of its duties, reform therefore had to be functional; it was understood as regularization of the bureaucracy in order to bring about its more efficient operation. This could be accomplished best by correcting one or another aspect of the bureaucracy, not by altering the body or the actual constitution of the institution. This mechanistic approach fit the theological view of the divine establishment of the papacy; by accepting this concept, the humanists avoided any theologically radical stance. The mechanistic approach was, however, an essential denial of the historical basis of any humanist reform plan.[8] What exists is implicitly justified not only by its very existence but also by God's special dispensation. The curial reformers lacked the means, or indeed the desire, to challenge the institution in any fundamental manner. This position did not mean that the curialists ignored the need for improvement on the part of the institution as well as the individual; rather, it reflected their belief that the way to curial reform was through legislation regulating the Curia's various components. The curialists' approach resulted in a compromise that combined the individual and institutional elements and made curial reform as advocated by the humanists and others both formal and ultimately ineffective.

The Curia and its institutions placed severe limits on the ability of humanists to respond to the reform needs of Rome. All curial reform plans, no matter what their source, centered on the person of the pope. This was not the result of the individualistic procedure of humanist rhetoricians; rather, the pope became the institution personified. No matter what the truth, the pope was portrayed as desirous of improvement and always in the process of reforming. Occasionally a reformer would note that the pope was not helping the forces of good as much as he could, and a few, very few, were willing to condemn one or two aspects of a pope's life or policies, usually after the pope's death, but no essential criticism of the person of the pope or his powers came from the Curia or its humanists.[9] Reformers emphasized the holy aspects of the successors of Peter and the propriety of their undertaking reform, not the actual attitude of a reigning pontiff toward reform.

A logical result of this emphasis on the papacy and the constitution of the Curia was a concentration on the clerical, especially high clerical, aspects of the Church. Ecclesiologically this meant that reform issued from the highest authorities in the Church and was directed in a hierarchical manner. The laity's needs were subsumed under clerical reform. In the eyes of the reformers, the defects and immorality of the laity resulted not only from their own deficiencies but in great part from the clergy's irresponsibility in not providing proper moral advice and models. This concern for hierarchy and clergy, so strong in Rome, contrasted with the general humanist solicitude for the secular problems of the laity. It represents yet another adjustment humanists underwent in Rome.

A more subtle limit imposed on the curial humanist reformers arose from their position in the bureaucracy. As the humanists' ability to capitalize on their position in the Curia grew, their desire to criticize the institution and demand essential reforms declined proportionally since any major alteration could adversely affect their financial and social positions. Many Roman humanists lamented the curial abuses surrounding them and sincerely wished for improvement; nevertheless, a major reorganization of the bureaucracy would have removed procedures that directly benefited them. Many humanists became wealthy or at least financially comfortable through their share in fees charged by the Curia. Humanists who rose to episcopal rank seldom spent time in their dioceses. Castellesi, for example, never visited England while he was bishop of two English sees. Mario Maffei, bishop of Aquino and of Cavallion, lived in Rome, Florence, and Volterra, and ignored the urgings of his close friend Jacopo Sadoleto to fulfill his episcopal duties.[10] The benefits accruing from the abuses were all too obvious to be relinquished summarily by those enjoying them.

The curial ambience also encouraged ambivalence on the part of humanist reformers toward the major instrument for Church reform in the quattrocento, the ecumenical council.[11] This was a legacy of the years of contention between the councils and the papacy during the Great Schism, when the popes had to defend their political and financial independence against the claims of the councils. The council fathers had directed much of their reforming zeal to criticizing the defects of the Curia and the papacy rather than the deficiencies in themselves. The councils became conduits for expressions of anti-Roman feeling, including those of disaffected curialists.[12] Both the Council of Constance (1417) and the Council of Basel (1431–1448) issued important calls for curial reform that could have undermined the pope's control of his own government.[13] The Curia and the councils viewed reform differently and succeeded in checking each other and preventing any significant changes. While most Christians looked to the councils for reform, Romans interpreted any conciliar program as directed at depriving the Holy See of its legitimate powers and sources of revenue. While this suspicion of conciliarism appeared less frequently in humanist reform proposals than in those of other curialists, some humanists followed curial prejudice in treating the councils as encroachers on papal privileges. Roman humanists and clerics wanted the pope to dominate any council. During the Fifth Lateran Council (1513–1517), the pope issued the council's reform legislation as his bulls.[14] For the curialists, any conciliar reform legislation naturally required papal implementation.

Whatever attitude a humanist or any concerned cleric brought to the reform of the Curia, he related it to the general reform of the Church and Christian society. Moral reform was never conceived of as purely Roman. Rome's reform would provide the example and machinery for the rest of Christendom. Curial reform was only the first, albeit the most vital, element in a program for the general improvement of Christian society. In this respect Roman reformers tacitly accepted the arguments of the conciliarists that Rome, being the source of much corruption, must first clean its own house, before any general improvement would be possible. Nevertheless, the Roman reformers had a certain parochial attitude toward their subject which caused them to ignore the difficulties of reform outside Rome and to underestimate the grievances expressed against Rome. They too willingly believed that whatever reform the papacy initiated would automatically be effective.

❧ I ❧

A variety of reform traditions helped to establish the Roman humanist reformers' essential principles. These traditions did not have any special relationship to humanism, since they developed from medieval experiences; however, they did form a collateral branch that provided humanists with much of the material they could reorganize to fit their own purposes.

The most important nonhumanist reform tradition in Rome was that of the reform bulls and plans issued by the various popes in the quattro- and early cinquecento.[15] The papal reforms were essentially administrative in nature. They all concurred in lamenting contemporary immorality and emphasizing the need for immediate relief. Several popes actually ordered the production of reform plans, but few of these were ever promulgated, which testifies to the limits of the papacy's will to reform. Although the genre extended back to the Avignon papacy, Martin V issued the first reform bull of the restored papacy.[16] Pius II contributed the first significant papal reform legislation in 1464.[17] His plan established the basic procedure repeated by his successors. Pius included the major ideas that were circulating in Roman reform circles: a strong papalism, a plea for peace among Christians in preparation for a crusade against the Turks, and the need to begin reform with regulation of the Curia. Although Pius expressed a theological preference for reform on the individual level,[18] his procedure was essentially the administrative-mechanistic one that characterized all curial reform programs.

In lamenting the evil state of the contemporary Church, Pius specifically cited avarice and its ecclesiastical offspring simony.[19] The pope promised to offer to the Church a fitting model for all to follow in remedying deficiencies. He provided rules and regulations for the various curial and Church offices, beginning with the College of Cardinals.[20] Many of these rules were purely technical in nature, such as those relating to the form of papal bulls, the handwriting of the papal scriptors, and payments for curial services. They all were aimed at making the centralized administration of the Church perform its duties more smoothly and act more morally.

Sixtus IV drew up the most comprehensive reform program after Pius's.[21] It, too, claimed to offer an example that others could follow in initiating reform. Sixtus's scheme gave special consideration to the papal household, the need to maintain efficiency and regularity in the government, and to limit the number of people in Rome who had no legitimate business there. These reforms addressed specific Roman problems.[22] Since excess breeds abuse and irregularity, the plan imposed strict limits on income, dress, and building.[23] For all its detail and careful presentation, however, Sixtus never issued his bull. It provided the guide for the reform bull ordered by Alexander VI in his one and only reform period following the murder of his favorite son, Juan, in 1497, but this, like its model, remained unimplemented.[24]

Julius II concentrated too fully on political and cultural activities to give much attention to reform, especially since it would have limited the income he so desperately needed for his wars. Nevertheless, he was sensitive to curial abuses and tried in small ways to provide some improvement. As his most personal reform, Julius issued a bull forbidding simony in papal elections. He was motivated by memories of the simoniacal practices that had characterized Alexander VI's and his own election, when cardinals' votes went to the highest bidder.[25] Of greater importance was the summoning of the Fifth Lateran Council with a mandate to reform.[26] Julius called the council for political rather than religious reasons; he wished to counter the French-dominated and antipapal Council of Pisa, which accused him of immoral behavior and called for a general reform of the Curia. The Fifth Lateran was meant to initiate reform in a manner that would not threaten the pope and the Curia. Despite this political motivation, the fathers of the council made some progress in refurbishing reform proposals dating as far back as Martin V's reign.

The reform program of the Fifth Lateran was expressed in final form in two bulls issued by Leo X: the *Pastoralis officii divina providentia* of December 13, 1513, and the *Supernae dispositionis arbitrio* of May 5, 1514.[27] The first bull dealt specifically with the Curia. Its major theme was the financial charges made by the Curia, which the bull sought to limit. It provided a price list for the services rendered by the various curial offices. The second bull was broader in intent. It outlined the duties of both clerics and laymen, stressing the moral lives of the cardinals. Simony, concubinage, blasphemy, unqualified priests, and witchcraft were all discussed as part of the moral degeneration of the Church. Together these two documents illustrate the movement of reform from curial regulation to general ecclesiastical and societal improvement. They are especially significant because they restated the traditional curial view of reform in a formal fashion immediately before the Reformation.

A second reform tradition in Rome paralleled the official papal reform bulls. Individuals, usually high clerics, proposed reform programs of their own. They usually covered the same topics the popes' plans did, but in less detail and with a greater theological orientation. A few, like Cardinal Domenico Capranica's *Advismenta super reformatione Papae et Romanae Curiae,* were directly related to conciliar pressures for reform.[28] Most, however, expressed the dissatisfaction of conscientious prelates with the sad state of the Church. Among these, two were especially prominent because of their authors. Domenico de' Domenichi (1416–1478), a doctor of theology, served as apostolic protonotary, bishop of Torcello (1448), as well as a diplomat under Pius II. A learned and devout man, he knew well the defects of the Curia and the Church. His *Tractatus de reformationibus Romanae Ecclesiae* is a learned discussion of the depravation of the Church and the need for reform.[29] He argued that reform must begin in the Curia with a list of the offices that required rehabilitation. In general his emphasis was on individual improvement rather than institutional reform.[30]

The pope must be especially solicitous of reform, Domenichi continued. He should initiate it first in the College of Cardinals, the group closest to him, and then proceed through each element in the bureaucracy. He expanded his reform by calling for the standardization of religious rites, orderliness in religious ceremonies, and the acceptance and reinvigoration of ancient customs. He was anxious that pluralism and nepotism be ended.[31] Similar to Domenichi's program was Nicholas of Cusa's reform program.[32] It, however, was more comprehensive; it began with curial abuses and soon passed on to general reform by urging the pope to send out to all Christian lands visitors whose duty would be to implement reform. More than most, Cusa argued the danger to salvation in an unreformed Church.

A further reform tradition with adherents in Renaissance Rome was the theological-mystical approach. Although it had elements in common with both humanist reform thought and curial institutional reform, it developed from a combination of older medieval ideas and recent mystical trends. Theological-mystical plans usually presented reform as a return to the purity of the early Church and provided elaborate theological accounts of the origin of its decline from its pristine period. This theological form, with its mystical additives, was not historical; its instruments of analysis were often drawn from Biblical texts, especially the Apocalypse, rather than from a detailed study of Church history. This strand could incorporate a variety of intellectual influences: Scholastic metaphysics; medieval mysticism, e.g., Joachimism or Lullism; and a taste for esoteric knowledge, especially of the Cabala. Its major representatives usually came from the ranks of the religious orders, with their strong medieval traditions. It often posited a contemporary moral decline as part of a broader epochal decline. In viewing decline and regeneration from a mystical perspective, these reformers projected an essentially ahistorical or metahistorical understanding of the Church and its development which separated them from humanist historicism. Giles of Viterbo, an Augustinian, blended the Scholasticism of his order with cabalistic and Joachimite views of history. He portrayed his own day as a time of both the deepest evils and the dawn of a new Golden Age based on the ten ages of the world.[33] Any contradictions in these claims were reconciled by a mystical interpretation of the true forces in history.

A moderate version of theological-mystical reform thought is the *Libellus de Re publica christiana, pro vera eiusdem Rei publicae reformatione* (ca. 1521), by the Observant Franciscan, Pietro Colonna Galatino (1464–1540).[34] Galatino's many works intermingled a variety of themes: Joachimism, the mystical metaphysics of Saint Bonaventure, and a deep study of Hebrew and the Cabala. He spent many years in Rome, served as papal penitentiary under Leo X and Adrian VI, and belonged to the Hebrew circle of Giles of Viterbo. His writings, most of which remain in manuscript form,[35] show a program of mystical interpretation of the Scriptures, the degenerate state of the Church, and the need for renewal.

The *Libellus,* which was dedicated to Leo X but readdressed to Adrian VI after the Medici pope's death (December 1521), discusses its subject from a mystical-hierarchical perspective. It organizes reform around the concept of the Church as the mystical body of Christ. Each member of the Church and Christian society assumes the functions of some corporeal element: the pope is the head, the cardinals the heart, the priests the ears, the emperor the neck, lesser kings the arms, and so on.[36] This mystical identification is extended to dress and adornments; the crown is victory, the ring fidelity, and the precious stones the virtues.[37] Unfortunately, these virtues are weak and the Christian Republic is deformed. Fraud, immorality, disobedience, ignorance, and luxury afflict the clergy and laity equally. The result of these deformations is the disunity of Christendom and the oppression by the Turks.[38] To counter these sins and their ill effects, Galatino proposes two papal initiatives. The first is the selection of only those men who are qualified to serve as clerics and prelates.[39] This solution is in keeping with the hierarchical position he states in the opening of the *Libellus.* The second calls for the unification of Christians by the pope and his leadership in a great crusade against the Turks with the object of liberating Jerusalem.[40] Galatino in his treatise united mystical elements and specifics of curial reform literature.

❧ II ❧

The humanist curial reformers used essentially the same themes that characterized papal and private reform plans and, to a lesser extent, the mystical-theological programs. There is an essential unity in the procedure humanists and nonhumanists employed in discussing abuses and improvement. The humanists, however, brought to their reforms strongly rhetorical and historical ideas that made their plans more immediate and provided a more conscious statement of the sources of abuses. In keeping with the rhetorical nature of humanism, the orations given at the papal court by humanists contained criticisms and pleas for reform. This genre has recently been studied in great detail.[41] The Fifth Lateran Council was especially successful in eliciting reform oratory.[42] However, while humanist orators included critical references to the state of the Church and the Curia and called for moral regeneration, the clerical audience that heard these orations did not always appreciate such topics. Jacopo Gherardi in his diary of Sixtus IV's reign remarked on a preacher who spent his time lambasting the clergy and who was not appreciated by his auditors.[43] Still, humanists did exploit their oratorical opportunities to express their dissatisfaction with the contemporary Church.

In a similar manner, a humanist occasionally detailed his criticism of the Church and society in individual treatises addressed to an important cleric. Benedetto Maffei (1429–1494), an influential curialist and a member of the Roman academy, followed this procedure in his *De moribus nostrorum temporum* (1483), which he dedicated to Cardinal Marco Barbo.[44] In the treatise Maffei relates three examples of children killing or defrauding their parents because of greed. Maffei interpreted these causes of parricide as proof of the general corruption of society and the need for change. He lacked, however, any real program of reform or analysis of the causes of this immorality. His one solution was to limiting the *oratores* (ambassadors) at the papal court. A uniquely Roman idea, it did not address the pressing problems of degeneration and reform.

Few men were in a better position to know the problems of the Curia and its traditions than Cardinal Adriano Castellesi, Raffaele Maffei, and Paolo Cortesi. Castellesi in particular represented a high curial humanist who, even though sensitive to religious problems, enjoyed too many of the fruits of the curial system to present any reforming stance. Still, even Castellesi was aware of the need for improvement among his contemporaries. In his short treatise *De Romanae*

Ecclesiae potestate (*ca.* 1492), which he dedicated to Cardinal Francesco Todeschini-Piccolomini, he collected a series of citations from canon law (rewritten in good Latin) which detailed the norms for the hierarchy and governance of the Church.[45] Its composition indicates that Castellesi realized that some improvement was needed, but he did not expand on its themes in his later writings.

Raffaele Maffei gave much fuller attention to the question of reform and produced a program that combined elements of the humanist, curial, and theological traditions. Although he prepared a complete plan in the *De Institutione Christiana*, his other writings also contain statements on the problems of the Church and the need for change. A theological conception of decline underlies Maffei's criticisms of abuses and his proposals for reform. He expressed the general principle that the Church has fallen from its pure state and must return to it. He gives this idea a Neo-Platonic basis: The Church has fallen from its ideal perfection and must work constantly in order to rectify this fault. Reform is always possible since God would never abandon his Church and leave it without the means for regeneration.[46] Still, the problems remain formidable. The clergy is unprepared for its duties and acts from cupidity.[47] Rome is a place where the unworthy are promoted and the libidinous find shelter.[48] Success in Rome implies moral failure. Maffei relates the lament of his close acquaintance in Rome Cardinal Cosimo Orsini (d. 1481), who after his election to the cardinalate and involvement in curial affairs longed for the peace of his monastery of Farfa.[49] Maffei's own experiences during the Borgia papacy perhaps moved him to leave Rome.

Although Maffei displayed a strongly pro-papal theology and ecclesiology, he willingly criticized what he perceived as papal failures. Indeed, in his *Commentaria Urbana* (1506), he developed a theory of the decline of the modern papacy.[50] He dated this contemporary decline from the reign of Paul II, who turned his attention away from the needs of the Church and his duties in order to satisfy his own pleasures by devoting himself to his art and gem collections.[51] This indifference to the good of the Church continued under Sixtus IV, whose nepotistic policies endangered the Church through the promotion of unworthy relatives.[52] The final example of papal decay was, naturally enough, Alexander VI, whose crimes were so great that Maffei felt it improper to discuss them in print.[53] This analysis continued in Maffei's *Brevis Historia* of Julius II and Leo X (*ca.* 1520), which criticizes Julius II for continuing in his reign the excesses of his predecessors and especially for the great human carnage caused by his wars (Maffei regarded Julius's policies in themselves as laudable).[54] None of these criticisms, however, moved Maffei to abandon his faith in the papacy as the reforming force.

Among the excesses of Renaissance Rome, Maffei singled out for special scrutiny the great building plans of the Renaissance popes, cardinals, and wealthy laymen.[55] His attitude contrasts markedly with that of most of his contemporaries, humanists and nonhumanists, who praised such building programs as proof of concern for religion or guarantees of immortality. Maffei judged expensive building enterprises as avaricious in nature and the result of the desire for display and luxury.[56] Such a combination of avarice and display, in Maffei's eyes, contributed to the papacy's abandonment of Christian virtue. From the popes and cardinals this disease spread to laymen, who could not afford a palace.[57] As remedy to this specific abuse Maffei argued that only necessary building should be undertaken, a requirement he proposed for ecclesiastical as well as secular structures.[58] This censure extended to the new St. Peter's begun by Julius II and continued by Leo. Maffei dismissed the building as not at that time necessary.[59] He rejected the traditional curial arguments favoring ecclesiastical magnificence as testimony to later generations of the liberality and religiosity of their times.[60] Evidence of religious fervor, countered Maffei, consists in following the simplicity of Christ.

Maffei's observations on avarice and ostentation continued in his consideration of the state of the religious orders, male and female. Like microcosms of the Church, the majority of the religious orders have fallen from the pristine purity exhibited by their founders. Acquisitiveness rather than the poverty of Christ governs them. Possessions have replaced simplicity and contemplation as the object of monastic life.[61] As a counter to such degeneration, Maffei supported the reform movement within the religious orders. This harsh attitude toward the orders reflected Maffei's own monastic proclivities and his deep study of Basil the Great, the great model of monastic learning and regularity of life.

These random remarks received their full development in the final two chapters of the *De Institutione Christiana*. These sections, entitled *De moribus et vitae genere curialium* and *Quomodo his malis occurratur,* stand apart from the body of the treatise.[62] They may, therefore, be read as a complete reform plan and as a plea to Leo X to initiate the necessary reforms. The scheme combines humanist moralistic and curial administrative-institutional reforms and utilizes the chief arguments of each. However, by virtue of its emphasis on curial reform as the beginning of a general reform of the Church, it does have a breadth not always found in the other curial reform plans. The themes Maffei developed show that he was familiar with a variety of reform ideas and anxious to provide them with a personal stamp.

Rome, the common fatherland, is the center of Maffei's reform design. Men come to the city for one of five reasons: *religio, quies, ambitio, avaritia,* and *voluptas.*[63] A modest Christian can find in Rome the center of religion and peace and a door to paradise. Its holy places give comfort and strength to believers and provide havens for exiles. But ambition, avarice, and illicit desire equally attract others, who corrupt the city; to such men Rome's sacred possessions are merely sources of revenue. Maffei provides a litany of the consequent depravations. The level of education in Rome is low. Curial posts go to the highest bidders, who scheme together to exploit the offices for their own good. Motivated only by greed, they blacken the name of the pope when he does not satisfy their demands. The courts respond only to money, and pious pilgrims are defrauded. Servants avoid their duties and spend their time telling lewd stories. Prelates' *familiae* abound in ignorant men. Rather than caring for the poor, supposedly religious men prefer to feed their pets. Brothels abound and sexual license goes unchecked. The Curia has become a danger to salvation.[64] In support of his complaints Maffei cites the great humanist Leon Battista Alberti, who spent several years in Rome, by comparing the Curia to a feast of fools and to the theater.[65] To Maffei " a place does not sanctify men, but men make a place holy" (*non locus homines sed homines locum sanctificant*).[66]

Maffei relies on the pope to correct these abuses. The pontiff must purge Rome of its evil morals and reestablish its primitive *libertas;* only in this manner can the members be brought in conformity to the head (*membra capiti congrua . . . reddantur*).[67] Implicit is the belief that the pope is not corrupt and intends to correct those who are. Maffei cites six specific topics the pope must address: the care of Rome and the Curia, the reform of the secular clergy, the improvement of the religious clergy, the review and authentication of religious writings, the revitalization of civil and ecclesiastical government, and, lastly, the restoration of peace among Christians. For Maffei, papal reform must be all-embracing; beginning with the Curia and Rome, it should extend to all Christendom.

Rome and the Curia receive Maffei's fullest attention. The pope must assure the distribution of curial offices according to merit so that even the poor can hope for appointment. The Curia's financial state must be regularized and special care must be given to using crusade and ransom revenues for their appointed ends. The financial demands of the Curia for the performance of its services need special correction. Lawyer's fees should be fixed to prevent unending litigation. Maffei comments that a petitioner must sell a house or a farm in order to raise sufficient funds to extract a papal indulgence from the Curia.[68] Once the curial bureaucracy has been corrected, the pope must turn to the city proper. He must expel prostitutes, panderers, gamblers, blasphemers, and others of their ilk. The city must be properly policed, especially the areas around the Curia. Care should be taken to guarantee a steady food supply. Churches and monasteries that have fallen into disrepair should be restored.[69] The pope must personally perform acts of charity and preach publicly. Seminaries, where the virtues and the liberal arts thrive, should be established.[70] The pope need look only to his predecessors for models.

Clergymen, the second object of Maffei's reform, are berated for living lives of splendor rather than apostolic simplicity. Again, Maffei points to the recent past as the beginning of these abuses. First, pluralism must be abolished; one church suffices for one priest. Next, the reservation of offices, which makes an ecclesiastical post functionally hereditary and results in unworthy succession, must be ended. In choosing men for ecclesiastical office, attention should be given to native residents who are familiar with local customs. The clergy must look to the physical state of their churches and maintain them in proper order.[71] The primary step in clerical reform, Maffei emphasizes, is the appointment of pastors whose lives display moderation and religious sensitivity; he realizes, however, that due to the long years of neglect this cannot be accomplished immediately.[72] The ancient vice of simony, which has survived all attacks, is a particular plague on the Church and must be eradicated.[73]

Maffei's third reform thrust focuses on the religious orders, all of which, he argues, have fallen from the high standards established by their founders. Their members have become great temporal empire builders rather than simple men pursuing lives devoted to prayer and contemplation. Maffei takes up the theme of the contentiousness of the religious orders, especially the Dominicans and Franciscans. To eliminate such excesses no one should attack a religious writer without first basing himself on another holy authority. In this way, both orthodoxy and intelligent investigation of sacred topics can be maintained.[74] In all of this Maffei strove to direct the orders back to the ideals of their founders and away from the excesses of wealth and intellectual pride.

The fourth reform, the call for the review and authentication of religious writings, is a unique element in Maffei's reform program but one very close to him as a scholar. In agreement with the papal reform bulls, Maffei calls for the pope to oversee the curial literary style so that it will correspond to the dignity of the Church and the papacy.[75] More serious problems arise, however, when historical and geographical inaccuracies enter into religious narratives, thereby allowing apocryphal stories to pass for the truth.[76] Even the Scriptures have been corrupted over the centuries as a result of misinterpretation and mistranslation.[77] Although these errors are not always dangerous to faith, the pope should correct them so that the dignity and decorum of the Church may be maintained. To accomplish this Maffei proposes textual criticism—the comparison of manuscripts.[78] He extends this procedure to religious rites, which vary from region to region, and calls for standardization.[79] (Maffei even contributed to this reform by composing offices and lives of saints according to stricter rules of historical accuracy.)[80] Further casualties of ignorance and irregularity are those papal laws which have lost their force and which should be reissued.[81]

The penultimate element in Maffei's plan centers on the deterioration of civil and ecclesiastical government. Previously Maffei had criticized the contemporary civil administration, and once he had written to Pietro Soderini, the ruler of Florence and a friend, to complain of the prevalence of evil government.[82] In his reform plan he noted that civil society had suffered a period of decline similar to that of the Church. Due to the passage of time and to the negligence of authorities, many evils had been tolerated, such as the factionalism of the Guelphs and Ghibellines in Italy.[83] Evil laws had been introduced, while good ones had been allowed to lapse. As a result of this, public morality had declined. In Maffei's judgment, the performance of the contemporary Christian princes as defenders of public morality had been greatly inferior to that of the Roman emperors.[84] Family feuds thrived while public morality went unpoliced.[85] The pope must urge civil rulers to perform their duties and restore public order.

The final and most important object of Maffei's reform plan was peace among Christians.[86] No topic was more central to the reform literature of the late Middle Ages and the Renaissance than the plea for peace. Maffei, like other reformers, argued that no other reform proposal could succeed unless there was general peace. To make peace the pope must act modestly and humanely in guiding the princes. He should dispatch legates to impress upon the Christian powers the need for peace and use of his spiritual powers to support this aim.[87] Maffei opposed the recent course of papal history with its reliance on military force; rather than use arms the pope should depend on his good example and his spiritual powers. Indeed, as history demonstrates, he argued, whatever the popes had gained by recourse to arms had ultimately bred evil.[88] The pope should leave the brandishment of arms to the secular powers and devote himself to imploring God to help them in their campaigns against his enemies, especially the Turks. In that way all people would be brought under papal obedience.[89]

Maffei's reform plan concludes with a strong reaffirmation of papal authority, reflecting both the accepted curial view of the centrality of papal power and Maffei's own hope in the person of the pope as the effective reformer, a hope that was especially strong with reference to Leo. The great and tremendous power of the pope stands above all others; no one may attempt to deprive him of his position in the Church save in the case of heresy. Papal power, which comes from God and reaches to heaven itself, requires that even an unworthy pope be tolerated.[90] For Maffei, the pope as the great guardian of Christendom enjoys universal authority.[91] Maffei's imperialistic conception of the papacy left only the "new" emperor, Leo, as the initiator of reform.[92]

Maffei's program drew on all the reform traditions available to him. While it lacked the detailed treatment of the curial offices common to the papal bulls, it displayed a comprehensiveness and Romanocentricism that rendered it significant in the history of curial reform. It promoted Rome as the initiator and director of reform and placed absolute trust in the pope. Maffei acknowledged the rights of the curial institutions and tried to work within their structures. He brought to this reform a theological sophistication and foundation not common to humanist reformers. Both his view of the decline from a perfect archetype and his concern for theological purity moved his proposals beyond the institutional limits of curial reform. As a humanist Maffei displayed a historical sensitivity to the origin of abuses and a confidence in the ability of humanist scholarship to advance reform. His strong sense of morality reached a logical conclusion in a call for individual and general reformation. He succeeded in synthesizing the various reform elements into one reform program. His skillful summation of the existing reform ideas did not provide him with an effective means of transcending their limits, however, and his program remained unimplemented like all the others.

❧ III ❧

Whether humanist, papal, or theological-mystical, all the reform proposals discussed so far in this chapter offered essentially general criticisms of and rules for the reformation of the Church and Christian society. Even the papal bulls, in their treatment of the curial offices and the clergy, centered on no individual group and offered no deep analysis of specific elements in the Curia. In contradistinction to these writings, Paolo Cortesi in his *De Cardinalatu* (1510) provided a procedure of great specificity, although it did not conflict with the established reform traditions.[93] The treatise concentrated on a small but vitally important body in the Curia and in Roman society generally, the College of Cardinals, a choice which allowed its author to investigate the needs and problems of the cardinals with great care and in an encyclopedic manner.

In presenting the *De Cardinalatu* as a reform treatise comparable to those of Cortesi's contemporaries, it is necessary to define reform in a specific and limited manner. Reform when applied to the *De Cardinalatu* refers to the regularization and rationalization of accepted procedures and rules rather than to a radical critique or alteration of established practices. It does not posit a perfect past which must be recovered. This restricted meaning of reform accounts for the weakness of the *De Cardinalatu* as a reform instrument. It did not offer radical solutions to problems and as a consequence historians have neglected it as a reform treatise.[94] Cortesi loyally accepted the essential strictures imposed by the Curia on its members, but he also promoted a rational procedure for avoiding the excesses that had characterized the recent history of the cardinalate. He accomplished this without diluting the powers and privileges of that body. Cortesi's selection of the cardinalate for detailed treatment reflected the importance of the College of Cardinals in the Church, in the Curia, and in the cultural life of Renaissance Rome.[95]

The history of the College of Cardinals throughout the later Middle Ages had been one of ever-increasing importance in the administration and ecclesiology of the Church.[96] As papal electors, administrators, legates, holders of great benefices and wealth, and often as relatives of the reigning pontiff, the cardinals individually and corporately ranked below only the pope in the ecclesiastical and curial bureaucracy. Cardinalate pretensions greatly increased during the Western Schism, when the rivalry between contending popes led many theologians and canon lawyers to turn to the college as the only institution capable of legitimately ending the chaos.[97] Legal theorists and ambitious cardinals proclaimed the college equal to the pope under certain circumstances and gave to it the right to depose and elect popes for the good of the Church and to end scandal. Although these claims were never generally accepted, they gave individual cardinals a putative justification for opposing papal orders when it served their purposes.[98] The cardinals tried to maintain control over the pope by forcing each participant in a conclave to sign an election capitulation affirming his intention to act only with the consent of the cardinals if elected pope. This extraordinary procedure did not lead to any lasting change in the relationship between pope and cardinals, however, for newly elected popes simply repudiated their election pacts.[99] The reestablished papacy did in time succeed in limiting the cardinals' claims to power through political and financial restraints. Nevertheless, throughout the quattrocento the cardinals maintained a position unique in Christendom and potentially threatening to a reigning pontiff.

In response to the increased prominence of the College of Cardinals in the later Middle Ages, a minor literary genre concerned with its position in the Church and vis-à-vis the papacy developed.[100] These treatises considered the college primarily from a theological and/or legal perspective. They idealized the college and treated its duties and powers as historically static. The college remained for them an object of academic treatment. Insofar as these writers considered reform, they approached it from a theoretical perspective and usually ignored the practical political and financial problems facing the cardinals in their day-to-day lives. Once established, this idealized genre changed little throughout the sixteenth century.[101] Cortesi's exposition of the college differed from the theological and legal approaches in concentrating on the real problems of the cardinals.

The reform of the cardinalate was not completely ignored in quattrocento reform literature. Papal bulls devoted attention to the position of the cardinals in administering the Church. The cardinals were actually perceived as one of the sources of disorder in the Curia. Even the Avignon papacy had realized the need to control the excesses of the cardinals, corporately and individually, and had legislated limits to the cardinals' *familiae* and to ostentation, but with little success.[102] Later popes continued to work to regulate the life style of the cardinals and to render them more subservient to their will and less the haughty princes or the special pleaders for various secular rulers. Institutionally, as the popes' immediate inferiors, the cardinals had to participate in any papally initiated reform.[103]

As a result of his association with important prelates in the Curia, Cortesi appreciated at first hand the value of the cardinals in the life of Rome and the Church. He realized that whatever their political limits individually, the cardinals provided vital cultural patronage in Rome. His critical mind gave him the tools necessary to deal with the cardinals' various problems. He carefully analyzed their constitution and needs and tried to integrate humanist values into the personal and official lives of the cardinals; in a sense he wished to remake the College in a more humanistic manner. Cortesi accepted the essentially medieval traditions that had formed the cardinalate, but he modified them with humanist educational and cultural values.[104]

The *De Cardinalatu* consists of three books arranged according to the *ordo naturae,* i.e., from particular to general. The first book, entitled *Liber ethicus et contemplativus* (contemplation encompassing study and religious activity) discusses the cardinal's personal moral character, intellectual development and culture. The second, *Liber economicus,* focuses on the cardinal as director of his own household (*familia*) and a great figure in Roman society. The third, *Liber politicus,* explains the cardinal's duties and rights as an adviser to the pope and as a co-ruler of the Church. Each book in turn proceeds according to the same deductive method. Book I opens with a discussion of personal moral virtues and concludes with a dissertation on the mass, a personal activity that brings the cardinal as a religious and moral leader into contact with the members of his *familia* as spectators. Book II initially considers the cardinal's finances, the foundation of his ability to offer patronage, and concludes with his relations with other members of Roman society as the dispenser of favors. The final book concentrates first on the cardinal's position vis-à-vis the pope, then on his duties as regulator of civil and commercial activities in Rome, and finally on his role as co-ruler of the Church. The final chapter of the treatise, called *De beatitudine,* logically concludes the progression, since the heavenly reward is the individual aim of each Christian and the fulfillment of Christianity.

In his discussion of individual topics in each section of the *De Cardinalatu,* Cortesi provided general norms for all aspects of human life; each rule offered the principles necessary to judge complex situations in a rational manner. In order to demonstrate the propriety of his general rules as well as make them more relevant, Cortesi offered an abundance of contemporary and near-contemporary illustrations. With few exceptions,[105] he avoided invoking examples from classical antiquity or the more distant Christian past, favoring instead those from recent political and social events. These functional illustrations emphasize the rules presented in the *De Cardinalatu,* thereby making it a practical handbook for both the cardinal's official duties and his private life. Cortesi believed that his rules were also valid for all men who held high positions and had to make decisions.[106] Thus his position emphasized an essential unity between secular and clerical needs.

Educationally Cortesi wished the cardinal to be learned in the traditional medieval clerical disciplines of theology and canon law,[107] but also sensitive to humanist values. Such an educational balance would enable a cardinal to distinguish the moral from the immoral and to judge and enjoy literary and scholarly productions. Although this role was essentially passive (i.e., the cardinal must have the knowledge to be a critic and evaluate other men and their work), Cortesi did insist that greatest fame belonged to those cardinals who actually contributed to the advancement of scholarship and wrote books.[108] This educational program was practical and was intended to produce a cultured, learned, and discriminating prince capable of appreciating the most exacting scholarship. Although it was hardly calculated to produce a simple Francis of Assisi as a cultural hero, it did have a moral dimension since Cortesi insisted that the proper education automatically implied the ability of the learned to understand and evaluate any dilemma and act in a moral manner.

Cortesi appreciated his religious prince's need for a large and steady income. The insecure financial state of the College of Cardinals was a major obstacle to curial and ecclesiastical reform, for it forced the cardinals to become adept at exploiting abuses for their own profit.[109] The problem stemmed from the unequal economic state of individual cardinals. The cardinals divided certain common revenues due to the college. These monies could be small since they varied annually and decreased as the number of cardinals increased. Cardinals who had family wealth or had obtained rich curial and ecclesiastical offices were independent of the common monies. Others depended on them and often found them inadequate; these men had to find other financial sources to meet their needs and to live in a manner expected of a prince. Many cardinals became rapacious office seekers or pledged their service to rich kings as cardinal-protectors.[110] Cortesi realized that such activities compromised the cardinal's moral, political, and religious character and made him undependable as a cultural patron. He therefore tried to devise a system to guarantee equality. He estimated that the annual income of the College of Cardinals should be 490,000 ducats. This sum he divided among the forty cardinals, what he considered to be the ideal number of princes. The resulting 12,000 ducats, he felt, would meet any cardinal's annual requirements.[111] If, in any year, the college's revenues fell below the necessary figure, then the pope should supply the added income so that all the cardinals could live in a manner befitting their dignity and not be jealous of their richer brothers.

Twelve thousand ducats a year was a large sum, but it was realistic in light of Cortesi's recommended life style. Cortesi's discussion of the cardinal's *familia* and palace has already been examined.[112] Here it should be noted that Cortesi's prescription of a large household and a splendid palace continued his rationalizing program. Magnificence was an attribute of a cardinal which all contemporaries accepted. Cortesi wished to direct this magnificence along lines that avoided extremes and that could serve to advance Rome's cultural life. Proper pay for the familiars, the employment of learned men, and an emphasis on the cardinal's moral duties were all directed toward controlling abuses. Equality of income, even though a large income, and a certain uniformity in household, even though a grand household, provided standards for every cardinal to follow. Such rules were necessary for the cardinal in regulating his life and those who depended on him.

Such wealth made the cardinal a major force in Rome's social life. Since he came into contact with many types of men, he had to regulate his relations with them carefully, especially when distributing financial largess and granting requests. This required detailed knowledge of human psychology, which in turn enabled him to judge the requests of petitioners and to select those most worthy of support.[113] Moreover, by understanding the psychological formation of other men, the cardinal could gauge his personal attitudes, such as his mode of speech, to fit the requirements of self-protection and justice.[114] A cardinal's correct and moderate attitude toward and relations with others displayed a moral and civic dimension; if the cardinal acted properly with others, then the opportunities for dissatisfaction and conflict would decrease and peace would become more secure.

Cortesi concluded the discussion of the cardinal's domestic life by detailing the types of liberality, magnificence, and charity which would bring him into contact with a large number of people. The cardinal should display his liberality to such deserving groups as those who were learned in theology, philosophy, and the liberal arts, and in particular, to men who cultivated the more difficult studies.[115] As a sign of his magnificence the cardinal should build hospitals, hospices, and monasteries, especially for the mendicant orders, which devote their time to theological studies and preaching.[116] In keeping with his supervision of learning, the cardinal should maintain a library and a public *studium* open to all men.[117] In anticipation of the reforms of the Council of Trent, Cortesi urged cardinals to establish seminaries for youths from their own regions in Rome so that they might be properly educated.[118] A cardinal's charitable acts should include both corporeal and spiritual components. He must be certain that his charity benefited only those deserving of help, such as the sick, Turkish captives, and refugees from political disorder.[119] In keeping with the aristocratic tendency of his day, Cortesi specified the poor and disenfranchised nobility as a proper group for cardinalate charity.[120] However, the group most worthy of help were those women who had suffered hardships.[121] Women who wished to enter the religious orders, widows who required help to keep their families together or to remarry, and young women who needed financial support to marry were all proper outlets for a cardinal's charitable activity.[122] All this necessitated money, and Cortesi viewed the cardinals' wealth as an opportunity for patronage and charity as well as display; he did not view wealth as a danger to a moral life.

Book III of the *De Cardinalatu* touches on a number of reform propositions. Politically the cardinal helps guide the government of the Church and the general good of Christian society. Cortesi displayed his curial background in noting that since the Church is a mixed government, consisting of ruler and aristocracy, it is better formed than other governments.[123] Even though the Church, being divinely established, will always survive, its rulers can affect the well-being of the believers in a number of ways. Cortesi therefore admonished the cardinal that a ruler could corrupt the state and its inhabitants and cause great evils if he misused his power and authority.[124]

In performing their official duties, Cortesi continued, the cardinals must care for the religious orders, serve as legates, rule the Church during a papal interregnum, act as judges, regulate secular life in Rome, and determine the proper disposition of religious ceremonies and acts.[125] Cortesi was anxious that the cardinals perform these duties rationally and religiously. As electors of the pope, for example, they were required to give careful consideration to their choice, avoid personal or selfish motives in their selection, and punish anyone who attempted simony in a papal election.[126] Cortesi recommended that a learned man be elected pope, but noted that he could accept a candidate who was simply well disposed to the educated.[127] In the consistory the cardinals must provide the pope with good advice, avoid flattery, and give proper consideration to the time, occasion, and means of any action they recommend.[128]

Since the cardinal's activity centered on Rome, Cortesi concentrated on the administration of the city and the Curia.[129] The cardinals must police the judicial offices of the Curia, particularly the Rota, and eradicate fraud and falsehood; they must also regulate the sale of offices.[130] Exact standards must be established and enforced in the coining of money.[131] Similarly, foreigners coming to Rome as pilgrims, as well as natives, must be protected from immoral business practices. This requires the supervision of every industry and service in Rome, from renting houses to the prices charged by butchers. Further, the public games and entertainments, which are occasions for illegal and immoral activities, must be controlled so that no hazard to human life will arise and no crime will be committed.[132] In all this the cardinals should have the physical and moral safety of the people foremost in their minds.

As collectively the second-highest authority in the Church and usually as bishops themselves, the cardinals have the special charge of overseeing episcopal appointments and administration.[133] First, the cardinals should insist that the men chosen for the episcopal office be free of evil characteristics and display moderate habits.[134] Once appointed, they must ensure that all candidates for the priesthood know Latin and music and be members of the diocese in which they are to be ordained.[135] The bishops must guarantee the proper administration of the sacraments and the punishment of evildoers in their dioceses. Synods should be held regularly in order to abrogate old laws and enact new ones.[136] Bishops should make regular visits to monasteries, nunneries, and other institutions.[137] While all of these activities implied that the bishop actually resided in his diocese, Cortesi did not specify this and certainly did not expect it of the curial cardinals.

Cortesi devoted an entire chapter to the great ecclesiastical abuse of simony. His treatment of this problem illustrates the ambiguities and limits of his reform thought.[138] His main concern was to distinguish between the proper and the improper means of obtaining a benefice and other forms of advancement. Cortesi knew the various personal considerations that affected the selection of men for office and led to irregularities, but he also realized that he could not alter the situation effectively. He therefore tried to establish norms that could circumscribe the dangers. Cortesi's essential criterion for advancement was simple: A worthy man has a right to promotion and an unworthy one does not.[139] A limited exchange of money or favors is acceptable provided the candidate is qualified. Even while trying to rationalize the way benefices were often obtained, Cortesi emphasized that simony was a serious threat to the Church and that the laws against it should be strengthened.[140]

A similar realistic attitude informed Cortesi's treatment of the selection of the cardinals themselves.[141] Although Cortesi understood the ultimate subservience of the cardinals to any papal decision in selecting new members of the college, he tried to provide some control over their selection in order to guarantee the integrity of the body.[142] He admitted that the rich were often preferred to the less wealthy, and the nobles to the nonnobles, and that a king's choice must often be accepted for political reasons, but even in these cases Cortesi expected that the candidate would be otherwise qualified.[143] In like manner he granted that the popes acted properly when they promoted members of their *familiae* or close friends who were outstanding in virtue.[144] Nor did he categorically oppose the choice of youths (*pueri*) when this was necessitated by political or similar considerations, although he remained suspicious of the practice.[145] His willingness to admit established procedures extended to nepotism, but Cortesi could hardly have initiated a strong critique on the subject since Julius II and his family were the outstanding examples of it.[146] Cortesi supported the status quo, but he also provided some restraints on its worst aspects by insisting upon certain fundamental requirements on the part of the candidate. A pope may select a relative provided the relative possesses qualities that make him worthy of a red hat.

Even though the administration of the Church and the direction of his own household are the cardinal's major duties, Cortesi maintained that those who excel in learning are more properly candidates for the cardinalate than are men who have essentially practical backgrounds. He argued that learning makes a man superior to all those who are engaged in practical activities, provides the perfect preparation for rational consideration of complex problems, and allows a man to act properly.[147] Significantly, Cortesi praised the College of Cardinals of earlier periods, when learned men filled its ranks.[148] Although Cortesi makes no explicit comparison between the college of his own day and that of previous times, there certainly is an implicit statement on the decline of the college. Finally, Cortesi maintained that those men who write books are the most deserving of selection as cardinals.[149] This argument was especially dear to Cortesi and his fellow humanists in Rome, who were anxious to earn ecclesiastical advancement through their scholarly production.

As regulators of the religious organization of the Church, the cardinals naturally concern themselves with the religious orders. This is the special obligation of those cardinals who serve as protectors of orders.[150] The cardinals must insist that the religious orders perform their duties and act in accordance with the canons of the Church and the examples of their founders; Cortesi provides a list of procedures that should guide the cardinal in administering the orders.[151] Although he did not stress the bad state of the contemporary orders, Cortesi's injunctions to the cardinals nevertheless indicate that he had reservations about the life styles of the orders and their value to the Church. Not surprisingly Cortesi gave careful consideration to the financial state of the orders, arguing that they be prevented from accumulating riches and holding private possessions.[152] Despite Cortesi's reservations concerning the excesses of the Scholastic mendicants, he still insisted that the orders make theology, scholarship, and preaching[153] their special concerns, especially since they must help defend the faith against heretical ideas.[154] But again he argued, as he had in the *Liber Sententiarum,* that the religious orders should engage in both humanistic and theological studies.[155]

Cortesi held a high enough opinion of the institutional power of the College of Cardinals to detail the circumstances under which the cardinals could properly censure a pope.[156] Although he emphasized that a pope could be removed from office only for manifest heresy,[157] he did concede that abuses and immoral acts, e.g., alienation of Church property, justified the cardinals' resistance to papal deeds. Cortesi treated this subject as had the theorists during the Great Schism; he conceived of cardinalate resistance not as a normal state but as an acceptable one only in the most critical circumstances. He had no desire for an independent source of authority to develop among the cardinals; he expected them to obey the pope. Certainly Cortesi preferred that the cardinals use fraternal admonition in order to deflect the pope from some activity they found improper,[158] but ultimately, like Maffei, he left the judgment of an unworthy pope to God.[159]

Cortesi's attitude toward the councils of the Church further reflected his curial background and prejudices.[160] Under normal circumstances, Cortesi insisted, only the pope has the power to summon an ecumenical council. Aware of recent history, he granted that under extraordinary conditions, such as a heretical pope or the prolonged illness of the pope, the cardinals could legitimately convene a council.[161] Cortesi furnished guidelines on who should attend such a council, specifying the bishops, secular rulers, theological experts, and humanists as advisers on select topics.[162] As a curialist Cortesi had a limited view of the utility of councils. He considered them to be extraordinary events required by some extreme need, as mechanisms for uniting Christians against a foreign threat or for dealing with heretics,[163] but not necessarily for other matters. Above all, a council must avoid initiating any internal strife within the Church or attempting any limitation on the power of the papacy.[164] Essentially Cortesi ignored the possibility of the councils' serving as reform instruments, and in response to recent Church history he circumscribed their usefulness to extraordinary occasions. A Church council was not a functional element in Cortesi's plans for the rationalization of the life and government of Christian society.

Although the *De Cardinalatu* was not primarily concerned with the question of reform of the Church and the Curia, it did touch upon the major problems confronting reform thought in the early cinquecento. Cortesi brought to these problems a thorough knowledge of the Roman and ecclesiastical machinery and a realistic appreciation of the possibilities of effecting improvement. His analyses of abuses and of programs for their correction did not go as far as those of other contemporaries in mandating a return to an apostolic model, but he did identify the same areas of abuse. Underlying Cortesi's approach was the belief that humanist learning constituted a vital element in man's ability to function at any level of society. He did not view his humanist approach and language as being in any fundamental way opposed to the traditional medieval claims of the cardinalate and the Curia; rather, he considered his ideas to be complementary to those teachings. Cortesi was optimistic about the ability of reason to provide the means of assessing any complex problems and offering a solution. Further, he believed that his treatise showed how reason could be used to establish the necessary rules for moral action, and that his audience was willing to accept his prescriptions. Ultimately he erred on all accounts, but he did express certain basic components of reform; he simply could not break through the structural limits imposed on him by his assent to the status quo in both fact and ideal.

In his detailed treatment of one of the major offices in the ecclesiastical and curial establishment, Cortesi provides valuable insights into the attitudes toward and possibilities for reform in Rome on the eve of the Reformation. Two things have become very clear. The first is that even when they did not publicize their ideas as part of any large-scale reform, the humanists certainly understood the deficiencies within the system and the need to broadcast them and propose solutions. The humanists' concern with morality made them natural reformers. Second, all the curial humanist reform plans were limited in their application because they remained within the established norms that had received the benediction of tradition. This did not mean that these humanists were blind to the real demands for reform, nor should they be faulted for not perceiving the essential structural changes that would have satisfied someone like Erasmus or that would be implemented after the Council of Trent. Rather, they were sensitive to the claims of the institutions they knew best and depended on, and they could not see how they could change the established forms without ruining their lives and the culture they had helped to build. To make the Curia an example of apostolic poverty might abolish its worst abuses, but that would hardly be practical if one believed its governmental and judicial roles were necessary. These humanists never doubted the need for the Curia as the director of the Church. Reform for them remained essentially moral, seldom institutional, and it always avoided extremes.

Theirs was an optimistic view which ignored fundamental questions and had no future.

Naturally, the Roman curialists looked to the pope for the impetus of reform. They believed that reform must be led by the pope or else it would be a danger to the curial structure. Their hope in Rome as an active agent in reform was not unique to them, but it was naïve nevertheless.[165] The humanists waited in vain for the pope to initiate reform. They resented Adrian VI's moves to limit abuses because these infringed on their established positions and prerogatives. When the humanistically educated Paul III tried to effect some improvement, his attempts were too weak even to accomplish the moderate programs sketched by Maffei and Cortesi. The Curia and those associated with it, even when they acknowledged the priority of reform, did not find the means by which to integrate it into the institutional framework. Reform remained essentially a moral attitude and not an active policy.

Conclusion

Paolo Cortesi's *De Cardinalatu* is a high point in the history of, and a valuable basis on which to assess, Roman humanism because it indicates the full integration of Renaissance humanist values into the clerical-curial world of pre-Reformation and pre-sack Rome. Cortesi's cardinal functioned at several levels: as a great prince in a territorial state, as the leader and protector of a large body of retainers, as the spiritual overseer of the Christian West, and as a connoisseur and propagator of humanist culture. In describing such a man, Cortesi had to relate all human and intellectual activities to humanist standards and models. His success in exploiting the cardinal as a Renaissance humanist ideal type analogous to Pontano's and Machiavelli's prince and Castiglione's courtier was all the more significant in its Roman setting since it required the adaptation of his humanist ideals to a body of well-defined medieval theories and practices. Cortesi's portrait is that of a man who is politically and socially a realist and devoted to the values of human reason and humanist learning as the proper guides to leading a moral life.

This idealized image of a cardinal reflected a century of humanist growth and assimilation in Rome. If like all ideals he did not exist (or in any case probably not in the College of Cardinals), the arguments and examples of the *De Cardinalatu* are no less important as mirrors of High Renaissance Roman humanism. Cortesi sought to define a normative model that could function in the actual world with all its ambiguities and dangers. It was a construction that differed from all other humanist ideal types, for it betrayed uniquely Roman qualities. First, it depended on the Latin classicism that defined Roman humanism and that Cortesi most fittingly epitomized in the archaic and erudite language he employed in the treatise itself. Second, it was concerned with the specifically Roman and clerical-curial responsibilities of the cardinal as co-governor of the Church and city.

The *De Cardinalatu* emphasizes the dual exploitation which characterized Roman intellectual life in the Renaissance and which this study has tried to describe and explain. The first was the success of the Curia and the papacy in ultimately co-opting humanist culture and making it a spokesman for its own political and religious ideals. The second was the other side of the procedure, the success of humanism in providing humanist ideals that easily blended with this clerical-curial world and helped to ensure for the humanists secure positions in that society. If Cortesi's cardinal patronized humanist culture, especially in its most magnificent and erudite forms, as a model for others and as proof of his own learning, he also controlled it through this very patronage. The humanist had to function within the limits imposed by the requirements of the Curia and the papacy.

Cortesi's humanist cardinal epitomized his own clericalized and bureaucratized society. While the re-formation of humanism to suit the Roman context had been slow and not always constant, the humanists in Rome did accommodate their secular studies and values to an essentially medieval and religious environment. They emphasized those qualities in their learning which were most acceptable to the administrative and propagandistic needs of the Curia, i.e., their secretarial skills and their ability to praise. In turn, the curial establishment allowed them to develop their intellectual interests in relative freedom and provided a measure of economic and social security. As a consequence Roman humanists displayed the same general employee loyalty that was found among others in the bureaucracy. They were conscious of their own and their families' needs and took the necessary steps to ensure their ability to meet them. They accepted both the ambiguities and opportunities offered by the Curia and Roman society. Even though they were aware of the compromises bureaucratic work could force on their scholarship, the Roman humanists extracted from their success a self-confident attitude toward their abilities.

It was this self-confidence which provided Cortesi with the means to fashion his cardinal as a humanist ideal and which allowed him and his associates to rewrite traditional theology to fit their own intellectual perceptions. If doubts were raised about this attitude, as Castellesi's treatise indicates, they were never so strong as to deflect contemporaries from undertaking them. Among themselves the Roman humanists believed that they had found the means of grafting their classical culture onto the dominant themes of the Curia and the Church. Once they had accomplished this they did not question the procedure. This security in their own abilities marked their attitude toward Scholasticism. In accepting Scholasticism in a form that rejected much of its development and tradition, these humanists proclaimed the ability of their classicized culture to deal competently with the medieval inheritance without requiring them to become professional theologians. The impetus behind their work was to unify different traditions within the limits of their classical ideals.

Such a sense of self-confidence, however, could become arrogant and prove itself sterile and incapable of defending its own ideals. Such was Roman humanism's fate at the time of the sack of Rome. The humanists had found an existent medieval ideology in the Curia and merely adapted their own thinking to it; they never criticized it or rethought its basis. They chose what suited them and ignored what did not, convinced that they knew what was essential in it and how to present it. The success of the humanists in grafting their thought and culture onto the medieval curial ideas and practices lasted as long as there were no strong outside attacks and as long as the Curia maintained its solid political and economic position. These presuppositions ended in the 1520s. With the dislocation of the world of High Renaissance Rome the Latin humanism of quattrocento Italy suffered a serious defeat. No better proof of the success of this tradition in adapting to its environment or of its ultimately dependence on stronger and potentially hostile forces exists, however, than Cortesi's ideal cardinal, in whom Roman humanism found its final expression.

Notes

INTRODUCTION

1. From R. P. Blackmur, *A Primer of Ignorance*, ed. Joseph Frank (New York: Harcourt, Brace and World, 1967), p. 126.

2. In general I have followed the definition advanced by Paul Oskar Kristeller in *Renaissance Thought*, 2 vols. (New York: Harper and Row, 1961–1965), but as modified by Eugenio Garin's insightful *Italian Humanism*, trans. Peter Munz (Oxford: Blackwell, 1965).

3. See, in general, Charles Trinkaus, *In Our Image and Likeness: Humanity and Divinity in Italian Humanist Thought* (Chicago: University of Chicago Press, 1970), esp. the introduction to vol. 1.

4. In addition to Trinkaus, *op. cit.*, vol. 1, pp. 294–321, and vol. 2, pp. 301–316, see John W. O'Malley, *Giles of Viterbo on Church and Reform: A Study in Renaissance Thought* (Leiden: Brill, 1968); *idem, Praise and Blame in Renaissance Rome: Rhetoric, Doctrine, and Reform in the Sacred Orators of the Papal Court, c. 1450–1521* (Durham, N.C.: Duke University Press, 1979); and O'Malley's collected articles, *Rome and the Renaissance: Studies in Culture and Religion* (London: Variorum Reprints, 1981).

CHAPTER 1

1. There is no large study devoted to Roman humanism in general. Much miscellaneous information can be found in Ludwig von Pastor, *History of the Popes*, ed. and trans. F. I. Antrobus *et al.*, vols. 1–11 (London/St. Louis: Herder, 1891–1910). However, Pastor was essentially unsympathetic to intellectual history generally and humanism in particular. His view of a "pagan" vs. a "Christian" Renaissance is unacceptable. Any reading of Pastor should be corrected by Vittorio Cian's review of the third volume of the German edition which covers the period dealt with in this study, in *Giornale storico della letteratura italiana*, 31 (1898), pp. 48–81. Cian deals specifically with the intellectual trends Pastor so often misunderstood. The other great German nineteenth-century history of Rome, Ferdinand Gregorovius, *History of the City of Rome in the Middle Ages*, trans. Annie Hamilton (London: Bell and Sons, 1900), vols. 5–8, is still valuable. For the first half of the quattrocento, see also Georg Voigt, *Die Wiederbelebung des classischen Alterthums oder das erste Jahrhundert des Humanismus*, 3d ed., vol. 2 (Berlin, 1893), and the Italian translation *Il risorgimento dell'antichità classica*, trans. D. Valbusa, vol. 2 (Florence, 1890); George Holmes, *The Florentine Enlightenment, 1400–1450* (New York: Pegasus, 1969); and L. Felici, "Gli umanisti alla corte pontificia: L'attività letteraria a Roma da Coluccio Salutati a Lorenzo

Valla," *Capitolium*, 48 (1973), pp. 30-40. Holmes makes some valuable observations on humanism in Rome, although it is not his primary focus. Also of use is the short survey by Aulo Greco, "Momenti e figure dell'umanesimo romano," in *Aspetti dell'umanesimo a Roma* (Rome: Istituto di studi romani, 1969), pp. 31-72. The general history of Rome, *Storia di Roma*, contains Pio Paschini's *Roma nel Rinascimento* (Bologna: Cappelli, 1940), which supplies a political history for the quattrocento and the first decades of the cinquecento. For more recent bibliography, see Alfred A. Strnad, "Papsttum, Kirchenstadt und Europa in der Renaissance," in *Rom in der Neuzeit: Politische, kirchliche und kulturelle Aspecte* (Vienna/Rome: Oesterreichische Akademie der Wissenschaften, 1970), pp. 20-52. On the general need for research on Renaissance Rome, see Amadeo Quondam, "Un'assenza, un progetto per una ricerca sulla storia di Roma tra 1465 e 1527," *Studi romani*, 27 (1979), pp. 166-175. The essays in *Scrittura, biblioteche e stampe a Roma nel Quattrocento*, 2 vols. (Vatican City: Biblioteca Apostolica Vaticana, 1980), provide valuable material on humanism in quattrocento Rome. Most recently, see V. De Caprio, "L'area umanistica romana (1513-1527)," *Studi romani*, 29 (1981), pp. 321-335.

2. See Peter Partner, *The Papal States under Martin V* (London: The British School at Rome, 1958); and Marc Dykmans, S.J., "D'Avignon à Rome: Martin V et le cortège apostolique," *Bulletin de l'Institut historique belge de Rome* 39 (1968), pp. 203-309.

3. For the political events, see Paschini, *Roma nel Rinascimento;* and, in general, Michele Monaco, "Avvenimenti politici economici e sociali," in *Aspetti dell'Umanesimo a Roma*, pp. 9-27.

4. Beginning with the years immediately after the French invasion, there is the general study by Peter Partner, *Renaissance Rome, 1500-1559: A Portrait of a Society* (Berkeley: University of California, 1977). For a later period that is of related interest, see Gerard Labrot, *Un Instrument polémique: L'Image de Rome au temps du Schisme, 1534-1667* (Lille: Université de Lille, 1978).

5. The papal *familia* and the Curia Romana overlapped to an extent, but they were essentially different and not coextensive. See Francesco Salerno, "Problemi costituzionali della Curia Romana," *Rivista italiana per le scienze giuridiche*, ser. 3, no. 10 (1959-1962), pp. 327-396, at pp. 349-350; and pp. 40-45 above.

6. On the relationship between humanism and the clergy, see the important article by Carlo Dionisotti, "Chierici e laici," in his *Geografia e storia della letteratura italiana* (Turin: Einaudi, 1967), pp. 47-73; Vincenzo De Caprio, "Intellettuali e mercato del lavoro nella Roma medicea," *Studi romani*, 29/1 (1981), pp. 29-46; Denys Hay, *The Church in Italy in the Fifteenth Century* (Cambridge: At the University Press, 1977), pp. 44-45; and Adriano Prosperi, "Intellettuali e chiesa all'inizio dell'età moderna," in *Storia d'Italia, Annali 4, Intellettuali e potere*, ed. Corrado Vivanti (Turin: Einaudi, 1981), pp. 161-252. On humanism and the religious orders, see Paul Oskar Kristeller, "The Contribution of the Religious Orders to Renaissance Thought and Learning," *American Benedictine Review*, 21/2 (1970), pp. 1-55, reprinted in *Medieval Aspects of Renaissance Learning: Three Essays*, ed. Edward P. Mahoney (Durham, N.C.: Duke University Press, 1974), pp. 95-158.

7. For our period, see Domenico Gnoli, "La Lozana andalusa e le cortegiane nella Roma di Leone X," *La Roma di Leone X* (Milan: Hoepli, 1938), pp. 185-216; and Jean Delumeau, *Vie économique et sociale de Rome dans la seconde*

moitié du XVIe siècle, vol. (Paris: Boccard, 1957), pp. 416-432, for the sixteenth century in general.

8. See Lawrence G. Duggan, "The Unresponsiveness of the Late Medieval Church: A Reconsideration," *Sixteenth Century Journal,* 9 (1979), pp. 3-26, at pp. 19-22.

9. See Leon Battista Alberti, *The Family in Renaissance Florence,* trans. Renée Neu Watkins (Columbia: University of South Carolina Press, 1969).

10. For example, see Flavio Biondo's "De verbis romanae locutionis," in *Scritti inediti e rari di Biondo Flavio,* ed. Bartolomeo Nogara, Studi e Testi #48 (Rome: Tipografia Poliglotta Vaticana, 1929), pp. 115-130; and Paolo Pompilio, "De antiquitate linguae latinae," excerpted by Giovanni Mercati in "Paolo Pompilio e la scoperta del cadavere intatto sull'Appia nel 1485," *Opere minori,* vol. 4, Studi e Testi #79 (Vatican City: Biblioteca Apostolica Vaticana, 1937), pp. 268-286. See also Chapter 4 above.

11. On Altieri, see *Dizionario biografico degli Italiani* (hereafter cited as *DBI*), vol. 2, pp. 560-561; see also Antonio M. Adorisio, "Cultura in lingua volgare a Roma fra Quattro e Cinquecento," in *Studi di biblioteconomia e storia del libro in onore di Francesco Barberi* (Rome: Associazione italiana biblioteche, 1976), pp. 19-36. On Italian poetry, see Chapter 3 above. Discussions of vernacular topics may have increased during the reign of Leo X. Niccolò Liburnio says that when he was in Rome (*ca.* 1517) he discussed Tuscan pronunciation and orthography with Girolamo Bonvisi and Andrea Cavalcanti; see Luigi Peirone, *Tradizione ed irrequietezza in Niccolò Liburnio* (Genoa: San Giorgio, 1968), pp. 26-27.

12. See Walther von Hofmann, *Forschungen zur Geschichte der kurialen Behörden vom Schisma bis zur Reformation* (Rome: Von Loescher, 1914), vol. 1, pp. 238-242.

13. On immigration to Rome and a breakdown of non-Romans in the city, see Delumeau, *Vie économique et sociale de Rome,* vol. 1, pp. 135-220. Naturally, most foreigners in Rome were not connected with humanism. On individual groups, see Arnold Esch, "Dal medioevo al rinascimento: uomini a Roma dal 1340-1450," *Archivio della Società romana di Storia Patria* (hereafter cited as *ASRSP*), 94 (1971), pp. 3-10; idem, "Florentiner in Rom 1400: Namenverzeichnis der ersten Quattrocento-Generation," *Quellen und Forschungen aus italienischen Archiven und Bibliotheken* (hereafter cited as *QFIAB*), 52 (1972), pp. 476-525; Renato Lefevre, "Fiorentini a Roma del'400: I Dati," *Studi romani,* 20/1 (1972), pp. 186-197; Benedetto Croce, *La Spagna nella vita italiana durante la Rinascenza,* 5th ed. (Bari: Laterza, 1968), chap. 5. On non-Italians, see Clifford W. Mass, "The German Community in Renaissance Rome: 1378-1528" (Ph.D. diss., University of Wisconsin, 1971); E. F. Jacob, "To and From the Court of Rome in the Early Fifteenth Century," in *Studies in French Language and Medieval Literature presented to Mildred K. Pope* (Manchester: Manchester University Press, 1939), pp. 161-181; Louis Madelin, "Le journal d'un habitant français de Rome au seizième siècle, 1509-1540 (Etude sur le manuscrit XLIII-98 de la Bibliothèque Barberini)," in *France et Rome* (Paris: Plon, 1913), pp. 197-262; José Rius, S.J., "Catalanes y Aragoneses en la Corte de Calixto III," *Analecta Sacra Tarraconensia,* 3 (1927), pp. 193-330; Manuel M. Boix, "Nicolas Conill: Un valenciano en la corte de tres papas (1403-1439)," *Anthologia annua* (Rome), 17 (1970), pp. 11-132; George B. Parks, *The English Traveler to Italy* (Rome: Edizioni di storia e letteratura, 1954); Christian Dury, "Les curialistes belges à Rome et l'histoire de la curie romaine

problème d'histoire de l'Eglise: L'exemple de Saint-Lambert à Liege," *Bulletin de l'Institut historique belge de Rome,* 50 (1980), pp. 131–160.

14. See p. 23 above.

15. On Valla, the humanist ambience at the Curia in his day, and his eventual entry into the Curia, see Mario Fois, S.J., *Il pensiero cristiano di Lorenzo Valla nel quadro storico-culturale del suo ambiente* (Rome: Gregoriana, 1969). Valla's dialogue, *De voluptate,* first developed in and represented the humanist curial ambience of the early quattrocento; see Lorenzo Valla, *On Pleasure* [*De Voluptate*], trans A. Kent Hieatt and Maristella Lorch (New York: Abaris Books, 1977), pp. 16–26.

16. See Friederich Gueldner, *Jacob Questenberg: Ein deutscher Humanist in Rom* (inagural-dissertation) (Wernigerode, 1905); and Giovanni Mercati, "Questenbergiana," *Opere minori,* vol. 4, 437–461.

17. On the popes, see Pastor, *History of the Popes,* vols. 1–8. Apart from a biography of Eugenius IV (Joseph Gill, *Eugenius IV, Pope of Christian Reunion* [Westminster, Md.: Newman Press, 1961]) and studies on Pius II (see n. 18 below) and Sixtus IV (see n. 19 below), there is little new material on the Renaissance popes as individuals. For political studies, see Joachim W. Stieber, *Pope Eugenius IV, the Council of Basel, and the Secular and Ecclesiastical Authorities in the Empire: The Conflict over Supreme Authority and Power in the Church* (Leiden: Brill, 1978); and John A. F. Thomson, *Popes and Princes, 1417–1517: Politics and Popes in the Late Medieval Church* (London: George Allen and Unwin, 1980).

18. On Pius, see R. J. Mitchell, *The Laurels and the Tiara: Pope Pius II, 1405–1464* (Garden City, N.Y.: Doubleday, 1962); and G. Paparelli, *Enea Silvio Piccolomini: L'umanesimo sul soglio di Pietro,* 2d ed. (Ravenna: Longo, 1978).

19. On Sixtus, see Pastor, *History of the Popes,* vol. 4; Dino Cortese, "Sisto Quattro: Papa Antoniano," *Il Santo,* 7 (1972), pp. 211–281; and Egmont Lee, *Sixtus IV and Men of Letters* (Rome: Edizioni di storia e letteratura, 1978), chap. 1.

20. See Voigt, *Die Wiederbelebung des classischen Alterthums,* vol. 2, pp. 2–4; and Valbusa's translation, *Il risorgimento dell'antichità classica,* vol. 2, pp. 3–5.

21. In general, see Garrett Mattingly, *Renaissance Diplomacy* (London: Cape, 1955). For an example, see Luigi Pesce, *Cristoforo Garatone trevigiano, nunzio di Eugenio IV* (Rome: Herder, 1975).

22. See Eugenio Marino, "Eugenio IV e la storiografia de Flavio Biondo," *Memorie domenicane,* n.s. 4 (1973), pp. 241–287; I have not seen Hester G. Gelber, "The Humanist as Bureaucrat: Humanism at the Court of Martin V" (M.A. thesis, University of Wisconsin, 1967).

23. For Nicholas, see Pastor, *History of the Popes,* vol. 2, pp. 165–214; Lena G. Gabel, "The First Revival of Rome, 1420–1484," in *Renaissance Reconsidered: A Symposium* (Northampton, Mass.: Smith College, 1964), pp. 13–25; Cesare Vasoli, "Profilo di un papa umanista: Tommaso Parentucelli," *Studi sulla cultura del Rinascimento* (Manduria: Lacaita, 1968), pp. 69–121; J. B. Towes, "Formative Forces in the Pontificate of Nicholas V," *Catholic Historical Review,* 54 (1968/1969), pp. 261–284; Caroll William Westfall, *In This Most Perfect Paradise* (University Park: Pennsylvania State University Press, 1974).

24. Holmes, *The Florentine Enlightenment,* chap. 5, lays great stress on the effect of the Curia's period of residence in Florence and the Council of Florence in aiding humanism in the Curia. On the council, see also Joseph Gill, *The Council of Florence* (Cambridge: At the University Press, 1959).

25. For a fuller discussion of the translations, see Costantino Cipolla, *L'azione letteraria di Niccolò V nel Rinascimento* (Frosinone: Tipografia 'Claudio Stracca,' 1900).

26. See A. D. Fraser-Jenkins, "Cosimo de Medici's Patronage of Architecture and the Theory of Magnificence," *Journal of the Warburg and Courtauld Institutes,* 33 (1970), pp. 162–170.

27. On Calixtus, see Pastor, *History of the Popes,* vol. 4; Peter Mallet, *The Borgias* (London: Phaidon, 1969), chap. 4; and Rius, "Catalanes y Aragoneses." On Pius as a patron, see Richard Boyd Hilary, "The Appointments of Pope Pius II (Enea Silvio Piccolomini), 1458–1464" (Ph.D. diss., University of Wisconsin, 1969); and *idem,* "The Nepotism of Pope Pius II, 1458–1464," *Catholic Historical Review,* 64 (1978), pp. 33–35.

28. See Roberto Weiss, *Un umanista veneziano: Papa Paolo II* (Venice: Istituto per la collaborazione culturale, 1958).

29. This is discussed in detail in Chapter 2.

30. See Lee, *Sixtus IV and Men of Letters,* chap. 1, for this criticism.

31. See Pastor, *History of the Popes,* vol. 4.

32. See Alfred A. Strnad, "Francesco Todeschini-Piccolomini: Politik und Mäzenarentum im Quattrocento," *Römische Historische Mitteilungen,* 8/9 (1964/ 65–1965/66), pp. 101–425.

33. See Pastor, *History of the Popes,* vol. 5; Emanuel Rodocanachi, *Le Pontificat de Jules II, 1503–1513* (Paris: Hachette, 1928); and n. 34 below.

34. See Biblioteca Apostolica Vaticana (hereafter cited as BAV), Ottob. Lat. 2377, ff. 232r–341r, *Raphaelis Volaterrani Breuis sub Iulio Leoneque Historia,* f. 235v; modern edition in John F. D'Amico, "Papal History and Curial Reform in the Renaissance: Raffaele Maffei's *Breuis Historia* of Julius II and Leo X," *Archivum Historiae Pontificiae,* 18 (1980), pp. 157–210, at p. 200.

35. BAV, Ottob. Lat. 2377, f. 234v; and D'Amico, "Papal History," p. 196.

36. On Leo, see Pastor, *History of the Popes,* vols. 6 and 7; Bonner Michell, *The Rome of Leo X* (Norman: University of Oklahoma Press, 1973); see also the revisionist study by Domenico Gnoli, "Il secolo di Leone X?" *La Roma di Leone X,* pp. 341–384. Thomas Rosco's *The Life and Pontificate of Leo X,* available in many editions, but especially useful in the Italian translation by Conte Luigi Bossi (Milan, 1816), which contains much material in the notes and appendices, remains useful. See also Emanuel Rodocanachi, *Le Première Renaissance de Rome au temps de Jules II et Léon X* (Paris: Hachette, 1912).

37. See Gnoli, "Il secolo di Leone X?"

38. See G. B. Picotti, *La giovinezza di Leone X* (Milan: Hoepli, 1927), pp. 265–267.

39. *Ibid.,* pp. 386–388.

40. *Ibid.,* pp. 341–344.

41. Pastor, *History of the Popes,* vol. 7.

42. For the negative view expressed by Vianesius Albergati, see E. Bache, "Les Commentaires de Vianesius Albergati," *Compte rendu des Séances de la Commission royale d'histoire,* ser. 5, no. 1 (1891), pp. 102–166.

43. On Clement, see Pastor, *History of the Popes,* vol. 7.

44. On the Italian episcopacy, see Hay, *The Church in Italy in the Fifteenth Century,* chap. 4.

45. See Giovanni Mercati, *Per la cronologia della vita e degli scritti di Niccolò*

Perotti arcivescovo di Siponto: ricerche, Studi e Testi #44 (Rome: Tipografia Poliglotta Vaticana, 1925); *Niccolò Perotti's Version of the Enchridion of Epic-
tetus,* ed. Revilo Pendleton Oliver (Urbana: University of Illinois Press, 1954);
and Joseph S. Salemi, "The Three Nicholases: Machiavelli and the Preface of
Perotti to the *Histories* of Polybius," *Allegorica,* 6 (1979), pp. 131-143.

46. For Bussi, see *DBI,* vol. 15, pp. 565-572; and Lee, *Sixtus IV and Men of
Letters,* index.

47. See Giovanni Andrea Bussi, *Prefazioni alle edizioni di Sweynheym e Pannartz prototipografi romani,* ed. Massimo Miglio (Milan: Il Polifilo, 1978); and
M. D. Feld, "Sweynheym and Pannartz, Cardinal Bessarion, Neoplatonism: Renaissance Humanism and Two Early Printers' Choice of Texts," *Harvard Library
Bulletin,* 30 (1982), pp. 282-335.

48. See *DBI,* vol. 17, pp. 424-429; Frank Rutger Hausmann, "Giovanni Antonio
Campano (1429-1477): Ein Beitrag zur Geschichte des italienischen Humanismus
im Quattrocento," *Römische Historische Mitteilungen,* 12 (1970), pp. 125-178;
Flavio de Bernardo, *Un vescovo umanista alla corte pontificia: Giannantonio
Campano (1429-1477)* (Rome: Gregoriana, 1975); and the review article by
Riccardo Fubini, "Umanesimo curiale del Quattrocento: Nuovi studi su Giovann'
Antonio Campano," *Rivista storica italiana,* 88 (1976), pp. 745-755.

49. On this, see Dieter Girgensohn, "Wie wird man Kardinal? Kuriale und
ausserkuriale Karrieren an der Wende des 14. zum 15. Jahrhundert," *QFIAB,* 57
(1977), pp. 138-162; and Thomson, *Popes and Princes,* chap. 3.

50. For Castellesi, see *DBI,* vol. 21, pp. 665-671. Basic works on Castellesi are
Girolamo Ferri, *De rebus gestis et scriptis Hadriani Cast. Cardinalis quo inprimis
autore latinitas restituta* (Faenza, 1771), where much material is published in the
appendices; Bruno Gebhardt, *Adriano von Corneto: Ein Beitrag zur Geschichte der
Curie und der Renaissance* (Breslau, 1886); and Pio Paschini, *Tre prelati illustri del
Rinascimento: Ermolao Barbaro-Adriano Castellesi-Giovanni Grimani* (Rome:
Lateranum, 1957). For further bibliography, see John F. D'Amico, "Humanism
and Theology at Papal Rome, 1480-1520" (Ph.D. diss., University of Rochester,
1977), pp. 100-113.

51. On Castellesi's offices, see Paschini, *Tre prelati illustri,* pp. 50-60.

52. See Alessandro Ferraioli, "Il matrimonio di Adriano Castellesi poi cardinale
e il suo annullamento," *ASRSP,* 42 (1919), pp. 295-301, where several documents
are published.

53. Castellesi's relations with England can be followed in J. J. Brewer, ed.,
Letters and Papers, Foreign and Domestic, of the Reign of Henry VIII (London:
HMSO, 1920). See also Maria Franca Mellano, *Rappresentanti italiani della Corona
inglese ai primi del Cinquecento* (Rome: Istituto di studi romani, 1970); and
William E. Wilkie, *The Cardinal Protectors of Engalnd: Rome and the Tudors
before the Reformation* (Cambridge: At the University Press, 1974). Several bulls
relating to Castellesi can be found in Thomas Rymer, *Foedera, Conventiones,
Literae, et cujuscunque generis Acta Publica* . . . (London, 1712), pp. 108-110,
290, 467-468, 515-516, 607-610, 622-624.

54. See Michele Monaco, ed., *Il 'De Officio Collectoris in Regno Angliae' di
Pietro Griffi da Pisa (1469-1516)* (Rome: Edizione di storia e letteratura, 1973);
and William E. Lunt, *Financial Relations of the Papacy with England, 1327-
1534* (Cambridge, Mass.: Medieval Academy of America, 1962).

55. Castellesi did not reside in his diocese; see Sir Henry Maxwell-Lyte, ed.,

The Registers of Oliver King, Bishop of Bath and Wells, 1496–1503, and Hadrian de Castello, Bishop of Bath and Wells, 1503–1518 (London: Somerset Record Society, 1939).

56. For Florido, see n. 103 below.

57. See Raffaele Maffei, *Raphaelis Volaterrani Commentariorum Urbanorum liber I[-XXXVIII]* (Rome, 1506), f. 318; but cf. Hay, *The Church in Italy*, p. 104.

58. Castellesi was accused, unjustly, of poisoning Alexander and Cesare Borgia at a dinner party. See Leopold von Ranke, *History of the Popes*, trans. E. Fowler (New York, 1901), vol. 3, pp. 180–181; and Susanne Schüller-Piroli, *Die Borgia Papste Kalixt III und Alexander VI* (Munich: Oldenbourg, 1980).

59. In 1518 Castellesi's episcopal finances were estimated by the Venetian ambassador in England to be 10,000 ducats a year; see Rowdon Brown, ed., *Calendar of State Papers and Manuscripts Relating to English Affairs Existing in the Archives and Collections of Venice and Other Libraries of Northern Italy* (London, 1864), vol. 1, #934.

60. For printing information, see Paschini, *Tre prelati illustri*, pp. 114–115.

61. See Dionisotti, *Gli umanisti e il volgare*, pp. 101–102.

62. See Ludwig Geiger, ed., *Johannes Reuchlins Briefwechsel* (rpt., Hildesheim: Olms, 1962), pp. 232–233, 247, 282–289; and, for a letter to Fisher, 1515, see "Notes from the College Records," *Eagle*, 32 (1916), pp. 145–146.

63. See Paschini, *Tre prelati illustri*, pp. 115, 117; and Chapter 5 above.

64. See Georg Ellinger, *Italien und der deutsche Humanismus in der Neulateinischen Lyrik*, vol. 1 (Berlin: De Gruyter, 1929), pp. 111–112.

65. See Chapter 5 above.

66. See Paschini, *Tre prelati illustri*, pp. 66–69. Castellesi's decision to flee was probably suggested by the recent imprisonment of the Cardinal S. Vitalis by Julius.

67. See *ibid.*, pp. 71–72; and A. Jäger, "Über Kaiser Maximilian I Verhältniss zum Papsthum," *Sitzungsberichte der K. Akademie der Wissenschaften: Philosophisch-historische Classe*, 12/2 (1854), pp. 195–236. On the disposition of the bishopric of Tournai, see the letters of Castellesi to the emperor in Trent, Biblioteca Comunale, 608, ff. 44r–45r; and Wilkie, *The Cardinal Protectors of England*, pp. 86–96.

68. See BAV, Borg. Lat. 257, ff. 26, 28, 32, 36, 49, 50, 101, 222–226, for the letters of Maso Albizzi, governor of Benevento, on papal oversight and grain shipments. A further sign of Castellesi's prominence was his appointment as chamberlain of the College of Cardinals in 1514 in succession to Cardinal Christopher Bainbridge; see D. S. Chambers, *Cardinal Bainbridge in the Court of Rome, 1509 to 1514* (Oxford: Oxford University Press, 1965), p. 111, n. 2.

69. See Alessandro Ferraioli, *La congiura dei cardinali contro Leone X* (Rome: R. Società Romana di Storia Patria, 1919); and Fabrizio Winspeare, *La congiura dei cardinali contro Leone X* (Florence: Olschki, 1957).

70. Paschini, *Tre prelati illustri*, pp. 104–105.

71. Entitled *De ecclesiae romanae potestate*, a copy is in BAV, Vat. Lat. 2934, ff. 403r–416r. The presentation copy is housed in, but not owned by Harvard University's Houghton Library, MS Typ. 171 H; see James Wardrop, "Six Italian Manuscripts in the Department of Graphic Arts," *Harvard University Library Bulletin*, 7/2 (1953), pp. 222–223. (I am grateful to the owner for permission to study this copy.) On Piccolomini as the English protector, see Wilke, *The Cardinal Protectors of England*, pp. 53–73.

72. On Castellesi's palace, the present Palazzo Giraud-Torlonia on the Via della Conciliazione, see William Mazière Brady, *Anglo-Roman Papers* (London, 1890), pp. 9–20; and Christoph L. Frommel, *Der Römische Palastbau der Hochrenaissance* (Tübingen: Wasmuth, 1973), vol. 2, pp. 207–215.

73. See Denys Hay, *Polydore Vergil* (Oxford: Oxford University Press, 1952). In addition to Vergil there was Filippo Beroaldo the Younger (see p. 44 above), Pescennio Francesco Negro (see Giovanni Mercati, "Pescennio Francesco Negro veneto protonotario apostolico," *Ultimi contributi alla storia degli umanisti,* Studi e Testi #91 [Vatican City: Biblioteca Apostolica Vaticana, 1939], pp. 84, 86–88), and Gian Vitale (see Girolamo Tumminello, "Gian Vitale, umanista del secolo XV," *Archivio storico siciliano,* n.s. 8 [1883], pp. 1–94, at pp. 35–36). Jacques Lefèvre d'Etaples mentions Lucas Pacioli as a *domesticus* of Castellesi; see *The Prefatory Epistles of Jacques Lefèvre d'Etaples and Related Texts,* ed. Eugene F. Rice, Jr. (New York: Columbia University Press, 1972), pp. 345, 347, 348.

74. See the breakdown of the education of early sixteenth century cardinals in Barbara McClung Hallman, "Italian Cardinals, Reform, and the Church as Property, 1492–1563" (Ph.D. diss., University of California at Berkeley, 1974), table 1.5.

75. For Ammannati, see *DBI,* vol. 2, pp. 802–803; for Todeschini-Piccolomini, see n. 32 above.

76. On Bessarion, see *DBI,* vol. 9, pp. 685–696.

77. On Dovizi, see Giuseppe Lorenzo Moncallero, *Il Cardinale Bernardo Dovizi da Bibbiena, umanista e diplomatico (1470–1520)* (Florence: Olschki, 1953).

78. I follow Max Weber's discussion of bureaucracy; see his "The Bureaucracy," *From Max Weber: Essays in Sociology,* ed. H. H. Gerth and C. Wright Mills (New York: Oxford University Press, 1964), pp. 196–244.

79. How many posts could the Curia offer to humanists in the Renaissance? Perhaps the best means of arriving at an approximate answer is to calculate the number of venal offices, which included almost all the nonspiritual posts but ignored the papal *familia.* Hofmann, *Forschungen zur Geschichte der kurialen Behörden,* vol. 2, pp. 106–107 and 168–169, prints two lists of venal offices. The first, dated 1509–1512, totals 939, but is incomplete because it excludes such posts as the *procuratores penitentiae.* The second, dated 1514, totals 2,220. This figure is somewhat inflated, however, by the presence of 401 *milites Sancti Petri,* one of the posts Leo created for purely financial reasons and which did not involve any active curial duties. If we add the number in the 1514 list for the missing offices of the earlier list, the 1509–1512 figure increases to 1,211. By the end of the second decade of the sixteenth century, almost two thousand curial offices might have been open to the humanists, depending on their qualifications. See also n. 106 below.

80. There exists no comprehensive history of curial development. On the Curia in general, see Niccolò del Re, *La Curia Romana,* 3d ed. (Rome: Edizioni di storia e letteratura, 1972); "Cour romaine," in *Dictionnaire de théologie catholique,* vol. 3/2 (Paris, 1923), cols. 1931–1983. For a general discussion of the problems encountered in studying the Curia, see Francesco Salerno, "Problemi costituzionali della Curia Romana," *Rivista italiana per le scienze giuridiche,* ser. 3, no. 101 (1959–1962), pp. 327–96; and Lajos Pasztor, "L'Histoire de la Curie romaine: Problème d'histoire de l'Eglise," *Revue d'histoire ecclésiastique,* 64 (1969), pp. 353–366. Important developments in curial organization occurred during the

Avignon period. See G. Mollat, *The Popes at Avignon*, trans. Janet Love (New York: Harper and Row, 1965), pp. 279–334; and Bernard Guillemain, *La cour pontificale d'Avignon (1309–1376): Etude d'une société* (Paris: Boccard, 1962). There is a general discussion of the Curia during the quattrocento and cinquecento in Xavier Bastida, "Guillermo Cassados: Su vida y sus obras," *Anthologia annua* (Rome), 20 (1973), pp. 203–751, at pp. 243–293. For archival collections of the Curia, see Leonard E. Boyle, *A Survey of the Vatican Archives and of Its Medieval Holdings* (Toronto: The Pontifical Institute for Medieval Studies, 1972).

81. See Geoffrey Barraclough, *Papal Provisions* (Oxford: Blackwell, 1935).

82. See William H. O'Neill, *Papal Rescripts of Favor* (Washington, D.C.: Catholic University of America Press, 1930); and *Dictionnaire de droit canonique*, vol. 7, pp. 607–635.

83. See the discussion in Henry Charles Lea, ed., *A Formulary of the Papal Penitentiary in the Thirteenth Century* (Philadelphia, 1892), introduction.

84. On the College of Cardinals, see pp. 227–228 above; see also Paul Maria Baumgartner, *Untersuchungen und Urkunden über die Camera Collegii Cardinalium für die Zeit von 1295 bis 1437* (Leipzig, 1898).

85. On the advocates, see Ottavio Pio Conti, *Origine, fasti e privilegi degli avvocati consistoriali: Memorie storiche* (Rome, 1898).

86. See G. Mollat, "Le Sacré Collège de Clement V à Eugene IV," *Revue d'histoire ecclésiastique*, 46 (1951), pp. 22–112, 566–594, at pp. 80–93.

87. On the *Rota*, see *Dictionnaire de droit canonique*, vol. 7, cols. 742–771; Hermann Hoberg, "Die Protokollbücher der Rotarsnotare von 1464 bis 1517," *Zeitschrift der Savigny-Stiftung für Rechtsgeschichte: Kanonistische Abteilung*, 60 (1953), pp. 177–227.; and Charles Lefebvre, "Le tribunal de la Rote Romaine et sa procedure au temps de Pio II," in *Enea Silvio Piccolomini: Papa Pio II*, ed. D. Maffei (Siena, 1968), pp. 199–211. For an example of the procedure of the *Rota*, see C. M. D. Crowder, "Four English Cases Determined in the Roman Curia during the Council of Constance, 1414–1418," *Annuarium Historiae Conciliorum*, 12 (1980), 315–411.

88. For both, see *Dictionnaire de droit canonique*, vol. 7, cols. 492–493, 1012–1018; Bruno Katterbach, O.F.M., *Referendarii utriusque Signaturae a Martino V ad Clementem IX et Praelati Signaturae Supplicationum a Martino V ad Leonem XII*, Studi e Testi #55 (Vatican City: Biblioteca Apostolica Vaticana, 1931); and Pietro Santini, *De Referendariorum ac Signaturae historico-iuridica evolutione* (Rome: Sapientia catholica, 1945).

89. For the *Camera*, see Guglielmo Felici, *La Reverenda Camera Apostolica: Studio storico-giuridico* (Vatican City: Biblioteca Apostolica Vaticana, 1940).

90. For the *Audientia*, see *Dictionnaire de droit canonique*, vol. 1, cols. 1389–1399; and Ernst Pitz, *Supplikensignatur and Briefexpedition an der römischen Kurie im Pontifikat Papst Calixts III* (Tübingen: Niemeyer, 1972).

91. See Lea, ed., *A Formulary*: Henry Charles Lea, "The Taxes of the Papal Penitentiary," *English Historical Review*, 8 (1893), pp. 424–438; Charles Homer Haskins, "The Sources of the History of the Papal Penitentiary," *American Journal of Theology*, 9 (1905), pp. 421–450; Emil Goller, *Die päpstliche Pönitentiarie von ihren Ursprüngen bis zu ihrer Umgestaltung unter Pius V* (Rome: Preussisches Historisches Institut, 1907–1911); "Pénitencerie Apostolique," *Dictionnaire de théologie catholique*, vol. 12/1, cols. 1128–1160; Filippo Tamburini, "Il primo registro di suppliche dell'Archivio della Sacra Penitenzieria Apostolica (1410–1411),"

Rivista di storia della Chiesa in Italia (hereafter cited as *RSCI*), 23 (1969), pp. 384–427; *idem*, "Un registoro di bolle de Sisto IV nell'Archivio della Penitenzieria Apostolica," in *Palaeografica, Diplomatica et Archivistica: Studi in onore di Giulio Battelli*, vol. 2 (Rome: Edizioni di storia e letteratura, 1979), pp. 375–405.

92. See n. 88 above for bibliography.

93. See Adolf Goller, *Aus der Camera Apostolica des 15. Jahrhunderts* (Innsbruck, 1899); Annie I. Cameron, *The Apostolic Camera and Scottish Benefices, 1418–1488* (London/Edinburgh: Humphrey Mildford, 1934); William E. Lunt, *Papal Revenues in the Middle Ages*, 2 vols. (New York: Columbia University Press, 1934); François Baix, *La Chambre Apostolique et les 'Libri Annatarum' de Martin V (1417–1431)* (Brussels/Rome: Palais des Académies, 1942), pp. cccxvi–cdii; Felici, *La Reverenda Camera Apostolica*; Michele Monaco, *La situazione della Reverenda Camera Apostolica nell'anno 1525* (Rome: Biblioteca editrice, 1960); and Jean Favier, *Les Finances pontificales à l'époque du Grand Schisme d'Occident, 1378–1409* (Paris: Boccard, 1966). See also the general discussion in Clemens Bauer, "Studie per la storia delle finanze papali durante il pontificato di Sisto IV," *ARSP*, 50 (1926), pp. 319–400; Peter Partner, "The 'Budget' of the Roman Church in the Renaissance Period," in *Italian Renaissance Studies*, ed. E. F. Jacob (London: Faber and Faber, 1960), pp. 256–78; *idem*, "Papal Financial Policy in the Renaissance and Counter-Reformation," *Past and Present*, 88 (1980), pp. 17–62 (esp. p. 19 for a chart of the papal financial organization); "Ecclesiastical Finances," *New Catholic Encyclopedia*, vol. 5, pp. 920–923; and Thomson, *Popes and Princes*, chap. 4.

94. See Peter Partner, *The Papal States under Martin V* (London: British School in Rome, 1958); Maria Luisa Lombardo, *La Camera Urbis: Premesse per uno studio sulla organizazione amministrativa della Città di Roma durante il pontificato di Martino V* (Rome: Centro di ricerca editore, 1970); Michele Monaco, *Il 'De Officio Collectoris in Regno Angliae' di Pietro Griffi da Pisa (1469–1516)* (Rome: Edizioni di storia e letteratura, 1973).

95. On the chancery in general, see Harry Bresslau, *Handbuch der Urkundenlehre für Deutschland und Italien*, vol. 1 (Leipzig: Hensius, 1912), pp. 287–352; Paulus Rabikauskas, S.J., *Diplomatica Pontificia (Praelectionum lineamenta)* (Rome: Gregoriana, 1972), pp. 75–140; and "Chancellerie apostolique," *Dictionnaire de droit canonique*, vol. 3, cols. 465–471. The fullest account is found in Walther von Hofmann, *Forschungen zur Geschichte der kurialen Behörden vom Schisma bis zur Reformation*, 2 vols. (Rome: Von Loescher, 1914); see also the general discussion in Thomson, *Popes and Princes*, chap. 5. Thomas Frenz is preparing a modern study of the chancery which will deal with exactly the years covered by this study; see the announcement of his "Die Urkundenexpedition der Päpste der Hochrenaissance—Struktur, Geschäftsgang und Personel von Datarie, Kanzlei und Secretaria Apostolica, 1417–1527," in his "Armarium XXXIV vol. 11 im Vatikanischen Archiv: Ein Formelbuch für Breven aus der Zeit Julius II," in *Römische Kurie. Kirchliche Finanzen. Vatikanisches Archiv. Studien zu Ehren von Hermann Hoberg*, ed. Edwin Gatz, vol. 1 (=*Miscellanea Historiae Pontificiae*, 45), pp. 197–213, at p. 200, n. 26.

96. See the article "Règles de la Chancellerie" in *Dictionnaire de droit canonique*, vol. 7, cols. 540–541.

97. For the protonotaries, see Gaetano Moroni, *Dizionario di erudizione storico-ecclesiastica*, vol. 56 (Venice, 1852), pp. 3–29. A summary of their statutes

is in Hofmann, *Forschungen zur Geschichte der kurialen Behörden,* vol. 2, pp. 143-145.

98. In addition to the references cited in n. 95, see the fuller, more modern study of the *correctores* by Brigide Schwarz, "Der Corrector litterarum apostolicarum: Entwicklung des Korrectoramts in der päpstlichen Kanzlei von Innocenz III bis Martin V," *QFIAB,* 54 (1974), pp. 122-191.

99. For the *collectores,* see Hofmann, *Forschungen zur Geschichte der kurialen Behörden,* vol. 1, pp. 138-142; prices for bulls varied according to their nature. Hofmann, *ibid.,* vol. 2, pp. 201-226, provides much material on the curial taxes. See, for example, *ibid.,* p. 218, where he details the provision of the bishopric of Freising at the beginning of the sixteenth century: the chancery received over 100 ducats; the plumbarium, about 30 ducats; and the registry of bulls, 21 ducats.

100. On papal bulls, see Rabikauskas, *op. cit.,* pp. 75-82; *Catholic Encyclopedia,* vol. 3 (1908), pp. 52-58; and *Dictionnaire de théologie catholique,* vol. 2/1, cols. 1124-1127.

101. I have followed Thomas Frenz, "Das Eindringen humanistiche Schriftformen in die Urkunden und Akten der päpstlichen Kurie im 15. Jarhhunderts," *Archiv für Diplomatik,* 19 (1973), pp. 287-418, and 20 (1974), pp. 384-506, at pp. 309-312. See also Ludwig Schmitz-Kallenberg, ed., *Practica Cancellariae Apostolicae saeculi XV. exeuntis* (Münster: Coppenroth, 1904); J. Haller, "Die Ausfertigung der Provisionen: Ein Beitrag zur Diplomatik der Papsturkunden des 14. und 15. Jahrhunderts," *QFIAB,* 2 (1899), pp. 1-40; and Antonio Era, "Il giureconsulto catalano Gironi Pau e la sua 'Practica Cancillariae Apostolicae,'" in *Studi di storia e diritto in onore di Carlo Calisse,* vol. 3 (Milan: Giuffrè, 1937), pp. 369-402.

102. See *Relatio olim habita, coram Fe. Re. Alexandro Papa VI, in Consistorio publico, per R. P. Dominos Petrum de Vicentia tunc Episcopum Caesenatensis et Camerae Apostolicae Auditorem, et Petrum Isuaglies Archiepiscopum Reginensis: tunc etiam Almae Vrbis Gubernatorem; Commissarios deputatos: Super Breuibus Apostolicis, per Bartholomeum, tunc Archiepiscopum Cusentinensis, eiusdem Sanctitatis suae Secretarium, confectis* (Rome, 1547).

103. See Hofmann, *Forschungen zur Geschichte der kurialen Behörden,* vol. 1, pp. 109-114. Some colleges developed special names, such as Jannisaries and Mameluckes; for these, see *ibid.,* vol. 2, pp. 149-150.

104. For discussion of the older literature on venality, see Felice Litva, S.J., "L'attività finanziaria della Dataria durante il periodo tridentino," *Archivum Historiae Pontificiae,* 5 (1967), pp. 79-174; and André-Jean Marquis, "Le Collège des Correcteurs et Scripteurs d'Archives: Contributions à l'étude des charges venales de la Curie Romaine," in *Römische Kurie. Kirchliche Finanzen. Vatikanisches Archiv,* vol. 1, pp. 459-472. Prof. Nelson Minnich, in his "'Incipiat judicium ad Domo Domini': The Fifth Lateran Council and the Reform of Rome," in *Reform and Authority in the Medieval and Reformation Church,* ed. Guy Fitch Lytle (Washington, D.C.: Catholic University of America Press, 1981), pp. 127-142, at p. 135, n. 30, cites a bull of Leo X (*Bulla super societatibus officiorum Romanae Curiae,* July 14, 1514 [Rome, 1514]) in which Leo discussed the financial implications of venality. Prof. Minnich informs me that Leo also stated that women could participate in venality.

105. On the datary, see Léonce Célier, *Les Dataires du XVe siècle et les origines de la Datarie Apostolique* (Paris: Fontemoing, 1910); Litva, *op. cit.;* and Nicola

Storti, *La storia e il diritto della Dataria Apostolica dalle origini ai nostri giorni* (Naples: Athena mediterranea, 1969). Only one humanist, Maffeo Vegio, held the office of datary; he served under Eugenius IV and Nicholas V.

106. See Litva, *op. cit.*, p. 134.

107. See Hofmann, *Forschungen zur Geschichte der kurialen Behörden*, vol. 2, pp. 168–169; and Lunt, *Papal Revenues*, vol. 2, pp. 536–537. For a slightly later list, see Emil Goller, "Hadrian VI. und der Ämterkauf an der päpstlichen Kurie," in *Abhandlungen aus dem Gebiete der mittleren und neueren Geschichte und ihrer Hilfswissenschaften* (Münster: Aschendorff, 1925), pp. 375–407.

108. Hofmann (*Forschungen zur Geschichte der kurialen Behörden*, vol. 1, p. 282, n. 4; vol. 2, p. 200) cites the value of 100 ducats *de camera* as being equal to 109 scudi *in auro;* see also Frank Rutger Hausmann, "Die Benefizien des Kardinals Jacopo Ammannati-Piccolomini," *Römische Historische Mitteilungen,* 13 (1971), pp. 27–68, at pp. 36–37.

109. See Litva, *op. cit.*, p. 135.

110. See the memoranda in Hofmann, *Forschungen zur Geschichte der kurialen Behörden*, vol. 2, pp. 233–236.

111. For a list of those appointed, see Michael Tangl, *Die päpstlichen Kanzleiordnungen von 1200–1500* (Innsbruck, 1894), pp. 184–185.

112. Julius's bull is in *Bullarum Diplomatum et Privilegiorum Sanctorum Romanorum Pontificum, Taurinensis editio,* ed. Francesco Gaude, vol. 5 (Turin, 1860), pp. 158 ff. See also Hofmann, *Forschungen zur Geschichte der kurialen Behörden*, vol. 2, pp. 150–152; Geoffrey Barraclough, *Public Notaries and the Papal Curia: A Calendar and a Study of a Formularium Notariorum Curie for the Early Years of the Fourteenth Century* (London: Macmillan, 1934), pp. 25–26; Josef Grisar, "Notare und Notariatsarchive im Kirchenstaat des 16. Jahrhunderts," in *Mélanges Eugène Tisserant,* vol. 4, Studi e Testi #234 (Vatican City: Biblioteca Apostolica Vaticana, 1964), pp. 251–300, at pp. 267–269; Marquis, "Le Collège des Correcteurs"; and J. Lesellier, "Notaires et Archives de la Curie Romaine (1507–1625): Les Notaires français à Rome," *Mélanges d'archéologie et d'histoire,* 49 (1932), pp. 250–275.

113. See Bresslau, *op. cit.*, pp. 307–308; and the recent general study of the *scriptores* in the quattrocento by Brigide Schwarz, *Die Organisation kurialer Schreiberkollegien* (Tübingen: Niemeyer, 1972).

114. For the abbreviators, see "Abbreviatores ou abbreviateurs de lettres apostoliques," *Dictionnaire de droit canonique,* vol. 1, cols. 98–106; I have not seen Thomas Frenz, "Die Gründung des Abbreviatorenkollegs durch Pius II. und Sixtus IV.," in *Miscellanea M. Giusti,* vol. 1 (Vatican City: Biblioteca Apostolica Vaticana, 1978). See also Brigide Schwarz, "Abbreviature officium et assistere vicecancellario in expeditione litterarum apostolicarum: Zur Entwicklung des Abbreviatorenamtes vom Grossen Schisma bis zur Gründung des Vacabalistenkollegs der Abbreviatoren durch Pius II," in *Römische Kurie. Kirchliche Finanzen. Vatikanisches Archiv.,* 2, pp. 789–824; and *idem,* "Die Abbreviatoren unter Eugen IV," *QFIAB,* 60 (1980), pp. 200–274. A list of *abbreviatores de parco maiori* can be found in Giovanni Ciampani, *De Abbreviatorum de parco maiori sive Assistentium S.R.E. Vicecancellario . . . dissertatio historica* (Rome, 1691).

115. See Tommaso Tommasio Gualteruzzi, *Venerabilis Collegii . . . Secretariorum Apostolicorum privilegia et iura diversa . . .* (Rome, 1597); Hofmann, *Forschungen zur Geschichte der kurialen Behörden*, vol. 1, pp. 142–157; Rabikauskas,

op. cit., pp. 95-100; P. Richard, "Origines et développement de la Secrétaire d'Etat apostolique (1417-1823)," *Revue d'histoire ecclésiastique*, 11 (1910), pp. 56-70, 505-529, 728-754; A. Serafino, "Le origini della Pontificia Segretaria di Stato e la 'Sapienti consilio' del Pio X," *Apollinaris*, 25 (1925), pp. 165-239. An interesting study of a humanist's off-again on-again relations with the Curia, especially the secretariat, is Germano Gualdo's "Francesco Filelfo e la Curia Pontificia: Una carriera mancata," *ASRSP*, 102 (1979), pp. 189-236.

116. On bulls and briefs, see n. 100 above. Karl August Fink, "Untersuchungen über die päpstlichen Breven des 15. Jahrhunderts," *Römische Quartalschrift*, 43 (1935), pp. 55-80; Charles Martial de Witte, O.S.B., "Notes sur les plus anciens régistres des brefs," *Bulletin de l'Institut historique belge de Rome*, 31 (1958), pp. 153-158; Karl August Fink, "L'origine dei brevi apostolici," *Annali della Scuola speciale per Archivisti e Bibliotecari dell' Università di Roma*, 11/1-2 (1971), pp. 75-81; Germano Gualdo, "I brevi 'sub plumbo,'" *ibid.*, pp. 82-121; *idem*, "Il 'Liber brevium de Curia anni septimi' di Paolo II: Contributo allo studio del breve pontificio," in *Mélanges Eugène Tisserant*, vol. 4, pp. 301-345; and Dieter Brosius, "Breven und Briefe Papst Pius II," *RQ*, 70 (1975), pp. 180-224. On their organization, see the discussion in Martino Giusti, *Studi sui registri di bolle papali* (Vatican City: Biblioteca Apostolica Vaticana, 1968).

117. See, in general, Frenz, "Das Eindringen," p. 306.

118. See Bresslau, *op. cit.*, pp. 311-322; and G. Opitz, "Die Sekretäre Franciscus de Sancto Maximo und Johannes de Sancto Martino: Bemerkungen zur Fruhzeit des päpstlichen Sekretariats," *QFIAB*, 30 (1940), pp. 189-206.

119. In *Bullarum, Taurinensis Editio*, vol. 5, pp. 330-339.

120. For Bracciolini, see Karl August Fink, "Poggio-Autographen kurialer Herkunft," in *Miscellanea Archivistica Angelo Mercati*, Studi e Testi #165 (Vatican City: Biblioteca Apostolica Vaticana, 1952), pp. 129-133; and James D. Folts, "In Search of the 'Civil Life': An Intellectual Biography of Poggio Bracciolini (1380-1459)" (Ph.D. diss., University of Rochester, 1976).

121. In general, see Voigt, *Die Wiederbelebung des classischen Alterthums*, vol. 2, bk. 5; for Bruni in the Curia, see Gordon Griffiths, "Leonardo Bruni and the Restoration of the University of Rome (1406)," *Renaissance Quarterly*, 26 (1972), pp. 1-10; for Loschi, see Luigi Pastine, "Antonio Loschi umanista vicentino," *Rivista d'Italia*, 18 (1915), pp. 831-879; for Trebizond, see John Monfasani, *George of Trebizond* (Leiden: Brill, 1976); and for Biondo, see pp. 70-71 above. Relatedly, see Giovanni Mercati, "Andreas de Florentia: Segretario apostolico," *Ultimi contributi alla storia degli umanisti I*, Studi e Testi #90 (Vatican City: Biblioteca Apostolica Vaticana, 1939), pp. 97-133.

122. For the advocates, see n. 85 above; and Roberto Weiss, "Un umanista e curiale del Quattrocento: Giovanni Alvise Toscani," *RSCI*, 12 (1958), pp. 322-333.

123. See Hofmann, *Forschungen zur Geschichte der kurialen Behörden*, vol. 2, pp. 152-155; and Folts, "In Search of the 'Civil Life,'" pp. 199-201. For Pius, see Hofmann, *Forschungen zur Geschichte der kurialen Behörden*, vol. 2, p. 25.

124. For Gherardi, see *Il diario romano di Jacopo Gherardi*, ed. E. Carusi, Rerum Italicarum Scriptores, 23/3 (Città di Castello: Lapi, 1904); *Dispacci e lettere di Giacomo Gherardi Nunzio pontificio a Firenze e Milano (11 Settembre 1487-10 Ottobre 1490)*, ed. E. Carusi, Studi e Testi #21 (Rome: Tipografia Poliglotta Vaticana, 1909); Gian Paolo Marchi, "Lettere pisane del nuncio pontificio

Giacomo Gherardi," *Italia sacra*, 16/2 (Padua: Antenore, 1970), pp. 659–686; Lee, *Sixtus IV and Men of Letters*, pp. 75–80; and *idem*, "Iacobo Gherardi and the Court of Pope Sixtus IV," *Catholic Historical Review*, 65 (1979), pp. 221–237.

125. On dei Conti, see his *Le storie de' suoi tempi dal 1475 al 1510* (Rome, 1883), 2 vols.; and "Vita di Sigismondo de Comitibus scritta dall'Abate Mengozzi," ed. D. Michele Faloci-Palgrani, *Bollettino di storia patria per l'Umbria*, 13/1 (1907), pp. 152–196. See also Lee, *Sixtus IV and Men of Letters*, pp. 80–83.

126. Gherardi's defense, entitled "Iacobus Volaterranus Secretarius Apostolicus ad Cardinales Deputatos super Controversia inter eosdem Secretarios et Advocatos Consistoriales," is in *Anecdota litteraria*, ed. G. Amaduzzi, vol. 1 (Rome, 1773), pp. 119–133; see also Hofmann, *Forschungen zur Geschichte der kurialen Behörden*, vol. 2, pp. 152–155.

127. Gherardi, *op. cit.*, pp. 131–132.

128. Dei Conti's defense, entitled "Sigismundi Comitii Fulginatis scriptoris breuium apostolicarum ad Sixtum iiii. Summum Pontificem pro secretariis," is in BAV, Vat. Lat. 2934, ff. 591r–603v; see also Hofmann, *Forschungen zur Geschichte der kurialen Behörden*, vol. 2, p. 152.

129. BAV, Vat. Lat. 2934, ff. 594r–v.

130. *Ibid.*, f. 595r.

131. *Ibid.*, f. 600v. Bartolomeo Roverella and Leonardo Griffo are mentioned.

132. This was a humanist *topos;* see Giannantonio Campano, *Opera omnia* (Rome, 1495), ff. 7v–8r.

133. BAV, Vat. Lat. 2934, ff. 601v–603v.

134. Hofmann, *Forschungen zur Geschichte der kurialen Behörden*, vol. 1, pp. 107–124; and Frenz, "Das Eindringen," pp. 428–470.

135. Andreas Kraus, "Die Sekretäre Pius II: Ein Beitrag zur Entwicklunsgeschichte des päpstlichen Sekretariats," *Römische Quartalschrift*, 53 (1958), pp. 25–80.

136. These were Jacopo Ammannati, Gregorio Lollio, Jacopo Gherardi, Gaspare Biondo, Andreas of Trebizond, Leonardo Dati, Niccolò Perotti, Mattia Palmieri, Marcello de' Rustici, Francesco Loschi, Lianoro de' Lianori. For de' Rustici, see Frenz, "Das Eindringen," p. 459; for Palmieri, see Cosenza, *Dictionary of the Italian Humanists*, vol. 3, pp. 2560–2564; for Loschi, see Hilary, "The Appointments," pp. 73, 83–84.

137. For Ammannati, see Frank-Rutger Hausmann, "Armarium 39, Tomus 10 des Archivio Segreto Vaticano: Ein Beitrag zum Epistolar des Kardinals Giacomo Ammannati-Piccolomini (1422–1479) und anderer Humanisten," *QFIAB*, 50 (1971), pp. 112–180.

138. On Dati, see Francesco Flamini, "Leonardo di Piero Dati," *Giornale storico della letteratura italiana*, 16 (1890), pp. 1–107; P. Tacchi-Venturi, "La pietra tombale di Leonardo Dati al Gesù di Roma," *ASRSP*, 52 (1929), pp. 491–500; Renato Lefevre, "Fiorentini a Roma nel'400: I Dati," *Studi romani*, 20 (1972), pp. 187–197, at pp. 189–191; Lee, *Sixtus IV and Men of Letters*, pp. 52–54. Dati was responsible for the first surviving collection of papal briefs; see Germano Gualdo, "Il 'Liber Brevium de Curia Anni Septimi' di Paolo II." For an example of Dati's humanistic abilities, see J. B. Berrigan, "Leonardo Dati: *Hiempsal Tragoedia:* A Critical Edition with Translation," *Humanistica Lovaniensia*, 25 (1976), pp. 84–145. For Perotti, see n. 45 above.

139. See Lee, *Sixtus IV and Men of Letters,* chap. 2, for details. Lee lists Leonardo Dati, Gaspare of Verona, Marcello dei Rustici, Francesco da Noceto, Sigismondo dei Conti, Benedetto Rasi, Leonardo Grifo, Domizio Calderini, Giovanni Andrea Bussi, Lianoro de' Lianori, Gaspare Biondo, Andreas of Trebizond, and Giovanni Pietro Arrivabene; for those not discussed elsewhere, see *ibid.,* Index. For Innocent VIII's secretaries, see Serafini, "Le origini," pp. 187-188; and Pio Paschini, "Fra curiali ed umanisti alla fine del Quattrocento," *Atti dell'Accademia degli Arcadi e scritti dei soci,* 16 (1932), pp. 173-184.

140. On Calderini, see *DBI,* vol. 16, pp. 597-605; and D. Coppini, "Il commento a Properzio di Domizio Calderini," *Annali della Scuola Normale Superiore di Pisa, Classe di lettere e filosofia,* ser. 3, no. 9/3 (1979), pp. 1119-1173.

141. See n. 46 above.

142. See Lee, *Sixtus IV and Men of Letters,* pp. 66-70; and *Scritti inediti e rari di Biondo Flavio,* ed. Bartolomeo Nogara, Studi e Testi #48 (Rome: Tipografia Poliglotta Vaticana, 1927), pp. xxi, lxxxvii, lxxxviii, cxxi, clxxi, clxxv, clxxvi, clxxix, clxxx, clxxxi.

143. On Andreas, see John Monfasani, *George of Trebizond,* pp. 236-237; and Lee, *Sixtus IV and Men of Letters,* pp. 70-73.

144. See Lee, *Sixtus IV and Men of Letters,* pp. 59-60.

145. See n. 138 above.

146. See Lee, *Sixtus IV and Men of Letters,* p. 54.

147. *Ibid.,* p. 56. For one example, see Leslie F. Smith, "Lodrisio Crivelli of Milan and Aeneas Silvius, 1457-1464," *Studies in the Renaissance,* 9 (1962), pp. 31-63; for other examples, see Kraus, "Die Sekretäre Pius' II," pp. 33-34.

148. See Lee, *Sixtus IV and Men of Letters,* p. 51, n. 13.

149. See *ibid.,* pp. 225-231, for a list of Grifo's benefices.

150. Lists of secretaries who served during the Renaissance can be found in Philippus Bonamicus, *De claris pontificiarum epistolarum scriptoribus* (Rome, 1770), pp. 123-234; Gaetano Luigi Marini, *Degli archiatri pontifici,* 2 vols. (Rome, 1784), vol. 1, pp. 154, 230, 241, 272, and vol. 2, p. 254; Hofmann, *Forschungen zur Geschichte der kurialen Behörden,* vol. 2, pp. 105-124; and Serafini, "Le origini."

151. See Lee, *Sixtus IV and Men of Letters,* pp. 54-56.

152. See n. 38 above.

153. On Sadoleto, see Alessandro Ferraioli, "Il Ruolo della Corte di Leone X," *ASRSP,* 38 (1915), pp. 215-452; and Richard Douglas, *Jacopo Sadoleto, 1477-1547: Humanist and Reformer* (Cambridge, Mass.: Harvard University Press, 1959).

154. See Ferraioli, "Il Ruolo di Leone X," *ASRSP,* 37 (1914), pp. 307-484; and *DBI,* vol. 8. pp. 133-151.

155. Bembo rewrote his papal letters and bulls in a more perfectly Ciceronian form after his retirement from the secretaryship; see Pastor, *History of the Popes,* vol. 8, pp. 482-511.

156. See Eugenio Garin, "The Humanist Chancellors of the Florentine Republic from Coluccio Salutati to Bartolomeo Scala," *Portraits from the Quattrocento,* trans. Victor A. and Elizabeth Velen (New York: Harper and Row, 1972), pp. 1-29. See also Ronald G. Witt, *Coluccio Salutati and His Public Letters* (Geneva: Droz, 1976); and Allison Brown, *Bartolomeo Scala, 1430-1497, Chancellor of*

Florence: The Humanist as Bureaucrat (Princeton: Princeton University Press, 1979).

157. On Naples, see Alan Ryder, *The Kingdom of Naples under Alfonso the Magnanimous: The Making of a Modern State* (Oxford: Clarendon Press, 1976), chap. 7; and Ennio I. Rao, "Alfonso of Aragon and the Italian Humanists," *Esperienze litterarie*, 4/1 (1979), pp. 43–57. For Pontano, see E. Pèrcopo, *La vita di Giovanni Pontano* (Naples: I.T.E.A., 1938).

158. On the papal library, see Jeanne Bignami-Odier, *La bibliothèque vaticane de Sixte IV à Pie X*, Studi e Testi #272 (Vatican City: Biblioteca Apostolica Vaticana, 1973).

159. On the founding of the Sixtine Library and its relationship to that of Nicholas V, see José Ruysschaert, "Sixte IV, fondateur de la Bibliothèque vaticane (15 juin 1475)," *Archivum Historiae Pontificiae*, 7 (1969), pp. 513–524.

160. On Tortelli, see Girolamo Mancini, "Giovanni Tortelli: Cooperatore di Niccòlo V nel fondare la Biblioteca vaticana," *Archivio storico italiano*, 78/2 (1920), pp. 161–282.

161. See Maria Donata Rinaldi, "Fortuna e diffusione del 'De Orthographia' di Giovanni Tortelli," *Italia medioevale e umanistica*, 11 (1973), pp. 227–261.

162. For Platina, see the introduction by G. Gaida to Platina's *Liber de Vita Christi et omnium pontificum, Rerum Italicarum Scriptores*, 3/1 (Città de Castello: Lapi, 1913); Leon-Pierre Raybaud, "Platina et l'humanisme florentin," in *Mélanges Pierre Tisset* (Montpellier: Université de Montpellier, 1970), pp. 389–405, and Richard J. Palermino, "Platina's History of the Popes" (M. Litt. thesis, University of Edinburgh, 1973).

163. See Maria Bertola, *I due primi registri di prestito della Biblioteca Apostolica Vaticana* (Vatican City: Biblioteca Apostolica Vaticana, 1942). Relatedly, see José Ruysschaert, "Les collaborateurs stables de Platina, premier bibliothècaire de la Vaticane," in *Palaeographica, Diplomatica et Archivistica: Studi in onore di Giulio Battelli*, vol. 2, pp. 575–591.

164. For Platina's work relating specifically to the Curia, see Heinrich Otto, "Das Avignoneser Inventar des päpstlichen Archivs vom Jahre 1366 und die Privilegiensammlungen des Fieschi und des Platina: Ein Beitrag zur Geschichte des Vatikanischen Archivs im 14. und 15. Jahrhundert," *QFIAB*, 12 (1909), pp. 132–188.

165. Among the other humanists working in the library were: Bartolomeo Manfredi di Pertinoro, Cristoforo Persona, Demetrio Guazzelli, Giovanni Lorenzi of Venice, Lorenzo Parmenio, Romolo Mammacino, Filippo Beroaldo the Younger, Zanobi Acciaiuoli, Girolamo Aleandro, Fabio Vigili and Fausto Sabeo. For these men, see Bignami-Odier, *op. cit.*

166. On Inghirami, see Annamaria Rugiadi, *Tommaso Fedra Inghirami: umanista volterrano* (1470–1516) (Amatrice: Scuola tipografica orfanotrofio maschile, 1933); Isabella Inghirami, "Notizie dei codici, degli autografi e delle stampe riguardanti le opere dell'umanista volterrano Tommaso Inghirami detto Fedro," *Rassegna volterrana*, 21/22 (1955), pp. 33–41; Nella Santorito Vichi, "Pingue e strabico, ma 'audace nelle imprese d'amore,'" *Almanacco dei bibliotecari italiani*, 1970, pp. 51–55; and Fabrizio Cruciani, "Il teatro dei ciceroniani: Tommaso 'Fedra' Inghirami," *Forum italicum*, 14 (1980), pp. 356–377.

167. See Luigi Pescetti, "Due carmi latini inediti di Tommaso Fedra Inghirami, 1470–1516," *Giornale storico della letteratura italiana*, 99 (1932), pp. 74–83;

and Roberto Weiss, "Un'orazione dimenticata di Tommaso Fedra Inghirami," *Rassegna volterrana*, 21/22 (1955), pp. 45-52. Two orations can be found in *Thomae Phaedri Inghirami Volaterrani orationes duae*, ed. P. A. Galletti (Rome, 1777). For Inghirami as a classical scholar, see the summary of G. Cambier's "Les annotations de Tommaso Inghirami à *l'editio princeps* des Argonautiques de Valerius Flaccus (Bologne, 1474)," *Revue belge de philologie et d'histoire*, 43 (1965), p. 1434.

168. Fedra's rhetoric textbook remains in manuscript form: BAV, Vat. Lat. 3370 and Ottob. Lat. 1485.

169. See Carlo Dionisotti, *Gli umanisti e il volgare fra Quattro e Cinquecento* (Florence: Le Monnier, 1968), p. 100.

170. In addition to *Orationes duae* (n. 167 above), see John M. McManamon, "The Ideal Renaissance Pope: Funeral Oratory from the Papal Court," *Archivum Historiae Pontificiae*, 14 (1976), pp. 5-70, at pp. 30-32; and O'Malley, *Praise and Blame*, index.

171. For Poliziano, see Vittore Branca-Manilio Pastore Stocchi, "La Biblioteca vaticana nella Seconda Centuria dei Miscellanea di Angelo Poliziano," in *Mélanges Eugène Tisserant*, vol. 6, pp. 141-159, at p. 152, n. 26.

172. See Bignami-Odier, *op. cit.*, pp. 26-27.

173. See Anselmo Albareda, "Il vescovo di Barcellona, Pietro Garcias bibliotecario della Vaticana sotto Alessandro VI," *La Bibliofilia*, 60 (1958), pp. 1-18.

174. See pp. 163-165 above.

CHAPTER 2

1. The colleges of the Curia Romana in the Renaissance have not been treated from a social perspective. For an earlier period, see Bernard Barbiche, "Diplomatique et histoire sociale: Les 'Scriptores' de la Chancellerie Apostolique au XIIIe siècle," *Annali della Scuola speciale per archivisti e bibliotecari dell'Università di Roma*, 12 (1972), pp. 116-129. For a discussion of the social origins of Belgians in the Curia, see Christian Dury, "Les Curialistes belges à Rome et l'histoire de la curie romaine, problème d'histoire de l'Eglise: L'Exemple de Saint Lambert à Liege," *Bulletin de l'Institut historique belge de Rome*, 50 (1980), pp. 131-160. See also Bernard Guillemain, *La Cour pontificale d'Avignon (1309-1376): Etude d'une société* (Paris: Boccard, 1962); and Brigide Schwarz, *Die Organisation kurialer Schreiberkollegien von ihrer Entstehung bis zur Mitte des 15. Jahrhunderts* (Tübingen: Niemeyer, 1972).

2. On the confraternities in Renaissance Rome, see Pio Paschini, *Roma nel Rinascimento* (Rome: Istituto di studi romani, 1940), pp. 460-464. For a specific example, see Paola Pavan, "Gli statuti della società dei raccomandati del Salvatore *ad sancta sanctorum* (1331-1496)," *ASRSP*, 101 (1978), pp. 35-96.

3. See Schwarz, *op. cit.*, pp. 161-166.

4. The one exception to this rule was the Roman Academy, which was reorganized under Sixtus IV as a religious *sodalitas*. This was a special case and is discussed in Chapter 4.

5. See Gaetano Moroni, *Dizionario di erudizione storico-ecclesiastica*, vol. 23 (Venice, 1843), pp. 147-156.

6. This definition is adapted from Moroni, *ibid.*, p. 27.

7. In addition to Moroni, see the discussion in Agostino Paravicini Bagliani, *Cardinali di Curia e 'familiae' cardinalizie dal 1227 al 1254*, 2 vols. (Padua: Antenore, 1972), vol. 2, chap. 6, and the bibliography there cited.

8. On the papal *familia* in general, see Moroni, *op. cit.*, vol. 23, pp. 27–126; "Famiglia pontificia," *Enciclopedia cattolica*, vol. 5, pp. 99–108; "Cour pontificale," *Dictionnaire de droit canonique*, vol. 4, cols. 726–729, and "Familiers du pape," *ibid.*, vol. 5, cols. 810–814; "Cour romaine," *Dictionnaire de théologie catholique*, vol. 3/2, cols. 1931–1983; Peter Partner, *Renaissance Rome, 1500–1559 A Portrait of a Society* (Berkeley: University of California Press, 1976), chap. 4. For specific examples, see Amato Pietro Frutaz, "La famiglia pontificia in un documento dell'inizio del secolo XIV," in *Palaeographia, Diplomatica et Archivistica: Studi in onore di Giulio Batelli* (Rome: Edizioni di storia e letteratura, 1979), vol. 2, pp. 277–323; François-Charles Uginet, ed., *Le 'Liber Officialium' de Martin V* (Rome: Archivio di Stato, 1975); George Bourgin, "La 'familia' pontificia sotto Eugenio IV," *ASRSP*, 27 (1904), pp. 203–224; Paolo Piccolomini, "La famiglia di Pio III," *ibid.*, 24 (1903), pp. 143–164; Alessandro Ferraioli, "Il Ruolo della Corte di Leone X" (*ibid.*, 34 [1911], pp. 363–391; 35 [1912], pp. 219–271, 483–539; 36 [1913], pp. 191–223, 519–584; 37 [1914], pp. 307–360, 453–484; 38 [1915], pp. 215–281, 425–452; 39 [1916], pp. 53–77, 537–576; 40 [1917], pp. 247–277; 41 [1918], pp. 87–110); and Léon Dorez, *La Cour de Pape Paul III d'après les Régistres de la Trésorerie secrète*, 2 vols. (Paris: Leroux, 1932).

9. See Moroni, *op. cit.*, vol. 23, p. 61, for a listing of these *veri familiares et commensuales papae;* see also E. von Ottenthal, *Regulae Cancelleriae Apostolicae: Die päpstlichen Kanzleiregeln von Johannes XXII bis zu Nicolaus V* (Innsbruck, 1888), p. 18.

10. See G. Mollat, *The Popes of Avignon, 1305–1378*, trans. Janet Love (New York: Harper and Row, 1963), pp. 310–318.

11. See Guillemain, *La Cour pontificale d'Avignon*, p. 493.

12. For Pius II's *familia*, see Moroni, *op. cit.*, vol. 23, pp. 54–57; for the other *familiae*, see n. 10 above. Papal *familiares* wore red-colored garments.

13. See Piccolomini, "La famiglia di Pio III."

14. See Ferraioli, "Il Ruolo di Leone X," 34 (1911), pp. 367–391, for the list.

15. Moroni, *op. cit.*, vol. 8, pp. 20–56.

16. *Ibid.*, vol. 9, pp. 6–14; and Emil Goller, "Die Kubiculare im Dienste der päpstlichen Hofverwaltung vom 12. bis 15. Jahrhundert," in *Papsstum und Kaisertum*, ed. Albert Brackmann (Munich: Münchner Drucke, 1926), pp. 622–647.

17. See Ferraioli, "Il Ruolo di Leone X" *ASRSP*, 36 (1913), p. 203.

18. See Moroni, *op. cit.*, vol. 62, pp. 83–93, and vol. 18, pp. 173–174.

19. *Ibid.*, vol. 25, pp. 185–192.

20. See Peter Partner, "Papal Financial Policy in the Renaissance and Counter-Reformation," *Past and Present*, 88 (1980), pp. 17–62, at p. 50. In his "The 'Budget' of the Roman Church in the Renaissance Period," in *Italian Studies*, ed. E. F. Jacob (London: Faber and Faber, 1960), pp. 256–278, at p. 263, Partner gives the figure of 30,000–40,000 ducats for the papal place under Sixtus IV. The *ducato d'oro* and the *fiorino d'oro* were of approximately equal value.

21. See Ferraioli, "Il Ruolo di Leone X," *ASRSP*, 41 (1918), pp. 105–107. The prelate was Bishop Tranquillo de Leonibus.

22. *Ibid.*, 34 (1911), p. 391.

23. See Vittorio Fanelli, "Il ginnasio greco di Leone X," *Studi romani,* 9 (1961), pp. 375–388.

24. For Beroaldo, see Ferraioli, "Il Ruolo di Leone X," *ASRSP,* 39 (1916), pp. 537–569; *DBI,* vol. 9, pp. 384–388; and Ettore Paratore, *Spigolature romane e romanesche* (Rome: Bulzoni, n.d.), pp. 75–114.

25. See Pio Paschini, *Tre illustri prelati del Rinascimento: Ermolao Barbaro-Adriano Castellesi-Giovanni Grimani* (Rome: Lateran, 1957), pp. 107–108. Paschini also cites attacks on Castellesi by the Roman poet Antonio Lelio.

26. See Ferraioli, "Il Ruolo di Leone X," *ASRSP,* 38 (1917), pp. 247–255; and Josef Klotner, *Kardinal Dominikus Jacobazzi und seine Konzilswerke: Ein Beitrag zur Geschichte der konziliaren Idee* (Rome: Gregoriana, 1948).

27. Ferraioli, "Il Ruolo di Leone X," *ASRSP,* 38 (1917), pp. 235–262.

28. For the cardinal's *familia,* see Moroni, *op. cit.,* vol. 23, pp. 126–147. For background, see Paravicini Bagliani, *op. cit.* For the Renaissance, see G. Dickinson, *Du Bellay in Rome* (Leiden: Brill, 1960), chap. 5; and Partner, *Renaissance Rome,* chap. 2.

29. See Ottenthal, *Regulae Cancelleriae Apostolicae,* index, s.v. "familiares cardinalium."

30. Moroni, *op. cit.,* vol. 23, p. 148.

31. See Martin Lowry, *The World of Aldus Manutius: Business and Scholarship in Renaissance Venice* (Ithaca, N.Y.: Cornell University Press, 1979), p. 215, n. 111, who lists only four cardinals; cf. Federico Ubaldini, *Vita di Mons. Angelo Colocci,* Studi e Testi #256 (Vatican City: Biblioteca Apostolica Vaticana, 1969), pp. 25–26, n. 32, for Medici.

32. On Calderini, see *DBI,* vol. 16, pp. 597–605.

33. See Guillemain, *La Cour pontificale d'Avignon,* chap. 2; and Mollat, *The Popes at Avignon,* pp. 305–309.

34. On this, see Denys Hay, "Renaissance Cardinals," *Synthesis* (Bucharest), 3 (1976), pp. 35–46.

35. See Partner, *Renaissance Rome,* p. 137. In the period before the sack this number might have been a bit inflated since Leo X created thirty-one cardinals at one time in 1517.

36. Printed in Domenico Gnoli, "*Descriptio Urbis* o censimento della popolazione di Roma avanti il Sacco borbonico," *ASRSP,* 17 (1894), pp. 375–520, at p. 387. Partner, *Renaissance Rome,* p. 75, n. 1, has announced a new study of this document.

37. See Dorez, *La Cour du Pape Paul III.*

38. For Cesarini, see *DBI,* vol. 24, pp. 180–182.

39. For Cajetan, see *Enciclopedia cattolica,* vol. 4, cols. 1506–1509.

40. Gnoli, *op. cit.,* pp. 386–388.

41. For a later period, see Pierre Hurtubise, "La 'Table' d'un cardinal de la Renaissance: Aspects de la cuisine et de l'hospitalité à Rome au milieu du XVIe siècle," *Mélanges de l'Ecole française de Rome: Moyen Age-Temps Modernes,* 92/1 (1980), pp. 249–282.

42. On the economic state of Renaissance cardinals, see D. S. Chambers, "The Economic Predicament of Renaissance Cardinals," *Studies in Medieval and Renaissance History,* 3 (1966), pp. 289–313; A. V. Antonovics, "A Late Fifteenth Century Division Register of the College of Cardinals," *Papers of the British School*

at Rome, 35 (1967), pp. 87–101; and Frank-Rutger Hausmann, "Die Benefizien des Kardinals Jacopo Ammannati-Piccolomini: Ein Beitrag zur Okonomischen Situation des Kardinals in Quattrocento," *Römische Historische Mitteilungen*, 13 (1971), pp. 27–80.

43. See the letter quoted in Moroni, *op. cit.*, vol. 23, p. 134.

44. See Kathleen Weil-Garris and John F. D'Amico, "The Renaissance Cardinal's Ideal Palace: A Chapter from Cortesi's *De Cardinalatu*," in *Studies in Italian Art and Architecture, 15th through 18th Centuries*, ed. Henry A. Millon (Rome: Elefante, 1980), pp. 88–89.

45. See Norman Zacour, "Papal Regulations of Cardinals' Households in the Fourteenth Century," *Speculum*, 50 (1975), pp. 434–455.

46. See Emanuel Rodocanachi, "Le Luxe des cardinaux romains de la Renaissance," *Revue des Questions historiques*, 89 (1911), pp. 414–432; and Hay, "Renaissance Cardinals."

47. See Weil-Garris and D'Amico, *op. cit.*, for bibliography.

48. See pp. 78–80 and 226–236 above.

49. *De Cardinalatu* (Castrum Cortesium, 1510), bk. 2, chap. 1, "De redditibus cardinalium," ff. F 3r–F 8v.

50. *Ibid.*, ff. F 3v–F 6r. Cortesi also argued that cardinals should be paid in cash.

51. *Ibid.*, ff. G 8v–H 1r. The text specifies 140 members, although the number 120 occurs in the side note. Cortesi specifically rejects the opinion of many that a staff of sixty servants would suffice.

52. *Ibid.*, f. G 8v.

53. See Weil-Garris and D'Amico, *op. cit.*, pp. 70–97, where the text and a translation are published.

54. See Gnoli, *"Descriptio Urbis,"* p. 387.

55. *De Cardinalatu*, ff. I 10v–12r.

56. See Weil-Garris and D'Amico, *op. cit.*, pp. 86–87.

57. *De Cardinalatu*, bk. 2, chap. 3, "De familia cardinalis," ff. G 7r–H 3r.

58. *Ibid.*, f. G 7v.

59. See Partner, *Renaissance Rome*, p. 121, for Julius and Leo. The description of the *familia* of the English cardinal Christopher Bainbridge in D. S. Chambers, *Cardinal Bainbridge in the Court of Rome, 1509 to 1514* (Oxford: Oxford University Press, 1965), pp. 112–120, demonstrates the English quality of much of his household.

60. *De Cardinalatu*, f. H 1v: ". . . dicimus his qui in maiorum gentium genere numerantur annua nummum quinquagena esse statuenda, quo sit honoratior in servitute virtus." The sidenote glosses this passage as follows: "Quod cappellanis et scutiferis debent dari 50 auri annuatim."

61. *Ibid.*, f. H 1v–2r.

62. See Weil-Garris and D'Amico *op. cit.*, pp. 80–81. Relatedly, see Nesca A. Robb, "The Fare of Prince: a Renaissance Manual of Domestic Economy," *Italian Studies*, 7 (1952), pp. 32–61, which discusses Domenico Romoli's *Lo Scalco* [The Steward] published in 1560 but probably written in the 1540s; Romoli had been a papal steward.

63. *De Cardinalatu*, ff. H 2v–3r.

64. *Ibid.*, f. G 8r; see also pp. 103–105 above.

65. See Weil-Garris and D'Amico, *op. cit.*, pp. 78–79.

66. *De Cardinalatu*, f. N 11v.

67. This point is made somewhat more strongly by Anna Gracci, "Studi su Paolo Cortesi da San Gimignano ed il suo 'De Cardinalatu,'" (thesis, University of Florence, 1967).

68. See *DBI*, vol. 9, pp. 686–696; and Ludwig Mohler, *Kardinal Bessarion als Theologe, Humanist und Staatsmann*, vol. 1 (Paderborn: Schöningh, 1923), pp. 325–335.

69. See Alfred A. Strnad, "Francesco Todeschini-Piccolomini: Politik und Mäzenatentum im Quattrocento," *Römische Historische Mitteilungen*, 8/9 (1964/ 65–1965/66), pp. 101–425, at pp. 321–349.

70. See Flavio di Bernardo, *Un vescovo umanista alla Corte pontificia: Giannantonio Campano, 1429–1477* (Rome: Gregoriana, 1975), pp. 206–209.

71. See pp. 36 and 97 above.

72. On Riario, see Egmont Lee, *Sixtus IV and Men of Letters* (Rome: Edizioni di storia e letteratura, 1978), index.

73. See Moroni, *op. cit.*, vol. 23, p. 134.

74. See C. Corvisieri, "Il trionfo romano di Eleonora d'Aragona nel giugno del 1472," *ASRSP*, 1 (1878), pp. 475–492, and 10 (1887), pp. 629–689.

75. On Cleofilo, see Giuseppe Zippel, "Un'apologia dimenticata di Pietro Riario," in *Scritti di storia e di filosofia d'arte* (Naples: Riccardi, 1908), pp. 329– 346; "Saggio bibliografico delle opere di Francesco," in *L'assedio di Fano nel 1463 narrato da Pietro Antonio Paltroni* (Fano, 1896), pp. 49–55; and Carlo Dionisotti, *Gli umanisti e il volgare fra Quattro e Cinquecento* (Florence: Le Monnier, 1968), chap. 3. Relatedly, see Giuseppe Frasso, "Un poeta improvvisatore nella 'familia' del Cardinale Francesco Gonzaga: Francisco Cieco da Firenze," *Italia medioevale e umanistica*, 20 (1977), pp. 395–400.

76. The letter is entitled *Octavius Cleophilus Baptistae Guarino, Antonio Citadino, Nicolao Leoniceno, Petro Bono, Ludovico Carboni, Lucae Ripae, Aristophilo Mamphredo, Beltramo Constabili, Lodovico Pictorio, amicis iocundissimis, S. P. D.* (Rome, 1498/1500); see *Gesamtkatalog der Wiegendrucke* (Leipzig, 1925), #7129.

77. *Ibid.*, ff. 3r–4v.

78. *Ibid.*, ff. 6v–7r; cf. Bartolomeo Platina, *De vita Christi et omnium Pontificum Maximorum*, ed. G. Zippel, *Rerum Italicarum Scriptores*, 3/1 (Città di Castello: Lapi, 1932), p. 407, for references to Riario and his cousin Giuliano della Rovere.

79. For Roverella, see Lee, *Sixtus IV and Men of Letters*, p. 58, n. 42; for Riario, see Armando Schiavo, "Profilo e testamento di Raffaele Riario," *Studi romani*, 8 (1960), pp. 414–429, at p. 425.

80. See Gian Paolo Marchi, "Un umanista nella Curia romana sul finire del XV secolo (ricerche umanistiche veronesi, V)," *Vita veronese*, 19 (1965), pp. 365– 373, at p. 366.

81. See Andrea Guarina da Salerno, *Scimmia*, ed. and trans. Giuseppina and Eugenio Battisti (Rome, 1970), pp. 94–97.

82. See Pio Paschini, "Una famiglia di curiali nella Roma del Quattrocento: I Cortesi," *RSCI*, 11/1 (1957), pp. 1–48, at p. 33. A poem written by Pamfilo Sasso on the death of Corsi ends," . . . turpi nam captus amore/Crimina damnavit Roma quod iste tua./Mortus est: poenas vero pro crimine solvet/Saeve manus; iustos nam movet ira deos." See Giorgio Rossi, "Alcune rime inedite di Jacopo

Corsi," *Giornale storico della letteratura italiana,* 26 (1885), pp. 390-397, at p. 390.

83. See Partner, *Renaissance Rome,* chap. 5.

84. See Francesco Priscianese, *Del governo della corte d'un signore in Roma,* ed. L. Bartolucci (Città di Castello, 1883). See Deoclecio Redig de Campos, "Francesco Priscianese, stampatore e umanista fiorentino del sec. XVI," *La Bibliofilia,* 40 (1938), pp. 160-183; I have not seen L. Vignali, "Nuove testimonianze sulla vita e le opere di Francesco Priscianese," *Studi e problemi di critica testuale,* 18 (1979), pp. 121-134.

85. Priscianese, *Del governo della corte,* pp. 7-21.

86. *Ibid.,* pp. 70-71.

87. *Ibid.,* pp. 21-23. In all, Priscianese estimated that 6,579 scudi would be necessary to maintain the lord's household for one year.

88. See L. Menapace, "Il banchiere di tre famosi pontificati: Il Magnifico Chigi," *Economia e storia,* 17/3 (1970), pp. 393-399; I have not seen *Il Magnifico Agostino Chigi* (Rome: Associazione banciaria italiana, 1970). See also G. Cugnoni, "Agostino Chisi, il Magnifico (e note)," *ASRSP* (2 [1879], pp. 37-83, 208-226, 475-490; 3 [1880], pp. 291-305, 422-448; 4 [1881], pp. 56-75, 195-216).

89. See Melissa M. Bullard, "*Mercatores Florentini Romanam Curiam Sequentes* in the Early Sixteenth Century," *Journal of Medieval and Renaissance Studies,* 6/1 (1976), pp. 51-71; and *idem, Filippo Strozzi and the Medici: Favor and Finance in Sixteenth-Century Florence and Rome* (Cambridge: At the University Press, 1980).

90. See Menapace, *op. cit.,* p. 397.

91. See Felix Gilbert, *The Pope, His Banker, and Venice* (Cambridge, Mass.: Harvard Unversity Press, 1980).

92. On Benigno, see *DBI,* vol. 8, pp. 512-513.

93. See José Ruysschaert, "Trois recherches sur le XVIe siècle romain, *ASRSP,* 94 (1971), pp. 10-29.

94. Gallo's poem is *De viridario Augustini Chisii* (Rome, 1511); Palladio's is *Suburbanum Augustini Chisii* (Rome, 1512).

95. On the university, see F. M. Renazzi, *Storia dell'Università degli Studi di Roma, detta communemente La Sapienza,* 2 vols. (Rome, 1804-1806).

96. See D. S. Chambers, "*Studium Urbis* and *gabella studii:* The University of Rome in the Fifteenth Century," in *Cultural Aspects of the Italian Renaissance: Essays in Honor of Paul Oskar Kristeller,* ed. Cecil H. Clough (Manchester: Manchester University Press, 1976), pp. 68-110.

97. For Brandolini, see *DBI,* vol. 14, pp. 40-42.

98. See John W. O'Malley, *Praise and Blame in Renaissance Rome: Rhetoric, Doctrine, and Reform in the Sacred Orators of the Papal Court, C. 1450-1521* (Durham, N.C.: Duke University Press, 1979), index. For examples of Brandolini's orations, see Charles Samaran, "Un français à Rome au XVe siècle: Guillaume Pérès condomois, Auditeur de Rote (1420?-1500)," *Annuaire-Bulletin de la Société de l'Histoire de France,* 31 (1931), pp. 181-218; and Aulo Greco, "La 'docta pietas' degli umanisti e un documento della Biblioteca Angelica," *Accademie e biblioteche d'Italia,* 48/3 (1979), pp. 210-238.

99. Entitled *Quae in Raphaelis Lippi Brandolini scriptis continentur,* this is found in BAV, Vat. Lat. 3590; the list was drawn up by F. Aeneas at the request of Balduino del Monte, Julius III's brother, at the pope's urging. On this, see

Gisbert Brom, "Einige Briefe von Raphael Brandolini Lippus," *RQ*, 2/2 (1888), pp. 175–206. Before coming to Rome, Brandolini had tutored in Naples; among his students there was Alfonso d'Argona, the illegitimate son of King Alfonso II; see *DBI*, vol. 3, p. 688.

100. See *DBI*, vol. 14, p. 42.

CHAPTER 3

1. Jean Delumeau, *Vie économique et sociale de Rome dans la seconde moitié du XVIe siècle*, 2 vols. (Paris: Boccard, 1957–1959), deals primarily with post-sack Rome and does not consider the humanists as a unique group. Recent scholarship has debated the extent to which the Italian family in the Renaissance was becoming nuclear. For the opposing views, cf. Richard A. Goldthwaite, *Private Wealth in Renaissance Florence: A Study of Four Families* (Princeton: Princeton University Press, 1968), and Francis William Kent, *Household and Lineage in Renaissance Florence: The Family Life of the Capponi, Ginori, and Rucellai* (Princeton: Princeton University Press, 1977). I have not dealt with this question for two reasons. The first is a lack of detailed information on a sufficiently large number of Roman families. The second is the clerical aspect, which altered normal family structure. A rich prelate, for example, could become the center of his family, but this was not a universal characteristic of Italian families and hence is not a basis for generalization.

2. For the earlier period, see Jean-Claude-Marie Vigueur, "Classe dominante et classes dirigeantes à Rome à la fin du Moyen Age," *Storia della Città*, 1 (1976), pp. 4–26.

3. On the Valla family, see p. 7 above.

4. For the social background of the Florentine humanists in the quattrocento, see Lauro Martines, *The Social World of the Florentine Humanists* (Princeton: Princeton University Press, 1963).

5. For the plots against the popes, see Pio Paschini, *Roma nel Rinascimento* (Bologna: Capelli, 1939), pp. 132–133 and 177–178.

6. See pp. 5–8 above for a general consideration of the clergy.

7. See p. 70 above.

8. On Naples, see the old but useful E. Gothein, *Il Rinascimento nell'Italia meridionale*, trans. (Florence: Sansoni, 1915); and *Storia di Napoli*, vol. 4/1 (Naples, 1974), pt. 1, chap. 5.

9. On Venice, see M. L. King, "The Patriciate and the Intellectuals: Power and Ideas in Quattrocento Venice," *Societas*, 5/4 (1974), pp. 295–312; and the more recent overview by Felix Gilbert, "Humanism in Venice," in *Florence and Venice: Comparisons and Relations*, vol. 1, *Quattrocento* (Florence: La Nuova Italia, 1979), p. 26.

10. See Martines, *op. cit.*; Gene Brucker, *The Civic World of Early Renaissance Florence* (Princeton: Princeton University Press, 1977); and Dale Kent, *The Rise of the Medici: Faction in Florence, 1426–1434* (Oxford: Oxford University Press, 1978).

11. On the city government, see Delumeau, *Vie économique et sociale de Rome*.

12. See Denys Hay, *The Church in Italy in the Fifteenth Century* (Cambridge: At the University Press, 1977), chap. 4.

13. See Domenico Gnoli, "*Descriptio Urbis* o censimento della popolazione di Roma avanti il Sacco borbonico," *ASRSP,* 17 (1894), pp. 375-520, at p. 389.

14. See pp. 3 and 21 above for the Curia and the Great Schism.

15. I have taken these population figures from Karl Julius Beloch, *Bevölkerungs-geschichte Italiens,* vol. 2 (Berlin: De Gruyter, 1939), pp. 1-6 and 147. Also useful for comparative purposes are population figures for Verona, which housed 14,000 in 1409, 14,225 in 1425, 20,800 in 1456, and 42,000 in 1502; see David Herlihy, "The Population of Verona in the First Century of Venetian Rule," in *Renaissance Venice,* ed. J. R. Hale (Totowa, N.J.: Littlefield, 1973), pp. 91-120, at p. 104.

16. Based on Gnoli, *op. cit.*

17. See Martines, *op. cit.*, pp. 271-286.

18. *Ibid.*, pp. 117-123.

19. *Ibid.*, pp. 123-127.

20. On Manetti, see pp. 120-122 above.

21. For Alberti, see Valerio Mariani, "Roma in Leon Battista Alberti," *Studi romani,* 7 (1959), pp. 635-646.

22. See Richard Boyd Hilary, "The Appointments of Pope Pius II (Enea Silvio Piccolomini), 1458-1464," (Ph.D. diss., University of Wisconsin, 1969).

23. See p. 74 above for the case of Alessandro Cortesi.

24. On the Accolti, see *DBI,* vol. 1, pp. 101-102, 103-104, 107-109. Smaller in dimension was the de Lellis family; see Walter Brandmüller, "Simon de Lellis de Teramo: Ein Konsistorialadvokat auf den Konzilien von Konstanz und Basel," *Annuarium Historiae Conciliorum,* 12, pt. 1/2 (1980), pp. 229-268.

25. See John Monfasani, *George of Trebizond* (Leiden: Brill, 1976), pp. 139-140; see p. 78 above for Paolo Cortesi's attempt to sell his secretaryship.

26. See p. 224 above.

27. The bull is printed in *Bullarum Diplomatum et Privilegiorum . . . Taurinensis Editio,* vol. 5, pp. 211-212.

28. For Biondo, see *DBI,* vol. 10, pp. 536-538.

29. For Biondo's antiquarian and historical scholarship, see Roberto Weiss, *The Renaissance Discovery of Classical Antiquity* (Oxford: Blackwell, 1964).

30. For Gaspare, see *DBI,* vol. 10, pp. 559-560; and Egmont Lee, *Sixtus IV and Men of Letters* (Rome: Edizioni di storia e letteratura, 1978), pp. 67-70; for examples of Gaspare's work as a notary, see Giuseppe Gatti, "Alcuni atti camerali rogati dal notaro Gaspare Biondo," *Studi e documenti di storia e diritto,* 1 (1886), pp. 59-83.

31. See Bartolomeo Nogara, ed., *Scritti ineditti e rari di Biondo Flavio,* Studi e Testi #48 (Rome: Tipografia Poliglotta Vaticana, 1927), p. clxxxi.

32. On Girolamo, see Carlo Dionisotti, "Resoconto di una ricerca interrotta," *Annali della scuola Normale Superiore di Pisa: Lettere, storia e filosofia,* ser. 2, no. 37 (1968), pp. 259-269.

33. See Gian Paolo Marchi, "Due corrispondenti veronesi di Ciriaco d'Ancona," *Italia medioevale e umanistica,* 11 (1968), pp. 317-329; and *idem,* "Lettere pisane del nuncio pontificio Giacomo Gherardi," *Italia sacra* (Padua: Antenore, 1970), pp. 659-686.

34. In addition to n. 35 below, see Gian Paolo Marchi, "Martino Rizzoni, allievo di Guarino Veronese," *Atti dell'Accademia di Agricoltura, Scienze e Lettere di Verona,* ser. 6, no. 17 (1965-66), pp. 291-325; *idem,* "Un umanista negli uffici della cancelleria pontificia," *Studi storici veronesi L. Simeoni,* 15 (1965), pp. 215-

235; *idem,* "Un umanista nella Curia romana sul finire del XV secolo (richerche umanistiche veronesi, V)," *Vita veronese,* 19 (1965), pp. 365-373.

35. See Gian Paolo Marchi, "Due corrispondenti veronesi di Ciriaco d'Ancona," pp. 317-328.

36. In addition to the Maffei of Volterra there was the Maffei of Verona. This family came to Rome in the second half of the quattrocento. Benedetto Maffei (d. 1491) was an abbreviator and writer (see p. 220 above); he married a Roman woman, Caterina Conti. Benedetto's brother Agostino (d. 1496) was a priest and *plumbarius* of the fisc; he might also have been a papal secretary. He was a prominent humanist, was close to Pomponio Leto, and was arrested with other members of the Roman Academy by Paul II (see pp. 96-97 above). Benedetto had one son, Achille (d. 1511), whose relationship to the Curia is uncertain. Achille's son Girolamo (dates uncertain) was a *maestro di strada.* Of Girolamo's four sons, three became priests and one, Mario, followed his father as *maestro di strada.* Of the priest-sons, two, Bernardino (1514-1553) and Marcantonio (1522-1583), became cardinals. The family was especially renowned for its excellent library. See Scipione Maffei, *Verona illustrata,* pt. 2 (Milan, 1825), pp. 261-275; and José Ruysschaert, "Recherche des deux bibliothèques romaines Maffei des XVe et XVIe siècles," *La Bibliofilia,* 60 (1958), pp. 306-355.

37. On the Cortesi family, see Pio Paschini, "Una famiglia di curiali nella Roma del Quattrocento: I Cortesi," *RSCI,* 11/1 (1957), pp. 1-43.

38. See *ibid.,* pp. 3-5.

39. See Ernst Pitz, *Supplikensignatur and Briefexpedition an der römischen Kurie im Pontifikat Papst Calixtus III* (Tübingen: Niemeyer, 1972), p. 106, who cites from a Lateran register: "Magister Antonius de Cortesiis, litterarum apostolicarum abbreviator, scriptor et familiaris apostolicus." See also Walther von Hofmann, *Forschungen zur Geschichte der kurialen Behörden vom Schisma bis zur Reformation,* 2 vols. (Rome: Von Loescher, 1914), vol. 2, pp. 43 and 65. In the *De hominibus doctis dialogus,* ed. and trans. Maria Teresa Graziosi (Rome: Bonacci, 1972), p. 62, Paolo Cortesi refers to his father as "princeps Collegii Duodecimvirum," i.e., head of the college of abbreviators. For an example of Cortesi's curial work, see Dieter Bosius, "Eine Reise an die Kurie im Jahre 1462: Der Rechenschaftsbericht des Lübecker Domherrn Albert Krummedeck," *QFIAB,* 58 (1978), pp. 411-440, at pp. 428-429. In the *Practica Cancellariae Apostolicae cum stilo et formis in Romana Curia usitatis . . .* (Venice, 1572), at pp. 120-127, there is a section entitled "Notabilia de expectativis, et aliis literas gratias concernentibus, excerpta ex notulis Antonii de Corthesis, et aliorum Abbreviatorum," which perhaps attests to Antonio Cortesi's prominence in his office.

40. A series of letters from Cortesi to members of the Medici family demonstrates this; see Florence, Archivio di Stato, Fondo Mediceo avanti il Principato, Filza X #463; XXX #231; LX #9, 94, 106; C #83.

41. See Paschini, "I Cortesi," p. 4; and Giovanni Antonazzi, "Lorenzo Valla e la Donazione di Costantino nel secolo XV con un testo inedito di Antonio Cortesi," *RSCI,* 4/2 (1950), pp. 223-234.

42. See p. 82 above.

43. For Lattanzio, see Paschini, "I Cortesi," pp. 5-7.

44. See Paolo Cortesi, *De Cardinalatu* (Castrum Cortesianum, 1510), f. M 6v.

45. Letter dated 1494, in Florence, Archivio di Stato, Archivio della Repubblica, Lettere varie, vol. 16, f. 408. According to G. V. Coppi, *Annali, memorie ed*

huomini illustri di San Gimignano (Florence, 1695), p. 390, Lattanzio served as one of the regulators of the Monte di Pietà in San Gimignano after its establishment in 1501.

46. Letter dated July 30, 1493, *ibid.*, f. 407. On the letters, see Guido Ristori, "Il carteggio di ser Francesco Baroni, *Rinascimento,* ser. 2, no. 17 (1977), pp. 279-303. Some letters from the group are printed in F. Pintòr, *Da lettere inedite di due fratelli umanisti (Alessandro e Paolo Cortesi): estratti ed appunti* (Perugia: Unione tipografica cooperativa, 1907), and in Libia Cortese Rossi, "La scapigliatura fiorentina," in *Ecumenismo della cultura,* vol. 3, ed. Giovannangiola Tarugi (Florence: Olschki, 1980), pp. 53-63. See also n. 48 below.

47. For Alessandro, see Paschini, "I Cortesi," pp. 7-26; and Florio Banfi, "Alessandro Tommaso Cortese, glorificatore di Mattia Corvino re d'Ungheria," *Archivio storico per la Dalmazia,* 23 (1937), pp. 135-160.

48. See Armando F. Verde, O.P., *Lo studio fiorentino, 1473-1503: Ricerche e documenti* (Pistoia: Memorie domenicane, 1977), vol. 3/2, pp. 20-30.

49. See Paschini, "I Cortesi," p. 8.

50. See Florence, Archivio di Stato, Mediceo avanti il Principato, Filza CII, #136; this letter is printed in Pintor, *op. cit.,* p. 18, and an Italian translation appears in Dino Cortese, "Sisto quarto papa antoniano," *Il Santo,* 7 (1972), pp. 211-271, at pp. 266-268.

51. In a letter to Baroni of January 28, 1487, Alessandro had also noted that "iam in urbe notor digito tamquam partium Medicianarum assertor acerrimus." See Pintor, *op. cit.,* p. 16; and Cortese, "Sisto quarto," p. 265. In this same letter Alessandro announced that he had rented one of his two houses in Rome to Gentile de' Bechi, bishop of Arezzo, a strong adherent of the Medici. Not only did the bishop have the same literary interests as Alessandro, but "Laurentiani ambo sumus." De' Bechi had actually defied Sixtus IV's interdict of Florence in 1478 because of his pro-Medici sympathies.

52. See Florence, Archivio di Stato, Archivio della Repubblica, Lettere varie, 16, f. 367; and Pintor, *op. cit.,* p. 29.

53. Pintor, *op. cit.,* p. 29: "Vivo et ho visso in casa mia honoratamente et e stata et e una achademia di letterati."

54. Florence, Archivio di Stato, Archivio della Repubblica, Lettere varie, 16, f. 371; and Pintor, *op. cit.,* p. 30.

55. Florence, Archivio di Stato, Archivio della Repubblica, Lettere varie, 16, f. 369; and Pintor, *op. cit.,* p. 31.

56. Florence, Archivio di Stato, Archivio della Repubblica, Lettere varie, 16, f. 371; and Pintor, *op. cit.,* p. 30.

57. Alessandro discusses this in the letter cited in n. 50 above; see also Pintor, *op. cit.,* pp. 23-24.

58. See Ladislas Havas, "Le Panégyrique de Cortesius et les relations diplomatiques entre Matthias Corvin et les relations diplomatiques entre Matthias Corvin et le Papauté," *Acta classica Universitatis Scientiarum Debreciensis,* 1 (1965), pp. 57-62. The poems are available in Abel Jenö, ed., *Irodalomtörteneti Emlekek* (Budapest, 1890), and J. Fógel, ed., *De laudibus bellicis Matthiae Corvini Hungariae Regis* (Leipzig: Teubner, 1934). For the Spanish poem, see *Gesamtkatalog der Wiegendrucke,* #7794.

59. See *Gesamtkatalog der Wiegendrucke,* #7795 and #7796, for his *Oratio in Epiphania* (Rome, 1483).

60. See Dino Cortese, ed., *Alexandri Cortesii ad Christianissimum Ludovicum Francorum Regem Opusculum* (Padua: Centro Studi Antoniani, 1976). For Fannese, see BAV, Vat. Lat. 2336; and A. Frugoni, ed., *Carteggio umanistico di Alessandro Farnese* (Florence: Sansoni, 1950), pp. 30, 39.

61. See the letter to Marco Maroldi della Bella, *magister sacri palatii*, on a recent archaeological discovery, in Pastor, *Geschichte der Päpste*, vol. 3/2 (Freiburg: Herder, 1965), pp. 1046–1047.

62. See BAV, Capponianus 235, ff. 18r–v, 83v–85r, 120v, 121v; and Isidoro del Lungo, *Florentia: Uomini e cose del Quattrocento* (Florence, 1897), pp. 250–253. See also Dino Cortese, "Il Poliziano a San Gimignano: Due epigrammi per Angelo Poliziano," in *Ecumenismo della cultura*, vol. 3, pp. 65–76.

63. See Cortesi, *De hominibus doctis dialogus* (ed. and trans. Graziosi), p. 58; and *idem, De Cardinalatu*, ff. K 5v and N 2r. Cortesi requested aid from Lorenzo de' Medici to help pay Alessandro's debts; see Pintor, *op. cit.*, p. 37, n. 3.

64. For further bibliography, see Paschini, "I Cortesi," pp. 26–48; Roberto Weiss, "Paolo Cortesi," in *Dizionario critico della letteratura italiana*, ed. Vittore Branca (Turin: Unione tipografico, 1974), vol. 1, pp. 633–636; John F. D'Amico, "Humanism and Theology at Papal Rome, 1480–1520" (Ph.D. diss., University of Rochester, 1977), chaps. 2, 3, 5; and Kathleen Weil-Garris and John F. D'Amico, "The Renaissance Cardinal's Ideal Palace: A Chapter from Cortesi's *De Cardinalatu*," in *Studies in Italian Art and Architecture, 15th through 18th Centuries*, ed. Henry A. Millon (Rome: Elefante, 1980), pp. 45–123. The exact date of Cortesi's birth is disputed. In her introduction to the *De hominibus doctis dialogus*, p. xiii, M. T. Graziosi proposed 1471, but this has been questioned and is probably incorrect; see Elena Miele's review in *La rassegna della letteratura italiana*, ser. 7, no. 82 (1978), pp. 254–256.

65. For Marullo as a teacher, see Rosario Tosti, "Per la biografia di Michele Marullo Taracaniota," in *Medievo e Rinascimento veneto . . . in onore de Lino Lazzarini*, vol. 1 (Milan: Antenore, 1979), pp. 557–570, at pp. 562–563. For Cortesi's education in Florence, see Verde, *Lo studio fiorentino*, vol. 3/2, p. 774. For Leto, see *De Cardinalatu*, ff. I 4v and NN 2v. One of the Cortesis' teachers in San Gimignano was Gioviano Crasso da Monopoli, a friend of Angelo Poliziano, see Giovanni Picotti, *Ricerche umanistiche* (Florence: Nuova Italia, 1955), p. 8; and Ida Maier, *Ange Politien: La formation d'un poete humaniste, 1469–1480* (Geneva: Droz, 1966), pp. 89–90.

66. Cortesi, *De hominibus doctis dialogus* (ed. and trans. Graziosi). For a more recent edition, see that by Giacomo Ferraù, Università degli Studi di Mesina, Facolta di Lettere e Filosofia, Centro di Studi umanistici, Studi e Testi #1 (Palermo: Il Vespro, 1979). See also Pintor, *op. cit.*, pp. 37–38, for the dedication. For further discussion of the dialogue, see pp. 128–129 above.

67. See Graziosi's introduction to Cortesi's *De hominibus doctis dialogus;* and Giacomo Ferraù, "Il 'De hominibus doctis' di Paolo Cortesi," *Umanità e storia: Scritti in onore di Adalchi Attisani* (Naples: Giannini, 1971), vol. 2, pp. 261–290. Ferraù, however, identifies the "Antonio" of the dialogue as Lelio Antonio Augusto rather than Giovanni Sulpizio.

68. See Léon Dorez, "Les maîtres intellectuels de pape Paul III," *Etudes italiennes*, 1 (1931), pp. 5–13; *idem, La Cour de pape Paul III*, vol. 1 (Paris: Leroux, 1932), chap. 1; A. Frugoni, "Per uno studio sulla giovinezza di Paolo III," *Annali della R. Scuola Normale di Pisa*, ser. 2, no. 9 (1940), pp. 202–210; and *idem, Il carteggio umanistico di Alessandro Farnese*.

69. See Benedetto Pecci, *L'umanesimo e la Cioceria* (Trani: Vecchi, 1912), pp. 28–111; and Cortesi, *De hominibus doctis dialogus* (ed. and trans. Graziosi), pp. xxiv–xxv.

70. The texts of Poliziano's and Cortesi's letters are available in *Prosatori latini del Quattrocento*, ed. Eugenio Garin (Milan: Riccardi, 1952), pp. 902–911; for analysis, see pp. 129–130 above.

71. See Paschini, "I Cortesi," pp. 27 and 37, for Cortesi's curial posts. Paschini (*ibid.*, p. 27, n. 107) notes that the document granting Paolo the scriptorship was countersigned by Raffaele Maffei.

72. See pp. 102–107 above.

73. Cortesi was in San Gimignano by May 18, 1503; see the letter in BAV, Autografi Ferrajoli, vol. 13, f. 1r.

74. Cortesi described the events in *De Cardinalatu*, ff. R 7r–v.

75. For Castellesi's letter, dated July 13, 1503, and probably directed to the monks of the Badia, see Girolamo Ferri, *De rebus gestis et scriptis Hadriani Castellensis Cardinalis . . .* (Faenza, 1771), pp. 61–62; for the letter to Maffei asking assistance, see Forlì, Biblioteca Comunale, Autografi Piancastelli, 670, no. 1.

76. The title is *In quattuor libros Sententiarum argutae Romanoque eloquio disputationes*, which was first published in Rome in 1504. See Chapter 6 for further discussion.

77. For the *De Cardinalatu*, see Weil-Garris and D'Amico, *op. cit.*, introduction. The text is discussed on pp. 49–53 and 226–236 above.

78. See Delio Cantimori, "Questioncine sulle opere progettate da Paolo Cortesi," in *Studi di bibliografia e di storia in onore di Tammaro de Marinis*, vol. 1 (Verona: Valdonega, 1964), pp. 273–280.

79. The letters in Florence, Biblioteca Nazionale Centrale, II-III-3, chronicle this. These letters have recently been printed; see Maria Teresa Graziosi, "Spigolature cortesiane," *Atti e memorie della Accademia Arcadia*, ser. 3, no. 7 (1977), pp. 67–84; see also the analysis in Weil-Garris and D'Amico, *op. cit.*, pp. 65–66.

80. On January 25, 1508, Theodore Gaza informed Cortesi that Julius had received the text (Florence, Biblioteca Nazionale Centrale, II-III-3, ff. 133r–v), but on March 8, 1508, Cardinal Vigerio noted that the pope had not read it (*ibid.*, ff. 130v–131r).

81. Some sources report that Cortesi was made bishop of Urbino before his death; however, this seems unlikely. See Paschini, "I Cortesi," p. 47.

82. See Maffei's introductory letter in the *De Cardinalatu* (unpaginated), and the letters to Severo Varini Piacentino, BAV, Barb. Lat. 2517, 11v–12r.

83. See Konrad Krautter, *Philologische Methode und humanistische Existenz: Filippo Beroaldo und sein Kommentar zum Goldenen Esel* (Munich: Fink, 1971).

84. On Giovanni Andrea (Gregorio) Cortesi, see Marvin W. Anderson, "Gregorio Cortese and Roman Catholic Reform," in *Sixteenth Century Essays and Studies*, ed. Carl S. Meyer, vol. 1 (St. Louis, Mo.: Foundation for Reformation Research, 1970), pp. 75–106.

85. The poem, "Io. Andreae Cortesii Mutinensis ad lectorem Ode Monocolos," can be found at the end of the *Liber Sententiarum* (Paris, 1513), f. 46r.

86. *De Cardinalatu*, f. R 12v.

87. On the Maffei family, see Pio Paschini, "Una famiglia di curiali: i Maffei di Volterra," *RSCI*, 7 (1953), pp. 337–376; and Ruysschaert, "Recherches des deux bibliothèques romaines."

88. For his curial offices, see Paschini, "I Maffei," pp. 337–340; and, for an example, see George Bourgin, "La 'familia' pontificia sotto Eugenio IV," *ASRSP*, 27 (1904), pp. 203–224.

89. See Ernst Pitz, *Supplikationsignatur und Briefexpedition an der römischen Kurie im Pontifikat Papst Calixtus III* (Tübingen: Niemeyer, 1972), index.

90. In addition to Pitz (*ibid.*), see Dieter Brosius, "Breven und Briefe Papst Pius' II," *Römische Quartalschrift*, 70 (1975), pp. 180–224, for reference to the "Registrum brevium apostolicorum mei G. de Vulterris secretarii de tempore domini Calisti pape tertii," in Archivio Segreto Vaticano, Arm. 39. 8.

91. Paschini, "I Maffei," p. 339.

92. *Ibid.*, pp. 341–342; and Jeanne Bignami-Odier, *La Bibliothèque vaticane de Sixte IV à Pie X*, Studi e Testi #272 (Vatican City: Biblioteca Apostolica Vaticana, 1973), pp. 27, 39.

93. Paschini, "I Maffei," pp. 343–344.

94. *Ibid.*, p. 341.

95. See Angelo Poliziano, *Della Congiura dei Pazzi (Coniurationis Commentarium)*, ed. A. Perosa (Padua: Antenore, 1958), pp. 19–20.

96. See Paschini, "I Maffei," p. 342.

97. See *ibid.*, pp. 344–356, 363–369; Benedetto Falconcini, *Vita del nobil-'uomo e buon servo di Dio, Raffaele Maffei detto il Volterrano* (Rome, 1735); John F. D'Amico, "A Humanist Response to Martin Luther: Raffaele Maffei's *Apologeticus*," *Sixteenth Century Journal*, 6/2 (1975), pp. 37–65; *idem*, "Papal History and Curial Reform in the Renaissance: Raffaele Maffei's *Breuis Historia* of Julius II and Leo X," *Archivum Historiae Pontificiae*, 18 (1980), pp. 157–210.

98. For an example of Maffei's activity in the Curia, see Tore Nyberg, "Der Geschäftsgang bei der Ausfertigung der Gründungsdokumente des Brigittenklosters Altomuster durch die Römische Kurie," *Archivum Historiae Pontificiae*, 9 (1971), pp. 209–248.

99. For the press, see *Catalogue of Books Printed in the XV Century Now in the British Museum*, pt. 4 (London: British Museum, 1916), pp. 46–48.

100. Paschini, "I Maffei," p. 345.

101. See Florio Banfi, "Raffaello Maffei in Ungheria," *L'Europa orientale*, n.s. 17 (1937), pp. 462–488.

102. See Paschini, "I Maffei," p. 344.

103. The Minucci family had humanist and curial connections; see Dennis E. Rhodes, "Un bibliofilo volterrano in Inghilterra alla fine del Quattrocento: Roberto Minucci," *Rassegna volterrana*, 53/54 (1979), pp. 17–23.

104. See the manuscripts in Forlì, Biblioteca Comunale, Autografi Piancastelli, 1340, nos. 51, 52, 53.

105. In Volterra, Biblioteca Comunale Guarnacciana, Archivio Maffei, 105, there is a document, unpaginated, noting that the dowry was 405 ducati d'oro paid in anticipation of 1,000 ducats, and that it was paid on February 19, 1515. In a letter to Paolo Riccobaldi from Mario Maffei, dated June 7, 1523 (Rome, Biblioteca Nazionale Centrale Vittorio Emanuele, Lettere autografe, A. 95. 12, 2), Mario provided Paolo with a list of his earnings from his scriptorship:

Introitus officii breuium an. M. D. XXII

November dedit duc.   7

December   „   „   9

M. D. XIII.

Ianuarius	dedit duc.		9
Februarius	,,	,,	17
Martius	,,	,,	23
Aprilis	,,	,,	13
Maius	,,	,,	13

Total, 91 ducats. The list of earnings is followed by a list of deductions.

106. Forlì, Biblioteca Comunale, Autografi Piancastelli, 1340, no. 49, addressed to his wife, Tita, dated April, 15, 1497, Rome.

107. See Raffaele Maffei, *Stromata*, BAV, Barb. Lat. 753, ff. 45r–v.

108. Paschini, "I Maffei," p. 353.

109. See the letter in Florence, Biblioteca Riccardiana, 974, ff. 58v–59r.

110. See letters in BAV, Barb. Lat. 2517, ff. 7r–11r; and Volterra, Biblioteca Comunale Guarnacciana, XLVII/II/2, #4 bis.

111. See Angelo Poliziano, *Epistolae* (Amsterdam, 1644), ff. 491–494.

112. See Benedetto Croce, *Poeti e scrittori del pieno e del tardo Rinascimento*, vol. 2 (Bari: Laterza, 1958), pp. 295–296.

113. In his *Commentaria Urbana* (Rome, 1506), f. 298v, Maffei was critical of George as a teacher, but he revised his opinion in his *Stromata*, BAV, Barb. Lat. 753, f. 301v, which contains retractions to the *Commentaria Urbana*.

114. See *Odissea Homeri per Raphaelem Volaterranum in latinum conversa* (Rome, 1510). See also Fernanda Ascarelli, *Annali tipografici di Giacomo Mazzocchi* (Florence: Sansoni, 1960), p. 44, #28; and BAV, Barb. Lat. 2517, ff. 24r–33v and Capponianus 169, for sections of the *Iliad*. For *Procopii de bello persico liber primus (–quartus) per Raphaelem Volaterranum conversa* (Rome, 1507), see Ascarelli, *op. cit.*, pp. 32, 10. For Xenophon, see n. 115 below.

115. Raffaele Maffei, *Raphaelis Volaterrani Commentariorum Urbanorum liber I [–XXXVIII]. Item Oeconomicus Xenophontis ab eodem latio conversus* (Rome, 1506); and BAV, Ottob. Lat. 1649.

116. Forlì, Biblioteca Comunale, Autografi Piancastelli, 1340, no. 6, contains a letter to Paolo Riccobaldo from Mario Maffei, who lists profits from curial offices: "Scriuo a messer Raffaello a quo reliqua, lofficio tuo e ualuto Aprile xvii ducati, di messer Raffaello xv et el mio xxv." The letter is undated, but may have been written in 1521.

117. See D'Amico, "A Humanist Response to Martin Luther"; and *idem*, "Papal History and Curial Reform in the Renaissance."

118. See Paschini, "I Maffei," p. 367.

119. Raffaele Maffei, *Opera Magni Basilii per Raphaelem Volaterranum nuper in latinum conversa* (Rome, 1515); see Ascarelli, *op. cit.*, pp. 91–92.

120. Raffaele Maffei, *Raphaelis Volaterrani De Institutione Christiana ad Leonem X Ponti. Max. libri octo. Eiusdem de prima philosophia ad Marium fratrem liber unus. De dormitione Beatae Mariae Virginis sermones duo Ioannis Damasceni et unus Andreae Hierosolimitani a greco in latinum per R. conversi* (Rome, 1518); see Ascarelli, *op. cit.*, pp. 124–126, 129; manuscript in BAV, Ottob. Lat. 992.

121. The autograph is BAV, Barb. Lat. 752; there is also a defective, seventeenth-century copy, Ottob. Lat. 2368.

122. After his death Mario Maffei and Paolo Riccobaldi erected a monument in Raffaele's honor in the Church of San Lino in Volterra.

123. Maffei wrote a Latin poem in hexameters on the founding of Rome; see Weiss, *The Renaissance Discovery of Classical Antiquity*, pp. 83–84.

124. For Mario, see Paschini, "I Maffei," pp. 356–363 and 369–376; Luigi Peschetti, "Mario Maffei (1463–1537)," *Rassegna volterrana*, 6 (1932), pp. 65–91; *idem*, "Le nozze di Lucrezia Borgia in una lettera inedita di Jacopo Gherardi a Mario Maffei," *ibid.*, 8 (1955), pp. 1–16; D'Amico, "Papal History and Curial Reform in the Renaissance," pp. 170–171.

125. Paschini, "I Maffei," p. 349–350.

126. Volterra, Biblioteca Comunale Guarnacciana, Archivio Maffei, 105, contains the following summary of Mario's offices: "sacritano vaticano, scrittore del Collegio di S. Giovanni in Laterano, canonico di Volterra, vescovo di Aquino, vescovo di Cavaillon nell'Avignonese, sopraintendente alla Fabbrica di S. Pietro in Vaticano, nunzio straordinario al re Luigi XII."

127. See Christoph Frommel, "Die Peterskirche unter Papst Julius II im Licht neuer Dokumente," *Römisches Jahrbuch für Kunstgeschichte*, 16 (1976), pp. 57–136, at pp. 72, 82, 93–94, 101.

128. See Paschini, "I Maffei," p. 359.

129. Mario accompanied Cardinal Francesco Soderini, the bishop of Volterra, into the conclave which elected Leo; see Peschetti, "Mario Maffei," p. 67, n. 2. Although identified with Soderini, whose brother had ruled Florence, Mario remained close to the Medici.

130. See Luigi Constantini, *La badia dei SS. Giusto e Clemente* (Lucca, 1915), pp. 24–28. Mario resigned in 1528 in favor of Giovanni Battista del Bava, a relative of Paolo Riccobaldi's.

131. See Rome, Biblioteca Nazionale Centrale Vittorio Emanuele, Lettere autografe, A. 95. 64, 1, for a letter in which Mario related that Leo had asked him to compose an epigram for windows he was constructing for the University of Rome.

132. See *ibid.*, A. 95. 34, 3; here Mario considered obtaining the recently vacant bishopric of Volterra, but "non mi pare expediente so vachio [?] et pagar di nuovo altre 1500 ducati. . . ." The letter is from 1530.

133. *Ibid.*, A. 95. 14, 6 (November 25, 1523); A. 95. 14, 7 (December 2, 1523); A. 95. 15, 2 (December 12, 1523); A. 95, 15, 4 (December 26, 1523); A. 96. 16, 3 (January 14, 1524). In the last of these letters, Mario wrote "delle stanze in Palazo non sene fora di speranze," and in postscript, "ho parlato con nostro Signore hoggi, et sponte mha detto che omnino io hauero le stanze, credo di certo non manchero." But the rooms never materialized.

134. These are listed in Volterra, Biblioteca Comunale Guarnacciana, Archivio Maffei, 105, unpaginated.

135. Maffei wrote numerous letters on these properties; they can be found in part in Rome, Biblioteca Nazionale Centrale Vittorio Emanuele, Lettere autografe, A. 95. 1–A. 95. 66.

136. Mario was still in Rome on September 1, 1526 (see *ibid.*, A. 95. 29, 2), but was in San Donnino, his villa near Volterra, on November 21, 1526 (*ibid.*, A. 95. 29, 4).

137. Jacopo Sadoleto urged Mario to go to his diocese; see Alessandro Ferraioli, "Il Ruolo di Leone X," *ASRSP*, 38 (1915), pp. 261–269. G. M. Giberti, Clement VII's datary and chief adviser, later in his life regretted helping Mario obtain a bishopric since he did not fulfill his episcopal duties; see Adriano Prosperi, *Tra*

evangelismo e controriforma: G. M. Giberti (1495-1543) (Rome: Edizioni di storia e letteratura, 1969), p. 201.

138. The dialogue is in Perugia, Biblioteca Comunale Augusta, Fondo Vecchio, J 115, ff. 104r-111r. (I am grateful to Prof. Alberto Grohman of the University of Perugia for obtaining a copy for me.) The poems are in BAV, Ottob. Lat. 2860, ff. 110r, 119r, 184r-v.

139. See Ascarelli, *op. cit.*, pp. 139-140, #144.

140. See p. 102 above.

141. See Jacopo Sadoleto, *Elogio della Sapienza*, trans. Antonio Altamura (Naples: Perioti, 1950).

142. See R. S. Maffei, "Blosio Palladio priore di S. Salvatore di Monte al Prunno," *Rassegna mensile di letteratura ed arte per la città di Volterra e suo territorio*, 1 (1898), pp. 82-83. For Blosio, see p. 111 above.

143. See Renato Lefevre, "Un prelato del'500: Mario Maffei e la costruzione di Villa Madama," *L'Urbe*, 33/3 (1969), pp. 1-11; and *idem*, "La 'Vigna del Cardinale de Medici' e il vescovo d'Aquino," *Strenna dei Romanisti*, 22 (1961), pp. 171-177.

144. See the letters in Rome, Biblioteca Nazionale Centrale, Vittorio Emanuele, Lettere autografe, A. 95. 44 and A. 95. 46.

145. *Ibid.*, A. 95. 45, 5, dated Rome, December 19, 1534. Mario wrote that he had purchased a scriptorship for Giulio for 400 ducats and was contemplating purchasing other offices.

146. *Ibid.*, A. 95. 25, 5 (September16, 1525).

147. Mario might have been expressing curial policy when he attacked Venice in an oration; see Paschini, "I Maffei," pp. 358-359. This occurred in 1510 when Julius II was warring against the Venetians.

CHAPTER 4

1. On the idea of Rome, see Franco Gaeta, "Sull'idea di Roma nell'umanesimo e nel Rinascimento (appunti e spunti per una ricerca)," *Studi romani*, 25 (1977), pp. 169-186.

2. See Flavio Biondo, *Scritti inediti e rari di Biondo Flavio*, ed. Bartolomeo Nogara, Studi e Test, #48 (Rome: Tipografia Poliglotta Vaticana, 1927), p. 115. For humanist rivalry, see John Monfasani, *George of Trebizond* (Leiden: Brill, 1976), pp. 109-111.

3. See pp. 38-39 above.

4. See Arnoldo della Torre, *Storia dell'Accademia platonica di Firenze* (Florence: Carnescchi, 1902); and M. Meylender, *Storia delle accademie d'Italia*, 6 vols. (Bologna: Cappelli, 1929).

5. See della Torre, *Storia dell'Accademia platonica, passim*.

6. See Erasmo Pèrcopo, *Vita di Giovanni Pontano*, ed. M. Manfredi (Naples: I.T.E.A., 1939), pp. 106-135.

7. On Leto and his academy, see Vladimiro Zabughin, *Giulio Pomponio Leto: Saggio Critico*, 3 vols. (Rome: La vita letteraria, 1909-1912); Arnoldo della Torre, *Paolo Marsi: Un contributo alla storia dell'Accademia pomponiana* (Rocca S. Casciano: Cappelli, 1903); Aristide Lesen, "Pomponio Leto Sabino," *Convivium*, 3/6 (1931), pp. 855-866; Josef Delz, "Ein unbekannter Briefe von Pomponius Laetus," *Italia medioevale e umanistica*, 9 (1966), pp. 417-440; Carlo de Frede, "Il concetto umanistico di nobiltà: Pomponio Leto e la sua famiglia," *Annali*

della facolta di lettere e filosofia de l'Università di Napoli, 2 (1952), pp. 205–226; I have not seen Annuziato Presta, "Pomponio Leto," *Almanacco Calabrese* (Rome), 22 (1973), pp. 63–100. Relatedly, see *idem,* "Rapporti fra umanesimo umbro e l'Accademia romana," in *L'umanesimo umbro: Atti del IX Convegno di Studi umbri* (Gubbio: Centro di Studi umbri, 1977), pp. 381–408.

8. On Pietro, see Delz, *op. cit.,*; and Maria Teresa Graziosi Acquaro, "Petri Odi Montopolitani carmina nunc primum e libris manuscriptis edita," *Humanistica Lovaniensia,* 19 (1970), pp. 7–113.

9. See Richard J. Palermino, "The Roman Academy, the Catacombs, and the Conspiracy of 1468," *Archivum Historiae Pontificiae,* 18 (1980), pp. 117–155.

10. On the suppression, see Palermino (*ibid.,*); Isidoro Carini, "La difesa di Pomponio Leto pubblicata ed illustrata," in *Nozze Cian=Sappa-Flandinet* (Bergamo, 1894), pp. 241–260; Eugenio Garin, "L'Accademia romana, Pomponio Leto e la congiura," in *Storia della letteratura italiana,* vol. 3 (Milan: Garganti, 1966), pp. 142–158; and A. J. Dunston, "Pope Paul II and the Humanists," *Journal of Religious History,* 7/4 (1973), pp. 287–306.

11. On this reform, see Walther von Hofmann, *Forschungen zur Geschichte der kurialen Behörden vom Schisma bis zur Reformation,* 2 vols. (Rome: Von Loescher, 1914), vol. 1, pp. 124–125.

12. On Platina, see pp. 35–36 above.

13. See Dunston, "Pope Paul II and the Humanists," pp. 299–304.

14. For Platina's relations with Cardinal Gonzaga and his family see A. Luzio-Renier, "Il Platina e i Gonzaga," *Giornale storico della letteratura italiana,* 13 (1889), pp. 430–440. In "Sweynheym and Pannartz, Cardinal Bessarion, Neoplatonism: Renaissance Humanism and Two Early Printers' Choice of Texts," *Harvard Library Bulletin,* 30 (1982), pp. 282–335, M. D. Feld argues for a series of connections between Cardinal Bessarion, Neo-Platonism, the academy, the German printers, and the suppression. He maintains that Leto and his followers sponsored Sweynheym and Pannartz's press and that when Paul attacked the academy, the printers sought protection by printing the *Speculum vitae humanae* of Roderigo Sanchez of Arevalo, the governor of Castel Sant'Angelo, where many of the academicians were incarcerated. Feld connects Bessarion with the fate of the academy. For him, Paul's attitude toward Leto's academy extended to Bessarion's and Ficino's academies. Bessarion, aware of this, bequeathed his library to the Republic of Venice, for fear Paul would seize it. Binding Bessarion to Leto's group was a devotion to Neo-Platonism; indeed, in Feld's telling, the Roman academy was a Neo-Platonistic institution. This writer finds this argument at variance with the obvious Latin and nonphilosophical inclinations of the Roman academy.

15. Carini, "La difesa," p. 160. See also the letter of Joannes Blanchus, Rome, February 18, 1468, to the Duke of Milan, Galeazzo Maria Sforza, in Emilio Motta, "Bartolomeo Platina e Papa Paolo II," *ASRSP,* 7 (1884), pp. 555–559, which mentions the poets "che sono Secretarij de cardinali" (p. 555); and Ludwig von Pastor, *History of the Popes,* ed. and trans. F. I. Antrobus *et al.* (London/St. Louis: Herder, 1891–1910), vol. 4, pp. 488–492.

16. See della Torre, *Paolo Marsi,* pp. 143 ff.; and Dunston, "Pope Paul II and the Humanists," pp. 295–296.

17. See Dunston, "Pope Paul II and the Humanists," pp. 301–302.

18. The belief that Antonio Settimuleio Campano died from the tortures he was subjected to while in prison is incorrect; see Flavio di Bernardo, *Un vescovo*

umanista alla Corte pontificia: Giannantonio Campano, 1429-1477 (Rome: Gregoriana, 1975), pp. 218-219.For further discussion of this, see Cortesi, *De hominibus doctis dialogus,* ed. and trans. Maria Teresa Graziosi (Rome: Bonacci, 1973), pp. 60, 104.

19. On Paul, see Roberto Weiss, *Un umanista veneziano: Papa Paolo II* (Venice: Istituto per la collaborazione culturale, 1958). See also Raffaele Maffei's negative assessment of Paul as pope in *Raphaelis Volaterrani Commentariorum Urbanorum liber I [-XXXVIII]* (Rome, 1506), ff. 315r-v.

20. Among Paul's secretaries were Lianoro dei Lianori and Leonardo Dati. One of the men imprisoned, Agostino Maffei, may also have been one of Paul's secretaries; see Dunston, "Pope Paul II and the Humanists," p. 298, n. 33.

21. See Igino Taù, "Il 'Contra Oblocutores et detractores poetarum' di Francesco da Fiano (con appendice di documenti biografici)," *Archivio italiano per la storia della pietà,* 4 (1961), pp. 255-350. See also Hans Baron, *The Crisis of the Early Italian Renaissance* (Princeton: Princeton University Press, 1955), vol. 2, pp. 401-408.

22. See Dunston, "Pope Paul II and the Humanists," pp. 301-302.

23. See Frank-Rutger Hausmann, "Giovanni Antonio Campano (1429-1477): Ein Beitrag zur Geschichte des italienischen Humanismus im Quattrocento," *Römische Historische Mitteilungen,* 12 (1970), pp. 121-171; and the discussion of academicians' poems in Federico Patetta, "Di una raccolta di componimenti e di una medaglia in memoria di Alessandro Cinuzzi senese paggio del conte Gerolamo Riario," *Bullettino senese di storia patria,* 6 (1899), pp. 151-176.

24. See Pastor, *op. cit.,* vol. 1, pp. 294-295; and Pio Paschini, *Roma nel Rinascimento* (Bologna: Cappelli 1940), pp. 132-134.

25. See Massimo Miglio, "'Viva la Libertà et Populo de Roma': Oratoria e politica a Roma: Stefano Porcari," *ASRSP,* (1974), pp. 5-37; see also Leon Battista Alberti, "The Conspiracy of Stefano Porcari," in *Humanism and Liberty: Writings in Freedom from Fifteenth Century Florence,* ed. and trans. Renée Neu Watkins (Columbia: University of South Carolina Press, 1978), pp. 107-115. Alberti was a papal secretary under Nicholas V.

26. See Carini, "La difesa"; and Platina's account of the conspiracy in his *Liber Vitae Christi et omnium Maximorum Pontificum,* conveniently available in *Prosatori latini del Quattrocento,* ed. Eugenio Garin (Milan: Riccardi, 1952), pp. 698-711. On Callimachus, see *DBI,* vol. 15, pp. 78-83; and Gioacchino Paparelli, *Callimaco Esperiente (Filippo Buonaccorsi)* (Salerno: Beto, 1971).

27. See Sabellico's life of Leto, in *Opera Pomponii Laeti* (Strasbourg, 1510), ff. 65r-67v.

28. See Martin Grabmann, *Mittelalterliches Geistesleben,* vol. 1 (Munich: Hueber, 1926), pp. 440-448; Paul Oskar Kristeller, *Medieval Aspects of Renaissance Learning,* ed. and trans. Edward C. Mahoney (Durham, N.C.: Duke University Press, 1974), index.

29. Letter in BAV, Vat. Lat. 9002, ff. 11r-18v, esp. f. 11v; see also Henri de l'Epinois, "Paul II et Pomponius Laetus," *Revue des questiones historiques,* 1 (1886), pp. 278-281.

30. For dei Giudici's encounter with the humanists over an anti-Semitic affair in Trent, see W. P. Eckert, "Il Beato Simonino negli 'Atti' del processo di Trento contro gli Ebrei," *Studi trentini di scienze storiche,* 44 (1965), pp. 193-221.

31. Raffaele Maffei, *Commentaria Urbana* (Rome, 1506), f. 299.

32. See Giovanni Battista de' Rossi, "L'Accademia di Pomponio Leto e le sue memorie scritte sulle pareti delle catacombe romane," *Bullettino di archeologia cristiana*, ser. 4, no. 1 (1890), pp. 81-94; G. Lumbroso, "Gli accademici alle catecombe," *ASRSP*, 12 (1890), pp. 221-239; H. Leclercq, "Laetus, Pomponius," in *Dictionnaire d'archéologie chrétienne et de liturgie*, 8/1 (Paris, 1928), cols. 1041-1051; and Palermino, *op. cit.*

33. This continues. See Mario Martini, *Domitius Palladius Soranus poeta (contributo alla storia dell'umanesimo)* (Frosinone: Casamari, 1969), chap. 4; and Roberto Bongiorno, "Fifteenth Century Anti-Christian Epicureanism and the Roman Academy," *Agora*, 2/2 (1973), pp. 60-67.

34. See della Torre, *Paolo Marsi*, chap. 4, for the reestablishment of humanism after Paul II.

35. See José Ruysschaert, "Les Manuels de grammaire latine composés par Pomponio Leto," *Scriptorium*, 8 (1954), pp. 98-107; *idem*, "A propos des trois premières grammaires latines de Pomponio Leto," *ibid.*, 15 (1961), pp. 65-75; A. J. Dunston, "A Student's Notes on Lectures by Giulio Pomponio Leto," *Antichthon*, 1 (1967), pp. 86-94.

36. See Jeanne Bignami-Odier, *La Bibliothèque vaticane de Sixte IV à Pie X*, Studi e Testi #272 (Vatican City: Biblioteca Apostolica Vaticana, 1973), pp. 21-22. Three collections of letters by Leto's academicians exist, including a series of Platina's from prison. For details on these, see Palermino, *op. cit.*, pp. 152-153. A full study of these letters will give some further details on the academicians' relationships.

37. For Guazzelli's benefices, see Robert Montel, "Un bénéficier de la Basilique Saint-Pierre de Rome: Demetrius Guasselli, 'custode' de la Bibliothèque vaticane (✝1511)," in *Mélanges de l'Ecole française de Rome: Moyen Age et Temps Modernes*, 85 (1973), pp. 421-454.

38. On Maffei, see Chapter 3, n. 36 above; Alfonso Bartoli, "La diaconia di Santa Lucia in Settimonio," *ASRSP*, 50 (1927), pp. 59-76; and B. L. Ullman, "Codices Maffeiani," *Studies in the Italian Renaissance* (Rome: Edizioni di storia e letteratura, 1955), pp. 373-382. On Fosforo, see Cortesi, *De hominibus doctis dialogus* (ed. and trans. Graziosi), pp. 104-105. On Demetrio, see Dunston, "Pope Paul II and the Humanists," p. 306.

39. For Farnese, see pp. 47 and 76 above.

40. On Altieri, see p. 7 above.

41. The *Opera Pomponii Laeti* includes the following sections: "De romanorum magistratibus," "De sacerdotiis," "De iurispertis," "De legibus ad M. Pantagathum," and "De antiquitatibus Urbis Romae libellus." See Fernanda Ascarelli, *Annali tipografici di Giacomo Mazzocchi* (Florence: Sansoni, 1961), pp. 38, 46, 96, 98; and B. L. Ullman, "The Dedication Copy of Pomponio Leto's Edition of Sallust and the 'Vita' of Sallust," *Studies in the Italian Renaissance*, pp. 365-372. Marsi published commentaries on Silius Italicus (Venice, 1492) and Ovid; see n. 66 below. Other academicians who produced commentaries were: Aurelio Brandolini on Virgil; Antonio Costanza da Piperno on Propertius and Ovid; and Cantalico on Juvenal's satires. Interesting is the reaction of Aldus Manutius to the type of Latin classicism represented in the Roman Academy. Aldus was born in Rome and studied with Calderini and Gaspare of Verona in Rome. He knew the Pomponian Roman humanist tradition, but his own work centered on Greek and avoided the type of commentaries favored by Leto's disciples; see Martin Lowry, *The World of*

Aldus Manutius: Business and Scholarship in Renaissance Venice (Ithaca, N.Y.: Cornell University Press, 1979), pp. 50–51.

42. See Margret Dietrich, "Pomponius Laetus Widererweckung des antiken Theaters," *Maske und Kothurn*, 3 (1957), pp. 245–267; and Klaus Neiiendam, "Le théâtre de la Renaissance à Rome," *Analecta Romana Istituti Danici*, 5 (1969), pp. 103–197.

43. On Roman humanist handwriting, see Giovanni Muzzioli, "Due nuovi codici autografi di Pomponio Leto: Contributo allo studio della scrittura umanistica," *Italia medioevale e umanistica*, 2 (1959), pp. 337–351; and Sergio Bertelli, "Un codice lucreziano dall'officina di Pomponio Leto," *Parola del Passato*, 20 (1965), pp. 28–38. Bartolomeo San Vito was its greatest scribe in the Roman Academy; see James Wardrop, *The Script of Humanism* (Oxford: Clarendon Press, 1963), pp. 19–35, 50–53.

44. For the place of oratory in Rome, see John W. O'Malley, *Praise and Blame in Renaissance Rome: Rhetoric, Doctrine, and Reform in the Sacred Orators of the Papal Court, c. 1450–1521* (Durham, N.C.: Duke University Press, 1979), chaps. 1 and 2. A large body of poetry and oratory is still in manuscript form. Much material is noted in Paul Oskar Kristeller, *Iter Italicum* (Leiden: Brill, 1963–67), vol. 2, which includes discussion of Rome and the Vatican Library.

45. See Federico Patetta, "Di una raccolta di componimenti e di una medaglia in memoria di Alessandro Cinuzzi senese paggio del conte Gerolamo Riario," *Bullettino senese de storia patria*, 6 (1899), pp. 151–176.

46. These poems were appended to the *Vitae Christi et omnium Maximorum Pontificum* in some editions.

47. See Roberto Weiss, "In obitv Vrsini Lanfredini: A Footnote to the Literary History of Rome under Pope Innocent VIII," *Italia medioevale e umanistica*, 2 (1959), pp. 353–366. There is, moreover, another collection of Neo-Latin poems written for Ludovico Lazzarelli, also a member of the academy and a poet respected especially for his *De fastis christianae religionis*. On this collection, see della Torre, *Paolo Marsi*, chap. 4; for Lazzarelli, see Paul Oskar Kristeller, "Marsilio Ficino e Ludovico Lazzarelli: Contributo alla diffusione delle idee ermetiche nel Rinascimento," *Studies in Renaissance Thought and Letters* (Rome: Edizioni de storia e letteratura, 1969), pp. 221–247. One other such collection of memorial poetry honors Domizio Calderini, but the poems are by Veronese humanists, not Romans; see Roberto Weiss, "In memoriam Domitii Calderini," *Italia medioevale e umanistica*, 3 (1961), pp. 309–321.

48. See Weiss, "In obitv Vrsini Lanfredini," pp. 354–355.

49. I have not listed all the known members of the academy, but rather have chosen a few examples which indicate the variety and activities of the academicians.

50. See pp. 31–32 above.

51. See *DBI*, vol. 19, pp. 154–157.

52. *Ibid.*, pp. 147–153.

53. See Cortesi, *De hominibus doctis dialogus* (ed. and trans. Graziosi), pp. 66–68.

54. On Brandolini, see *DBI*, vol. 14, pp. 26–28; the fullest account is Elizabeth Mayer, "Aurelio Brandolini Lippo alla Corte di Mattia Corvino," *Biblioteca della Accademia d'Ungheria*, 14 (1938), pp. 3–51. See also Lynn Thorndike, "Lippus Brandolinus *De Comparatione Reipublicae et Regni:* A Treatise in Comparative

Political Science," in his *Science and Thought in the Fifteenth Century* (New York: Hafner, 1963), pp. 233–260; Charles Trinkaus, *In Our Image and Likeness: Humanity and Divinity in Italian Humanist Thought* (Chicago, Ill.: The University of Chicago Press, 1970), vol. 1, pp. 297–321, and vol. 2, pp. 601–613; John F. D'Amico, "Humanism and Theology in Papal Rome, 1480–1520" (Ph.D. diss., University of Rochester, 1977), chaps. 2 and 5; Wilhelm Kölme, "Menschliche Existenz in der Sicht des Augustineremetin und Humanisten Aurelio Brandolini," in *Secundum regulam vivere: Festschrift für P. Norman Bachmund, O. Praem.*, ed. Gert Melville (Windberg: Poppe, 1978), pp. 321–334; and O'Malley, *Praise and Blame in Renaissance Rome*, index.

55. For the *De laudibus*, see BAV, Vat. Lat. 5008 (defective), and Urb. Lat. 739. Selections are printed in E. Muntz, *Les Arts à la Cour des Papes*, pt. 3 (Paris, 1883), pp. 56–60, 112, 118, 135–136, 162–163, 167, 189–192, 201–202; and Giuseppe de Luca, "Un umanista fiorentino e la Roma rinnovata da Sisto IV," *La Rinascita*, 1 (1938), pp. 74–90.

56. Cardinal Marco Barbo called Brandolini "the Christian Orpheus."

57. See BAV, Ottob. Lat. 438 and 121; this work is discussed on pp. 146–147 above. Brandolini also dedicated his *De ratione scribendi* to the cardinal's nephew, Agostino. There is a mutilated copy in Siena, Biblioteca Comunale, H. VII. 13, bearing the Piccolomini coat of arms. An older version is found in the *Grammatices rudimenta*, BAV, Reg. Lat. 155; see also O'Malley, *Praise and Blame in Renaissance Rome*, pp. 44–50.

58. *Lippi Brandolini Oratio pro Sancto Thoma Aquinate Romae in templo Sanctae Mariae Minervae ad Cardinales et Populum habita* (Rome, 1485–1490). See *Gesamtkatalog der Wiegendrucke*, #5016; and John W. O'Malley, "Some Renaissance Panegyrics of Aquinas," *Renaissance Quarterly*, 27/2 (1974), pp. 174–192, at pp. 176–177, 191–192.

59. See BAV, Reg. Lat. 1368: *Lippi Brandolini Florentini Oratio pro clarissimo viro Antonio Lauredano oratore veneto ad principem et Senatum venetum illustrissimum*. Another of Brandolini's orations, *Lippi Brandolini pro Laurentio Justino equite et iureconsulto praestantissimo oratio in funere eius habita* (Rome, Biblioteca Angelica, 1503, ff. 215r–227r) was delivered in December 1487.

60. Brandolini's poem is entitled simply "Lippus Brandulinus [*sic*] de morte Platynae."

61. See *DBI*, vol. 14, p. 26.

62. See Federico Patetta, *Venturino de Prioribus*, Studi e Testi #149 (Vatican City: Biblioteca Apostolica Vaticana, 1950), pp. 67–77.

63. This is *Dialogus de humanae vitae conditione et toleranda corporis aegritudine ad Matthiam Corvinum*. The text is available in Abel Jenö, ed., *Irodalomtörteneti Emlekek* (Budapest, 1890), pp. 1–75; see also Trinkaus, *op. cit.*, vol. 1, pp. 297–306.

64. For an example and study of Brandolini's preaching, see John M. McManamon, S.J., "Renaissance Preaching, Theory and Practice: A Holy Thursday Sermon of Aurelio Brandolini," *Viator*, 10 (1979), pp. 354–373.

65. See Luigi Rava, "Un dalmata coronato in Campidoglio: Elio Lampridio Cerva," *Accademia delle scienze dell'Istituto di Bologna: Classe di scienze morali. Rendiconti*, ser. 2, no. 3 (1918–1919), pp. 142–150.

66. Pietro Marsi, a member of the academy, summarized the occasion as follows: "Constet ergo omnibus et nostrae in primis Academiae XX die Aprilis esse

Palilia et natalem Urbis. Quem diem sodalitas nostra literaria religiosissime colit, propter festum ss. martyrum Victoris, Fortunati et Genesii eiusdem sodalitatis protectorum, quod eodem die a fidelibus cunctis celebratur" (*Commentaria in Ovidii fastos* [Venice, 1520], quoted in de' Rossi, "L'Accademia di Pomponio Leto," p. 83). See also Mario Martini, *Domitius Palladius Soranus Poeta*, pp. 61-66, where Soranus's *Carmen in Romae Urbis Genethliacum* appears with an Italian translation; on Martini's book, see Godelieve Tournoy-Thoen, "La laurea poetica del 1484 all'Accademia romana," *Institut historique belge de Rome, Bulletin* 42 (1972), pp. 211-235. The celebrations continued into the cinquecento; I have not seen B. Bilinski, "Un umanista diplomatico polacco Erasmo Ciolek-Vitellius al Natale di Roma del 1501," *Strenna dei Romanisti*, 40 (1979), pp. 73-88.

67. On Biondo, see *DBI*, vol. 10, pp. 536-538; Roberto Weiss, "Biondo Flavio archeologo," *Studi romagnoli*, 14 (1963), pp. 335-341; *idem, The Renaissance Discovery of Classical Antiquity* (Oxford: Blackwell, 1964), chap. 2; Angelo Mazzocco, "Biondo Flavio and the Antiquarian Tradition" (Ph.D. diss., University of California at Berkeley, 1973). I have not seen P. W. H. Spring, "The Topographical and Archeological Study of the Antiquities of the City of Rome, 1420-47" (diss., University of Edinburgh, 1971). More generally, see E. Mandowsky and Charles Mitchell, *Pirro Ligorio's Roman Antiquities* (London: The Warburg Institute, 1963), chap. 2; and Gianfilippo Carettoni, "La scoperta dei monumenti romani," *Aspetti dell'umanesimo a Roma* (Rome: Istituto di studi romani, 1969), pp. 75-84.

68. For Leto, see Giovanni Battista de' Rossi, "Note di topografia romana raccolte dalla bocca di Pomponio Leto e testo pomponiano alla Notitia Regionum Urbis Romae," *Studi e documenti di storia e diritto*, 3 (1892), pp. 74-86; and Weiss, *The Renaissance Discovery of Classical Antiquity*, pp. 76-78. Leto even united poetry and archaeology; see D. G. Merin, "Les Distiques de Pomponio Leto sur les stations liturgiques du Carême," *Revue bénédictine*, 35 (1923), pp. 20-23.

69. On Raphael and the antiquarian tradition, see Weiss, *The Renaissance Discovery of Classical Antiquity*, pp. 94-96; and Pier Nicola Pagliara, "La Roma antica di Fabio Calvo: Note sulla cultura antiquaria e architettonica," *Psicon*, 8/9 (1977), pp. 65-87.

70. See Roberto Weiss, "Andrea Fulvio antiquario romano (ca. 1470-1527)," *Annali della Scuola Normale Superiore di Pisa*, ser. 2, no. 28 (1959), pp. 1-44; the reprint of *Illustrium Imagines di Andrea Fulvio* (Rome, 1522; rpt., Rome, 1967), with notes by Weiss; and Weiss, *The Renaissance Discovery of Classical Antiquity*, pp. 86-89, 178-179.

71. Weiss, "Andrea Fulvio," pp. 3-4.

72. *Ibid.*, pp. 15-34; and Ascarelli, *op. cit.*, pp. 64, 114-115.

73. Weiss, "Andrea Fulvio," pp. 6-7; see Ascarelli, *op. cit.*, pp. 41-42, for Albertini's *De mirabilibus novae et veteris Vrbis Romae* (1510).

74. See de' Rossi, "L'Accademia di Pomponio Leto."

75. See A. Silvagni, *Inscriptiones Christianae Urbis*, 1 (Rome: Befani, 1922), pp. xxxviii-xl; Zabughin, *Giulio Pomponio Leto*, vol. 2, pp. 187 ff.; and Weiss, *The Renaissance Discovery of Classical Antiquity*, pp. 96-98.

76. Sabino was also connected with Questenberg; see Giovanni Mercati, "Questenbergiana," *Opere Minori*, vol. 4, Studi e Testi #79 (Vatican City: Biblioteca Apostolica Vaticana, 1937), pp. 456-457. For Sabino's university career, see *Lettera dell'Abate Gaetano Marini al ... Monsignor Giuseppe Muti Paparurri già*

Casali nella quale s'illustra il Ruolo de' Professori dell'Archiginnasio romano per l'anno MDXIV (Rome, 1794), pp. 29–31.

77. See Carmine Gioja, *Gli orti colocciani in Roma* (Foligno, 1893), p. 9; Rodolfo Lanciani, *The Golden Age of the Renaissance in Rome* (London: Constable, 1906); and Fedele Baiocchi, "Sulle poesie latine di Francesco M. Molza, saggio," *Annali della R. Scuola Normale Superiore di Pisa, filosofia e filologia*, 18 (1905), pp. 67–91.

78. See pp. 76–80 above.

79. Vincenzo Calmeta, *Prose e lettere edite e inedite (con appendice di altri inediti)*, ed. Cecil Grayson (Bologna: Commissione per i testi di lingua, 1959), pp. 60–77, "Vita del facondo poeta vulgare Serafino Aquilano per Vincenzo Calmeta composta." On Calmeta, see *ibid.*, Grayson's introduction. For Serafino, see R. Grazotto, "Onde musicali nella corrente poetica di Serafino dell'Aquila," *Musurgia Nova* (Milan, 1959), chap. 1; and Barbara Bauer-Formicini, *Die Strambotti des Serafino dell'Aquila* (Munich: Fink, 1967).

80. The bishop is the rather obscure Leonardo Corvino. See Mario Cosenza, *Biographical and Bibliographical Dictionary of the Italian Humanists . . . 1300–1800* (Boston: Hall, 1962), vol. 2, p. 1124.

81. Cornelio is Cornelio Benigno; see p. 58 above. Cortesi called him his *familiaris* (*De Cardinalatu*, f. q 2v) and mentioned a work in which Cornelio treated "grammaticae voculationes quam musici servantur phthongi." He also advocated Cornelio as one worthy of being patronized (*ibid.*, f. N 12r).

82. Aretino is Bernardo Accolti, l'Unico Aretino (1458–1535); see *DBI*, vol. 1, pp. 103–104. Cortesi mentioned him as a fine extemporaneous poet; see *De Cardinalatu*, ff. Q 14r-v, M 8r.

83. Calmeta, *op. cit.*, p. 64, also noted that there was *tanta fraterna emulazione* between Cortesi, his academicians, and Serafino.

84. *Ibid.*, pp. 63–64: "Fioriva medesimamante in Roma a quel tempo la nostra Accademia in casa di Paulo Cortese, giovene per dottrina, grado e affabilità in la Corte assai reverito, per modo che non casa di corteggiano ma officina di eloquenza e recettaculo d'ogni inclita virtù se potteva chiamare. Concorrevano ivi ogni giorno gran multidudine de elevati ingegni: Gianlorenzo Veneto, Petro Gravina, Montepiloso Episcopo, Agapito Gerardino, Manilio, Cornelio e molti altri eruditi, sotto la cui ombra altri de minore etade, che de amplettere la virtù tuttavia erano desiderosi, a soggiornare e prendere delettazione ancora se reducevano. Erano de' poeti vulgari in grandissimo pregio li ardori de lo Aretino né ancora de' nostri frammenti si faceva poca essistimazione. Serafino adunque, il quale più meco che con altra persona vivente ebbe commercio, de frequentare medesimamente questa Accademia prese deliberazione. . . ."

85. On these men, see Alessandro D'Ancona, "Del secentismo nella poesia cortigiana del secolo XV," *Pagine sparse di letteratura e di storia* (Florence: Sansoni, 1914), pp. 63–181, at pp. 90–91. Acquaro, "Note su Paolo Cortesi," p. 357, adds Jacopo Corsi to Cortesi's academy; Cortesi praised Corsi's poetic skills in the *De Cardinalatu*, f. Q 12v. Michael Mallet, *The Borgias* (London: Paladin, 1972), p. 212, adds Adriano Castellesi, Cardinal Giovanni Vera (Cesare Borgia's old tutor), and Michele Ferno. Ferno wrote his description of Alexander VI's coronation for Cortesi; see Michele Ferno, *Historia nova Alexandri VI ab Innocentii obitu VIII* (Rome, 1493), f. 3r, on which see L. Hain, *Repertorium bibliographicum*, 4 vols. (Stuttgart, 1826–1838), #6978.

86. See Pierre de Nolhac, "Giovanni Lorenzi, bibliothècaire d'Innocent VIII," *Mélanges d'archéologie et d'histoire*, 8 (1888), pp. 3–18; Pio Paschini, "Un ellenista veneziano del Quattrocento: Giovanni Lorenzi," *Archivio veneto*, 32/33 (1943), pp. 114–146; *idem, Il carteggio fra il Card. Marco Barbo e Giovanni Lorenzi (1481–1490)*, Studi e Testi #137 (Vatican City: Biblioteca Apostolica Vaticana, 1948); A. Albareda, "Intorno alla fine del bibliotecario apostolico Giovanni Lorenzi," in *Miscellanea Pio Paschini*, vol. 2 (Rome: Lateranum, 1949), pp. 191–204.

87. On Persona, see Pio Paschini, "Un ellenista romano del Quattrocento e la sua famiglia," *Atti dell'Accademia degli Arcadi*, 21 (1939–1940), pp. 45–46.

88. See Hofmann, *Forschungen zur Geschichte der kurialen Behörden*, vol. 2, p. 85.

89. Cortesi mentions Lorenzi several times in a positive manner in *De Cardinalatu;* see ff. L 4r-v, I 7r, and C 5v-6r.

90. See Charles B. Schmitt, "An Unstudied Fifteenth Century Latin Translation of Sextus Empiricus by Giovanni Lorenzi (Vat. Lat. 2990)," in *Cultural Aspects of the Renaissance: Essays in Honor of Paul Oskar Kristeller*, ed. Cecil H. Clough (Manchester: Manchester University Press, 1976), pp. 244–261; and Ascarelli, *op. cit.*, pp. 37–38, 76, 86–87, 156.

91. See C. Cansacchi, "Agapito Geraldini di Amelia primo segretario di Cesare Borgia (1450–1515)," *Bollettino di storia patria per l'Umbria*, 58 (1961), pp. 44–87; and Luigi Michelini Tocci, "Agapito, bibliotecario 'docto, acorto e diligente' della biblioteca urbinate alla fine del Quattrocento," in *Collectanea Vaticana in honorem Anselmi M. Card. Albareda a Biblioteca Apostolica habita*, Studi e Testi #220 (Vatican City: Biblioteca Apostolica Vaticana, 1962), pp. 245–280. Antonio Geraldini (d. 1489) was a relative of Agapito's also in the Curia; see Cortesi, *De hominibus doctis* (ed. and trans. Graziosi), pp. 68–69 and 106.

92. See Cansacchi, *op. cit.*, for Geraldini's career.

93. Cortesi, in *De Cardinalatu*, f. L 2v, discusses Guidobaldo of Urbino's receiving visitors despite his illness and Agapito's service to him. There is no indication that Agapito ever served Guidobaldo. Michelini Tocci, *op. cit.*, pp. 177–178, argues that this was not our Geraldini, but rather Agapito of Urbino, who is known to have served the duke. Possibly Cortesi did not remember the anecdote correctly or his editors added the surname incorrectly after his death. Cansacchi (*op. cit.*, p. 56) seems to misunderstand the anecdote and for some reason changes Guidobaldo to Cesare Borgia.

94. Cortesi, *De Cardinalatu*, f. L 6v, mentions his mordant tongue (also mentioned on f. N 6v.)

95. On Giustolo, see Augusto Campana, "Dal Calmeta al Colocci: Testo nuovo di un epicedio di P. F. Giustolo," in *Tra latino e volgare per Carlo Dionisotti*, ed. G. Bernardoni et al., vol. 1 (Padua: Antenore, 1974), pp. 267–330; and Annuziato Presta, "Rapporti fra l'umanesimo umbro e l'Accademia romana," pp. 395–400.

96. See Vladimiro Zabughin, "Pierfrancesco Giustolo da Spoleto e gli 'errori di Omero,'" *Giornale storico della letteratura italiana*, 67 (1916), pp. 456–458.

97. See R. Garnett, "A Laureate of Caesar Borgia," *English Historical Review*, 17 (1902), pp. 15–19; and Presta, "Rapporti."

98. See *DBI*, vol. 15, pp. 669–671.

99. Antonio Altamura, *L'umanesimo nel Mezzogiorno d'Italia* (Florence: Bibliopolis, 1941), pp. 134–136.

100. Cortesi mentions him as a familiar of Cardinal Barbo; see *De Cardinalatu*, f. G 8r.

101. *Ibid.*, f. D 1r. Alessandro's death also elicited a poem, "Querimonia in morte Alexandri Cortesii ad Hemolaum Barbarum," by Battista Mantovano; see *Opera Omnia Baptistae Mantuani Carmelitae* (Bologna, 1502), ff. 94v-97r.

102. See Altamura, *op. cit.*, p. 134.

103. See Cosenza, *Dictionary of the Italian Humanists*, vol. 2, pp. 1671-1672.

104. See Altamura, *op. cit.*, pp. 114-115. Cortesi, in *De Cardinalatu*, ff. N 12r and M 5v, praises him.

105. O'Malley, *Praise and Blame in Renaissance Rome*, pp. 66, 94, 118, 152, 163.

106. For the *strambotti* of Cortesi and his academicians (in BAV, Vat. Lat. 5170 and Urb. Lat. 729), see Giovanni Zannoni, "Strambotti inediti del sec. XV," *Rendiconti della R. Accademia dei Lincei*, ser. 5, no. 1 (1892), pp. 371-387; Mario Menghini, "Poesi inedite del sec. XV," *Rassegna bibliografica della letteratura italiana*, 3 (1895), pp. 17-27; and Grazotto, *op. cit.*

107. On Petrarchism, see *Enciclopedia italiana*, vol. 27, pp. 23-24; Giorgio Santangelo, *Il Petrarchismo del Bembo e di altri poeti del'500* (Rome: I.E.C.E., 1962); and Bauer-Formiconi, *op. cit.*

108. Cortesi, *De Cardinalatu*, f. K 2r: "At vero carminum modi hi numerari solent qui maxime octasticorum, aut trinariorum ratione constant: quod quidem genus primus apud nostros Franciscus Petrarcha instituisse dicitur, qui edita carmina caneret ad lembum; nuper autem Seraphinus Aquilanus princeps eius generis renovandi fuit; a quo ita est verborum et cantuum coniunctio modulata nexa, ut nihil fieri posset eius modorum ratione dulcius." My translation is adapted from Nino Perotta, "Music and Cultural Tendencies in Fifteenth Century Italy," *Journal of the American Musicological Society*, 19 (1966), pp. 147-161, at p. 155.

109. Calmeta, *op. cit.*, pp. 32-36 (chap. 7, "Per molti essempi che cosa sia servare il decoro").

110. *Ibid.*, p. 34.

111. See Domenico Gnoli, "Orti letterari nella Roma di Leone X," *Nuova Antologia*, 65 (1930), pp. 3-19, 137-148 (reprinted in his *La Roma di Leone X*, pp. 136-163); and Baiocchi, *op. cit.*, pp. 67-91.

112. On Colocci, see Federico Ubaldini, *Vita di Mons. Angelo Colocci*, ed. Vittorio Fanelli, Studi e Testi #256 (Vatican City: Biblioteca Apostolica Vaticana, 1964); and Vittorio Fanelli, *Ricerche su Angelo Colocci e sulla Roma cinquecentesca*, Studi e Testi #283 (Vatican City: Biblioteca Apostolica Vaticana, 1979). Several relevant studies are in *Atti del Convegno di studi su Angelo Colocci* (Jesi: Amministrazione comunale, 1972); see also Carmine Gioja, *Gli orti colocciani in Roma* (Foligno, 1893).

113. See Ubaldini, *op. cit.*, p. 4.

114. *Ibid.*, p. 22.

115. See *ibid.*, pp. 22-23, for a listing of these offices.

116. *Ibid.*, p. 23.

117. See Fanelli, "Le case e la raccolte archeologiche del Colocci," *Richerche*, pp. 111-134.

118. See S. Lattes, "A proposito dell'opera incompiuta 'De ponderibus et messuris,' di Angelo Colocci," in *Atti su Colocci*, pp. 97-108.

119. See R. Avesani, "Appunti del Colocci sulla poesia mediolatina," *ibid.*,

pp. 109–132; J. Scuderi Ruggieri, "Le traduzioni di A. Colocci dal castigliano," *ibid.*, pp. 177–196; Valeria Bertolucci Pizzorusso, "Note linguistiche e letterarie di Angleo Colocci in margine ai canzonieri portoghesi," *ibid.*, pp. 197–203; and Aulo Greco, "L'Apologia delle 'Rime' di Serafino Aquilano di Angelo Colocci," *ibid.*, pp. 205–219. See also Fanelli, "Aspetti della Roma cinquecentesca: Note sulla diffusione della cultura iberica a Roma," *Ricerche*, pp. 154–167.

120. See Francesco Barberi and Emilio Cerulli, "Le edizioni greche in Gymnasio mediceo ad Caballinum montem," in *Atti su Colocci*, pp. 61–76; and Fanelli, "Il ginnasio greco di Leone X a Roma" *Ricerche*, pp. 91–110. Colocci also tried to attract Aldus Manutius to Rome to establish his 'academy'; see Lowry, *op. cit.*, pp. 213–214.

121. The letter is most conveniently found in Ubaldini, *op. cit.*, pp. 67–75, with abundant notes. Similar to Sadoleto's letter, but written while the academies were still active, is Fedra Inghirami's letter to Andrea Umiliato in *Marquardi Gudii et doctorum virorum ad eum epistolae* (The Hague, 1714), pp. 139–140.

122. Speaking of Fedra and Camillo Porzio, Sadoleto writes: "Nam illa ornamenta et lumina linguae latinae Phaedrus et Camillus Porcius magno cunctorum incommodo jamdiu morte erepta nobis sunt: in quibus sedem sibi videbatur statuisse eloquentia" (Ubaldini, *op. cit.*, p. 71).

123. On Goritz and his academy, see Ludwig Geiger, "Der älteste römische Musenalmanach," *Vierteljahrschrift für Kultur und Literatur der Renaissance*, 1 (1886), pp. 145–161; Th. Simar, *Christophe de Longueil, humaniste (1488–1522)* (Louvain: Peeters, 1911), pp. 194–203; and Ph. P. Bober, "The 'Coryciana' and the Nymph Corycia," *Journal of the Warburg and Courtauld Institutes*, 40 (1977), pp. 223–239.

124. See Simar, *op. cit.*, p. 196.

125. *Ibid.*, pp. 196–202.

126. The list of members of Goritz's academy, *Corytianae Academiae fato functi qui sub Leone floruerunt*, can be found in Florence, Archivio di Stato, Carte Strozziane, filza 353, f. 16v, but is most conveniently available in Ubaldini, *op. cit.*, app. 4, pp. 114–115.

127. For the statue and its place in the academy, see Gnoli, "Orti letterari," pp. 151–155; and Virginia Anne Bonito, "The Saint Anne Altar in Sant'Agostino: Restoration and Interpretation," *The Burlington Magazine*, 124 (1982), pp. 268–280.

128. On the *Coryciana*, see Geiger, *op. cit.*, and José Ruysschaert, "Les Péripéties inconnues de l'édition des 'Coryciana' de 1524," in *Atti su Colocci*, pp. 45–60.

129. On Arsilli, see *DBI*, vol. 4, pp. 342–343.

130. See Simar, *op. cit.*, for some examples; for a discussion of such classicism in religious writings, see Chapter 6 above.

131. Arsilli began his poem as follows: "Felices Musae, felix quas protulit aetas, / Cum foret Augusto Principe Roma potens." The *De poetis urbanis* can be found most conveniently in William Roscoe, *The Life and Pontificate of Leo the Tenth* (Liverpool, 1805), appendix.

132. On Longueil and his encounter with the Roman academy, see Simar, *op. cit.*, and Domenico Gnoli, *Un giudizio di lesa romanità sotto Loene X* (Rome, 1891).

133. In addition to note 132, see Marius Bevilacqua, "De Celso Mellino eiusque in Longolium oratione," *Latinitas*, 23/1 (1975), pp. 53–56.

134. See George B. Parks, "Did Pole Write the 'Vita Longolii?'"*Renaissance Quarterly*, 26 (1973), pp. 274–285; and Alvin Vos, "The 'Vita Longolii': Additional Considerations about Reginald Pole's Authorship," *ibid.*, 30 (1977), pp. 324–333.

135. See Roberto Valentini, "Erasmo di Rotterdam e Pietro Corsi a proposito di una polemica fraintesa," *Rendiconti dell'Accademia Nazionale dei Lincei, Classe di scienze morali, storiche e filologiche*, ser. 6, no. 12 (1937), pp. 896–922.

136. For Blosio, see G. Amaduzzi, ed., *Anecdota litteraria*, vol. 2 (Rome, 1773), pp. 167–190; and Giulio Battelli, "Un umanista romano del Cinquecento," *La Bibliofilia*, 43 (1941), pp. 16–23. See also pp. 86 and 134–137 above. I have not seen A. Lesen, "Blosio Palladio e il cenacolo letterario di Gian Goritz," *Terra Sabina* (Rome), 4 (1926), pp. 37–44.

137. For an example of his oratorical talents, see *Anecdota litteraria*, vol. 2, pp. 191–206.

138. For Mario Maffei, see pp. 85–88 above.

CHAPTER 5

1. See the magisterial work of Charles Trinkaus, *In Our Image and Likeness: Humanity and Divinity in Italian Humanism*, 2 vols. (Chicago: University of Chicago Press, 1970), esp. the introduction to vol. 1.

2. See Eugenio Garin, *Italian Humanism: Philosophy and Civic Life in the Renaissance*, trans. Peter Munz (New York: Harper and Row, 1965); and George Holmes, *The Florentine Enlightenment, 1400–1450* (New York: Pegasus, 1969), chap. 8.

3. See Paul Oskar Kristeller, *The Philosophy of Marsilio Ficino*, trans Virginia Conant (Gloucester, Mass.: Peter Smith, 1964); and Garin, *Italian Humanism*, chaps. 3 and 4.

4. Encounters were most common between humanists and members of the religious orders, especially the mendicants; see pp. 145–147 above.

5. See Paul Oskar Kristeller, *Renaissance Thought: Its Classical, Scholastic, and Humanistic Strains* (New York: Harper and Row, 1961).

6. See Richard Scholz, "Eine ungedruckte Schilderung der Kurie aus d. J. 1438," *Archiv für Kulturgeschichte*, 10 (1912), pp. 399–413; F. P. Luiso, "Studi su l'epistolario e le traduzioni di Lapo da Castiglionchio," *Studi italiani di filologia classica*, 7 (1899), pp. 205–299; Massimo Miglio, "Une lettera di Lapo da Castigliocio il giovane a Flavio Biondo," *Storiografica pontificia del Quattrocento* (Bologna: Patron, 1975), pp. 31–59, 189–201; and Riccardo Fubini, in *DBI*, vol. 22, pp. 44–51.

7. On Orsini, see Erich Koenig, *Kardinal Giordano Orsini (+1438): Lebensbild aus der Zeit der grossen Konzilien und des Humanismus* (Studien und Darstellungen aus dem Gebiete der Geschichte, vol. 5, pt. 1) (Freiburg im Breisgau: Herder, 1906); Ludwig von Pastor, *History of the Popes* ed. and trans. F. I. Antrobus *et al.* (London/St Louis: Herder, 1891–1910), vol. 1, pp. 272–273; and W. A. Simpson, "Cardinal Giordano Orsini (+1438), as a Patron of the Church and a Patron of the Arts: A Contemporary Panegyric and Two Descriptions of the

Lost Frescoes in Monte Giordano," *Journal of the Warburg and Courtauld Institutes*, 29 (1966), pp. 135–159.

8. The dialogue's full title is *Dialogus super excellentia et dignitate Curie Romane supra certas policias et curias antiquorum et modernorum contra eos qui Romanam Curiam diffamant;* it was published in Richard Scholz, "Eine humanistische Schilderung der Kurie aus dem Jahre 1438," *QFIAB*, 16 (1914), pp. 108–153. There is a partial edition and Italian translation in Eugenio Garin, ed., *Prosatori latini del Quattrocento* (Milan: Ricciardi, 1952), pp. 170–211. I cite from Scholz's edition.

9. See *DBI*, vol. 22, p. 48.

10. Scholz ed. p. 116.

11. *Ibid.*, pp. 131–132. On Traversari, see Charles Stinger, *Humanism and the Church Fathers: Ambrogio Traversari (1386–1439) and Christian Antiquity in the Italian Renaissance* (Albany: State University of New York Press, 1977).

12. Scholz ed. pp. 136–137. Flavio Biondo, in his *De verbis romanae locutionis* (in *Scritti inediti e rari di Biondo Flavio*, ed. Bartolomeo Nogara, Studi e Testi #48 [Rome: Tipografia Poliglotta Vaticana, 1924], p. 125), complains that the foreigners who came to the Curia Romana spoke extremely poor Latin.

13. Scholz ed., pp. 145–155.

14. See *DBI*, vol. 22, pp. 49–50. For the currency of such views, see Miglio, *Storiografia pontificia*, pp. 122–153.

15. See John W. O'Malley, "The Vatican Library and the School of Athens: A Text of Battista Casali, 1508," *Journal of Medieval and Renaissance Studies*, 7 (1977), pp. 271–287.

16. The *Oratio* is in J. Vahlen, "Laurentii Vallae Opuscula Tria," reprinted in Lorenzo Valla, *Opera Omnia*, ed. Eugenio Garin (rpt.; Turin: Bottega d'Erasmo, 1962), vol. 2, pp. 280–286. On this oration, see Mario Fois, S.J. *Il pensiero cristiano di Lorenzo Valla nel quadro storico-culturale del suo ambiente* (Rome: Gregoriana, 1969), pp. 441–444; and Trinkaus, *op. cit.*, vol. 2, pp. 765–766.

17. See, in general, Fois, *op. cit.*

18. Garin, *Prosatori latini del Quattrocento*, p. 596. On Valla's linguistic theories in the *Elegantiae*, see Lawrence J. Johnson, "The 'Linguistic Imperialism' of Lorenzo Valla and the Renaissance Humanists," *Interpretation*, 7 (1978), pp. 29–49; and David Marsh, "Grammar, Method, and Polemic in Lorenzo Valla's 'Elegantiae,'" *Rinascimento*, 19 (1979), pp. 91–116.

19. See J. B. Staegmüller, "Die Idee von der Kirche als Imperium Romanum im kanonischen Recht," *Theologische Quartalschrift*, 18 (1898), pp. 50–801; Franz Kamper, "Roma aeterna und sancta Dei Ecclesia Rei publicae Romanorum," *Historisches Jahrbuch*, 19 (1921), pp. 240–249; Werner Goez, *Translatio Imperii: Ein Beitrag zur Geschichte des Geschichtsdenkens und der politischen Theorien im Mittelalter und in der frühen Neuzeit* (Tübingen: Mohr, 1958); and Robert Folz, *The Concept of Empire in Western Europe*, trans. Sheila Ann Ogilvie (London: Arnold, 1969).

20. Giannozzo Manetti, *Vita Nicolai V. Summi Pontificis*, ed. Lodovico Antonio Muratori, in *Rerum Italicarum Scriptores*, 3/2 (Milan, 1734), cols. 929–940. See also J. Pagnotti, "La *Vita* di Niccolo V scritta da Giannozzo Manetti," *ASRSP*, 14 (1891), pp. 411–436; and Laura Onofri, "Sacralità, immaginazione e proposte politiche: La *Vita* di Niccolo V di Giannozzo Manetti," *Humanistica Lovaniensia*, 28 (1979), pp. 27–77.

21. For Manetti's scholarship, see Trinkaus, *op. cit.*, vol. 2, pp. 578–601.

22. Manetti, *Vita Nicolai V*, cols. 928–940. For this, see Torgil Magnuson, *Studies in Roman Quattrocento Architecture* (Rome: Tipografia del Senato, 1958); and Carroll William Westfall, *In this Most Perfect Paradise* (University Park: Pennsylvania State University Press, 1974).

23. Manetti, *Vita Nicolai V*, col. 913.

24. See p. 9 above.

25. Manetti, *Vita Nicolai V*, col. 926.

26. *Ibid.*, cols. 935–936.

27. *Ibid.*, cols. 946–957.

28. *Ibid.*, col. 954.

29. See, in general, John F. D'Amico, "Papal History and Curial Reform in the Renaissance: Raffaele Maffei's *Breuis Historia* of Julius II and Leo X," *Archivum Historiae Pontificiae*, 18 (1980), pp. 157–210.

30. On Platina, see pp. 35–36 above. Zeno's *Vitae Pontificum* is BAV, Vat. Lat. 5942, and Chigi F. VIII. 198; see Miglio, *Storiografia pontificia*, pp. 17–19 and 181–182.

31. See Miglio, *Storiografia pontificia*, pp. 207–208.

32. See Julius II's master of ceremonies, Paride de' Grassi's, *Diarium*, as excerpted in J. I. von Döllinger, *Beiträge zur politischen, kirchlichen und Cultur-Geschichte der sechs letzten Jahrhunderte*, vol. 3 (Vienna, 1882), pp. 363–364.

33. See Stanislaus von Moos, "The Palace as a Fortress: Rome and Bologna under Julius II," in *Art and Architecture in the Service of Politics*, ed. Henry A. Millon and Linda Nochlin (Cambridge, Mass.: MIT Press, 1978), pp. 46–79, at p. 47. See also Elisabeth Schröter, "Der Vatikan Hügel Apollons und der Musen: Kunst und Panegyrik von Nikolaus V. bis Julius II," *RQ*, 75 (1980), pp. 208–240.

34. D'Amico, *op. cit.*, p. 201.

35. See G. Zippel, ed., *Le Vite di Paolo II di Gaspare da Verona e Michele Canensi*, in *Rerum Italicarum Scriptores*, 3/16 (Città di Castello: Lapi, 1904–1911), p. 16 and n. 6. On Gaspare's history, see A. Andrews, "The 'Lost' Fifth Book of the Life of Pope Paul II by Gaspare of Verona," *Studies in the Renaissance*, 17 (1970), pp. 7–45.

36. Zippel, *Le Vite*, p. 16 and n. 4.

37. See Remigio Sabbadini, *Storia del Ciceronianismo e di altre questioni letterarie nell'età della Rinascenza* (Turin, 1885); Izora Scott, *Controversies over the Imitation of Cicero* (New York: Columbia University Press, 1910). My interpretation of Ciceronianism has elements in common with and different from that of Giuseppe Toffanin. Toffanin viewed Cicero as the great representative of learning and as a figure being continually incorporated into Christian thought. While this is of course largely true, it seems to me that Ciceronianism had a particular element unique to Renaissance Rome which cannot be read as paradigmatic for all Christian history. See Toffanin's *Il Cinquecento (Storia della letteratura italiana)* (Milan: Vallardi, 1929); *idem, History of Humanism*, trans. E. Gianturco (New York: Las Americas, 1955); and *idem, La religione degli umanisti* (Bologna: Zanichelli, 1950). See also the writings of his various disciples, including Giulio Vallese, "L'umanesimo al primo Cinquecento: Da Cristoforo Longolio al *Ciceronianismo* di Erasmo," *Le parole e le idee*, 1 (1959), pp. 107–123; *idem*, "Erasmo e Cicerone: Le Alle *Tuscalone*," *ibid.*, 11 (1969), pp. 265–272; *idem, Studi da Dante ad Erasmo di letteratura umanistica*, 2d ed. (Naples: Scalabrini, 1966); and Donato

Gagliardi, *Il Ciceronianismo nel primo Cinquecento e Ortensio Lando* (Naples: Morra, 1967).

38. See the discussion of the ideological importance of Cicero's Latinity in Karl Otto Apel, *L'idea di lingua nella tradizione dell'umanesimo da Dante a Vico,* trans. Luciano Tosti (Bologna: Mulino, 1975), chaps. 5 and 6; see also Jerrold E. Seigel, *Rhetoric and Philosophy in Renaissance Humanism: The Union of Eloquence and Wisdom, Petrarch to Valla* (Princeton: Princeton University Press, 1968).

39. See Paolo Portoghesi, *Rome in the Renaissance,* trans. Pearl Sanders (London: Phaidon, 1977), chap. 1; and William Harrison Woodward, *Desiderius Erasmus Concerning the Aim and Method of Education* (Cambridge, 1897; rpt., New York, 1963), pp. 51-60.

40. See Hans Baron, "Cicero and the Roman Civic Spirit in the Middle Ages and Early Renaissance," *Bulletin of the John Rylands Library,* 22/1 (1958), pp. 72-97.

41. See Mario Di Cesare, *Vida's Christiad and Vergilian Epic* (New York: Columbia University Press, 1964).

42. See Portoghesi, *op. cit., passim.*

43. See Vincenzo Fontana and Paolo Marchelli, eds., *Vitruvio e Raffaello: Il De Architectura di Vitruvio nella traduzione inedita di Fabio Calvo Ravennate* (Rome: Officina, 1975).

44. For the elements of Ciceronian style, see Harold C. Gotoff, *Cicero's Elegant Style: An Analysis of the Pro Archia* (Urbana: University of Illinois Press, 1979).

45. See Paul Antin, *Recueil sur Saint Jérôme* (Brussels: Latomus, 1968), pp. 71-100.

46. See Harold Hagendahl, *The Latin Fathers and the Classics* (Göteborg: Elanders Boktryckeri Aktidbolag, 1958); for a broader interpretation, see Charles Norris Cochrane, *Christianity and Classical Culture: A Study of Thought and Action from Augustus to Augustine,* 2d ed. (New York: Galaxy, 1957).

47. See Harold Hagendahl, *Augustine and the Latin Classics* (Göteborg: Elanders Boktryckeri Aktidbolag, 1967).

48. See C. J. Classen, "Cicerostudien in der Romania im 15. und 16. Jahrhundert," in *Cicero: Ein Mensch seiner Zeit,* ed. G. Radke (Berlin: Gruyter, 1968), pp. 198-245; also, in general, see M. L. Clarke, "Non Hominis Nomen, Sed Eloquentiae," in *Cicero,* ed. T. A. Dorey (New York: Basic Books, 1965), pp. 81-107.

49. See Salvatore I. Camporeale, O.P., *Lorenzo Valla: Umanismo e teologia* (Florence: Istituto Nazionale di Studi sul Rinascimento, 1972).

50. See pp. 76-77 above. I cite from Paolo Cortesi, *De hominibus doctis dialogus,* ed. and trans. Maria Teresa Graziosi (Rome: Bonacci, 1972). On the *Dialogus,* see Sabbadini, *op. cit.,* pp. 32-45; L. Dorez, "Les Maîtres intellectuels de Paul III, d'après le 'Dialogue sur les Savants' de Paolo Cortesi," *Etudes italiennes,* n.s. 1 (1931), pp. 5-13; *idem, La Cour de Pape Paul III,* vol. 1 (Paris: Leroux, 1932), pp. 19-24; Aresenio Frugoni, "Per uno studio sulla giovinezza di Paolo III," *Annali della R. Scuola Normale Superiore di Pisa,* ser. 2, no. 9/3 (1940), pp. 202-210; Maria Teresa Graziosi Acquaro, "Note su Paolo Cortesi e il Dialogo 'De hominibus doctis,'" *Annali: Sezione romanza,* 10/2 (1968), pp. 355-376; Anna Gracci, "Studio su Paolo Cortesi da San Gimignano ed il suo 'De Cardinalatu'" (thesis, Univeristy of Florence, 1967), pp. 28-34; Donald Wilcox, *The De-*

velopment of Florentine Humanist Historiography in the Fifteenth Century (Cambridge, Mass.: Harvard University Press, 1959); Giacomo Ferraù, "Il 'De hominibus doctis' di Paolo Cortesi," *Umanità e storia: Scritti in onore di Adalchi Attisani* (Naples: Giannini, 1971), vol. 2, pp. 261-290.

51. On imitation, see n. 37 above. For the older literature, see Riccardo Scrivano, "Il concetto di imitazione nel Rinascimento," *Cultura e letteratura nel Cinquecento* (Rome: Ateneo, 1966); and G. W. Pigman III, "Versions of Imitation in the Renaissance," *Renaissance Quarterly*, 33 (1980), pp. 1-32.

52. Cortesi, *De hominibus doctis dialogus* (ed. and trans. Graziosi), pp. 50-52. Cortesi played an important role in advancing Renaissance understanding of Ciceronian periodic sentence structure.

53. *Ibid.*, pp. 62-64.

54. The exchange is printed in Latin and Italian translation in Garin, *Prosatori latini del Quattrocento,* pp. 902-911. There is an English translation in Scott, *op. cit.,* pp. 17-22. See also Sabbadini, *op. cit.,* pp. 32-34; and Giorgio Santangelo, *Il Bembo critico e il principio d'imitazione* (Florence: Sansoni, 1950), pp. 48-49. For the application of the theory to art, see Eugenio Battisti, "Il concetto d'imitazione nel Cinquecento: Da Raffaello a Michelangelo," *Commentarii,* 7 (1956), pp. 86-104.

55. See *De hominibus doctis dialogus* (ed. and trans. Graziosi), introduction, p. xxxi.

56. Garin, *Prosatori latini del Quattrocento,* pp. 902-904.

57. *Ibid.*, p. 902.

58. *Ibid.*, p. 906.

59. *Ibid.*

60. *Ibid.*: "Illa enim ridicula imitatrix tantum deformitates et vitia corporis depravata similitudine effingit; hic autem vultum, incessum, statum, motum, formam, vocem denique et figuram corporis repraesentat, et tamen habet in hac similitudine aliquid suum, aliquid naturale, aliquid diversum, ita ut cum comparertur dissimiles inter se esse videantur."

61. *Ibid.*, p. 908: "Ego autem statuo non modo in eloquentia, sed in aliis etiam artibus necessariam esse imitationem. Nam et omnis doctrina ex antecedenti cognitione paratur, et nihil est in mente quin fuerit prius in sensibus perceptum."

62. *Ibid.*: "Sic eloquentiae una est ars, una forma, una imago. Qui vero ab ea declinant, saepe distorti, saepe claudi reperiuntur."

63. See Isidoro del Lungo, *Florentia: Uomini e cose del Quattrocento* (Florence, 1897), pp. 250-253, for Poliziano's letter to Alessandro Cortesi complaining of Roman criticism of his translation of Herodianus. On the differences between Rome and Florence as humanist centers, see Vittorio Rossi, *Il Cinquecento (Storia della letteratura italiana,* 8th ed. (Milan: Vallardi, 1964), chap. 7, esp. pp. 302-303.

64. On Pico, see Charles B. Schmitt, *Gianfrancesco Pico della Mirandola (1469-1533) and his Critique of Aristotle* (The Hague: Nijhoff, 1970). Pico's and Bembo's letters are in Giorgio Santangelo, ed., *Le Epistole 'De Imitatione' di Giovannfrancesco Pico della Mirandola e di Pietro Bembo* (Florence: Olschki, 1954); for English translations, see Scott, *op. cit.,* vol. 2, pp. 1-18. See also Giorgio Santangelo, "La polemica d'imitazione," *Rinascimento,* 1 (1950), pp. 323-339; M. Pompilio, "Una fonte italiana del *Ciceronianus* d'Erasmo," *Giornale italiano di filologia,* 8/3 (1955), pp. 193-207; and Dante della Terza, "*Imitatio,* Theory and Practice: The Example of Bembo the Poet," *Yearbook of Italian Studies,* 1 (1971), pp. 119-141.

65. Santangelo, *Le Epistole,* pp. 35-36.

66. See Santangelo, *Il Bembo critico e il principio d'imitazione:* and Hamletus Tondini, "De Ciceronianae Imitationis ortu et progressione ab exordio renatarum litterarum ad P. Bembum," *Latinitas,* 1960, pp. 166-181.

67. Santangelo, *Le Epistole,* pp. 56-57: "Quae hoc in genere toto Pice, ea esse lex potest: primum, ut qui sit omnium optimus, eum nobis imitandum proponamus: deinde sic imitemur, ut assequi contendamus: nostra demum contentio omnis id respiciat, ut quem assequuti fuerimus, etiam praetereamus."

68. *Ibid.,* pp. 65-66.

69. *Ibid.,* pp. 71-72.

70. *Ibid.,* p. 75.

71. See pp. 16-19 above. The full text appears in Richard Ketel, *De elegantiori Latinitate comparanda scriptores selecti* (Amsterdam, 1713). See also Carlo Dionisotti, *Gli umanisti e il volgare fra Quattro e Cinquecento* (Florence: Le Monnier, 1968), pp. 101-102. Jacob Burckhardt, *The Civilization of the Renaissance in Italy,* trans. S. G. C. Middlemore (New York: Harper and Row, 1958), vol. 1, p. 258, considered Castellesi a milestone in the development of Ciceronianism.

72. See *De sermone,* in Ketel, *op. cit.,* p. 3v, on Cicero's Latin: "Illa enim sublimitas quanquam imitabilis illa quidem videtur cupienti, nihil tamen est experienti minus: audendum tamen, et ita annitendum, ut quod assequi non possumus, imitari saltem voluisse videamur."

73. See Dionisotti, *op. cit.,* p. 102.

74. See Santangelo, *Il Bembo critico e il principio d'imitazione.*

75. BAV, Vat. Lat. 7928, "Laudatio M. T. Ciceronia per T. Phedrum," f. 1r; and BAV, Vat. Lat. 3745, ff. 1r-8r, "Constantini Foelicii de Castro Durantis utriusque iuris periti ad Leonem X Pont. Max. in libros de coniuratione Catalinae ac exilio et redditu M. Tulli Ciceronis praefatio." See also John W. O'Malley, "The Discovery of America and Reform Thought at the Papal Court in the Early Cinqecento," in *First Images of America: The Impact of the New World on the Old,* ed. Fredi Chiapelli (Berkeley: University of California Press, 1976), pp. 185-200.

76. See Cicero, *De oratore,* vol. 1 ed. and trans. E. W. Sutton and H. Rackham, Loeb Classical Library (Cambridge, Mass.: Harvard University Press, 1942), pp. 10-11.

77. See, for example, the dedicatory letter of Jacopo Mazzocchio to Adrian VI in the 1522 edition of Albertini's *Opusculum de mirabilibus novae et veteris urbis Romae,* f. A 2r; see also Inghirami's oration, *In laudem omnium sanctorum oratio,* in Volterra, Biblioteca Comunale Guarnacciana, LIII. 4. 8. This oration received much comment in its time. Writing to Adriano Castellesi, Mario Maffei noted: "Phaedrus orationem habuit in qua cum multa de imperio Christianorum ornate disseruisset peroratione se ad Iulium Pontificem vertit, ac totum in eius laude consumpsit quem viventem inter sanctos jam retulit ob illius egregia opera singula memorans quae fecit, quaeque animo facere concipit" (BAV, Barb. Lat. 2517, f. 59v); see also Fedele Baiocchi, "Sulle poesie latine di Francesco M. Molza, saggio," *Annali della R. Scuola Normale di Pisa, filosofia, e filologia,* 18 (1905), p. 7, n. 1.

78. Blosio Palladio, *Oratio totam fere romanam historiam complectans habita in aedibus Capitolinis XI kal. maii MDXXI ab anonymo auctore die, qua dedicata fuit marmorea Leonis X Pont. Max. statua, nunc primum in lucem edita, ac notis illustrata,* ed. Rudolfini Venuti (Rome, 1735). BAV, Vat. Lat. 5297, ff. 133r-210r,

contains the oration and attributes it to Blosio Palladio. See also Domenico Gnoli, *Un giudizio di lesa romanità sotto Leone X* (Rome, 1891), p. 35, for the attribution. On Blosio, see pp. 86 and 111 above.

79. See Hans Henrik Brummer and Tore Jansen, "Art, Literature, and Politics: An Episode in the Roman Renaissance," *Konsthistorisk Tidskrift*, 45 (1976), pp. 79–93.

80. Blosio, *Oratio*, pp. 122–123.

81. *Ibid.,* pp. 8–9.

82. *Ibid.,* p. 10.

83. *Ibid.,* p. 12.

84. *Ibid.,* pp. 46–47, 93, 98. Blosio argued that Latin literature outlived the empire and was its chief glory (*ibid.,* pp. 73–74).

85. *Ibid.,* p. 48: "Jam vero T. Livius quasi tuba proclamarat, nullam umquam Rem publicam, aut majorem, aut sanctiorem, bonisque exemplis ditiorem fuisse."

86. *Ibid.,* pp. 108–110.

87. *Ibid.,* pp. 123–124: ". . . Deus in hac Urbe caput, ac sedem religionis statuit, ubi maxime eam natam, auctam, roboratamque perspexit. Itaque si Deo ita placitum fuerat, ut Romanum Imperium tamquam humanum concideret, laetari prorsus debemus, quod ruina prioris Imperii, initium melioris fuit. Siquidem illi Christianum successit, hoc est Caelum terris, lux tenebris, vita morti, aeterna caducis." See also *ibid.,* p. 117, where Blosio maintained that God loved the Romans for their virtues.

88. *Ibid.,* pp. 116, 119.

89. *Ibid.,* p. 122.

90. *Ibid.,* p. 125: "Addidit et Deus nostris temporibus foelicitatem siquidem novus terrarum orbis nostris majoribus ignotus ad occidentem Hispanis, ad orientem Lusitanis classibus adapertus, Romanas leges accepit, Romanoque Pontifici, et Christianis legibus paret."

91. *Ibid.,* pp. 126–127.

92. *Ibid.,* 132. Blosio said that Leo X lowered taxes, which he did not do.

93. *Ibid.,* p. 155: "Quanta nuper sapientia consilioque Lutheranam heresim in Germania invalescentem fere excussit?"

94. *Ibid.,* pp. 157–160.

95. *Ibid.,* pp. 161–162.

96. On the Campidoglio, see F. Saxl, "The Capitol during the Renaissance— A symbol of the Imperial Idea," *Lectures,* vol. 1 (London: Warburg, 1957), pp. 200–214.

97. Blosio, *Oratio,* p. 166: "Quare, et Te non jam Jupiter, sed Virgo Capitolina Dei Parens, quae hujus Urbis, et collis reliquiis praesides Romamque et Capitolium tutaris. . . ."

98. For Erasmus and Italian humanists, see Pierre de Nolhac, *Erasme en Italie* (Paris, 1925); August Renaudet, *Erasme et l'Italie* (Geneva: Droz, 1954); and Delio Cantimori, "Erasmo e la vita morale e religiosa italiana nel secolo XVI" and "Erasmo e l'Italia," *Umanesimo e religione nel Rinascimento* (Turin: Einaudi, 1975), pp. 400–487.

99. See James K. McConica, "Erasmus and the 'Julius': A Humanist Reflects on the Church," in *The Pursuit of Holiness in Late Medieval and Renaissance Religion,* ed. Charles Trinkaus and Heiko A. Oberman (Leiden: Brill, 1974), pp. 444–471.

100. See Julien Gerard Michel, "Etude sur le *Ciceronianus* d'Erasn e avec une édition critique" (thesis, University of Paris, 1951).

101. See Myron P. Gilmore, "Italian Reaction to Erasmian Humanism," in *Iterarium italicum*, ed. Heiko A. Oberman (Leiden: Brill, 1975), pp. 61–115; and Silvana Seidel Menchi, "Alcuni atteggiamenti della cultura italiana di fronte a Erasmo," in *Eresia e riforma nell'Italia del Cinquecento: Miscellanea I* (De Kalb/Chicago: Northern Illinois University/Newberry Library, 1974), pp. 71–133.

102. See Raymond Marcel, "Les dettes d'Erasme envers l'Italie," in *Actes du Congrès Erasme* (Amsterdam: North Holland Publishing Co., 1971), pp. 159–173.

103. See *DBI*, vol. 21, pp. 75–78; Seidel Menchi, *op. cit.*, pp. 89–116; and O'Malley, "The Vatican Library and the School of Athens."

104. The manuscript is Milan, Biblioteca Ambrosiana, G 133 inf., ff. 82v–87v; see Seidel Menchi, *op. cit.*, pp. 97–98.

105. Milan, Biblioteca Ambrosiana, G 133 inf., f. 83v. Casali mentioned the following members of the academy: Portio, Sadoleto, Bembo, Gravina, Fabiano, Colotio, Motta, Cornelio, Jovio, Capella, Petrasancta, Pimpinella, Casanova, Elmo, Thamyra, Blosio, Laelio, Pierio, Curtio, Sanazario, Summontio, Haltrensio, Vopisco, Sessa, Naugerio, Bombasio, Amiterino, Camertibus, Parrhasio, Marcello, Diacetio, Modesto, Siculo, Arcade, Scio, Molosso, Anselmo, Cataneo, and Pio.

106. *Ibid.*, f. 84r: ". . . sic enim Ro. Academiam appellaverim ubi sunt semper omnium linguarum, gentium, nationumque commercia. . . ."

107. *Ibid.*, f. 84v: "Nam quid me litteras graecas ignorare contendis. . . ."

108. *Ibid.*, f. 84v.

109. *Ibid.*, f. 86r.

110. *Ibid.*, f. 86r: ". . . qui Christianum dogma decretumque te eversurum facilius putasti simulatiose religionis qua tanquam gladio abutereris atque iterum Christum iugulares."

111. *Ibid.*, f. 86r: "Atque id quidem minus flagitiosum esset, si unus tu pseudochristianus in tuo delirio insanires. . . ."

112. On the *Ciceronianus*, see the edition and Italian translation by Angelo Gambaro (Brescia: La Scuola, 1965), and especially Gambaro's important introduction. For criticisms of Gambaro's edition, see Giulio Vallese, *Da Dante ad Erasmo*, pp. 109–110, n. 18; p. 118, n. 48; and pp. 124–125, n. 65. For an English translation, see Scott, *op. cit.* See also F. Férère, "Erasme et le Ciceronianisme au XVIe siècle," *Revue de l'Agenais et des Anciennes Provinces du Sud-Ouest*, 3, 4, and 5 (1924), pp. 176–182, 283–294, and 342–357; Scott, *op. cit.*, chap. 3; Pierre Mesnard, "L'Année érasmienne," *Etudes*, 328 (February 1968), pp. 236–255; *idem*, "La Religion d'Erasme dans le 'Ciceronianus,'" *Revue thomiste*, 78 (1968), pp. 268–272; and G. W. Pigman III, "Imitation and the Renaissance Sense of the Past: The Reception of Erasmus' *Ciceronianus*," *Journal of Medieval and Renaissance Studies*, 9/2 (1979), pp. 155–177. See also nn. 100 and 101 above.

113. Erasmus, *Ciceronianus* (ed. Gambaro) p. 188.

114. See Mesnard, "L'année érasmienne" and "La religion d'Erasme."

115. Erasmus, *Ciceronianus* (ed. Gambaro), p. 162; Scott, *op. cit.*, p. 75.

116. Erasmus, *Ciceronianus* (ed. Gambaro), pp. 140–150.

117. *Ibid.*, p. 262; Scott, *op. cit.*, p. 112.

118. Erasmus, *Ciceronianus* (ed. Gambaro), pp. 282–284.

119. *Ibid.*, pp. 296–300, where Cortesi is criticized.

120. See *ibid.*, p. 270, for a discussion of an anti-Luther oration by Longueil;

see *Christophori Longolii orationes* (Florence, 1524; rpt., Boston: Gregg Press, 1967).

121. Erasmus, *Ciceronianus* (ed. Gambaro), pp. 304–306.

122. *Ibid.*, p. 308.

123. See A. Joly, *Etude sur J. Sadolet (1477–1547)* (Caen, 1857), chap. 1; and G. Zappacosta, *Francesco Maturanzio: Umanista perugino* (Bergamo: Minerva italica, 1970), chap. 3.

124. See Marc Fumaroli, "Cicero Pontifex Romanus: La tradition rhétorique du College romain et les principes inspirateurs de mécenat des Barberini," *Mélanges de l'Ecole française de Rome: Moyen Age et Temps Modernes*, 90/2 (1978), pp. 797–835; and *idem, L'Age de l'Eloquence: Rhétorique et "res literia" de la Renaissance au seuil de l'epoque classique* (Geneva: Droz, 1980). For the later history of Ciceronianism and anti-Ciceronianism, see Morris W. Croll, *"Attic" and Baroque Prose Style: The Anti-Ciceronian Movement*, ed. J. Max Patrick, Robert O. Evans, and John M. Wallace (Princeton: Princeton University Press, 1966).

CHAPTER 6

1. On humanist theology in general, see Charles Trinkaus, *In Our Image and Likeness: Humanity and Divinity in Italian Humanist Thought*, 2 vols. (Chicago: University of Chicago Press, 1970).

2. On the university, see F. M. Renazzi, *Storia dell'Università degli Studi di Roma, detta comunemente La Sapienza* (Rome, 1803–1804), vol. 1, pp. 155–242, and vol. 2, pp. 1–78; and Raymond Creytens, O.P., "Le 'Studium Romanae Curiae' et le Maître du Sacré Palais," *Archivum Fratrum Praedicatorum*, 12 (1942), pp. 5–83.

3. See George Holmes, *The Florentine Enlightenment, 1400–1450* (New York: Pegasus, 1969), pp. 118–121; and "Il 'Contra Oblocutores et Detractores Poetarum' di Francesco da Fiano (con appendice di documenti biografici)," ed. Igino Taù, *Archivio italiano per la storia della pietà*, vol. 4 (1964), pp. 255–350.

4. See John W. O'Malley, *Giles of Viterbo on Church and Reform* (Leiden: Brill, 1968); and Jared Wicks, S.J., "Thomism between Renaissance and Reformation: The Case of Cajetan," *Archiv für Reformationsgeschichte* 68 (1977), pp. 9–33.

5. Most prominently, Pedro Garcia, who is discussed on p. 165 above. See also Giovanni di Napoli, *Giovanni Pico della Mirandola e la problematica dottrinale del suo tempo* (Rome: Desclée, 1965), pp. 90–92.

6. The Latin text is in J. Vahlen, "Lorenzo Valla über Thomas von Aquino," *Vierteljahrsschrift für Kultur und Litteratur der Renaissance*, 1 (1886), pp. 384–396; there is an English translation in Leonard A. Kennedy, ed., *Renaissance Philosophy: New Translations* (The Hague: Mouton, 1973), pp. 17–26. On this oration, see Mario Fois, S.J., *Il pensiero cristiano di Lorenzo Valla nel quadro storico-culturale del suo ambiente* (Rome: Gregoriana, 1969), pp. 456–469; Hanna H. Gray, "Valla's *Encomium of St. Thomas Aquinas* and the Humanist Conception of Christian Antiquity," in *Essays in History and Literature presented by Fellows of the Newberry Library to Stanley Pargellis*, ed. H. Bluhm (Chicago: Newberry Library, 1965), pp. 37–51; John W. O'Malley, S.J., "Some Renaissance Panegyrics of Aquinas," *Renaissance Quarterly*, 27/2 (1974), pp. 164–200; *idem*, "The Feast of Thomas Aquinas in Renaissance Rome: A Neglected Document and Its Import,"

RSCI, 35/1 (1981), pp. 1-27, for the setting; and Salvatore I. Camporeale, O.P., "Lorenzo Valla tra Medioevo e Rinascimento: Encomion s. Thomae—1457," *Memorie dominicane*, 7 (1976), pp. 3-190.

7. On Brandolini, see pp. 99-100 above. I have used the copy dedicated to Cardinal Francesco Todeschini-Piccolomini; see BAV, Ottob. Lat. 438, "Lippi Brandolini Epithoma in sacram Judeorum historiam ex volumine quam bibliam appellant et Josepho historico fidelissimo." Another copy is BAV, Ottob. Lat. 121. See Trinkaus, *op. cit.*, vol. 2, pp. 825-826 and n. 111. On Biblical scholarship in the Renaissance, see *ibid.*, pp. 563-614; and Salvatore Garofalo, "Gli umanisti italiani del secolo XV e la Bibbia," *Biblica*, 27 (1948), pp. 338-375.

8. BAV, Ottob. Lat. 438, ff. 3v-4r.

9. *Ibid.*, f. 4v.

10. *Ibid.*, ff. 4v-5r.

11. *Ibid.*, f. 5r: "Postremo qui suspicemini me non esse theologum quum sciatis me Christianum esse, et de Deo non modo loqui non imperite quod theologi nomen efficit, verum etiam non inscite scribere videatis?"

12. *Ibid.*, ff. 7v-8r: "Est igitur (ut videtis) eloquentia cum ob eam quam affert rebus dignitatem ac speciem tum ob eam quam habet in persuadendo vim divinis rebus vel maxime necessaria."

13. *Ibid.*, f. 8v.

14. *Ibid.*, f. 6r: "Proinde a nobis biblia nostra oratione immutata dicatur, modo eam a vobis vostris commentatiunculis constet esse depravatam atque corruptam. Sit sane id quod nos agimus bibliam innovare, modo sciatis vos rem perdere atque abolere."

15. For Cortesi's life, see pp. 76-81 above.

16. I cite from *Pauli Cortesii Protonotarii Apostolici in quattuor libros Sententiarum argutae Romanoque eloquio disputationes* (Paris, 1513). For other editions, see Fridericus Stegmüller, *Repertorium Commentariorum in Sententias Petri Lombardi* (Würzburg: Schöningh, 1947), pp. 298-299; Pio Paschini, "Teologia umanistica," *RSCI*, 11 (1957), p. 254; Anna Gracci, "Studio su Paolo Cortesi da San Gimignano ed il suo 'De Cardinalatu'" (thesis, University of Florence, 1967), chap. 2; and Giovanni Farris, *Eloquenza e teologia nel 'Prooemium in Librum Primum Sententiarum' di Paolo Cortesi* (Savona: Sabatelli, n.d. [1972]).

17. On Peter Lombard and his work, see the article "Sentences (Commentaires sur les)," in *Dictionnaire de théologie catholique*, vol. 14/2, cols. 1860-84,; Philippe Delahaye, *Pierre Lombard: Sa vie, ses oevres, sa morale* (Montreal: Institut d'Etudes Medievales, 1961); and Joseph de Ghellinck, S.J., *Le mouvement théologique du XIIe siècle*, 2d ed. (Bruges, 1948), pp. 213-249. See also Battista Mondon, S. X., *St. Thomas Aquinas' Philosophy in the Commentary to the Sentences* (The Hague: Nijhoff, 1975); and M.-D. Chenu, *Toward Understanding Saint Thomas*, trans. A.-M. Landry, O.P., and D. Hughes, O.P. (Chicago: Henry Regnery Co., 1964), pp. 264-276. Two of Cortesi's Roman contemporaries wrote similar works. Giles of Viterbo wrote *Commentarium secundum mentem Platonis* (see Jules Pasquier, "Un Essai de théologie platonienne à la Renaissance: Le Commentaire de Gilles de Viterbe sur le première livre des Sentences," *Recherches de science religieuse*, 13 [1923], pp. 293-312, and 419-436); and Cardinal Francesco Ponzetto wrote *Summa brevis theologiae* (Rome, 1512). While not a commentary on the *Sentences*, Ponzetto's *Summa* was similar to Cortesi's tract. For a later ex-

ample, see Walter L. Moore, Jr., ed., *In Primum Librum Sententiarum Annotatiunculae D. Iohanne Eckio Praelectore* (Leiden: Brill, 1976).

18. See John F. D'Amico, "Beatus Rhenanus, Tertullian, and the Reformation: A Humanist's Critique of Scholasticism," *Archiv für Reformationsgeschichte*, 71 (1980), pp. 37–63.

19. For a discussion of this, see the introduction by Bohdan Kieszkowski to Giovanni Pico della Mirandola's *Conclusiones sive These DCCCC* . . . (Geneva: Droz, 1973), pp. 97–100.

20. See Farris, *op. cit.*, pp. 22–35, where the Latin text from the Basel, 1540, edition is printed with an Italian translation. For an English translation, see Kennedy, *op. cit.*, pp. 32–37, where, at p. 35, *de principe* is translated as "about the fundamental truth (i.e. theology)." In fact, however, *de principe* refers to the *De Cardinalatu* in its earlier form as a book on the prince.

21. See Chapter 3 above.

22. Barbaro's letter is printed in Ermolao Barbaro, *Epistolae, orationes et carmina*, ed. V. Branca (Florence: Bibliopolis, 1943), vol. 1, #68, pp. 84–86. Pico's letter can be found in Latin, with an Italian translation, in Eugenio Garin, ed., *Prosatori latini del Quattrocento* (Milan: Ricciardi, 1952), pp. 804–823; see *ibid.*, pp. 844–863, for the rest of the correspondence. English translations can be found in Quirinus Breen, "Giovanni Pico della Mirandola on the Conflict of Philosophy and Rhetoric," *Journal of the History of Ideas*, 12 (1952), pp. 384–412; "Melanchthon's Reply to G. Pico della Mirandola," *ibid.*, pp. 412–426; and in A. Fallico and H. Shapiro, eds., *Renaissance Philosophy*, vol. 1 (New York: Harper and Row, 1968), pp. 105–117. See also Hanna H. Gray, "Renaissance Humanism: The Pursuit of Eloquence," *Journal of the History of Ideas*, 42/3 (1963), pp. 497–514. Pico's letter is dated June 3, 1485.

23. Garin, *op. cit.*, p. 812. See also John F. D'Amico, "Paolo Cortesi's Rehabilitation of Giovanni Pico della Mirandola," *Bibliothèque d'Humanisme et Renaissance*, 44 (1982), pp. 37–51, at pp. 40–42.

24. Garin, *op. cit.*, p. 818.

25. See Karl Otto Apel, *L'idea di lingua nella tradizione dell'umanesimo da Dante a Vico*, trans. Luciano Tosti (Bologna: Mulino, 1975), chap. 6.

26. Garin, *op. cit.*, p. 818.

27. For the relations between Pico and Cortesi, see the material cited in Pio Paschini, "Una famiglia di curiali nella Roma del Quattrocento: I Cortesi," *RSCI*, 11/1 (1957), pp. 31–32; and D'Amico, "Paolo Cortesi's Rehabilitation of Giovanni Pico della Mirandola," p. 40.

28. I cite from Cortesi, *In quattuor libros Sententiarum*, f. 4r, and from the English translation in Kennedy, *op. cit.*, p. 32.

29. Cortesi, *In quattuor libros Sententiarum*, f. 4r; Kennedy, *op. cit.*, p. 32.

30. Cortesi, *In quattuor libros Sententiarum*, f. 4r: "Ex quo confiteri necesse, eiusmodi philosophiae speciem litteratam et artificiosam videri, quae ad naturae pulchritudinem statuatur. Quod si artificiosa dicatur, nemini dubium esse debet, eam speciem philosophiae studiis esse aptiorem quae suavis quam quae absona feratur, propterea quod suavitas cum in intelligendi sensum irrepat, philosophiae studia amplificat." For an English translation, see Kennedy, *op. cit.*, p. 33.

31. Cortesi, *In quattuor libros Sententiarum*, f. 4v; Kennedy, *op, cit.*, p. 34.

32. Cortesi, *In quattuor libros Sententiarum*, f. 4v; Kennedy, *op. cit.*, p. 35.

33. Cortesi, *In quattuor libros Sententiarum*, f. 4v: "...meo...iudicio ...natura semper pulchritudinem cum utilitate suopte quodam foedere coniungit...." For an English translation, see Kennedy, *op. cit.*, p. 34.

34. Cortesi, *In quattuor libros Sententiarum*, f. 4v; Kennedy, *op. cit.*, p. 35.

35. Cortesi, *In quattuor libros Sententiarum*, f. 5r; Kennedy, *op. cit.*, p. 35.

36. Cortesi, *In quattuor libros Sententiarum*, f. 45v: "Ammonere enim philosophos et humaniores volumus, ut uberius et illustrioribus litteris hoc scribendi studium aggrediantur."

37. Cortesi was not alone in lamenting this state. In his introduction to the life of St. Eugenia, Antonio Lollio, a member of the *familia* of Cardinal Francesco Todeschini-Piccolomini, noted the distaste for religious topics on the part of contemporaries because of the bad style used by religious writers. Lollio also called for a return to good Latin style in religious writings. See BAV, Chigi F. IV. 83, ff. 1r–v. On Lollio, who died in 1486, see Alfred A. Strnad, "Studia Piccolomineana: Vorarbeiten zu einer Geschichte der Bibliothek der Päpste Pius II und III," in *Enea Silvio Piccolomini: Papa Pio II*, ed. D. Maffei (Siena, 1968), pp. 253–254.

38. Cortesi, *De Cardinalatu* (Castrum Cortesium, 1510), ff. R 10v–11r.

39. *Ibid.*, f. R. 10v: "Siquidem quanquam philosophorum doctrina multum praestat explicatione naturae, iudicari tamen notando potest, multa saepe in ea misceri solere falsa, semperque in ea aliquem relinqui dubitandi nodum, id accidere crebro consuesse, propterea quod sit in ea sita ratione naturae, quae facile potest suopte inscitiae errore falli, quod contra ei scientiae generi evenire solet, cum ea sit in divina quadam supra progredientem naturam constituta luce, quae falli nullo modo potest."

40. *Ibid.*, ff. R 10v–11r: "Quo magis est mihi saepe cum quodam superstitioso concionatorum genere certamen, qui cum minus se in dicendo sine piaculo uti artificii epolitione credant, concionantemque affirmant divino oportere afflatu loqui, non intelligunt Deum haudquaquam uti theolepto concionatore semper, sed adiecto interdum artificio dicendi hominum mentes movere vehementius; ex quo facile intellectu sit, perinde hominis referre artificio uti in dicendo, ut Dei intersit dirigere in concionando linguam."

41. *Ibid.*, f. T 1r.

42. *Ibid.*, ff. T 1r–v: "Quotus enim ex politiorum litteratorum coetu quisque ita suapte eruditione comptus reperiri potest, qui aut opinetur se posse quippiam eruere ex octo Alberti de phisica disciplina libris, aut se credat ex Ioannis Scoti theoria hausturum quicquam? sive quis est item humaniorum litterarum peritior, qui se eius D. Thomae epitomes partem millesimam intellecturum speret, in quo de usia divina disputatur?"

43. Farris, *op. cit.*, pp. 36–38, makes a short comparison of Cortesi's work with Aquinas's *Summa* and the *Sententiae*.

44. Cortesi, *Liber Sententiarum*, f. 6v: "Nos vero quanquam theologiam videamus unum esse scientiae genus, id tamen expletum et absolutum esse dicimus, vimque ad hominum absolutionem ex divinitatis luce nancisci, hominemque maxime absoluere cum ad munia recta, tum ad facultatem contemplandi veri. Ex quo eam partim praxin, partim contemplationem esse volumus. At cum omne scientiae genus finis mensione expendamus, extremumque huius scientiae finem in aetheriis sedibus principis veri contemplationem esse dicamus, constare debere inter sanos volumus eam imprimis in contemplandi quodam genere versari." Cf. Thomas Aquinas, *Commentum in primum librum Sententiarum Magistri Petri Lombardi*

(in *Sancti Thomae Aquinatis . . . Opera Omnia* [Parma, 1858], vol. 6), Prologus, quaes. 1, art. 3, quaestiun. 3 (p. 7): "Respondeo dicendum, quod ista scientia, quamvis sit una, tamen perfecta est et sufficiens ad omnem humanam perfectionem, propter efficaciam divini luminis, ut ex praedictis patet. Unde perficit hominem et in operatione recta et quantum ad contemplationem veritatis: unde quantum ad quid practica est et etiam speculative. Sed, quia scientia omnis principaliter pensanda est ex fine, finis autem ultimus istius doctrinae est contemplatio primae veritatis in patria, ideo principaliter speculativa est." See also Thomas Aquinas, *Summa Theologiae*, Ia. I. 4. In addition, see the English Dominicans' translation and discussion of the *Summa*, vol. 1 (New York: McGraw-Hill, 1964), pp. 58–87.

45. Cortesi, *Liber Sententiarum*, ff. 8r–9r.

46. *Ibid.*, ff. 8r–v: "In eiusmodi enim controversia Divo Thomae valde in ore est a Deo singularum rerum genera pernosci. Contra quem ex caesia disciplina Aureolus multa Scoteo genere conscripsit, affirmans cum flaccescentium ratiuncularum genera afferre, quibus singula a Deo percipi probare conetur. Nec ita ab eo Averroim feriri dicit, ut cadendi necessitatem inducat. Tantumdemque aculeorum affert argutus inficiator Garro. Sed praeter caeteros ingenii gloria abundans Gregorius Ariminensis, articulatim argumentorum genera retexit, qui quidem multa eius deturbandi causa conari videretur, si diligentior Aquitaneorum verborum aestimator putaretur. At vero ex philosophorum genere Averrois maxime talum [intersit?], cum a Deo singularum rerum genera percipi posse negavit. . . . Ex eadem quoque Arabum disciplina Algazellus et Avicenna, nobile recentium philosophorum par, quamquam minime a Deo singula percipi posse negent. Eum tamen catholice singula rerum genera agnoscere volunt, non quidem quatenus per se singula existant. In quo sane non intelligunt se Deo inscitiam internoscendi dare. At mihi quidem videtur, cum singularum rerum agnitio ad hominum expletam absolutionem pertineat, necesse esse ut eadem a Deo pernoscantur."

47. *Ibid.*, ff. 35v–36v.

48. The question of the indulgences and their relationship to penance can be found in Adolph Harnack, *History of Dogma*, trans. N. Buchanan (rpt.; New York: Dover, 1961), vol. 6, pp. 234–269.

49. Cf. Aquinas, *Summa Theologiae*, III. 90. 2.

50. Cortesi, *Liber Sententiarum*, f. 36r.

51. See Chenu, *op. cit.*, pp. 100–125; and Josef Pieper, *Guide to Thomas Aquinas* (New York: New American Library, 1964), pp. 94–105, for a discussion of medieval Latin.

52. See n. 44 above. Another example is the *imago Dei* idea. See Peter Lombard, *Sententiae* (in *Sancti Thomae Aquinatis . . . Opera Omnia*, vol. 7), Dist. XVI (p. 523): "Factus est ergo homo ad imaginem Dei et similitudinem secundum mentem, qua irrationalibus antecellit: sed ad imaginem secundum memoriam, intelligentiam et dilectionem; ad similitudinem secundum innocentiam et justitiam, quae in mente rationali naturaliter sunt. Vel imago consideratur in cognitione veritatis, similitudo in amore virtutis; vel imago in aliis omnibus, similitudo in essentia: quia immortalis et indivisibilis." Cortesi, *Liber Sententiarum*, f. 20r: ". . . hominem Dei esse simulacrum, non quidem absolutum simulacrum, sed tanquam ad similitudinem expressum, negamusque primigenio homini Deum notum fuisse de facie, nisi sopito ei, et phantasmate sevocato Deum esse concedimus." Cf. Aquinas, *Commentum* (in *Sancti Thomae Aquinatis .'. . Opera Omnia*, vol. 7), Dist. XVI, quaes. 1, art. 1 and 2 (pp. 523–525); see also Delahaye, *op. cit.*, pp. 28–30.

53. Cortesi, *Liber Sententiarum*, f. 36r: "Nos autem in Senatu summum quoddam imperii genus constitutum dicimus, cui reliqui pareant. Ex quo in quosdam circunscriptum dominatum nanciscantur. Cum autem aetheriarum clavium usus aliquod imperii ius flagitare videatur, ob eam causam dicimus eum qui summi imperii potestate nitatur, iisdem uti in unum quenque posse."

54. *Ibid.*: "Itaque ob eam causam Christi divorumque litatum quasi R. P. aerariumque quoddam dicemus. In quod tanquam in urnam generatim quisque usque eo vectigal iniiciat, quoad expleatur. Nec tamen expletam futuram dicimus, nisi in busto deflagrati et cinefacti mundi. Ex quo tam multiplicem indulgendi facultatem oriri volumus."

55. *Ibid.*: "Sed multi theologorum tunicati, qui velut mirmillones aut Thraces in vulgi coetu gladiatoria spectacula edunt, hoc indulgentiae munus tanquam inutilem explodunt, affirmantes inutile[m] muneralem ambitum videri."

56. J. Duns Scotus, *Opera Omnia* (Paris, 1639; rpt., Hildesheim: Georg Olms, 1968), vol. 8, p. 275: "Sicut ergo imperatori deberet sententiare aliquem obedire debere Proconsuli, contempto praecepto curatoris, id est, inferioris Proconsule, si contradiceret Proconsuli, ita etiam, si essent sub eodem dominio ordinata, scilicet, quod aliquis esset servus Titii, et Titius Petri, magis deberet Imperator cogere servum servire Petro, quia superior est Titio, quam Titio, si Titius vellet uti servo illo contra dominium Petri; ergo maxime debet Princeps zelare, pro dominio servando supremi Domini, scilicet Dei, et per consequens non solum licet, sed debet Princeps auferre parvulos a dominio parentum volentium eos educare contra cultum Dei, qui est supremus, et honestissimus dominus, et debet eos applicare cultui divino." Cortesi, *Liber Sententiarum*, f. 34r: "Ex quo etiam a multis interrogationes interponuntur, num repugnantium parentum liberi hac debeat aspersione lustrari. Eidem Scoto qui in quocumque disputationum genere usque eo pervenire vult, quousque intelligentiae acies intendi potest, invitorum parentum liberos ante pubem hoc rore suffundi posse placet; idque publici consilii principis permagni interesse affirmans cui infantes in R. P. descriptione sunt iure commissi. Nam cum maius regale imperii genus, quam ius parentum arbitretur, permagni putat interesse regis eum praescribere parendi modum quo inferius genus superiori subsit. Idque ut saepe solet similitudine connectit. Nam si quispiam, inquit, Q. Flaminii servus fuerit, ipseque Flaminius Cn. Sempronii servus dicatur, vehementius laborandum esse regi opinatur, ut is magis Cn. Sempronio quam Q. Flaminio pareat, si modo eo Q. Flaminius ad Cn. Sempronii imperii perniciem uti velle videatur. Ex quo apertum esse permagni interesse regis, summi heri imperium dominatumque tueri. Ob eam causam minime regibus interdictum putat, quin possint ex invitorum parentum gremio infantes evellere, ne parvi detestatique cultus traditione inquinentur, nefarieque in parente[m] Deum armentur." After reviewing Aquinas's counterarguments, Cortesi concluded that before a child reaches the age of reason, he should not be dealt with against his parents' will. On this question, see Steven W. Rowen, "Ulrich Zasius and the Baptism of Jewish Children," *Sixteenth Century Journal,* 6/2 (1975), pp. 3–25.

57. See Carlo Dionisotti, "Umanistici dimenticati?" *Italia medioevale e umanistica,* 4 (1961), pp. 287–321, at p. 302; many interesting things are said about humanist Latin in this article. See also Hubert Jedin, *The History of the Council of Trent,* trans. Ernest Graf, vol. 1 (St. Louis, Mo.: Herder, 1957), p. 159.

58. The manuscript is BAV, Vat. Lat. 2222, ff. 135r–v. The creed begins:

Unum credo Deum caeli rerumque parentem
Qui liquido solus vires infundit Olympo
Quique est omnipotens; mundum terrasque creavit
Quaeque invisa oculis, et quae nos cernere [?] contra
Concessum, totumque potens, et Christus Jesus
Creditur esse dea genitus patris unica proles.

For Pompilio, see Giovanni Mercati, "Paolo Pompilio e la scoperta del cadavere intatto sull'Appia nel 1485," *Opere minori*, vol. 4, Studi e Testi #79 (Vatican City: Biblioteca Apostolica Vaticana, 1937), pp. 268-286; and Carlo Dionisotti, *Gli umanisti e il volgare fra Quattro e Cinquecento* (Florence: Le Monnier, 1968), chap. 3.

59. Manuscript entitled *Nicomachius in Tridentonem*, BAV, Vat. Lat. 4511, f. 11r: "Ego, igitur, heus inquam tibi dico parmensis, cum deos invocem non Iovem utique Phebum vel Martem intellexi, qui quod sibi non habent, nequaquam in sui cultores conferre possunt, sed Petrum Paulum Hieronymum nostrumque simul Iacobum quo novello Deo celicolas iam omnes laetari non dubito sicuti et Christianum et religiosum hominem decet intelligi volui." (I am indebted to Prof. James Butrica for calling my attention to this text.) Similarly, when composing a liturgical text, Agostino Patrizi, a papal master of ceremonies, apologized for using technical and liturgical vocabulary rather than classical terms; see Jean Mabillon and Michael Germain, *Museum Italicum*, 2 vols. (Paris, 1687-1689), vol. 2, p. 586. (I am grateful to Prof. Nelson Minnich for providing this reference.)

60. On this, see Averil and Alan Cameron, "Christianity and Tradition in the Historiography of the Late Empire," *Classical Quarterly*, 14/2 (1964), pp. 316-328.

61. See Harald Hagendahl, *The Latin Fathers and the Classics* (Göteborg: Elanders Boktryckeri Abtidbolag, 1958), pt. 3, chap. 2, for ample examples.

62. See Loren Partridge and Randolph Starn, *A Renaissance Likeness: Art and Culture in Raphael's Julius II* (Berkeley, Calif.: Unversity of California Press, 1980), for an attempt to relate Raphael to the High Renaissance Roman culture.

63. See Georg Weise, *L'ideale eroico del Rinascimento* (Naples: Edizioni scientifiche italiane, 1961), vol. 1, pp. 296-297.

64. See Gunnar Danbolt, "Triumphus Concordiae: A Study of Raphael's Camera della Segnatura," *Konsthistorisk Tidskrift*, 44 (1975), pp. 70-84.

65. See Paul Oskar Kristeller, "Thomism and the Italian Thought of the Renaissance," *Medieval Aspects of Renaissance Learning: Three Essays*, ed. and trans. Edward P. Mahoney (Durham, N.C.: Duke University Press, 1974).

66. See Cortesi, *Liber Sententiarum*, f. 13v; cf. Aquinas, *Commentum*, Prologus, quaes. 3, art. 1, p. 5.

67. Cortesi, *Liber Sententiarum*, f. 14r.

68. *Ibid.*, f. 13v.

69. *Ibid.*, f. 42v.

70. Cortesi, *De Cardinalatu*, f. T 2r. In discussing Averroës in the *Liber Sententiarum*, f. 15v, Cortesi wrote: "Nos vero id Averroim ad intelligentiam possibilem (Faciamus enim hoc verbum tractando tritus). . . ."

71. Cortesi, *De Cardinalatu*, f. T 2v: "Sed permagni refert cum res in disputationem cadit, ut quaerendum videatur, quot utrinque inter se disceptantium

numerari queant, in quo quidem ei est maxime adhaerescendum parti, quae est numero maior iudicanda, siquidem dubitari non debet quin id sit verius iudicium putandum, quod pluribus visum iri cernitur, quam quod sit commune cum paucis. Eodemque modo ea sunt rationum argumentorumque genera expendenda, quibus sint iacta fundamenta opinantum, idque fieri debere ratione probatur, cum perspicuum sit, nec his rebus esse assentiendum subito quarum sit obstructa difficultas, nec ab his esse desciscendum, quae intelligantur verae magis videri qam falsae."

72. *Ibid.*, f. T 3r.

73. On Thomas's influence in the Renaissance, see Kristeller, "Thomism and the Italian Thought of the Renaissance." For Scotus's influence, see Giovanni di Napoli, "Duns Scoto nel Rinascimento italiano," in *Regnum Hominis et Regnum Dei*, ed. Camille Berube, vol. 2 (Rome: Societas Internationalis Scotistica, 1978), pp. 265–282.

74. Cortesi, *Liber Sententiarum*, f. 10v.

75. *Ibid.*, f. 42r; cf. Aquinas, *Commentum* (in *Sancti Thomae Aquinatis . . . Opera Omnia*, vol. 7), Dist. L, quaes. 2, art. 1, quaestiun. 2 (p. 1252).

76. Cortesi, *Liber Sententiarum*, f. 38v; cf. Aquinas, *Commentum* in *Sancti Thomae Aquinatis . . . Opera Omnia*, vol. 2), Dist. XXVI, quaes. 1, art. 2 (p. 920). Scotus opposed matrimony as a sacrament; see Harnack, *op. cit.*, vol. 6, p. 274.

77. Cortesi, *Liber Sententiarum*, ff. 43v–44r.

78. Cf. Cortesi, *De Cardinalatu*, bk. I, chap. 1, on the cardinal's virtues, and the final chapter, on beatitude.

79. See Kathleen Weil-Garris and John F. D'Amico, "The Renaissance Cardinal's Ideal Palace: A Chapter from Cortesi's *De Cardinalatu*," in *Studies in Italian Art and Architecture, 15th through 18th Centuries*, ed. Henry A. Millon (Rome: Elefante, 1980), p. 115, n. 104.

80. In the *Liber*, f. 27v, Cortesi recalled: "Sed nobis pueris praeter caeteros flagrantius homo doctus Vincentius [de Castronovo] insuper Aquinateum patrocinium suscepit, in eaque causa ducentenis sexagenis testibus usus. Contra quos maxime concurrit armata caesiorum phalanx." For the doctrine of the Immaculate Conception, see *Dictionnaire de théologie catholique*, vol. 7/1, cols. 846–1218, esp. cols. 1120–1124.

81. Cortesi, *Liber Sententiarum*, f. 28v; cf. *idem, De Cardinalatu*, ff. T 2v–3r.

82. See Cortesi, *Liber Sententiarum*, f. 37r, on holy orders: "Ex quo praeclare dux Sententiarum ait ordinis sacrum signum quoddam esse Senatus, quo spiritus imperium initiato tribuatur. Quam quidem diffinitionem Divus Thomas maxime probat, affirmans mirifice ordini consentaneam videri, quatenus scilicet Senatus sacrum dicatur. Sed in eadem curuli sella confessor Scotus negat eiusmodi sacrum spiritus imperium ad actum quempiam in Senatu nancisci. Cum quo ab Aquinatibus summa contentione pugnatur. In qua quidem re utrumvis concedi potest. . . ."

83. See *ibid.*, ff. 21r–v, for Cortesi's discussion of Adam's sin.

84. See Jerome, *De viris inlustribus*, ed. G. W. Herdin (Leipzig, 1870), p. 14.

85. This has been discussed in detail in D'Amico, "Paolo Cortesi's Rehabilitation of Giovanni Pico della Mirandola," pp. 37–51.

86. On the dispute and Pico's condemnation, see di Napoli, *Giovanni Pico della Mirandola*, chaps. 2 and 3; Henri de Lubac, *Pic de la Mirandole* (Paris: Aubier Montaigne, 1974), chap. 2; *Une controverse sur Origène à la Renaissance: Jean Pic de la Mirandole et Pierre Garcia*, ed. and trans. Henri Crouzel, S.J. (Paris: J. Vrin, 1977); and Pico, *Conclusiones sive Theses DCCCC . . . .*

87. See D'Amico, "Paolo Cortesi's Rehabilitation of Giovanni Pico della Mirandola," p. 42.

88. See Pico, *Conclusiones sive Theses DCCCC . . .* , p. 66, #13; and D'Amico "Paolo Cortesi's Rehabilitation of Giovanni Pico della Mirandola," pp. 43–44.

89. See Pico, *Conclusiones sive Theses DCCCC . . .* , p. 66, #8; and D'Amico, "Paolo Cortesi's Rehabilitation of Giovanni Pico della Mirandola," p. 44.

90. See Pico, *Conclusiones sive Theses DCCCC . . .* , p. 66, #14; and D'Amico, "Paolo Cortesi's Rehabilitation of Giovanni Pico della Mirandola," p. 44.

91. On Garcia, see A. Albareda, "Il vescovo di Barcellona, Pietro Garcia, bibliotecario della Vaticana sotto Alessandro VI," *La Bibliofilia*, 60 (1958), pp. 1–18; and D'Amico, "Paolo Cortesi's Rehabilitation of Giovanni Pico della Mirandola," pp. 44–45. The title of Garcia's work is *Petri Garsie Episcopi Ussellensis ad Sanctissimum Patrem et Dominum Innocentium Papam VIII in Determinationes Magistrales contra Conclusiones Apologales Ioannis Pici Mirandulani. . . . .* (Rome, 1489), Hain #7492.

92. See Cortesi, *Liber Sententiarum*, f. 25v; and D'Amico, "Paolo Cortesi's Rehabilitation of Giovanni Pico della Mirandola," p. 45.

93. See Pico, *Conclusiones sive Theses DCCCC . . .* , pp. 21–22. Vittorio Cian also made this point in his review of the third volume of Pastor's *Geschichte der Päpste* in *Giornale storico della letteratura italiana*, 24 (1897), p. 443.

94. See Chapter 8 below.

95. For *theologia rhetorica*, see Trinkaus, *op. cit.*, vol. 2, pp. 770–771.

96. The letters can be found in Adalbert Horawitz and Karl Hartfelder, eds., *Briefwechsel des Beatus Rhenanus* (Leipzig, 1886), pp. 57–61.

97. See John F. D'Amico, "Beatus Rhenanus and Italian Humanism," *Journal of Medieval and Renaissance Studies*, 9/2 (1979), pp. 237–260.

98. This is the opinion of Farris (*op. cit.*, p. 7).

99. Leopold von Ranke, *History of the Popes*, trans. E. Fowler, vol. 1 (rpt. 1901 ed.; New York: Ungar, 1966), p. 335, notes that Cortesi dealt with scholastic theology "in a well-written classical work, full of wit and spirit."

CHAPTER 7

1. On Castellesi, see pp. 16–19 above. The full title of the treatise is *De Vera Philosophia ex quattuor Doctoribus Ecclesiae.*

2. See the article "Fidéisme" in the *Dictionnaire de théologie catholique*, vol. 6/1, cols. 174–236.

3. On the place of astrology in Renaissance thought, see Eugenio Garin, *Lo zodiaco della vita: La polemica sull'astrologia dal Trecento al Cinquecento* (Rome: Laterza, 1976).

4. On skepticism, see Richard H. Popkin, *The History of Scepticism from Erasmus to Descartes* (New York: Harper and Row, 1964), chaps. 1 and 2, for the period considered here; Charles B. Schmitt, *Cicero Scepticus: A Study of the Influence of the Academia in the Renaissance* (The Hague: Nijhoff, 1972); *idem*, "The Recovery and Assimilation of Ancient Scepticism in the Renaissance," *Rivista di storia della filosofia*, 27/4 (1972), pp. 363–384.

5. See the general remarks of Leszek Kolakowski in "Intellectuals against Intellect," *Daedalus*, Summer 1972, pp. 1–15.

6. See Donald Weistein, *Savonarola and Florence: Prophecy and Patriotism in the Renaissance* (Princeton: Princeton University Press, 1970).

7. The general history of the Roman academies support this; see Chapter 4 above.

8. On humanist patristic studies, see August Buck, "Der Rückgriff des Renaissance-Humanismus auf die Patristik," in *Festschrift Walther von Wartburg*, ed. K. Baldinger (Tübingen: Niemeyer, 1968), vol. 1, pp. 153–175; Charles Stinger, *Humanism and the Church Fathers: Ambrogio Traversari (1386–1439) and Christian Antiquity in the Italian Reniassance* (Albany: State University of New York Press, 1977); and John F. D'Amico, "Beatus Rhenanus, Tertullian, and the Reformation: A Humanist's Critique of Scholasticism," *Archiv für Reformationsgeschichte*, 71 (1980), pp. 37–63.

9. See p. 9 above.

10. See Pio Paschini, *Tre prelati illustri del Rinascimento: Ermolao Barbaro-Adriano Castellesi-Giovanni Grimani* (Rome: Lateranum, 1957), p. 110.

11. On Giles, see John W. O'Malley, *Giles of Viterbo on Church and Reform* (Leiden: Brill, 1968); on Galatino see pp. 218–219 above.

12. There was a tradition of antirationalism among Jewish thinkers in Italy which might have been communicated to those Christians engaged in Hebrew studies, especially study of the Cabala; see Isaac E. Barzilay, *Between Reason and Faith: Anti-Rationalism in Italian Jewish Thought, 1250–1650* (The Hague: Mouton, 1967).

13. See Schmitt, *Cicero Scepticus*, for discussion.

14. For this type of skepticism, see Letizia A. Panizza, "Lorenzo Valla's *De Vero Falsoque Bono*, Lactantius, and Oratorical Scepticism," *Journal of the Warburg and Courtauld Institutes*, 41 (1978), pp. 76–107.

15. I cite from the Rome, 1514, edition. The first edition was published in Bologna in 1507; for the Rome edition see Fernanda Ascarelli, *Annali tipografici di Giacomo Mazzocchi* (Florence: Sansoni, 1961), pp. 76–78, #74. In the eighteenth century Benedetto Passionei issued a corrected edition (Rome, 1776). I have used Passionei's edition only for corroboration and references and because of its rarity have not cited it regularly. On the *De Vera Philosophia*, see Girolamo Ferri, *De rebus gestis et scriptis Hadriani Castellensis Cardinalis quo inprimis autore latinitas restituta* (Faventia, 1771), pp. xxxix–lix; Bruno Gebhardt, *Adriano von Corneto: Ein Beitrag zur Geschichte der Curie und der Renaissance* (Breslau, 1886), pp. 54–64; Paschini, *Tre prelati illustri*, pp. 114–117; and *idem*, "Teologia umanistica," *RSCI*, 11 (1957), pp. 253–255.

16. Castellesi, *De Vera Philosophia*, f. A 1v: "Cum ex inclyto tuo Angliae Regno Henrice Regum maxime Innocentio VIII Pontefice quaesture munere functus Romam rediissem, essetque tum mihi et iuveni et studiorum cupido cum doctissimis viris frequens congressus admodum animo commovebar plerosque obstinate negare sine Aristotelis doctrina quod eam vel solam philosophiam dicerent Sacram Scripturam intelligi posse, asseverarentque ipsum Aristotelem et caeteros philosophos in caelo esse, eruditissimos quosque theologos qui Aristoteli et humanis rationibus addicti non fuerint sacras litteras ignorare videremque scholas ac religiosorum conventus omnes non tam Sacrae Scripturae quam humanae philosophiae studio resonare. . . ." An Italian translation of the letter can be found in Giovanni di Napoli, "Religione e filosofia nel Rinascimento," in *Il pensiero della Rinascenza e della Riforma*, vol. 9, *Grande antologia filosofica* (Milan: Mazarotti, 1964), p. 1990.

17. Castellesi, *De Vera Philosophia*, f. A lv: "... perquirere et scrutari coepi quattuor Doctores Ecclesiae clarissima fidei nostrae lumina, quibus ipsi aut salva fide non credere aut sine suo periculo detrahere non auderent, ex quorum libris ea colligi quae ad ipsam Scripturam intelligendam et eorum comprimendam opinionem visa sunt pertinere. ..."

18. On Benetus, see Jacques Quétif and Jacques Echard, *Scriptores Ordinis Praedicatorum* ..., vol. 2 (Paris, 1771), pp. 49–50; and Angelus Walz, O.P., *Compendium Historiae Ordinis Praedicatorum* (Rome: Angelicum, 1948), pp. 451, 478.

19. See Friedrich Lauchert, *Die italienischen literarischen Gegner Luthers* (Freiburg im Breisgau: Herder, 1912), pp. 668–670, 686; and Ascarelli, *op. cit.*, pp. 58, 64.

20. Castellesi was a cardinal-protector of the Dominicans; see Stephen L. Forte, O.P., *The Cardinal Protectors of the Dominican Order* (Rome: S. Sabina, 1959), p. 67. Hieronymus Armenius, O.P., dedicated his exposition of Psalm 109 to Castellesi; see BAV, Vat. Lat. 3899, ff. 93r–97v.

21. While neither man makes any claim on this matter, it is a logical supposition.

22. Castellesi, *De Vera Philosophia*, ff. A 2r–v.

23. *Ibid.*, f. A 2v. Benetus also mentioned that Bishop Albertus Vilnensis was among those who requested a second edition.

24. See p. 18 above.

25. See pp. 17–18 above.

26. On Renaissance Augustinianism, see Paul Oskar Kristeller, "Augustine and the Early Renaissance," *Studies in Renaissance Thought and Letters* (Rome: Edizioni di storia e letteratura, 1969), pp. 355–372; Pietro Paolo Gerosa, *Umanesimo cristiano del Petrarca: Influenza agostiniana-attinenze medievali* (Turin: Bottega d'Erasmo, 1966); Charles Béné, *Erasme et Saint Augustin sur l'humanisme d'Erasme* (Geneva: Droz, 1969); William J. Bouwsma, "The Two Faces of Humanism: Stoicism and Augustinianism in Renaissance Thought," in *Itinerarium Italicum*, ed. Heiko A. Oberman and Thomas A. Brady, Jr. (Leiden: Brill, 1975), pp. 3–60. The title *De Vera Philosophia* is Augustinian.

27. I cannot offer here a full bibliography of Augustinian philosophy, but for a few references, see Ronald H. Nash, *The Light of the Mind: St. Augustine's Theory of Knowledge* (Lexington: The University Press of Kentucky, 1969); Robert E. Cushman, "Faith and Reason in the Thought of St. Augustine," *Church History*, 19 (1951), pp. 271–294; John Heil, "Augustine's Attack on Scepticism: The *Contra Academicos*," *Harvard Theological Review*, 65/1 (1972), pp. 99–116; Elaine Limbrich, "Montaigne et Saint Augustin," *Bibliothèque d'Humanisme et Renaissance*, 34 (1972), pp. 49–64; Frederick Van Fleteren, O.S.A., "Authority and Reason, Faith, and Understanding in the Thought of St. Augustine," *Augustinian Studies*, 4 (1973), pp. 33–71. See also the general study by Etienne Gilson, *The Christian Philosophy of St. Augustine* (New York: Random House, 1960); and the essays in Markus, ed., *Augustine: A Collection of Critical Essays* (Garden City, N.Y.: Doubleday, 1972). For Augustine's attitude toward pagan culture, see Harald Hagendahl, *Augustine and the Latin Classics* (Göteborg: Elanders Boktryckeri Aktidbolag, 1967).

28. Castellesi, *De Vera Philosophia*, f. A 1r, from Augustine's *De Doctrina Christiana*, bk. II, chap. 7, par. 9; text can be found in Migne, *Patrologia Latina*

(hereafter cited as *PL*) (Paris, 1844-1899), vol. 34, col. 39. I provide the appropriate citation to Migne whenever possible.

29. Castellesi, *De Vera Philosophia*, f. A 4r; Augustine, *Quaestiones LXXXIII*, quaest. 48 (*PL*, vol. 40, col. 21).

30. Castellesi, *De Vera Philosophia*, ff. B 5v-6r; Pseudo-Augustine, *De cognitione verae vitae*, chap. 4 (*PL*, vol. 40, col. 1009).

31. Castellesi, *De Vera Philosophia*, f. B 8r. Castellesi cited from Ambrose, *De virginitate* (which he misidentifies as *De viduis*), chap. 14 (*PL*, vol. 16, col. 289); and from Augustine, *Epistula CXVIII*, chap. 5, no. 2 (*PL*, vol. 33, col. 448).

32. Castellesi, *De Vera Philosophia*, f. C 2r: "Catholica ecclesia per orbem difusa, tribus modis probatur existere; quicquid in ea tenetur aut auctoritas est Scripturarum, aut traditio universalis, aut certe propria et particularis instructio, sed auctoritate tota constringitur." Castellesi attributed this to Augustine, *De Fide Catholica*, but in his edition (Rome, 1776), p. 40, Passionei noted that it is not found in Augustine's writings.

33. Castellesi, *De Vera Philosophia*, f. C 2r: "[Ego vero] Evangelio non crederem, nisi me auctoritas catholicae ecclesiae commoneret." Castellesi mistakenly attributed this to Augustine, *De Doctrina Christina*, but it is from Augustine, *Liber contra Epistolam Manichei, quam vocant Fundamenti*, chap. 5, par. 6 (*PL*, vol. 42, col. 176).

34. See Robert J. O'Connell, S.J., "Action and Contemplation," in *Augustine: A Collection of Critical Essays*, ed. Markus, pp. 38-58.

35. Castellesi, *De Vera Philosophia*, f. C 4v; Augustine, *De utilitate credendi*, chap. 16, par. 34 (*PL*, vol. 42, cols. 89-90).

36. Castellesi, *De Vera Philosophia*, f. C 5r; Castellesi wrongly cited Gregory the Great's *Commentarium super Ezechielem*, but he actually quoted from Augustine's *De Trinitate*, bk. I, chap. 8, par. 17 (*PL*, vol. 42, col. 832); and bk. VII, chap. 4, par. 6, (*PL*, vol. 42, col. 95).

37. Castellesi, *De Vera Philosophia*, f. C 6v-7r; Augustine, *Quaestiones LXXXIII*, quaes. 46, par. 2 (*PL*, vol. 40, cols. 30-31). For Augustine's Neo-Platonism, see John J. O'Meara, "Augustine and Neo-Platonism," *Recherches Augustiniennes*, 1 (1958), pp. 91-111; and A. H. Armstrong, "St. Augustine and Christian Platonism," in *Augustine: A Collection of Critical Essays*, ed. Markus, pp. 3-37.

38. Castellesi, *De Vera Philosophia*, f. C 7r; Augustine, *De Trinitate*, bk. I, chap. 2, par. 4 (*PL*, vol. 42, col. 822). See also Castellesi, *De Vera Philosophia*, f. C 8r; Ambrose, *Praefat. in Psalmum XLVI 'Deus refugium et virtus'* (*PL*, vol. 14, col. 1136).

39. Castellesi, *De Vera Philosophia*, f. D 1r: "Ordo autem recte progrediendi describitur per ipsum Augustinum *De Trinitate* cum dicit: '[Et] certe cum inconcusse crediderint Scripturis Sanctis [tanquam veracissimis testibus], agant orando [et] quaerendo et bene vivendo ut intelligant.' Sed quid oranti, quid legenti contingat, Ambrosius *De Officiis* describit, dicens: 'Christum alloquimur, cum oramus, sed illum audimus, nobis loquentem cum oracula divina legimus.' Sed quae sint legenda ostendit Hieronymus *Super Quaestione X, de verbis Apostoli*, dicens: 'Elementis veteris testamenti, ut ad Evangelicam plenitudinem veniat sancti viri eruditur infantia, unde centesimus decimus octavus Psalm., et omnes alii qui litteris praenotantur, per ethicam nos ducunt ad theologicam [theoricam in *PL*], et ab elementis occidentis litterae quae destruitur transire faciunt ad spiritum vivificantem.'" Augustine, *De Trinitate*, bk. XV, chap. 27, par. 49 (*PL*, vol. 42, col. 1096);

Ambrose, *De officiis ministrorum*, bk. I, chap. 20 (*PL*, vol. 16, col. 50); Jerome, *Epistola ad Algasiam*, Ep. CXXI (*PL*, vol. 22, col. 1035).

40. Castellesi, *De Vera Philosophia*, f. D 2r; possibly quoting Pseudo-Augustine, *Liber exhortationis, vulgo De salutaribus documentis ad quemdam comitem*, chap. 28 (*PL*, vol. 40, col. 1047). See also Castellesi, *De Vera Philosophia*, f. D 2r; Jerome, *Epistola ad rusticum monachum*, Ep. CXXV (*PL*, vol. 22, cols. 1075–1085).

41. Castellesi, *De Vera Philosophia*, f. D 5r; Gregory the Great, *Homilias XL in Ezechielem*, Hom. I, chap. X, par. 4 (*PL*, vol. 22, col. 1878); Jerome, *Epistula LV* (*PL* vol. 22, cols. 560–565).

42. Castellesi, *De Vera Philosophia*, f. D 6r; Pseudo-Augustine, *Scala Paradisi*, chap. 10 (*PL*, vol. 40, col. 1002).

43. Castellesi, *De Vera Philosophia*, f. D 6r-v; Pseudo-Augustine, *Scala Paradisi*, chap. 10 (*PL*, vol. 40, col. 1002).

44. Castellesi, *De Vera Philosophia*, f. D 8r; Augustine, *De Doctrina Christiana*, bk. III, chap. 2, par. 2 (*PL*, vol. 34, cols. 65–66).

45. Castellesi, *De Vera Philosophia*, f. D 8v; Augustine, *De Genesi ad litteram*, bk. I, chap. 21, par. 41 (*PL*, vol. 34, col. 262).

46. Castellesi, *De Vera Philosophia*, ff. E 3v-4r; Augustine, *De Doctrina Christiana*, bk. III, chap. 28, par. 39 (*PL*, vol. 34, col. 80).

47. Castellesi, *De Vera Philosophia*, f. E 5r: "Patet ergo quod neque in obscuris, neque in apertis divinarum Scriptuarum locis humana coniectura aut opinio quae mundi philosophia est, aliquid temere diffinire debet, sed his omnibus revelationem necessariam esse ostendit."

48. *Ibid.*, ff. F 1v-25; Augustine, *Sermo 354, ad continentes alias 53*, chap. 6, par. 6 (*PL*, vol. 39, col. 1566).

49. Castellesi, *De Vera Philosophia*, ff. F 7r-8r; Jerome, *Epistula LXXXII*, (*PL*, vol. 22, col. 739); Ambrose, *Hexameron*, bk. II, chap. 1, par. 3 (*PL*, vol. 14, col. 145); and *idem*, *Super Psalmum XLIII* (*PL*, vol. 14, col. 1123).

50. Castellesi, *De Vera Philosophia*, f. G 1r: "Dialectici, quorum Aristoteles princeps est, solent argumentationum retia tendere, et vagam rhetoricae libertatem in syllogismorum spineta concludere." Jerome, *Commentariorum in Epistolam Titum*, chap. 3 (*PL*, vol. 26, col. 631).

51. Castellesi, *De Vera Philosophia*, f. G 1v; Ambrose, *De Incarnationis Domini Sacramento*, chap. 9, pars. 89–90 (*PL*, vol. 16, col. 840).

52. Castellesi, *De Vera Philosophia*, f. G 2r; Jerome, *Commentarium in Esaiam*, bk. III, chap. 7, par. 1 (*PL*, vol. 24, col. 102).

53. Castellesi, *De Vera Philosophia*, f. G 2v: "Sed videre etiam licet quam parum ad Sacram Scripturam rhetoricam artem hi quattuor doctores, fidei nostrae lumina, putaverint pertinere; et primo quid eloquentissimus Hieronymus senserit in Epistola ad Iulianum in qua dicit: 'Nos leporem artis rhetoricae contemnentes, et puerilis atque plausibilis eloquii venustatem, ad Sanctarum Scripturarum gravitatem confugimus.'" Jerome, *Epistula CXVIII, alias ad Juliam* (*PL*, vol. 22, col. 961).

54. Castellesi, *De Vera Philosophia*, f. G 4v; Augustine, *De Doctrina Christiana*, bk. IV, chap. 6, par. 10 (*PL*, vol. 34, col. 93).

55. Castellesi, *De Vera Philosophia*, f. G 5v: "Astrologia, et geometria, et alia huiusmodi ideo despecta sunt a nostris, quia nihil ad salutem pertinent, sed magis mittunt in errorem, et a Deo avocant." This citation is not from Augustine, as

Passionei in his edition, p. 155, n. 4, noted; Passionei suggested Augustine's *De ordine disciplinae*, bk. II, chap. 15 (*PL*, vol. 32, cols. 1014-1015).

56. Castellesi, *De Vera Philosophia*, f. G 7r; Augustine, *Confessionum Lib.V*, chap. 5, par. 9 (*PL*, vol. 32, col. 709).

57. Castellesi, *De Vera Philosophia*, f. H 1v; Augustine, *Epistula CX, alias CXXXI ad Memorium*, par. 2, (*PL*, vol. 33, col. 368).

58. Castellesi, *De Vera Philosophia*, ff. H 3r-v and 6r; Pseudo-Ambrose, *De vocatione omnium gentium*, bk. I, chap. 3 (*PL*, vol. 17, col. 1078).

59. Castellesi, *De Vera Philosophia*, f. H 2v: "Haec tortuosa argumentatio est, an ecclesiasticam simplicitatem inter philosophorum spineta concludemus? Quid Aristoteli et Paulo? quid Platoni et Petro?" Jerome, *Dialogus contra Pelagianos*, bk. I, par. 14 (*PL*, vol. 23, col. 539). See also Castellesi, *De Vera Philosophia*, f. H 4r; Jerome, *Epistula XIV, ad Helidorum*, par. 11 (*PL*, vol. 22, col. 354). Pythagoras is condemned on f. H 4r of Castellesi's *De Vera Philosophia;* Epicurus and the Stoics, on f. H 5r.

60. A side note on f. H 4r of Castellesi's *De Vera Philosophia* reads: "Platonem, Aristotelem et alios philosophos esse in inferno cum diabolo."

61. Castellesi, *De Vera Philosophia*, ff. I 6r-v; Augustine, *De Doctrina Christiana*, bk. I, chaps. 40-42 (*PL*, vol. 34, cols. 53-65).

62. A side note on ff. I 8v-9r of Castellesi's *De Verum Philosophia* reads: "Philosophos Patriarchas fuisse haereticorum." The text reads "Pulchre quidam nostrum ait: 'Philosophi Patriarchae haereticorum, Ecclesiae puritatem perversa maculavere doctrina.'" Jerome, *Epistula CXXXIII, ad Ctesiphontem*, par. 2 (*PL*, vol. 22, col. 1118).

63. Castellesi, *De Vera Philosophia*, f. K 2r; Augustine, *De Civitate Dei*, VIII, chap. 1 (*PL*, vol. 41, cols. 224-225). See also Castellesi, *De Vera Philosophia*, f. K 3r, probably paraphrasing Augustine, *De Civitate Dei*, bk. XXII, chap. 22 (*PL*, vol. 41, cols. 784-785).

64. Castellesi, *De Vera Philosophia*, ff. K 4r-8v; cf. *ibid.*, f. K 4r: "Et quae omnia cum ita sint recte Sacrae Scripturae auctoritas cum doctrina, tum veritate atque simplicitate super omnia laudatur, de quibus laudibus aliqua subnectemus."

65. Castellesi, *De Vera Philosophia*, f. K 4v; Ambrose, *Hexameron*, bk. III, chap. 6, par. 50 (*PL*, vol. 14, cols. 166-169).

66. Castellesi, *De Vera Philosophia*, ff. K 6r-v; excerpts from Augustine, *Sermo XXXXVIII, ad Fratres in Eremo* (*PL*, vol. 40, cols. 1304-1306), according to Passionei (p. 232, n. 7).

67. Castellesi, *De Vera Philosophia*, f. K 8r: "Et Augustinus in *Epistola ad Volusianum*, 'Quae mens avida aeternitatis, vitaeque praesentis brevitate permota, contra divinae auctoritatis culmen lumenque contendat? Quae disputationes, quae litterae quorumlibet philosophorum, quae leges quarumlibet civitatum duobus praeceptis, ex quibus Christus dicit totam legem, prophetasque pendere, ullo modo sunt comparandae? "Diliges Dominum Deum tuum ex toto corde tuo, et ex tota anima tua, et ex tota mente tua, et proximum tuum tanquam te ipsum" [Matthew 22: 37, 39]. Hic physica, quoniam omnes omnium naturarum causae in Deo creatore sunt; hic ethica, quoniam vita bona et honesta non aliunde formatur, quam cum ea quae diligenda sunt, quemadmodum diligenda sunt, diliguntur, hic est Deus et proximus; hic logica, quoniam veritas lumenque animae rationalis, nonnisi Deus est.'" Augustine, *Epistula CXXXVII*, chap. 4, pars. 16-17 (*PL*, vol. 33, col. 524).

68. For an example of the medieval Augustinian reaction to elements in Scho-

lasticism, see Gordon Leff, *Brandwardine and the Pelagians* (Cambridge: At the University Press, 1957).

69. See Popkin, *op. cit.*

70. For Pico's treatise, see the edition in *Johannis Francisci Pici Mirandulae Opera quae extant Omnia . . .*, vol. 2 (Basel, 1601); see Charles B. Schmitt, *Gianfrancesco Pico della Mirandola (1469–1533) and His Critique of Aristotle* (The Hague: Nijhoff, 1967).

71. For the relations between Savonarola and Gianfrancesco Pico's uncle, see Paolo Rocca, *Giovanni Pico della Mirandola nei suoi rapporti di amicizia con Gerolamo Savonarola* (Ferrara: Universita degli Studi, 1964).

72. See Schmitt, *Gianfrancesco Pico*, for the *Examen Vanitatum*.

73. *Johannis Francisci Pici . . . Opera*, f. AA 1r.

74. *Ibid.*, f. AA 2r.

75. *Ibid.*, f. AA 3r.

76. *Ibid.*, f. AA 5r.

77. *Ibid.*, f. BB 1r.

78. *Ibid.*, f. CC 2v.

79. See Jacopo Sadoleto, *Elogio della Sapienza (De laudibus philosophiae)*, ed. Antonio Altamura and Giuseppe Toffanin (Naples: Pironti, 1950).

80. *Ibid.*, p. 26.

81. *Ibid.*, p. 65.

82. *Ibid.*, p. 67–75.

83. The full title is *B. Pauli Justiniani et Petri Quirini Eremitarum Camaldulensium Libellus ad Leonem X Pontificem Maximum;* it is available in *Annales Camaldulenses Ordinis Sancti Benedicti*, ed. J. B. Mittarelli and A. Costadoni (Venice, 1773), cols. 612–719.

84. See Felix Gilbert, "Cristianismo, umanesimo e a bolla 'Apostolici Regiminis' del 1513" *Rivista storica italiana*, 79 (1967), pp. 976–990.

85. See Gebhardt, *op. cit.*, pp. 74–80; and Ludwig von Pastor, *History of the Popes*, ed. and trans. F. I. Antrobus *et al.* (London/St. Louis: Herder, 1891–1910), vol. 5, pp. 143–146. Cf. Paschini, *Tre illustri prelati*, pp. 114–117; and Delio Cantimori, *Erectici italiani del Cinquecento* (Florence: Sansoni, 1967), pp. 8–10.

86. See Georg Ellinger, *Italien und der deutsche Humanismus in der neulateinischen Lyrik*, vol. 1 (Berlin: Gruyter, 1929), pp. 111–112.

87. Outside Italy, Castellesi became something of an authority on the question of the relationship between faith and reason. In *Probatissimorum Ecclesiae doctorum sententiae, qui non detrahunt quidem ethnicorum philosophiae, sed eam prorsus vituperant, abiiciunt, despiciunt ut Christiani hominis studio indignissimam impiamque et pestilentem* (n.p., n.d.), Castellesi is cited with Church Fathers, Scholastics (including Aquinas), and contemporaries (e.g., Gianfrancesco Pico) as one who maintained the correct balance between Sacred Scripture and philosophy. For Castellesi's letter to Henry VII, see *ibid.*, f. C 2r.

CHAPTER 8

1. For biographical details on Maffei, see pp. 82–85 above.

2. On the *Commentaria Urbana*, see p. 84 above. Throughout this chapter, I cite from the first edition (Rome, 1506).

3. *Commentaria Urbana*, f. 3r.

4. *Ibid.*, f. 140r.

5. See pp. 83–85 above for Maffei's concern for his family.

6. For a list of Italian patristic scholars, see Paul Oskar Kristeller, "Erasmus from an Italian Perspective," *Renaissance Quarterly*, 23/1 (1970), pp. 1–14, at pp. 8–9.

7. On Basil, see *Dictionnaire de théologie catholique*, vol. 2/1, cols. 441–459. For the element of Basil's thought which will most interest us, see Werner Jaeger, *Early Christianity and Greek Paideia* (Cambridge, Mass.: Belknap Press, 1961); L. V. Jacks, *St. Basil and Greek Literature* (Washington, D.C.: Catholic University of America Press, 1939); and John Ferguson, *Clement of Alexandria* (New York: Twayne, 1974).

8. See Luzi Schucan, *Das Nachleben von Basilius Magnus 'ad adolescentes': Ein Beitrag zur Geschichte des christlichen Humanismus* (Geneva: Droz, 1973).

9. See BAV, Barb. Lat. 2517, f. 12r; see also Vittorio Branca and Manlio Pastore Stocchi, "La Biblioteca Vaticana nella seconda centuria del Miscellanea di Angelo Poliziano," in *Mélanges Eugène Tisserant*, vol. 4, Studi e Testi #236 (Vatican City: Biblioteca Apostolica Vaticana, 1964), pp. 141–159, at p. 147.

10. See BAV, Barb. Lat. 2517, f. 37r; also Branca and Stocchi, *op. cit.*, p. 148, n. 19.

11. See Maria Bertola, ed., *I due primi registri di prestito della Biblioteca Apostolica Vaticana: Codici Vaticani Latini 3964, 3966* (Vatican City: Biblioteca Apostolica Vaticana, 1942), pp. 106–107. For the sketch see *Commentaria Urbana*, f. 256. In his *De Honesta Disciplina* (Rome: Bocca, 1955), pp. 178–179, Maffei's contemporary Pietro Crinito composed a chapter entitled "De ingenio et eruditione Gregorii Nazianzeni et Basilii, et quo affectu ac studio simul ab humanis litteris ad sacras et divinas concesserint."

12. Raffaele Maffei, trans., *Opera Magni Basilii, per Raphaelem Volaterranum nuper in latinum conversa* (Rome: Mazzocchi, 1515); see Fernanda Ascarelli, *Annali tipografici di Giacomo Mazzocchi* (Florence: Sansoni, 1961), pp. 91–92. Schucan, *op. cit.*, pp. 123–124, confuses Maffei with Raffaele Regio; on this error, see Luigi Peschetti, "Raffaele Regio non 'Volaterranus,'" *Rassegna volterrana*, 20 (1952), pp. 1–5. See the introduction to Basil's *Opera omnia* in *Patrologica Graeca*, vol. 29 (Paris, 1857), pp. ccxlvii–vii, ccl, cclv, and cclxii, for printing information that indicates the popularity of Maffei's translations. Maffei's translations were used by the circle around Lefèvre d'Etaples; see Eugene F. Rice, Jr., *The Prefatory Epistles of Jacques Lefèvre d'Etaples and Related Texts* (New York: Columbia University Press, 1972), pp. 186–187, 244, 366, 420.

13. Maffei, *Opera Magni Basilii*, f. A 1v.

14. *Ibid.*: "Ubi nihil antiquius habui quam quem prius laudabam lectitabamque ethicorum decimum vitae institutione ac animi exercitatione complecti. Verum quoniam is demum indicis potius quam doctoris eorum quae agenda meditandaque forent partes haberet, ad sacra volumina confugi."

15. *Ibid.*: "Quamobrem plura me in hoc genere cogitantem ad convertendos demum magni Basilii sermones tanta cum cupiditate incensus ut non toto vertente anno rem prorsus absolveram. Res in his variae ut ipse facile perpendes et stilo patrio id est asiatico exuberantique conscriptae."

16. *Ibid.* Desiderius Erasmus criticized Maffei's translations of Basil; see his 1532 letter of dedication to Jacopo Sadoleto in his own translations of Basil,

Opus Epistolarum Des. Erasmi Roterdami, ed. P. S. Allen (Oxford: Clarendon Press, 1934), vol. 9, #2611, pp. 435-440. Benedetto Falconcini, *Vita del nobil' uomo e buon servo di Dio Raffaele Maffei detto il Volterrano* (Rome, 1722), pp. 151 ff., compared Maffei's and Basil's lives. For Erasmus and Basil, see G. Chantraine, S.J., "Erasme et Saint Basile," *Irenikon,* 54/4 (1974), pp. 451-493.

17. See Eugenio Garin, "Alessandro d'Alessandro e Raffaele de Volterra," *Rinascimento,* 1 (1950), pp. 102-103.

18. On these translations, see pp. 84-85 above.

19. See Raffaele Maffei, *De Institutione Christiana* (Rome, 1518), ff. 0 5v and M 6v; bk. 1, chap. 14, and bk. 5, chaps. 42 and 43; and *idem, Stromata,* BAV, Barb. Lat. 753, ff. 42r, 70v, and 87r. Maffei also translated Gregory of Nazianzus' life of Basil; see Sister Agnes Clare Way, "S. Gregorius Nazianzenus," in *Catalogus Translationum et Commentariorum,* ed. P. O. Kristeller *et al.,* vol. 2 (Washington, D.C.: Catholic University of America Press, 1971), p. 144.

20. Raffaele Maffei, trans., *Raphaelis Volaterrani De Institutione Christiana ad Leonem X Ponti. Max. libri octo. Eiusdem De Prima Philosophia ad Marium fratrem liber unus; de dormitione Beatae Mariae Virginis sermones duo Ioannis Damasceni et unus Andreae Hierosolimitani e greco in latinum per R. conversi* (Rome, 1518). See Pio Paschini, "Teologia umanistica," *RSCI,* 11 (1957), pp. 253-255.

21. On Lactantius, see *Dictionnaire de théologie catholique,* vol. 8/2, cols. 2425-2444.

22. Maffei, *De Institutione Christiana,* dedicatory letter, no foliation: "Alios alia tenet animos contemplatio, ego vero semper eam potissimam censui quae sanctorum librorum eruditionem, gerendorum omnium viam, finem denique quem tantopere spectamus hominibus ostenderet."

23. *Ibid.*: "Meum autem imprimis opus, huius artis procerum arculas et myrobrechia quantum meae tenuitati fas erit excutere, eosque veluti palantes per arua milites ad unam aciem cogere, simulque et ordine et stilo alio interpolare, denique novae aliquid veterum partibus foeturae adicere sum conatus."

24. *Ibid.*: "Aquinate nihilominus ut antesignano caeteris praelato. Is enim primus morem in utramque partem disserendi post Socraticos illos seculis renovavit, ac dogmati christiano corroborando coniunxit, tantaque in hac facultate dicendi copia pollet, ita in disputando vehemens, in distinguendo luculentus, in inveniendo locuples apparet, ut suorum temporum ac post eum succedentium princeps haberi sine controversia possit."

25. This is evidenced by the *De Prima Philosophia.* The *De Prima Philosophia,* a standard discussion of metaphysical topics dealing with being *qua* being, depends on Scotus. On Scotus in the Renaissance, see pp. 161-163 above.

26. See Paul Oskar Kristeller, *Le Thomisme et la pensée italienne de la Renaissance* (Montreal: Institut d'Etudes Medievales, 1967); and *idem, Medieval Aspects of Renaissance Learning: Three Essays,* ed. and trans. Edward P. Mahoney (Durham, N.C.: Duke University Press, 1974). See also Ardis B. Collins, *The Secular is Sacred: Platonism and Thomism in Marsilio Ficino's Platonic Theology* (The Hague: Nijhoff, 1974).

27. Cf. Maffei, *De Institutione Christiana,* bk. 2, chaps. 1-8, and Aquinas, *Summa Theologiae,* Ia. 50-64.

28. Maffei, *De Institutione Christiana,* ff. 22r, 23r-v.

29. Maffei, *Stromata,* BAV, Barb. Lat. 753, f. 18v.

30. See *Patrologia Graeca*, vol. 8 (Paris, 1860), pp. 15-16. Maffei knew of Clement's writings, including the *Stromateis;* see Maffei, *Commentaria Urbana,* f. 203r. For Clement's *fortuna*, see Walter H. Wagner, "A Father's Fate: Attitudes toward and Interpretations of Clement of Alexandria," *Journal of Religious History*, 6/3 (1971), pp. 209-231.

31. For Clement and the *Stromateis*, see *Dictionnaire de théologie catholique*, vol. 3/1, cols. 137-199; E. F. Osborn, *The Philosophy of Clement of Alexandria* (Cambridge: At the University Press, 1957); and Henry Chadwick, *Early Christian Thought and the Classical Tradition* (New York: Oxford University Press, 1964).

32. See Angelo Poliziano, *Miscellaneorum Centuria Secunda*, ed. Vittore Branca and Manlio Pastore Stocchi (Florence: Olschki, 1978), index for Clement. For Crinito, see his *De Honesta Disciplina* (Rome: Bocca, 1956).

33. Maffei, *Stromata*, BAV, Barb. Lat. 753, f. 225v: "Quemadmodum in fide catholica in qua omnes pariter boni ac fideles eodem pariter spiritu concurrunt, ad unum Deum et omnium patrem complectendum, verum aliis alia saepe via et modus alius excogitatur, ut cuique ex natura, ex humoribus, ex fortuna, ex gratia simul plus minusque vivatur. Itemque in doctrinis saepe optimorum doctorum diversae sint [?], omnium tamen ad unum bonum pariter et verum vestigandum concurrentur. Quod et sanctissimos viros et ipsos apostolos evenisse interdum legimus." The text seems defective here.

34. *Ibid.*, f. 181v.

35. *Ibid.*, f. 182v.

36. Maffei, *De Institutione Christiana*, ff. 14r-15r.

37. *Ibid.*, f. 22r.

38. *Ibid.*, ff. 23v-24r.

39. *Ibid.*, f. 73r.

40. *Ibid.*, f. 18r.

41. *Ibid.*, f. 52v.

42. Maffei, *Stromata*, BAV, Barb. Lat. 753, f. 25v.

43. *Ibid.*, f. 12r.

44. Maffei, *De Institutione Christiana*, f. 65r.

45. *Ibid.*, ff. 34v-35r.

46. *Ibid.*, f. 48r; cf. Maffei, *Stromata*, BAV, Barb. Lat. 753, f. 41r.

47. Maffei, *De Institutione Christiana*, f. 66r; cf. *idem*, *Stromata*, BAV, Barb. Lat. 753, f. 212r.

48. Maffei, *De Institutione Christiana*, f. 83r: "Dyalecticae captionibus quid opus viro christiano, cui per sophismata dogma nostrum probare nisi qua [*sic*] his adversarios interdum refellimus omnino supervacuum."

49. Maffei, *Stromata*, BAV, Barb. Lat. 753, ff. 113r-v.

50. Maffei, *De Institutione Christiana*, f. 103r.

51. *Ibid.*, f. 48r.

52. *Ibid.*, f. 52v.

53. Maffei, *Stromata*, BAV, Barb. Lat. 753, f. 111r: "Quot sectae ad hunc usque diem vigent quis non videt minorem prae illis nostram esse portionem? Cui dicerem 'Nolite timere pusillus grex, complacuit enim patri dare vobis regnum.' Sectas autem iam inde [ab] apostolorum tempore statim cepisse Pauli epistola satis ostendit ubi ait 'Ego sum Apollo, ego Pauli'.... [After criticizing the religious orders, he continues:] Et ut quondam ab his exordio 'Ego sum Apollo, Ego Pauli' contendentes dictitabant, sic item hodieque 'Ego Thomista, ego Scotista, ego

meorum qualiscunque, tu tuorum opinionis adsertor'. Venenum profecto pestilens ambitionis loco religionis ad convivium hoc sacrum adducunt; dum nonnulli de fama ingenii magis quam de rei veritate sollicitantur."

54. *Ibid.*, f. 117r: "Primum sese ac proprias animas scotizant, id est tenebrant, id enim latine dicerem, quum se alios inlustrare dicant. Deinde ad perfectam theologiae cognitionem, aut degustationem tales nunquam veniunt, quum ille [*sic*] potius metaphysici quam perfecti theologi partes habeant. Tertio ut usu videmus ex auditoribus tales raro fructum referunt desideratum. Postremo contentiones maximas atque sectas fidelibus praesertim theologorum excitant scholis. Nam religiosorum dissidia longasque sine fructu saepe disertationes et insuper et seditiones et tumultus ex huiuscemodi provenire causa dum sui quisque magistri cui sit addictus sententiam praeferre cupit conspicere licet."

55. In the *Commentaria Urbana*, f. 275r, Maffei related the disputations of the religious orders to the advent of humanistic studies in the tre- and quattrocento.

56. Maffei, *Stromata*, BAV, Barb. Lat. 753, f. 26v; cf. Cortesi's evaluation of Pico, pp. 163-165 above.

57. The tract is published in Kristeller, *Le Thomisme et la pensée italienne de la Renaissance*, pp. 137-184. On the treatise, see Aquinas Sullivan, O.C.D., "A Contribution to the History of Intellectual Freedom: The 'Opus Aureum in Thomistas' of Blessed Baptista Mantuanus, O. Carm. (1447-1516)," in *De Doctrina Ioannis Scoti: Acta Congressus Internationalis*, vol. 4 (Rome, 1968), pp. 155-169; and Romano Rosa, "Tomismo e Antitomismo in Battista Spagnoli Mantovano (1447-1516)," *Memorie domenicane*, n.s. 7 (1976), pp. 227-264.

58. Maffei, *De Institutione Christiana*, f. R 4v.

59. Maffei, *Stromata*, BAV, Barb. Lat. 753, f. 113v: "Tantum [*sic*] eloquentiae studia ea sunt natura ut magis in delectatione quam utilitate versentur. Ex quo in his verborum cultus et orationis apta dispositio et inventionis decor plus quam rei aut materiae sustantia [*sic*] tenent aures quae pars quum longe ab eis deficiat antiquis totam sibi hanc laudem vindicantibus, non in eodem similiter habetur pretio, nisi forte et haec ea contineat quae sint operae pretium audire aut legere."

60. *Ibid.*, ff. 184v-185r.

61. Maffei, *De Institutione Christiana*, f. 82v. In the *Stromata*, BAV, Barb. Lat. 753, f. 113r, Maffei lamented that those who studied only for the purpose of showing off their talents were common throughout Italy.

62. Maffei, *Stromata*, BAV, Barb. Lat. 753, f. 114r.

63. Maffei's *De origine urbis*, in Vergilian hexameters, is discussed in Roberto Weiss, *The Renaissance Discovery of Classical Antiquity* (New York: Humanities Press, 1969), pp. 83-84.

64. See John F. D'Amico, "A Humanist Response to Martin Luther: Raffaele Maffei's *Apologeticus*," *Sixteenth Century Journal*, 6/2 (1975), pp. 37-56; and *idem*, "Papal History and Curial Reform in the Renaissance: Raffaele Maffei's *Breuis Historia* of Julius II and Leo X," *Archivum Historiae Pontificiae*, vol. 18 (1980), pp. 157-210.

65. Maffei, *Stromata*, BAV, Barb. Lat. 753, f. 23v.

66. *Ibid.*, f. 24v.

67. Maffei complained of Paolo Cortesi's use of "Apuleian" Latin in his introductory letter to the *De Cardinalatu* (1510), and in two letters: BAV, Bar. Lat. 2517, ff. 11v-12r. Maffei also condemned Apuleius in the *Stromata* (BAV, Barb. Lat. 753, f. 113v).

68. Maffei, *Stromata*, BAV, Barb. Lat. 753, f. 24r: "Cavenda rursus profana quaedam quamvis latina, ut divus pro sancto, concinnator sive orator pro praedicatore, quod ego in scriptis meis si quando per inconsiderantiam posuerim libenter retractaverim. Mirorque sane id a quibusdam gravibus religiossimisque plane viris inter quos Beatus Jacobus Picens ut ego manu illius vidi conscriptum minime observatum. Praeterea pro passione sive morte Domini nostri quidam magis latine minus tamen religiose supplicium dicunt, hoc enim sontibus [?] potius convenire videtur." On Jacopo, see Dionysius Lasci, O.F.M., *De vita et operibus s. Iacobi de Marchia* (Falconara M. [Ancona]: Biblioteca francesca, 1974). Maffei had been favorable to the Franciscan in the *Commentaria Urbana,* f. 293r.

69. Maffei, *Stromata*, BAV, Barb. Lat. 753, f. 110v: "Adeo ut qui nunc hanc videndi [*sic*] formulam Romanae praesertim Curiae totque in tambulonum et supervacuorum et neutilum [?] hominum inanes ventres ex illorum fructibus pasci et insignia gentilitia pro christianis anteferri totque faleros [*sic*] ornatas mulas contra Deum et fidem esse praedicaret, non sane audiretur proque Arretico [*sic*] ac a dogmate catholico descinente [*sic*] taxaretur."

70. Maffei, *De Institutione Christiana*, f. 83r: "Plus igitur Apostoli nudo sermone sine verborum apparatu ac dialecticorum acumine seu tragica vocis facilitate quam schola omnis [*sic*] phylosophorum omnesve Indorum aut Aegyptiorum sapientes prophetaeque persuadere potuerunt."

71. See pp. 224–225 above.

72. Maffei, *De Institutione Christiana*, f. 79r.

73. *Ibid.*, f. 74r.

74. Maffei, *Stromata*, BAV, Barb. Lat. 753, f. 69v.

75. Maffei, *De Institutione Christiana*, f. 52v: "Oris enim confessio fit ad salutem ait Paulus. Cicero item in oratione sit medicina peccati confessio."

76. *Ibid.*, f. 9v: ". . . nec propterea dogmati adversum nostro fallitur."

77. Maffei, *Stromata*, BAV, Barb. Lat. 753, ff. 46r and 106v–107r; and *idem, De Institutione Christiana*, f. 79v.

78. Maffei, *Stromata*, BAV, Barb. Lat. 753, ff. 41r, 97r-v, and 294r.

79. *Ibid.*, f. 116v.

80. *Ibid.*, ff. 116v–117r. One should not overemphasize these attacks on Plato. Even in Rome, Platonism and its chief Renaissance exponent, Ficino, had many friends. Although Maffei did not expand on the topic, he also rejected the use of the Talmud and the Cabala in interpreting Scripture; see Maffei, *De Institutione Christiana*, ff. 81v–82r.

81. See Lynda Gregorian Christian, "The Figure of Socrates in Erasmus' Works," *Sixteenth Century Journal*, 3/2 (1972), pp. 1–10. Relatedly, see Mary Louise Carlson, "Pagan Examples of Fortitude in the Latin Christian Apologists," *Classical Philology*, 43 (1948), pp. 93–104.

82. Maffei, *Stromata*, BAV, Barb. Lat. 753, ff. 11v, 78r, 176r, and 183r.

83. *Ibid.*, ff. 170r-v.

84. *Ibid.*, ff. 13v, 17r, and 78v–79r; and Maffei, *De Institutione Christiana*, ff. 7r, 18r.

85. Maffei, *Stromata*, BAV, Barb. Lat. 753, f. 10r: "Quanquam Chilonis unius e septem sapientibus illud est, Nosce te ipsum, Christiano tamen homini ac plane perfecto tantum licet, cui ex fide dona spiritus adduntur [*sic*]." Among the sermons of Basil that Maffei translated was "Attende tibi ipsi," which was based on

Chilo's dictum. Marsilio Ficino also emphasized self-knowledge; see Collins, *op. cit.*, pp. 3, 7, 8, 111.

86. Maffei, *Stromata*, BAV, Barb. Lat. 753, f. 11v.

87. Maffei, *De Institutione Christiana*, ff. 75r, 83r.

88. On voluntarism among Italian humanist theologians, see Charles Trinkaus, *In Our Image and Likeness: Humanity and Divinity in Italian Humanist Thought*, 2 vols. (Chicago: University of Chicago Press, 1970), vol. 1, pp. 167–168 and 318–319, and vol. 2, pp. 701–702.

89. Maffei, *De Institutione Christiana*, f. 100v.

90. See Maffei, *Stromata*, BAV, Barb. Lat. 753, ff. 203v–204r, for the chapter entitled "Bene velle magis quam bene intelligere difficile ac rarum."

91. *Ibid.*, f. 69v.

92. *Ibid.*, f. 68v.

93. *Ibid.*, f. 176r.

94. *Ibid.*, ff. 183r–v.

95. Maffei, *De Institutione Christiana*, f. 93r; and *idem*, *Stromata*, BAV, Barb. Lat. 753, f. 11v.

96. Maffei, *Stromata*, BAV, Barb. Lat. 753, f. 13v.

97. Maffei, *De Institutione Christiana*, f. 117v: "Imaginem pictor si absolvere voluerit Apellis aut Polygnosti tabellam sibi proponet, philosophus Socraticos, orator Ciceronem, poeta Maronem sive Homerum. Siquis opes aut potentiam spectat Croesi divitias aut Alexandri Caesarisve gesta ante oculos habebit; eadem et in moribus et vita spirituali ratio. Quid potius quam Domini vestigia sequi, ut ait Paulus, imitatores mei estote sicut et ego Dei [1 Cor. 11:1]." The ideas of imitation and archetype were patristic, and were especially prominent in the thought of Gregory of Nyssa, Basil the Great's brother; see Gerhart B. Ladner, *The Idea of Reform*, rev. ed. (New York: Harper and Row, 1967), pp. 90–101.

98. Maffei, *De Institutione Christiana*, f. 117v: "Quum natura sit ita institutum eveniatque plerumque et infra Archetypi praestantiam apographum existat ac eo minus quo illud imperfectius, iterdumque ita ruit, ut nullam prorsus habeat laudem. Quamobrem levare oculos in montes admonemur et ad conditoris sapientiam quantum liceat per imitationem adcedere."

99. Maffei, *Stromata*, BAV, Barb. Lat. 753, f. 126r.

100. *Ibid.*, ff. 11v–12r.

101. *Ibid.*, f. 11v.

102. *Ibid.*, f. 19r.

103. Maffei, *De Institutione Christiana*, f. 117r.

104. Maffei, *Stromata*, BAV, Barb. Lat., 753, f. 68r. Despite the seeming parallels between Maffei's teachings and the Nominalist doctrine of *facere quod in se est*, no direct connection appears to have been involved.

105. *Ibid.*, f. 72v.

106. *Ibid.*, f. 99v.

107. *Ibid.*, f. 80r.

108. *Ibid.*, ff. 80v–81r.

109. *Ibid.*, f. 67v.

110. *Ibid.*, f. 84v: "Quemadmodum pauperi uxorem ducere non expediat quod in re angusta cura familiaris maximum sit animae salutis impedimentum; diviti autem

contra modo ad virtutum [*sic*] prono quod per facultates multa praeclara geri possint."

111. See Sister M. G. Murphy, *St. Basil and Monasticism* (Washington, D.C.: Catholic University of America Press, 1930).

112. Maffei, *Stromata*, BAV, Barb. Lat. 753, f. 170v.

113. Maffei, *Commentaria Urbana*, ff. 410v–411r.

114. Maffei, *Stromata*, BAV, Barb. Lat. 753, ff. 136r, 232r–233r.

115. See n. 83 above.

116. Maffei, *De Institutione Christiana*, f. 54r: "Nam et homines exemplo vitae seu officio aliquo promerendi, similiter et auxilii ferendi aut capiendi utilitate [*sic*], si quid forte opus, multae saepe oriuntur occasiones quibus in [*sic*] Dei gratiam, quam imprimis expetimus, et perfectam assequi virtutem facile possimus; virorum item prudentium et theologorum perita facundia [*sic*] et iuges in ecclesia exhortationes et demum spiritualia cuncta fomenta in urbe, non in agro comperies."

117. *Ibid.*, f. 54v: "Dominus quoque ipse urbes aut frequentiam non abhorruit, desertum pro tempore coluit et in secretum se recepit ut reconditos divinitatis thesauros inde turbis promeret."

118. Maffei, *Stromata*, BAV, Barb. Lat. 753, f. 26v.

119. Maffei, *De Institutione Christiana*, ff. 79v, 83v.

120. Maffei, *Stromata*, BAV, Barb. Lat. 753, f. 128v.

121. *Ibid.*, ff. 156v, 163r–v. Maffei cited Leo I's *Sermo LXXXXII* (*PL*, vol. 54, cols. 422-423), a popular text in Rome; see John W. O'Malley, *Praise and Blame in Renaissance Rome: Rhetoric, Doctrine, and Reform in the Sacred Orators of the Papal Court, c. 1450-1521* (Durham, N.C.: Duke University Press, 1979), p. 210 and note.

122. Maffei, *Stromata*, BAV, Barb. Lat. 753, ff. 110r–v.

123. *Ibid.*, f. 111v: "Postremo C. Cysar [*sic*] omnia temeritate subvertit, divina humanaque confundit, patriam invasit, denique imperium per vim sibi corripiens hereditarium posteris usque ad Constantinum reliquit qui et idem una cum fide ad extremum accepta successoribus per manus tradens Urbem [?] Romae pontifici cessit. Imperium igitur tanta olim iniuria ex tyrannideque adeptum sacrum iustumque nunc facit ecclesia."

124. See Maffei, *Commentaria Urbana*, f. 328r, for indications of Maffei's reservations about the Donation.

125. See D'Amico, "A Humanist Response to Martin Luther," pp. 37-56. I cite from the autograph copy, BAV, Ottob. Lat. 992, ff. 279r–286r. The treatise was written in 1520; see D'Amico, "Papal History and Curial Reform in the Renaissance," p. 164, n. 31.

126. For Prierias and his writings, see D'Amico, "A Humanist Response to Martin Luther," p. 37, n. 1.

127. Maffei changed the title of the treatise from *Genii Romani in Martinum Lutherum Apologeticus* to *Nasi Romani in Martinum Lutherum Apologeticus;* see D'Amico, "A Humanist Response to Martin Luther," p. 50, for the significance of this change.

128. BAV, Ottob. Lat. 992, f. 279r: "Recepta postmodo fide non minora ac prius edidi exempla."

129. *Ibid.*, f. 279v.

130. *Ibid.*, f. 280r.

131. *Ibid.*, f. 280r.

132. *Ibid.*, f. 280v: "Hoc ferme modo Aeresiarchae sua decreta plena veneni ac pestilentiae contra Romanum Pontificem Ecclesiamque Catholicam ediderint, auctores se melius Scripturas enarrandi fecerunt. Per canones Deique verba omnia sua probaverunt, eaque perperam interpretantes immo potius distrahentes atque lacerantes ad omnem persuasionem praesto parata obicere. Dum nihil periculosius, nihil cum maiori animarum damno tentatur."

133. *Ibid.*, f. 285v: "Ingens Dei sapientia facit ut bona non solum ex bonis sed etiam malis eliciat, sic e sentibus rosas, e stercore fruges et demum e serpentum venenis medicamenta quandoque salutifera promat."

CHAPTER 9

1. On reform in general, see Hubert Jedin, *The History of the Council of Trent*, trans. Ernest Graf, vol. 1 (St. Louis, Mo.: Herder, 1957). For general surveys, see *idem, Riforma cattolica o controriforma?* trans. Marola Guarducci (Brescia: Morceliana, 1967); Romeo de Maio, *Riforme e miti nella Chiesa del Cinquecento* (Naples: Guida, 1973), pp. 11-29; and Alfred A. Strnad, "Renaissance, Humanismus und Kirchenreform: Zu einigen Neuerscheinungen," *Römische Historische Mitteilungen*, 16 (1974), pp. 231-280. See also Denys Hay, *The Italian Church in the Fifteenth Century* (Cambridge: At the University Press, 1977), chap. 5.

2. See Gerhart B. Ladner, *The Idea of Reform* (Cambridge, Mass.: Harvard University Press, 1959).

3. Any number of tracts could be cited; Matthew of Cracow's *De Praxi Romanae Curiae*, ed. Wladyslaw Senko (Warsaw: Zakład Narodowy im. Ossolińskich, 1969), is an example of their geographical diversity.

4. See Eugenio Garin, "Desideri di riforma nell'oratoria del Quattrocento," *La cultura filosofica del Rinascimento italiano* (Florence: Sansoni, 1961), pp. 166-182. As in so much else, Petrarch began the process; see his *Liber sine nomine*, trans. Norman Zacour (Toronto: Pontifical Institute of Medieval Studies, 1973).

5. See August Buck, "Der Rückgriff des Renaissance Humanismus auf die Patristik," in *Festschrift Walther von Wartburg*, ed. K. Baldinger, vol. 1 (Tübingen: Niemeyer, 1968), pp. 153-175; and Charles Stinger, *Humanism and the Church Fathers: Ambrogio Traversari (1386-1439) and Christian Antiquity in the Italian Renaissance* (Albany: State University of New York Press, 1977).

6. For Roman curialist and humanist-curialist reform thought, see Léonce Célier, "L'Idée de réforme à la Cour pontificale du Concile de Bâle au Concile de Lateran," *Revue des questions historiques*, 86 (1904), pp. 418-435; John W. O'Malley, "Historical Thought and the Reform Crisis of the Early Sixteenth Century," *Theological Studies*, 28 (1967), pp. 531-548; *idem*, "The Discovery of America and Reform Thought at the Papal Court in the Early Cinquecento," in *First Images of America: The Impact of the New World on the Old*, ed. Fredi Chiappelli, (Berkeley: University of California Press, 1976), pp. 185-200; and *idem, Praise and Blame in Renaissance Rome: Rhetoric, Doctrine, and Reform in the Sacred Orators of the Papal Court, c. 1450-1521* (Durham, N.C.: Duke University Press, 1979), chap. 8.

7. See, for example, Poggio Bracciolini's *Oratio ad Patres Reverendissimos*, in *Opera Omnia*, ed. R. Fubini (rpt., Turin: Bottega d'Erasmo, 1964); and

Riccardo Fubini, "Un'orazione di Poggio Bracciolini sui vizi del clero scritta al tempo del Concilio di Costanza," *Giornale storico della letteratura italiana,* 82 (1965), pp. 24–33.

8. An example of this lack of historical consciousness is Platina's *Vitae Christi et omnium Pontificum,* in which the author condemns certain abuses but attempts no institutional criticisms; see, on this, Richard J. Palermino, "Platina's *History of the Popes*" (M. Litt. thesis, University of Edinburgh, 1973).

9. See O'Malley, *Praise and Blame in Renaissance Rome,* pp. 216–217.

10. The relevant correspondence is discussed in Alessandro Ferraioli, "Il Ruolo di Leone X," *ASRSP,* 38 (1915), pp. 261–269.

11. See especially Jedin, *History of the Council of Trent;* and Francis Oakley, *Council over Pope: Towards a Provisional Ecclesiology* (New York: Herder and Herder, 1960), pt. 1, pp. 33–101.

12. See Pardon E. Tillinghast, "An Aborted Reformation: Germans and the Papacy in the Mid-Fifteenth Century," *Journal of Medieval History,* 2/1 (1976), pp. 57–79; and Joachim W. Stieber, *Pope Eugenius IV, The Council of Basel, and the Secular and Ecclesiastical Authorities in the Empire* (Leiden: Brill, 1978). For an example of a conciliar reform by a curialist, see Franco Gaeta, *Lorenzo Valla: Filologia e storia nell'Umanesimo italiano* (Naples: Istituto italiano per gli studi storici, 1955), pp. 211–253; and G. Billanovich, "Leonardo Teronda, umanista e curiale," *Italia medioevale e umanistica,* 1 (1958), pp. 379–381.

13. See Joseph Gill, *Constance et Bâle-Florence* (Paris: L'Orante, 1965); and M. Spinka, ed., *Advocates of Reform: From Wyclif to Erasmus* (Philadelphia: Westminster Press, 1953), pp. 91–184.

14. For the Fifth Lateran Council and its reform program, see pp. 217 and 220 above.

15. See Célier, "L'Idée de réforme"; and *idem,* "Alexandre VI et la réforme de l'Eglise," *Mélanges d'archéologie et histoire de l'Ecole française de Rome,* 27 (1907), pp. 65–124.

16. For Avignon, see Norman Zacour, "Papal Regulation of Cardinals' Households in the Fourteenth Century," *Speculum,* 50 (1975), pp. 434–455. Martin V's reform bulls are published in J. I. von Döllinger, *Beiträge zur politischen, kirchlichen, und Cultur-Geschichte der sechs letzten Jahrhunderte,* vol. 2 (Regensburg, 1863), pp. 335–344.

17. For background, see Ludwig von Pastor, *History of the Popes,* ed. and trans. F. I. Antrobus *et al.* (London/St. Louis: Herder, 1891–1910), vol. 3, chap. 7. The text of Pius's reform is printed in Rudolf Haubst, "Der Reformentwurf Pius des Zweiten," *Römische Quartalschrift,* 49 (1954), pp. 188–242, and is summarized in Pastor, *op. cit.,* vol. 3, pp. 397–403.

18. See Haubst, *op. cit.,* p. 208.

19. *Ibid.,* p. 209.

20. *Ibid.,* pp. 211–236.

21. Sixtus's reform bull exists in two manuscripts: BAV, Vat. Lat. 3883 and Vat. Lat. 3884. While the two copies are essentially the same, Vat. Lat. 3884, at f. 119v, has a section, *de datario,* which is lacking in Vat. Lat. 3883, and at f. 132v the section *Circa executionem reformationum* has been added. On one of these manuscripts, see John J. Sawicki and Phillip H. Stump, "New Evidence of the Reform Committee at the Council of Constance in Vat. Lat. 3884," *Bulletin*

of Medieval Canon Law, n.s. 8 (1978), pp. 50-55. Sections are published in M. Tangl, *Die päpstlichen Kanzleiordnungen von 1200 bis 1500* (Innsbruck, 1894), pp. 379-385; and in Walther von Hofmann, *Forschungen zur Geschichte der kurialen Behörden vom Schisma bis zur Reformation* (Rome: Von Loescher, 1914), vol. 2, pp. 230-231. The parts relating to cardinals are in Christopher Hoffmann, ed., *Nova Scriptorum ac Monumentorum ... Collectio*, vol. 1 (Leipzig, 1731), pp. 517-520. Célier, "Alexandre VI et la réforme," p. 94, collates the manuscripts with sections of the bull published in Tangl.

22. BAV, Vat. Lat. 3883, ff. 14v, 20v.

23. *Ibid.*, ff. 20r-v.

24. See Célier, "Alexandre VI et la réforme"; and Pastor, *op. cit.*, vol. 4, appendix.

25. On Julius, see Pastor, *op. cit.*, vol. 4, pp. 446-447. The bull, *Cum tam divino*, is reprinted in *Bullarum diplomatum ... Taurinensis Editio*, vol. 5, pp. 405-406; see also J. B. Sägmüller, *Die Papstwahlen und die Staaten von 1447 bis 1555 (Nikolaus V bis Paul IV)* (Tübingen, 1890), pp. 7-10.

26. See O. De la Brosse, *Lateran V et Trente* (Paris: L'Orante, 1975); C. J. Hefele and J. Hergenroether, *Histoire des Conciles*, vol. 8/1 (Paris: Letouzey, 1917); Jedin, *History of the Council of Trent*, pp. 117-138; Nelson H. Minnich, "Concepts of Reform Proposed at the Fifth Lateran Council," *Archivum Historiae Pontificiae*, 7 (1969), pp. 163-251; Richard J. Schoeck, "The Fifth Lateran Council: Its Partial Successes and Its Larger Failures," in *Reform and Authority in the Medieval and Reformation Church*, ed. Guy Fitch Lytle (Washington, D.C.: Catholic University of America Press, 1981), pp. 99-126, and Nelson H. Minnich, "*Incipiat Indicium a Domo Domini*: The Fifth Lateran Council and the Reform of Rome," *ibid.*, pp. 127-142.

27. The *Pastoralis officii divina providentia* can be found in *Bullarum diplomatum ... Taurinensis Editio*, vol. 5, pp. 571-601; the *Supernae dispositionis arbitrio* is in J. D. Mansi, comp., *Sacrorum Conciliorum Nova et Amplissima Collectio*, vol. 32 (Paris: Welter, 1902), cols. 874-886.

28. BAV, Vat. Lat, 4039, ff. 16v-18v. See also O'Malley, *Praise and Blame in Renaissance Rome*, pp. 212 and 221; and n. 12 above.

29. The tract was published in Brescia in 1495; see L. Hain, *Repertorium bibliographicum* (Stuttgart, 1826-1838), #6321. See also Hubert Jedin, *Studien über Domenico de' Domenichi (1416-1478)* (Mainz: Akademie der Wissenschaften und der Literatur, 1957), pp. 247-250; Heribert Smolinsky, *Domenico de' Domenichi und seine Schrift 'De Potestate Pape et termino eius': Edition und Kommentar* (Münster: Aschendorff, 1976); and O'Malley, *Praise and Blame in Renaissance Rome*, index. I have not seen Franco Gaeta, *Domenico Domenichi De reformationibus Romanae Curiae* (Aquila, n.d.).

30. Domenichi, *Tractatus*, f. A 3r.

31. *Ibid.*, ff. B 1r-v.

32. The text is in Stephan Ehses, "Der Reformentwurf des Kardinal Nikolaus Cusanus," *Historisches Jahrbuch*, 32 (1911), pp. 274-297. See also Jedin, *History of the Council of Trent*, p. 123; and D. Sullivan, "Nicholas Cusa as Reformer: The Papal Legation to the Germans, 1451-1452," *Medieval Studies*, 36 (1974), pp. 382-428. I have not seen Erwin Iserloh, *Reform der Kirche bei Nikolas von Kues*, Vorträge des Instituts für Europaische Geschichte, Mainz, no. 38 (Wiesbaden:

F. Steiner, 1965). Relatedly, see Pio Paschini, "Una predica inefficace (Propositi di riforma ecclesiastica alla fine del sec. XV)," *Studi romani,* 1 (1952), pp. 31-38.

33. See John W. O'Malley, *Giles of Viterbo on Church and Reform* (Leiden: Brill, 1968); *idem,* "Giles of Viterbo: A Reformer's Thought on Renaissance Rome," *Renaissance Quarterly,* 20/1 (1967), pp. 1-11; *idem,* "Man's Dignity, God's Love, and the Destiny of Rome: A Text of Giles of Viterbo," *Viator,* 3 (1972), pp. 389-416.

34. On Galatino, see Arderinus Kleinhans, O.F.M., "De vita et operibus Petri Galatini, O. F. M., scientiarum biblicarum cultoris (c. 1460-1540)," *Antonianum,* 1 (1926), pp. 145-178 and 327-356; and Benigno F. Perrone, "Il 'De re publica christiana' nel pensiero filosofico e politico di Pietro Galatino," in *Studi di storia pugliese in onore di Giuseppe Chiarelli,* ed. Michele Paone, vol. 2 (Galatina: Congedo, 1973), pp. 499-632. For the text of the *Libellus,* see BAV, Vat. Lat. 5578, ff. 86r-106v; and the edited version in Perrone, *op. cit.,* pp. 609-632.

35. Kleinhans, *op. cit.,* pp. 150-179, describes Galatino's works. Unfortunately the manuscripts have deteriorated and in many places are illegible.

36. Perrone, *op. cit.,* pp. 611-625.

37. *Ibid.,* pp. 625-627.

38. *Ibid.,* pp. 627-628.

39. *Ibid.,* p. 630.

40. *Ibid.,* pp. 631-632.

41. See O'Malley, *Praise and Blame in Renaissance Rome;* and John M. McManamon, "The Ideal Renaissance Pope: Funeral Oratory from the Papal Court," *Archivum Historiae Pontificiae,* 14 (1976), pp. 5-70.

42. See n. 26 above. Giles of Viterbo's sermon was the most famous oration given at the council; see Clare O'Reilly, "'Without Councils We Cannot Be Saved . . .': Giles of Viterbo Addresses the Fifth Lateran Council," *Augustiniana,* 27 (1972), pp. 166-204. In addition, there were other reform-oriented sermons and tracts. For Pico della Mirandola's "Ad Leonem Decimum Pontificem Maximum et Concilium Lateranense Johannis Francisci Pico Mirandulae Domini, de Reformandis Moribus Oratio," see William Roscoe, *Vita et Pontificato di Leone X,* trans. G. Bossi (Milan, 1817), vol. 8, pp. 106-119; and Charles B. Schmitt, "Gianfrancesco Pico della Mirandola and the Fifth Lateran Council," *Archiv für Reformationsgeschichte,* 61/2 (1970), pp. 161-178. For the *B. Pauli Justiniani et Petri Quirini Ermitarum Camaldulensium Libellus ad Leonem X Pontificem Maximum,* see *Annales Camaldulenses Ordinis Sancti Benedicti,* ed. J. B. Mittarelli and A. Costadoni (Venice, 1773), vol. 9, cols. 612-719; and Silvio Tramontin, "Un programma di riforma della Chiesa per il Concilio Lateranese V: Il *Libellus ad Leonem X* dei Veneziani Paolo Giustiniani e Pietro Querini," in *Venezia e i Concili* (Venice: Quaderni del Laurentianum, 1963), pp. 67-93. For Raffaele Brandolini's *Oratio ad Lateranense Concilium,* see BAV, Ottob. Lat. 813; Milan, Biblioteca Ambrosiana, Z 65; John F. D'Amico, "Humanism and Theology at Papal Rome, 1480-1520" (Ph.D. Diss., University of Rochester, 1977), pp. 380-384; and O'Malley, *Praise and Blame in Renaissance Rome,* index.

43. Jacopo Gherardi, *Il Diario Romano di Jacopo Gherardi,* ed. E. Carusi, in *Rerum Italicarum Scriptores,* 23/3 (Città di Castello: Lapi, 1904), p. 40.

44. The treatise remains in manuscript form; see Florence, Biblioteca Nazionale Centrale, Cl. VI. 191, ff. 1v-36r. On Maffei, see Scipione Maffei, *Verona illustrata,*

pt. 2 (Milan, 1825), pp. 261-263; and Alfonso Bartoli, "La diaconia di Santa Lucia in Settizonio," *ASRSP,* 50 (1927), pp. 59-73.

45. The manuscripts are BAV, Vat. Lat. 2934, and the dedication copy, MS. Typ. 171 H, Houghton Library, Harvard University, Cambridge, Mass. For details, see p. 18 above.

46. Raffaele Maffei, *Stromata,* BAV, Barb. Lat. 753, ff. 11v-12r, 99r-v, 105r-v.

47. Raffaele Maffei, *De Institutione Christiana,* ff. 136v-137r; for the full title, see n. 120, p. 270, above.

48. Maffei, *Stromata,* BAV, Barb. Lat. 753, f. 99v.

49. *Ibid.,* f. 124v.

50. For full reference to Maffei's *Commentaria Urbana,* see n. 115, p. 270, above.

51. Maffei, *Commentaria urbana,* f. 315r.

52. *Ibid.,* f. 315v.

53. *Ibid.,* f. 318r: "Has igitur animi dotes magnis obruerat vitiis, quae narrare non attinet, tantum referam quae vulgus adspexit."

54. See John F. D'Amico, "Papal History and Curial Reform in the Renaissance: Raffaele Maffei's *Breuis Historia* of Julius II and Leo X," *Archivum Historiae Pontificiae,* 18 (1980), pp. 157-210.

55. Maffei, *De Institutione Christiana,* ff. 128r-129r: "De opibus aedificiis sumptibusque reliquis non necessariis."

56. *Ibid.,* f. 128v.

57. See *ibid.*

58. *Ibid.:* "Ego vero tantum abesse puto ut ex hoc aliquis laudem promereatur ullam ut longe prudentissimum sanctumque plane virum existimem qui quum maxime possit nunquam nisi forte necessaria aedificaverit. Necessaria namque domus est si eam constructam mercari aut uti minime liceat?"

59. See D'Amico, "Papal History and Curial Reform in the Renaissance," p. 197.

60. On this, see Massimo Miglio, *Storiografia pontificia del Quattrocento* (Bologna: Patron, 1975), pp. 119-153.

61. Maffei, *De Institutione Christiana,* ff. 136r-v.

62. *Ibid.,* ff. 139r-143v. These two chapters form a separate section within the *De Institutione Christiana.* They might have been part of a larger work on moral philosophy. On the genesis of these chapters, see D'Amico, "Papal History and Curial Reform in the Renaissance," p. 181, n. 107.

63. Maffei, *De Institutione Christiana,* f. 139r.

64. *Ibid.,* ff. 140r-v.

65. *Ibid.,* f. 140v. Maffei might be recalling Alberti's *Pontifex,* in *Opera inedita et pauca separatim impressa,* ed. G. Mancini (Florence, 1890), pp. 67-121; see D'Amico, "Papal History and Curial Reform in the Renaissance," p. 182, n. 111.

66. Maffei, *Stromata,* BAV, Barb. Lat. 753, f. 62r.

67. Maffei, *De Institutione Christiana,* f. 141r; and D'Amico, "Papal History and Curial Reform in the Renaissance," p. 182, n. 112.

68. Maffei, *De Institutione Christiana,* ff. 141r-v; and D'Amico, "Papal History and Curial Reform in the Renaissance," p. 182, n. 113.

69. Maffei, *De Institutione Christiana,* f. 141r.

70. *Ibid.*, f. 141v: "Denique virtutes omnis simul et artes liberales constructo Atheneo fovere, cui magis quam tibi in studiis educato conveniet?"

71. *Ibid.*; and D'Amico, "Papal History and Curial Reform in the Renaissance," p. 183, n. 116.

72. Maffei, *De Institutione Christiana*, f. 142r; and D'Amico, "Papal History and Curial Reform in the Renaissance," pp. 183-184, n. 119.

73. Maffei, *De Institutione Christiana*, f. 142r; and D'Amico, "Papal History and Curial Reform in the Renaissance," p. 184, n. 120.

74. Maffei, *De Institutione Christiana*, f. 142r; and D'Amico, "Papal History and Curial Reform in the Renaissance," p. 184, n. 123.

75. In the *Stromata*, BAV, Barb. Lat. 753, ff. 113v-114r, Maffei specifies a clear, but not ornate, curial style.

76. Maffei, *De Institutione Christiana*, f. 142r: "Deinde ea quae Apochrypha dicuntur ut multa et varia in sanctorum historiis et aliis commentariis quae rursus horis canonicis et aliis ceremoniis adscribuntur, non solum ineptae inconditeque [sic], sed etiam quod omnino detestandum falsa ut Constantini baptismum contra duorum praecipuorum doctorum Hieronymi et Ambrosii auctoritatem narratum."

77. See *ibid.*, f. 142r, for some examples.

78. *Ibid.*, f. 142v: "Antigraphum cum apographo diligentissime conferat, ne qua menda flagitiosae lectionis sensum moretur aut interpellet."

79. *Ibid.*: "In sacrificiis quoque ac cerimoniis multa praeter ritum orthodoxum apud barbaras praesterim nationes leguntur audiunturque. Haec itaque et his similia quanquam fidei sustantiae [sic] maioribus roboratae munimentis minime derogant, lectionis attamen iucunditatem, lectoris eruditi consolationem, ritus demem ecclesiae venustatem atque decorem talis per ignorantes homines suborta negligentia satis est apta impedire."

80. These can be found in BAV, Ottob. Lat. 992, Ottob. Lat. 2377, and Barb. Lat. 2517; see also D'Amico, "Papal History and Curial Reform in the Renaissance," p. 185, n. 128.

81. Maffei, *De Institutione Christiana*, f. 142v.

82. See the letters dated 1505 in BAV, Barb. Lat. 2517, ff. 7r-11r.

83. Maffei, *De Institutione Christiana*, f. 142v; and D'Amico, "Papal History and Curial Reform in the Renaissance," p. 185, n. 129.

84. Maffei, *De Institutione Christiana*, f. 142v; and D'Amico, "Papal History and Curial Reform in the Renaissance," p. 185, n. 130.

85. Maffei, *De Institutione Christiana*, f. 142v: "Insuper odiis inimicitiisque privatis quae totas per orbem evertunt familias."

86. *Ibid.*: "Postremo autem sextoque loco omnium maximum, principum scilicet populorumque pacis studium reservavi. Quo ferme sublato, frustra sunt caeteri quidem conatus."

87. *Ibid.* On March 13, 1518, Leo dispatched four legates—one each to England, France, Spain, and the empire—to encourage a Turkish crusade; see Kenneth M. Setton, "Pope Leo X and the Turkish Peril," *Proceedings of the American Philosophical Society*, 113 (1969), pp. 367-434, at pp. 398-400.

88. Maffei, *De Institutione Christiana*, ff. 142v-143r; and D'Amico, "Papal History and Curial Reform in the Renaissance," p. 186, n. 133.

89. Maffei, *De Institutione Christiana*, f. 143r; and D'Amico, "Papal History and Curial Reform in the Renaissance," p. 186, n. 134.

90. Maffei, *De Institutione Christiana*, f. 143r; and D'Amico, "Papal History and Curial Reform in the Renaissance," p. 187, n. 135.

91. Maffei, *De Institutione Christiana*, f. 143r: "Hunc [the pope] Aethiopes, Indi, Armenii, remotissimaeque ac barbarae nationes, nec Italiae nomen saepe audientes, uṭ Petri successorem colunt, adeunt, per legatos in Synodis excipiunt."

92. *Ibid.*, f. 143v: "Leo, papa sanctissime, non tam dissimulanter, aut ex exercitationis gratia declamare quam iure, atque ordine quum ad te scriberem narrare sum nisus, qui unus omnium mitissimus quum existas, si ad beatam naturam indolemque tuam studium ac diligentiam omnibus expectatam perseveranter adhibueris, nihil te in terris divinius, nihil tuis seculis felicius fuerit, gratia tamen ac benignitate domini nostri Iesu Christi cui gloria et imperium in aeterna secula."

93. On the *De Cardinalatu*, see pp. 78–80 above. For a fuller bibliography, see Kathleen Weil-Garris and John F. D'Amico, "The Renaissance Cardinal's Ideal Palace: A Chapter from Cortesi's *De Cardinalatu*," in *Studies in Italian Art and Architecture, 15th through 18th Centuries*, ed. Henry A. Millon (Rome: Elefante, 1980), pp. 45–123.

94. See Delio Cantimori, "Questioncine sulle opere progettate da Paolo Cortesi," in *Studi di bibliografia di storia in onore di Tammaro de Marinis*, vol. 1 (Verona: Valdengo, 1963), pp. 273–280. Hubert Jedin did not consider the *De Cardinalatu* to be a reform tract, but he did not view it as being opposed to reform either; see his "Vorschläge und Entwürfe für Kardinalsreform," *Römische Quartalschrift*, 42 (1934), pp. 305–332 (also available in Italian translation as "Proposte e progetti di riforma del Collegio cardinalizio," in *Chiesa della fede: Chiesa della storia*, ed. A. Destro, A. M. Fidora, and G. Poletti [Brescia: Morelliana, 1972], pp. 156–192, at pp. 172–173).

95. Cortesi originally planned to write a work on the secular prince, but upon the suggestion of Cardinal Ascanio Sforza, he changed his topic to the pope and finally to the cardinal. There can be no better example of the clericalization of humanistic thought in the Curia than the transformations of the *De Cardinalatu;* for details on these changes, see Weil-Garris and D'Amico, *op. cit.*, pp. 64–65.

96. On the cardinalate in the High and Later Middle Ages, see Giuseppe Alberigo, *Cardinalato e Collegialità: Studi sull'ecclesiologia tra l'XI e il XIV secolo* (Florence: Vallecchi, 1969), where an ample bibliography is cited.

97. In addition to Alberigo, see Brian Tierney, *Foundations of the Conciliar Theory: The Contribution of the Medieval Canonists from Gratian to the Great Schism* (Cambridge: At the Unversity Press, 1955). See also Bernard Arle, *Beiträge zur Geschichte des Kardinalskollegiums in der Zeit vom Konstanzer bis zum Tridentiner Konzil: Erste Halfte: Die Jahre vom Regierungsantritt Martin V bis zum Tode Sixtus IV. (1417–1484)* (Bonn: Rhenania-Verlag, 1914); Paolo Brezzi, *Lo sviluppo dell'assolutismo nello stato pontificio (secoli XV–XVI)*, vol. 1 (Bologna: Patron, 1967), pp. 86–114; Denys Hay, "Renaissance Cardinals," *Synthesis*, 3 (1976), pp. 35–46; and John A. F. Thomson, *Popes and Princes, 1417–1517* (London: George Allen and Unwin, 1980), chap. 3.

98. For an outline of cardinalate opposition to the papacy, see Jean Lulves, "Die Machtbestrebungen des Kardinalskollegiums gegenüber dem Papsttum," *Mitteilungen des Instituts für Österreichische Geschichtsforschung*, 35 (1914), pp. 455–483.

99. On the election pacts, see Jean Lulves, "Päpstliche Wahlkapitulationen:

Ein Beitrag zur Entwickelungsgeschichte des Kardinalats," *QFIAB*, 12 (1909), pp. 212-231; Walter Ullman, "The Legality of the Papal Electoral Pacts," *Ephemerides iuris canonici* (Rome, 1962), pp. 2-35; and *idem*, "Julius II and the Schismatic Cardinals," in *Schism, Heresy, and Religious Protest*, ed. Derek Baker (Cambridge: At the University Press, 1972), pp. 177-193.

100. See Giglilia Soldi Rondinini, "Per la storia del Cardinalato nel secolo XV (con l'edizione del trattato *De Cardinalibus* di Martino Garati da Lodi)," *Memorie dell'Istituto lombardo: Accademia di scienze e lettere*, 33/1 (1973), pp. 7-91. Several quattrocento treatises dealing with the cardinalate are in *Tractatus universi iuris . . .* , vol. 13/1, *Tractatus illustrium utraque tum pontificii, tum caesarei iuris facultate iurisconsultorum de potestate ecclesiastica* (Venice, 1584). See also J. B. Sägmüller, *Zur Geschichte des Kardinalates: Ein Traktat des Bischofs von Feltre und Treviso Teodoro de' Lolli über das Verhältniss von Primat und Kardinalat* (Rome, 1893); and Harry Hynes, *The Privileges of Cardinals: Commentary with Historical Notes* (Washington, D.C.: Catholic University of America Press, 1945).

101. Some examples of the cinquecento tracts are Girolamo Manfredi, *De perfecto cardinali S. R. Ecclesiae liber* (Bologna, 1584); *idem, De maiestate . . . cardinalium* (Bologna, 1591); Fabio Albergati, *Del Cardinale . . . libri tre* (Bologna, 1599); Girolamo Botero, *Dell'ufficio del cardinale libri due* (Rome, 1599); and G. Piatti, S.J., *De cardinalis dignitate et officio* (Rome, 1602). See also Jedin, "Proposte e progetti di riforma del Collegio cardinalizio."

102. See Norman Zacour, "Papal Regulations of Cardinals' Households in the Fourteenth Century," *Speculum*, 50 (1975), pp. 434-455; and Guillaume Mollat, "Contributions à l'histoire du Sacre Collège de Clement V à Eugène IV," *Revue d'histoire ecclésiastique*, 46 (1951), pp. 566-594.

103. For a broader study of the college and reform, see Barbara McClung Hallman, "Italian Cardinals, Reform, and the Church as Property, 1492-1563" (Ph.D. diss., University of California at Berkeley, 1974).

104. *De Cardinalatu* was Cortesi's last experiment in humanist Latin. He chose to write the treatise in highly archaic and erudite Latin, which emphasized his unitary approach to the ecclesiastical establishment and to literary theory; in his eyes, such a literary language was proper for the Church and its government. In contradistinction to the Ciceronianism of his earlier writings, *De Cardinalatu* has a highly involved syntax and contains uncommon vocabulary. As a result, the reader is given every aspect of the cardinal's life in a noncontemporary language, which imbues the rules offered with a normative and historically static quality.

105. An interesting exception to this rule was Cortesi's citation of the Hohenstaufen family of emperors, which represents the curial view of these emperors as the great enemies of the Church and the papacy; see, for examples, *De Cardinalatu*, ff. A 5r-v, A 6v, C 5r, G 5v, I 3v, R 13v, and T 6r.

106. Cortesi, *De Cardinalatu*, introductory letter, no foliation: "Ex quo facile intelligi poterit hos libros non modo Senatui, sed etiam utiles caeterorum dignitati fore, cum maxime in colendae virtutis ratione consistant, in qua sit appetendorum extimum et vita beata sita."

107. *Ibid.*, bk. 1, chap. 6, ff. D 8r-E 3r.

108. *Ibid.*, chap. 8, ff. E 4r-8r: "De Cardinalibus qui aliquid scripti reliquerunt."

109. On the economic state of the College of Cardinals, see D. S. Chambers, "The Economic Predicament of Renaissance Cardinals," in *Studies in Medieval and Renaissance History*, 3 (1966), pp. 289-313.

110. For a detailed study of cardinal-protectors, see William E. Wilkie, *The Cardinal Protectors of England: Rome and the Tudors before the Reformation* (Cambridge: At the University Press, 1974).

111. Cortesi, *De Cardinalatu*, ff. F 6v-7v.

112. See pp. 50-51.

113. Cortesi, *De Cardinalatu*, bk. 2, chap. 4, "De amicitia," ff. H 3v-8v; and chap. 8, "De audientia," ff. K 3r-L 3v.

114. *Ibid.*, chap. 9, "De sermone" ff. L 4r and N 3v; and chap. 10, "De metaphoris in sermone utendis," ff. N 4r-9v.

115. *Ibid.*, f. N 11v.

116. *Ibid.*, ff. N 12v-NN 1v.

117. *Ibid.*, f. NN 2r.

118. *Ibid.*, f. NN 2v.

119. *Ibid.*, ff. NN 3r-4r.

120. *Ibid.*, f. NN 5r: "Ex quo nulla causa dubitandi datum quin Senatores esse debeant ad bene de eo nobilium hominum genere promerendum prompti; qui rebus suis eversis in exilii afflicta egestate vivant; quique fortunam tegunt pudendo et reticendo suam."

121. *Ibid.*, ff. NN 5v-6r: "Sed ex omnium hominum genere maxime est imbecilitas iuvanda mulierum. Nam quemadmodum a natura cernimus omnia imbecilliora foveri solere diligentius, ut facile ab ea videmus, et arbores cortice, et fruges spica vestituque custodiri aristarum, sic censemus esse a Senatore in foeminarum imbecillitate faciendum, ut quo plus eas vident egere solere opis, eo plus his praesidii adhibendum putent."

122. *Ibid.*, ff. NN 7r-v.

123. *Ibid.*, bk. 3, chap. 1, "Quod papa cum Collegio est perfectior et durabilior Res pu. omnibus Re pu. humanitus inventis," ff. O 3r-P 1v.

124. *Ibid.*, ff. O 4v-5r.

125. *Ibid.*, chap. 2, "De potestate Cardinalium," ff. P 2r-5v. Cortesi had planned to add a chapter on ceremonies, but it never appeared (f. O 6v).

126. *Ibid.*, chap. 4, "De electione papae," ff. P 6r-Q 1v, esp. f. P 8v.

127. *Ibid.*, f. Q 1v.

128. *Ibid.*, chap. 5, ff. Q 2r-6v.

129. *Ibid.*, chap. 6, "De rebus urbanis consistorialibus," ff. Q 6v-q 1r.

130. *Ibid.*, ff. Q 6v-7r.

131. *Ibid.*, ff. Q 8r-9r.

132. *Ibid.*, ff. Q 11v-15v.

133. *Ibid.*, chap. 7, "De praelatis maioribus et rebus ecclesiasticis ad Consistorium pertinentibus," ff. q 1v-r 1r.

134. *Ibid.*, ff. q 2r, 3 r-v.

135. *Ibid.*, ff. q 2r-v.

136. *Ibid.*, ff. q 2v-3r.

137. *Ibid.*, ff. q 5r-r 1r.

138. *Ibid.*, chap. 8, "De simonia quatenus de ea potest tractari in Consistorio," ff. r 1v-6r. Cortesi specified three types of simony: "unum quod sermone, alterum quod obsequio, tertium quod pecunia continetur."

139. *Ibid.*, ff. r 1v-2r.

140. *Ibid.*, ff. r 5v-6r: "Quocirca dubitari hoc loco nullo modo debet, quin Senatus in orbis terrarum vigilia intersit, Pont. Max. admonere rogando, si minus

Rei pu. statum convulsum iri cupiat, uti rursum severiori velit sancire iu ssu, ne cui sit sacerdotia aut fana nundinari licitum, neve cuipiam permittat id munerale genus inire quaestus quod sit industriae innocentis hostis, pestis urbis, Rei pu. naufragium orbisque ruina terrarum."

141. *Ibid.*, chap. 9, "De creatione cardinalium," ff. r 6v-R 3v.

142. *Ibid.*, f. r 6v.

143. *Ibid.*, ff. r 6v-7r.

144. *Ibid.*, ff. r 8r-v.

145. *Ibid.*, ff. R 1r-v.

146. *Ibid.*, ff. r 8r-v.

147. *Ibid.*, R 3r: "At vero si dignitas suapte naturae praestantia expendatur, dubitatio nulla esse potest quin concedendum sit iustiorem Senatui dari causam cooptandi eos qui doctrinae magnitudine scientiaeque dignitate florent, quatenus scilicet scientia est progrediendi ratione prior aut quatenus in praestantiori rerum genere consistit."

148. *Ibid.*, "Itaque iure avorum memoria accepimus, nullos fere senatores esse factos, qui non essent doctrinarum maximarum gnari."

149. *Ibid.*, f. R 3v: "Ex quo satis exploratum esse potest, eos in primis in Senatum debere legi, quorum virtus sit, commentando et scribendo cognita, cum scriptio maxime sit animi recte dictantis et disponentis index, in quo sit tota vitae constituta ratio."

150. *Ibid.*, chap. 10, "De protectione rel'gionum," ff. R 4r-11v.

151. *Ibid.*, ff. R 5r-8r.

152. *Ibid.*, ff. R 7r-v.

153. *Ibid.*, ff. R 10v-11r.

154. *Ibid.*, ff. R 11v-112r.

155. See p. 153 above.

156. Cortesi, *De Cardinalatu*, bk. 3, chap. 11, ff. R 14r-18r (foliation is irregular at this point).

157. *Ibid.*, f. R 14r: "Nos autem cum videmus lege esse obiurgatoria cautum necui sit Pon. Maximi repraehendendi ius, nisi quatenus perduellionatus postulari possit, facile affirmamus pro caetero scelerum genere minus Senatui potestatem ad tribus corrependi dari, cum cuiusvis hominis sit scire, eum qui proprio magistratu caeteros iudicaturus sit, nullius sententia damnari posse."

158. *Ibid.*, ff. R 5v-6r.

159. *Ibid.*, f. R 17r.

160. *Ibid.*, chap. 12, "De conciliis," ff. R 7v-S 3v.

161. *Ibid.*, ff. R 17v-18r.

162. *Ibid.*, f. S 1v. Cortesi mentioned Raffaele Maffei as one who should be called to attend a council.

163. *Ibid.*, ff. S 1v-2v. Cortesi recommended Giles of Viterbo and Fedra Inghirami as preachers for a council (*ibid.*, f. S 2r); Giles gave the opening oration for the Fifth Lateran Council, and Fedra was its secretary.

164. *Ibid.*, f. S 3r-v.

165. See Oddone Ortolani, "The Hope of Italian Reformers in Rome," in *Italian Reformation Studies in Honor of Laelius Socinus*, ed. John Tedeschi (Florence: Le Monnier, 1965), pp. 13-20.

Index

Abbreviatores, 26–29, 36, 71–75, 92, 103, 104, 107
Academic Skepticism, 171
Academies, humanist, 89–112; Platonic, 116, 204. *See also* Roman Academy
Acciaiuoli, Zanobi, 256 n. 165
Accolti family, 69
Adam, 113, 197
Adrian VI, 11–12, 86, 111, 219, 237
Advocates, consistorial, 31
Aeneas, F., 262 n. 99
Aeneid, 125
Agapito of Urbino, 280 n. 93
Alberti, Leon Battista, 6, 68
Albertini, Francesco, 101
Aldobrandini, Tita (Cortesi), 73
Aleandro, Girolamo, 256 n. 165
Alexander VI, 6, 10, 17, 25, 26, 36, 65, 71, 84, 103, 105, 108, 123; and Church reform, 217, 221
Alexander of Hales, 161
Alfonso, King of Naples, 120
Alfonso, Prince of Bisceglie, 59
Alfonso d'Aragona, 263 n. 99
Algazel, 155
Alidosi, Francesco, Cardinal, 46
Altieri, Marc'Antonio, 7, 97
Ambrose, Saint, 171, 174, 177
Ammannati-Piccolimini, Jacopo, Cardinal, 15, 19, 32, 33, 53, 92, 254 n. 136
Ancona, 18, 71
Andreas of Trebizond, 33, 254 n. 136, 255 n. 139
Andrew of Jerusalem, 192
Andronicus, Livius, 132
Angelo of Recanati, Bishop, 117
Angels, 194, 197
Ann, Saint, 109
Anselm of Canterbury, 161
Anti-Aristotelianism, 179, 182
Anticlericalism, 94, 95
Anti-intellectualism, 169–170
Antiphilosophy, 169, 170, 172, 184, 185

Antirationalism, 169, 300 n. 12
Antirhetoric, 179
Appelles, 158
Apocalypse, 218
Apollo, 198
Apostles, 184, 201
Apuleianism, 79
Apuleius, 79, 132
Aquinas, Thomas, Saint, 14, 100, 146, 153, 158, 160–164, 180, 193–194, 197, 199, 100, 103. *See also* Thomists
Aquilano, Serafino Ciminelli, 102, 106
Archaeology, 75, 98, 101, 170; and the Roman Academy, 98, 101
Archetypes, 205
Architecture, 121, 125
Archivist of the Curia, 28
Aretino, Pietro, 102
Arianism, 175
Aristotelians, 198
Aristotle, 84, 86, 95, 130, 152, 155, 156, 161, 172, 179, 180, 182, 185, 191, 192, 197, 203
Arminius, Hieronymus, O.P., 301 n. 20
Arrivabene, Giovanni Pietro, 255 n. 139
Ars dicendi, 32
Arsilli, Francesco, 109
Ascoli, 107
Assyrians, 135
Astrology, 170, 179
Athenasius, Saint, 173
Audientia, 23, 26
Auditores, 23, 24, 26, 59
Augustine of Hippo, Saint, 135, 152, 171, 174–177, 181, 205; and humanists, 174, 175; and Neo-Platonism, 175–177
Aulus Gellius, 14
Auscultator, 26
Austria, 18
Authoritarianism, 124, 130
Averroës, 155
Avicenna, 155
Avignon, 30, 41, 46, 48, 65, 228

Badia of Florence, 78
Barbaro, Ermolao, 101, 149
Barbaro, Francesco, 70
Barberini, 142
Barbo, Marco, Cardinal, 103, 104, 220
Barbo, Pietro, Cardinal, 71. *See also*
    Paul II
Baroni, Francesco, 73, 74
Basil the Great, Saint, 85, 191, 192,
    203, 204, 206, 210, 222
Bechi, Gentile de', Bishop of Arezzo,
    266 n.51
Bembo, Pietro, 11, 34, 43, 108, 110,
    131, 132
Benetus, Cyprianus, O.P., 173
Benigno, Cornelio, 58, 279 n.81
Bernard of Clairvaux, 169
Beroaldo, Filippo, the Younger, 44–45,
    256 n.165
Bessarion, Cardinal, 13, 19, 33, 53, 90,
    97
Biondo, Flavio, 31, 32, 70, 72, 101
Biondo, Francesco, 71
Biondo, Gabriele, 71
Biondo, Gaspare, 71, 81, 254 n.136,
    255 n.139
Biondo, Girolamo, 71
Biondo, Paolo, 71
Biondo family, 70–72
Blasphemy, 217
Bonaventure, Saint, 219
Boniface IX, 27
Borgia, Cesare, 6, 103, 104, 280 n.93
Borgia, Giovanni, Cardinal, 103, 104
Borgia, Juan, 217
Borgia, Rodrigo, Cardinal, 16, 54, 165.
    See also Alexander VI
Bramante, 11, 26
Brandolini, Aurelio, 59, 99, 100, 146,
    147, 149, 200–201, 275 n.41
Brandolini, Raffaele, 43, 59, 60, 100,
    108, 200
Briefs, papal, 25, 29, 30, 81
Brugnoli, Raffaele, 123
Bruni, Leonardo, xiv, 31, 34, 67, 191
Bullatores, 26
Bulls, papal, 23–26, 29, 30; price of,
    251 n.99; specific, 30, 70, 216, 217,
    228
Buonaccorsi, Filippo (Callimachus Ex-
    periens), 94–95
Bureaucracy, and humanists, 4, 7, 10,
    19, 20, 25, 39
Bussi, Giovanni Andrea, Bishop of Aleria,
    14, 15, 33, 53, 255 n.139

Cabala, 165, 171, 218, 219
Caesar, Julius, 14, 73, 122, 208
Cajetan (Tommaso da Vio, Cardinal), 47,
    145
Calabria, Duke of, 73
Calandini, Filippo, Cardinal, 15
Calderini, Domizio, 33, 53, 255 n.139,
    275 n.41, 276 n.47
Calixtus III, 9, 14, 29, 69, 81
Calligraphy, humanist, 30
Calmeta, Vincenzo, 102–103, 105, 106
Calvo, Marco Fabio, 126
Camera Apostolica, 16, 23, 24, 26, 27,
    58, 71, 81
Camera Collegii Cardinalium, 23
Camerarius, Cardinal, 24
Campano, Angelo, 15
Campano, Antonio Settimuleio, 273–
    274 n.18
Campano, Giannantonio, Bishop of
    Teramo, 14–15, 53, 200
Campeggio, Tommaso, Cardinal, 138
Cancellaria Apostolica, 25–29
Canensi, Michele, 122
Cantalico, Giambattista, 53, 275 n.41
Capranica, Domenico, Cardinal, 99, 218
Capranica, Giovanni Battista, Bishop of
    Fermo, 99
Caraffa, Oliviero, Cardinal, 34
Cardinals, 4, 12, 15, 16, 19, 21, 23, 24,
    25, 41, 45–56. *See also* College of
    Cardinals *and individual names*
Careerism, in the Curia, 5
Carvajal, Juan de, Cardinal, 14
Casali, Giovanni Battista, 138
Cassiodorus, 173
Castellesi, Adriano, Cardinal, xvii, 16–
    19, 44, 51, 78, 200, 202, 208, 210,
    220–221. Works: *De modo loquendi*,
    17, 174; *De Romanae Ecclesiae potes-
    tate*, 18, 174, 220, 221; *De sermone
    latino*, 17, 18, 132–133, 171; *De Vera
    Philosophia*, 17, 169–195; *Venatio*,
    187
Castiglionchio, Lapo da, 117–118
Castiglione, Baldassare, 5, 108, 238
Celibacy, 5, 6, 69
Cerva, Elio Lampridio, 100
Cesarini, Alessandro, Cardinal, 47
Chamberlains, 42, 71, 107
Chaplains, 42, 46, 52, 58, 60
Charles I of Spain, 18
Charles VII of France, 101
Chigi, Agostino, 58
Christ, 109, 137, 154, 157

Christian empire, 134, 136, 208
Christ's Blood, 197
Chrysostom, John, 191
Church Fathers, 100, 146, 155, 161, 167, 170, 173, 189, 191, 199, 203, 207, 210, 212. *See also* Doctors of the Church, Latin; Patristics, Greek
Cicero, 14, 17, 31, 76, 93, 123-129, 130-134, 153, 174, 203
Ciceronianism, 11, 17, 34, 36, 76-79, 98, 100, 105, 110, 123-134, 137-140, 143, 149, 150, 158, 163, 183, 195, 202, 285 n.37
Cinuzzi, Alessandro, 98
Cistercians, 26
Civic humanism, 3, 4, 66
Classicism, 97, 98, 150, 156-159, 186, 187, 188
Clement of Alexandria, 195, 202
Clement VII, 11, 111
Cleofilo, Ottavio, 54
Clericalization. *See* Humanism, clericalization of
Cleric of the Registry, 26
Cleric of the *Camera*, 16, 24, 71
Cola di Rienzo, 62
Collectores taxae plumbi, 25-26
College of Cardinals, 7, 16, 17, 48, 49, 86, 122, 227-238
Colocci, Angelo, 107-108
Colonna, Pompeo, Cardinal, 47
Colonna family, 39
Columella, 91
Computator, 26
Concubinage, in Rome, 6, 217
Confraternities, in Rome, 38
Confraternity of Divine Love, 38
Confraternity of S. Spirito, Sassia, 82
Consensus doctorum, 162
Consilium de emendanda ecclesia, 80
Consistory, 25, 31
Contemplation, 154, 177, 178, 206
Conti, Sigismondo dei, 31-33, 99, 191, 255 n.139
Contrario, Andrea, 129
Cornelio. *See* Benigno, Cornelio
Correctores litterarum apostolicarum, 25, 28
Corsi, Jacopo, 56, 103
Cortesi, Alessandro, 73-76, 88, 104
Cortesi, Antonio, 72-73
Cortesi, Antonio (son of Lattanzio), 73
Cortesi, Caterina, 73, 82
Cortesi, Giovanni Andrea (Gregorio), Cardinal, 80

Cortesi, Lattanzio, 73, 79, 80
Cortesi, Paolo, xvii, 16, 49-53, 55, 59, 73, 76-80, 128-131, 169, 186-188, 197, 199, 200, 201, 208, 210, 220, 238-240; academy of, 77, 102-107; on the cardinalate *familia*, 49-53; and Church reform, 227-238; Latin of, 76-77, 79-80, 128-131, 156-158; and Pico, 150-151; and Poliziano, 77, 128-131. Works: *De Cardinalatu*, 49-53, 57, 73, 78-80, 153, 162-164, 166, 167, 227-238; *De hominibus doctis dialogus*, 76-77, 128-129, 163; *In quattuor libros Sententiarum*, 78, 80, 148-168, 194
Cortesi family, 72
Corvinus, Matthias, of Hungary, 75, 82, 100
Coryciana, 105, 109, 111, 158
Cosmopolitanism, in the Curia, 7, 12, 43
Council of Constance, 215
Council of Florence, 9
Council of Basel, 215
Council of Pisa, 217
Council of Trent, 231, 236
Counterfeiting, of bulls, 26
Counter-Reformation, 142
Courtesans, in Rome, 5, 6
Crinito, Pietro, 195
Curial humanism, xvi, 4, 66, 208
Curial pluralism, 20
Curia Romana, 4, 5, 7, 10, 11, 16, 19-35; colleges of, 23, 24, 25, 26, 28, 42; number of posts in, 248 n.79; organizational diagram of, 22
Cyprian, Saint, 14, 173

Dalmatia, 72
Dante, 106
Datary, 6, 24, 26, 27
Dati, Leonardo, 33, 254 n.136, 255 n.139
Decorum, 106
Demetrio, Pietro, 96
Depositarius generalis, 24
Dionisotti, Carlo, 36
Diplomacy, 13
Doctors of the Church, Latin, 13, 171-174, 181-182. *See also* Ambrose; Augustine; Gregory I; Jerome
Domenichi, Domenico de', Bishop of Torcello, 218
Dominicans, 173, 198, 224
Donation of Constantine, 73, 119, 208
Dovizi, Bernardo, Cardinal, 19

Durandus of Saint-Pourçain, 161

Elijah, 108
Ecclesiae consuetudo, 207
Eclecticism, 128, 138, 141
Eloquence, 32, 148, 151
Encyclopedic theology, 190, 196
Englishmen, in Rome, 51
Epicurus, 161
Epigrammata Antiquae Urbis, 86, 111
Episcopacy, and humanism, 12–16
Erasmus, Desiderius, xvi, 138–143, 167–
   168, 202, 208
Eucharist, 155, 197, 198
Eugenius IV, 9, 31, 41, 65, 81, 93, 94
Exodus, 180

Familiae, xvii, 5, 38–60; general characteristics of, 39–40; and Church reform,
   223, 228, 229
—cardinalate, 15, 19, 34, 45–57; cost of,
   54; humanists in, 45, 46, 52–54, 56,
   71, 77; size of, 46, 47, 50, 229, 230;
   staff of, 54
—papal, 4, 14, 21, 24, 40–45; members
   of, 42
—secular, 49, 57–60; humanists in, 58–
   60
Families, humanist, xvii, 5, 38, 61–88;
   dynasticism of, 68–70
Farnese, Alessandro, Cardinal, 46, 47,
   75, 76, 87, 108. *See also* Paul III
Feld, M. D., 273 n. 14
Ferrara, 4, 34
Festus, 105
Ficino, Marsilio, 5, 90, 116, 204, 205
Fideism, 17, 148, 170
Fifth Lateran Council, 36, 215, 217,
   220, 322 n. 163
Fisher, John, 17
Flaminio, Marcantonio, 59
Flavius Panthagathus. *See* Capranica,
   Giovanni Battista
Florence, xiii, xv, xviii, 3, 12, 34, 62, 64,
   66, 67, 76, 83, 90, 99, 100, 116, 130,
   131, 170, 183, 191, 195, 204, 214
Florido, Bartolommeo, 17, 26
Foix, Cardinal de, 75
Forteguerra, Scipione (Cateromachus),
   46
Fossanova, monastery of, 26
France, 16, 110
Francesco da Fiano, 93
Franciscans, 160, 198, 224
Francis of Assisi, 184, 230

Fratres barbati, 26
Frenchmen, in Rome, 7, 43, 51
Fuensalida, Giovanni, 36
Fulvio, Andrea, 101

Galatino, Pietro Colonna, 171, 219
Gallo, Egidio, 59
Gallo, Niccolò, 123
Garcia, Pietro, 36, 165
Gaspare of Verona, 53, 255 n. 139,
   275 n. 41
George of Trebizond, 31, 53, 69, 84,
   93
Geraldini, Agapito, 102–104, 280 n. 93
Germans, in Rome, 13, 45, 111
Gherardi, Jacopo, Bishop of Aquino,
   31–34, 53–54, 82, 220, 254 n. 136
Ghibellines, 225
Giberti, Gian Matteo, 6, 271 n. 137
Giles of Viterbo, Cardinal, 47, 108, 145,
   171, 219, 321 n. 163
Giovanni d'Aragona, Cardinal, 82, 104
Giovio, Paolo, 109
Giudici, Battista da Finale dei, Bishop
   of Ventimiglia, 95
Giustiniani, Paolo, 186
Giustolo, Piero Francesco, 103–104
Golden Age, 124, 135, 150, 219
Gonzaga, Francesco, Cardinal, 92
Goritz, Johannes, 107, 108–109, 115,
   135
Grace, 197, 205
Gratia, 21, 24
Gravina, Pietro, 102, 105
Great Schism, 3, 21, 28, 65, 212, 215,
   227
Greek, 8, 9, 13, 14, 16, 35, 43, 53, 58,
   71, 97, 101, 104, 108, 121, 159, 170,
   275 n. 41
Greek Fathers. *See* Patristics, Greek
Gregory I (the Great), 171, 174
Gregory of Nazianzus, 191
Gregory of Nyssa, 191
Grifo, Leonardo, 33, 255 n. 139
Grimani, Domenico, Cardinal, 46
Guarino da Verona, 13, 82
Guazzelli, Demetrio, 96, 100, 256
   n. 165
Guelphs, 225
Guidobaldo of Urbino, 280 n. 93

Hahn, Ulrich, 15
Hebrew, 16, 17, 58, 120, 171, 219, 300
   n. 12
Hell, 154, 158

Henry VII of England, 17, 172
Heresy, 92, 95, 158
Hierarchialism, in Rome, 8
Homer, 192
Homosexuality, in Rome, 92–94
Horace, 130
Humanism: civic, 3, 4, 66; clericalization of, 5; defined, xiv; exploitation of, by the Curia, 238–239. *See also* Curial humanism
Humanist historiography, of the popes, 120–123
Humanists. *See* Roman humanists
Hungary, 45, 82, 83, 100

Illegitimacy, in Rome, 6
Imitation: literary, 106, 128–132; moral, 205–206
Immaculate Conception, 157, 163
Imperia, 6
Imperialism, 124–126
Indulgences, 155
Inghirami, Tommaso Fedra, 16, 36, 82, 108, 134, 142, 185, 196, 321 n.163
Innocent VIII, 6, 7, 10, 30, 33, 75, 103
Inscriptions, 101, 102, 111
Irreligion, 92, 95

Janissaries, 74
Jerome, Saint, 14, 127, 132, 147, 152, 158, 163, 171, 177, 210
Jerusalem, 219
Jesuits, 142
Joachimism, 218, 219
Job, 210
John of Damascus, 192
Jove, 158
Judaizers, 141
Julius II, 9–12, 17, 26–28, 36, 44, 48, 51, 58, 65, 70, 82, 95, 122, 123, 125, 137, 138, 142, 149, 163, 190, 191; and Church reform, 217, 221, 222
Julius III. *See* Monte, Giovanni Maria del
Jupiter, 137, 158

Lactantius, 127, 171–173, 192
Lanfredini, Orsini, 98
Laocoön, 34
Last Judgment, 154, 162
Latin, 7, 150, 155, 156, 157; history of, 132–133; and the humanists, 7, 20, 29, 30, 35, 52, 53, 58, 76, 90, 93, 96, 105, 106, 118, 119, 123, 126, 195, 201

Lelio, Antonio, 136, 207, 267 n.67
Leo I, 14, 136, 207
Leo X, 6, 11, 12, 17, 19, 30, 41–47, 51, 58, 60, 85, 87, 105, 108, 109, 111, 122, 123, 125, 135, 136, 137, 138, 142, 186, 192, 207; and Church reform, 217, 219, 221, 226; *familia* of, 41–45. *See also* Medici, Giovanni de', Cardinal
Leto, Pomponio, 76, 91–97, 100–102, 104, 115, 158, 200
Lianori, Lianoro de', 254 n.136, 255 n.139
Libellus ad Leonem X, 186
Librarianship, papal, 35–37, 43, 256 n.165
Libraries: cardinalate, 53; papal (*see* Vatican Library)
Liburnio, Niccolò, 243 n.11
Litterae apostolicae. See Bulls, papal
Liva, Cardinal, 15
Livy, 135
Logic, 179; attack on, 182
Lollio, Gregorio, 254 n.136
Lombard, Peter, 148, 149, 154, 161, 193
Longueil, Christophe de, 110, 140, 141
Loredan, Antonio, 100
Lorenzi, Giovanni, 102–103, 256 n.165
Loschi, Antonio, 31
Loschi, Francesco, 254 n.136
Louis XI of France, 75
Lucan, 14
Lullism, 218
Luther, Martin, 80, 137, 138, 143, 168, 173, 208, 209, 210
Lutheranism, 140

Machiavelli, Niccolò, 238
Maffei, Agostino, 96
Maffei, Antonio, 73, 82
Maffei, Benedetto, 220
Maffei, Gerardo di Giovanni, 81–82
Maffei, Giovanni Battista, 82
Maffei, Giovanni Battista (son of Antonio), 82
Maffei, Giuliano, Bishop of Bertinoro, 82
Maffei, Giulio, 87
Maffei, Lucilla, 83
Maffei, Mario, 78, 82, 83, 85–88, 102, 108, 111, 112, 185, 191, 214, 269 n.105
Maffei, Raffaele, xvii, 10, 11, 16, 17, 79, 80, 82–85, 86, 87, 95, 111, 123,

Maffei, Raffaele *(continued)*
188, 235-237, 322 n.162; and Aristotle, 203; on Church and Roman
Empire, 208; and Church reform,
220-226; on Christian tradition, 209;
on diligence, 206; on eloquence, 195,
200-202; on Martin Luther, 208-210;
on Neo-Platonism, 203-204; and pagan
writers, 202-203; on Rome as a cultural model, 208-209, 210-211; on
Scholasticism, 197-199, 224; on silence and solitude, 206-207. Works:
Brevis Historia, 84, 201, 221; *Commentaria Urbana,* 83, 84, 190, 191,
192, 203, 204, 210, 221, 222; *De In-
stitutione Christiana,* 85, 189, 192-
198, 201, 202, 204, 221, 222; *De
Prima Philosophia,* 102, 106, 203;
*Nasi Romani in Martinum Lutherum
Apologeticus,* 84, 201, 208-210;
Stromata, 85, 189, 195, 196, 202,
203, 204, 206, 207; translations of
Basil the Great, 85, 193, 196, 206
Maffei family of Verona, 265 n.36
Maffei family of Volterra, 72
Magister registri supplicationum, 26, 71,
74, 103, 107
Mammacino, Romolo de, 43, 256 n.165
Manetti, Giannozzo, 68, 120-122
Mantua, 13, 14
Manutius, Aldus, 275-276 n.41
Marca, Jacopo della (Jacobus Picens),
201
Margania, Lucrezia, 71
Mariano, Fra, 42
Marriage, in Rome, 5, 6, 16
Mars, 158
Marsi, Pietro, 200, 277-278 n.66
Martial, 14
Martin V, 3, 9, 31; and Church reform,
216
Marullo, Michele, 76, 84
Maximilian I, 18
Mazzochio, Jacopo, 86
Medici, Cosimo de', 9, 35, 120
Medici, Giovanni de', Cardinal, 33, 44,
45, 75, 80. *See also* Leo X
Medici, Giulio de', 6, 7, 46, 87. *See also*
Clement VII
Medici, Lorenzo de', 74, 75, 76, 82, 83,
128
Medici family, 64, 72, 73, 74, 75, 90,
116
Meditation, 177
Mellini, Celso, 110

Mercatores sequentes Curiam Romanam,
58
Michelangelo Buonarotti, 11
Michele, Giovanni, Cardinal, 71
Minucci, Tita di Bartolomeo (Maffei),
83
Modena, 34, 80
Monte, Antonio del, Cardinal, 59
Monte, Balduino del, 262 n.99
Monte, Giovanni Maria del, 59
Monte Cassino, abbacy of, 75
Monte family, 69
Montepiloso, Bishop of, 102
Montone, Braccio da, 15
Morality, 181-182
Mysticism, and Church reform, 218-
219

Naples, 4, 7, 13, 14, 34, 64, 68, 73, 90,
99, 103, 104, 105, 107, 120
Neapolitans, in Rome, 7, 51
Neopaganism, xv, 92, 95, 140, 141, 186,
187
Neo-Platonism, xiv, 2, 90, 175, 176,
177, 182, 203, 205, 221, 273 n.14
Nicene Creed, 158
Nicholas of Cusa, Cardinal, 14, 218
Nicholas of Lyra, 14
Nicholas V, xiii, 4, 9, 10, 12, 14, 27, 32,
35, 94, 120-122, 170
Nicholas of Cusa, Cardinal, 14, 218
Nicholas of Lyra, 14
Notaries, 23, 24, 27, 107
Numa, 123
Numerus, 129

Odi, Pietro da Montopoli, 91
Officialis collectoriae plumbi, 71
Oliva, Alessandro, Cardinal, 15
Olympus, 109, 158
Oratio, 177
Orsini, Cosimo, Cardinal, 221
Orsini, Giordano, Cardinal, 117
Orsini family, 39
Orsino, Battista, 103
Ovid, 14, 135, 275 n.41

Padua, 110
Palestrina, 101
Palilia, 96, 99-100
Palladio, Blosio, 59, 86, 108, 111, 134-
137, 142
Palmieri, Mattia, 254 n.136
Pannartz, Arnold, 14, 273 n.14
Papal states, 24

Paris, 161
Paris (city), 14, 158
Parmenio, Lorenzo, 43, 256 n.165
Patristics, Greek, xiv, 13, 170, 173, 191, 195, 203
Paul, Saint, 158, 180, 198, 203
Paul II, 9, 10, 12, 15, 28, 29, 36; and the Roman Academy, 92–97, 122, 123, 221
Paul III, 47, 75, 80, 111. *See also* Alessandro Farnese, Cardinal
Pazzi Conspiracy, 68, 82, 83
Pelagianism, 175, 206
Penance, 155
Perotti, Niccolò, 13, 14, 15, 33, 53, 254 n.136
Persona, Cristoforo, 103, 256 n.165
Pertinoro, Bartolomeo Manfredi di, 256 n.165
Perugia, 13, 15, 77
Peruzzi, Baldassare, 58
Peter, Saint, 158, 180
Peter Lombard. *See* Lombard, Peter
Peter's pence, 16, 17, 18, 24
Petrarch, Francesco, 106, 115, 124, 169
Peutinger, Konrad, 167
Phaëthon, 158
Phoebus, 158
Piacentino, Severo, 80
Piccolomini, Aeneas Silvius. *See* Pius II
Pico della Mirandola, Gianfrancesco, 131–132, 183–186, 200
Pico della Mirandola, Giovanni, 76, 149, 150, 163–164, 199
Pindarus. *See* Santesio, Gentile
Piombo, Sebastiano del, 26, 58
Piperno, Antonio Costanza da, 275 n.41
Pisa, 73, 76
Pisanello, 106
Pius III, 10, 41, 53. *See also* Todeschini-Piccolomini, Francesco, Cardinal
Platina, 34–36, 77, 92–97, 100, 122
Plato, 90, 116, 131, 152, 155, 161, 172, 180, 187, 203
Plutarch, 103
Poggio Bracciolini, Gian Francesco (father), xiv, 31, 34, 44, 67, 115, 128
Poggio Bracciolini, Giovanni Francesco (son), 44
Pole, Reginald, 110
Poles, 42, 43
Polirone, monastery of, 80
Poliziano, Angelo, 5, 11, 36, 76–77, 84, 128–131, 138, 141, 149, 195
Pompilio, Paolo, 158

Pontano, Giovanni, 35, 90, 104, 105, 238
Ponzetti, Francesco, Cardinal, 47
Popes, and humanism, 8–12, 98. *See also individual names*
Preachers, and rhetoric, 153
Predestination, 197
Prierias, Silvester, O.P., 208
Printing, in Rome, 14, 15
Priscianese, Francesco, 57–59
Procopius, 83
Propertius, 275 n.41
Prophecy, 170
Protonotaries, apostolic, 7, 16, 25, 42, 77
Ptolemy II Philadelphus, 121
Purgation, of the Christian soul, 176–177
Pyrrhonism, 171

Questenberg, Jacob, 7, 8, 43, 103
Quintilian, 128
Quinzano, 72
Quirini, Pietro, 186

Rale (Rhallus), Constantinus, 43
Raphael Sanzio, 11, 58, 101, 108, 126, 159
Ransano, Pietro, Bishop of Nocera, 100
Rasi, Benedetto, 255 n.139
Referendarius, 23, 26, 41
Reform, Church, xviii, 212–237; limits of, 214
Reformation, 12, 117, 169, 217
Register of supplications, 26, 42
Regulae Cancellariae Apostolicae, 20, 25
Republicanism, 92, 94, 95
Rescribendarius, 26
Reuchlin, Johannes, 17, 44
Rhallo, Manilio Cabacio, 102, 104, 105
Rhenanus Beatus, 167
Riario, Galeotto, Cardinal, 104
Riario, Girolamo, Count, 74, 98
Riario, Pietro, Cardinal, 14, 15, 36, 46, 54
Riario, Raffaele, Cardinal, 51, 54, 55
Riario family, 82
Riccobaldi, Paolo del Bava, 83, 84, 87, 269 n.105
Richard of Media Villa, 161
Rizzoni, Benedetto, 55, 71–72
Rizzoni, Giacomo, 71
Rizzoni family, 71–72
Roman Academy, 10, 12, 15, 35, 54,

Roman Academy *(continued)*
71, 76, 89-112, 290 n.105; poetry
and oratory in, 98, 105, 106, 108,
109, 112; as *sodalitas*, 92, 96, 278
n.66; suppression of, 92-97. *See also*
Archaeology; Colocci, Angelo; Cortesi,
Paolo; Goritz, Johannes; Leto, Pomponio; Rome, *horti* in
Roman Empire, 66, 122, 132, 135-137,
208
Roman humanists: attraction of Rome
to, 66-67; clericalization of, 69; decline of, 110-112; dynasticism among,
69-70; ideology of, 115-143
Romano, Giulio, 58
Romans, 7, 51, 47, 66
Rome: Campidoglio, xiii, 137; Castel
Sant'Angelo, 26, 74, 93; catacombs
of, 96, 101; Church of Sant'Agostino,
47, 108; college for Greek studies in,
43-44; governor of, 24; *horti* in, 107-
108; Palazzo Venezia (San Marco), 93;
Parione, 86, 102; Quirinal Hill, 91;
sack of, 3, 11, 108, 204; St. John Lateran, 85, 138; St. Peter's, 85, 87, 121,
123, 138, 222; Santa Maria in Aracoeli, xiii; SS. Apostoli, 14, 54; University of (the *Sapienza*), 59; Villa
Farnesina, 59. *See also* Curia Romana;
Vatican
Rota, 7, 23, 41, 107
Rovere, Domenico della, Cardinal, 55,
71
Rovere, Franciotti della, Cardinal, 46
Rovere, Giuliano della, Cardinal, 46, 56,
99. *See also* Julius II
Roverella, Bartolomeo, Cardinal, 55, 94,
96
Ruolo. See Leo X, *familia* of
Rustici, Marcello dei, 33, 254 n.136,
255 n.139

Sabellico, Marc Antonio, 95
Sabeo, Fausto, 256 n.165
Sabino, Pietro, 101
Sacra Penitentiaria Apostolica, 24, 27
Sacred Scripture, 17, 146, 153, 169,
171-174, 176-178, 180-184, 191,
196, 199, 201, 202, 209, 225
Sadoleto, Jacopo, 11, 34, 43, 86, 108,
138, 214
Salutati, Coluccio, xiv, 34, 67
Salviati, Giovanni, Cardinal, 47
Sanchez, Roderigo, 273 n.14
San Gimignano, 72, 73, 76, 77, 78, 80

Sanseverino, Francesco, Cardinal, 56
Sanseverino family, 91
Sansovino, Andrea, 109
Santesio, Gentile, 44, 45
Saraceni, Ippolita (Cortesi), 73
Savonarola, Girolamo, 44, 169, 170,
183
Scala, Bartolomeo, 34
Scholasticism, 144, 149, 153, 166-169,
171, 173, 190, 197, 199, 202, 210,
218; attack on, by humanists, 172,
184; hostility of, to humanism, 144,
145, 165
Scholastic Latin, 150, 155, 156
Scholastics, 141, 150, 155, 164, 165,
174, 193-196, 199
Scientia, 178, 184
Scotland, 16, 17
Scotus, John Duns, 157, 158, 160-161,
162, 163, 197, 198, 199
Scotists, 155, 157, 168, 174, 198, 199;
criticism of, 168, 174
Scriptores litterarum apostolicarum, 16,
26, 28, 29, 30, 41, 71, 72, 73, 77, 81,
82, 83, 84, 85, 87, 103
Secretaries: apostolic, 16, 25, 28, 29-
35, 42, 67, 71, 74, 77, 81, 103, 107,
254 n.136, 255 n.139; in the *familia*,
58, 60
Seghieri, Lucia di Giovanni (Maffei), 81
Senate, 125, 135, 136, 155
Seneca, 93, 203
Sextus Empiricus, 103, 171, 183
Sforza, Ascanio, Cardinal, 79, 102, 319
n.95
Signatura gratiae, 23, 24
Signatura justitiae, 23
Silius Italicus, 14
Simony, 217, 233
Sixtus IV, 7, 8, 9, 14, 15, 23, 27, 28,
29, 31, 32, 33, 35, 43, 53, 54, 68, 70,
71, 74, 82, 90, 97, 99, 103, 115, 122,
163; and Church reform, 216, 217,
220
Sixtus V, 20
Skepticism, 169-188
Socrates, 94, 104, 193, 204
Sodalitas, of Saints Victor, Fortunato,
and Genesio, 96, 278 n.66. *See also*
Roman Academy
Soderini, Pietro, 83
Sollicitor litterarum apostolicarum, 16,
74, 107
Spagnoli, Battista Mantovano, 199-200
Spain, 75

Spaniards, in Rome, 7, 36, 43
Sperulo, Francesco, 103
Stable hands, 42, 51. See also *Familiae*
Stewards, 42, 52. See also *Familiae*
Strabo, 14
Strambotti, 104, 105, 106
Sulpizio, Giovanni, 76–77, 267 n. 67
Sweynheym, Konrad, 14, 273 n. 14

Tacitus, 44
Talmud, 44
Taxator litterarum apostolicarum, 96, 103
Taxes, curial, 25, 26, 251 n. 99
Tertullian, 169, 173
Theologia erudita, 167
Theologia rhetorica, 167, 174
Theological language, 155–157
Theology: dialectics in, 148–149, 165, 202; as a science, 154. *See also* Encyclopedic theology
Thomists, 157, 162, 164, 198–200
Thucydides, 159
Tiberius, 123
Todeschini-Piccolomini, Francesco, Cardinal, 15, 18, 19, 53, 73, 76, 99, 221. *See also* Pius III
Toffanin, Giuseppe, 285 n. 37
Torrella, Gaspare, 36
Tortelli, Giovanni, 35
Tranquillo de Leonibus, Bishop, 258 n. 21
Translatio Imperii, 119
Traversari, Ambrogio, 118
Treasurer-general of the Roman church, 16, 24, 107
Trinity, 161, 179
Trivulzio, Agostino, Cardinal, 47
True philosophy. *See* Castellesi, *De Vera Philosophia*
Turks, 9, 82, 83, 216, 219, 226
Tuscan, 58
Tuscany, 7, 72, 73, 82
Tutors, 19, 59, 60

Ulysses, 210
Undersecretaries, 58, 60
Ungetti, Filippo, Cardinal, 103
Urban VI, 81
Urban VIII, 142

Valla, Lorenzo, 7, 73, 91, 97, 118–119, 125, 128, 146, 147, 171
Valla family, 62, 69
Vatican, 9, 40, 41, 45, 159
Vatican Library, 14, 35, 82, 96, 170, 191
Venality, of offices, 20, 27–29, 69
Venice, 13, 14, 17, 64, 68, 93, 94, 100, 186
Vergil, 14, 125
Vergil, Polydore, 18
Vergilianism, 18
Vernacular studies, 7, 97, 105, 243 n. 11
Verona, 71, 72, 108
Vice-chancellor, cardinalate, 24, 25, 26
Vida, Girolamo, 125
Vigili, Fabio, 256 n. 165
Virgin Mary, 109, 137, 197
Vitelleschi, Giovanni, 71
Vitruvius, 125–126
Volterra, 72, 75, 81–85, 87, 111, 189, 190, 191, 210, 214; Badia of Ss. Giusto and Clemente, 75, 86; Church of San Lino, 85, 270 n. 122; San Donnino, 86
Voluntarism, 181

Will, 177, 181
William of Ockham, 161
Witchcraft, 217
Wolsey, Thomas, Cardinal, 18
Women, in Rome, 5

Xenophon, 152, 192
Ximenes de Cisneros, Francisco, Cardinal, 48

Zeno, Battista, Cardinal, 54
Zeno, Jacopo, 122

The Johns Hopkins University Press

RENAISSANCE HUMANISM IN PAPAL ROME

This book was composed in IBM Baskerville text and VIP Garamond No. 3 display type by Horne Associates, Inc., from a design by David Horne. It was printed on S. D. Warren's 50-lb. Sebago Eggshell paper and bound in Holliston Roxite A cloth by The Maple-Vail Book Manufacturing Group.